ICSA STUDY TEXT

FINANCIAL DECISION MAKING

Second edition

JENNY ROBERTSON

First edition published 2012

Published by
ICSA Publishing Ltd
Saffron House,
6–10 Kirby Street,
London EC1N 8TS

Designed and typeset by Paul Barrett Book Production, Cambridge
Printed by Hobbs the Printers Ltd, Totton, Hampshire

British Cataloguing in Publication Data
A catalogue record for this book is available from the British Library.

ISBN 978-1-860726-811

Contents

How to use this study text

ICSA study texts developed to support ICSA's Chartered Secretaries Qualifying Scheme (CSQS) follow a standard format and include a range of navigational, self-testing and illustrative features to help you get the most out of the support materials.

Each text is divided into three main sections:

- introductory material
- the text itself, divided into Parts and Chapters, and
- additional reference information.

The sections below show you how to find your way around the text and make the most of its features.

Introductory material

The introductory section of each text includes a full contents list and the module syllabus which reiterates the module aims, learning outcomes and syllabus content for the module in question.

The text itself

Each **part** opens with a list of the chapters to follow, an overview of what will be covered and learning outcomes for the part.

Every **chapter** opens with a list of the topics covered and an introduction specific to that chapter. Chapters are structured to allow students to break the content down into manageable sections for study. Each chapter ends with a summary of key content to reinforce understanding, as well as end of chapter examination-standard questions to test your knowledge further.

Part opening

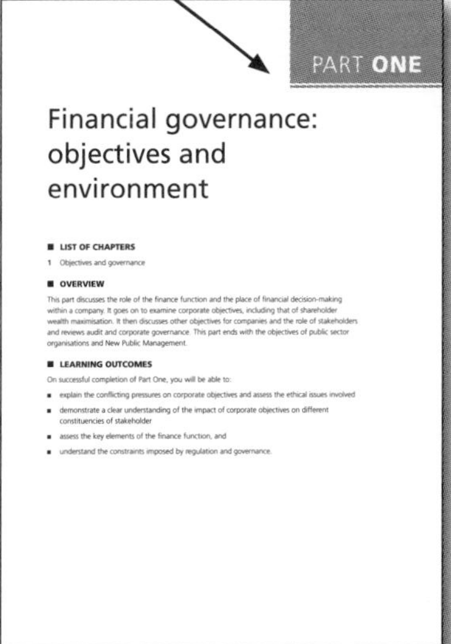

PART ONE

Financial governance: objectives and environment

■ LIST OF CHAPTERS

1 Objectives and governance

■ OVERVIEW

This part discusses the role of the finance function and the place of financial decision-making within a company. It goes on to examine corporate objectives, including that of shareholder wealth maximisation. It then discusses other objectives for companies and the role of stakeholders and reviews audit and corporate governance. This part ends with the objectives of public sector organisations and New Public Management.

■ LEARNING OUTCOMES

On successful completion of Part One, you will be able to:

- explain the conflicting pressures on corporate objectives and assess the ethical issues involved
- demonstrate a clear understanding of the impact of corporate objectives on different constituencies of stakeholder
- assess the key elements of the finance function, and
- understand the constraints imposed by regulation and governance.

Chapter opening

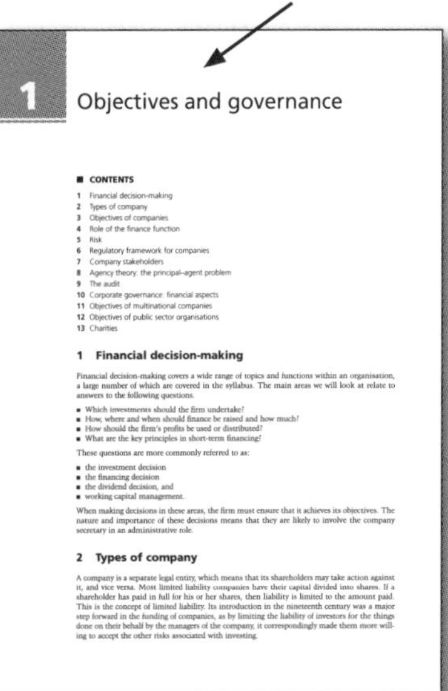

1 Objectives and governance

■ CONTENTS

1 Financial decision-making
2 Types of company
3 Objectives of companies
4 Role of the finance function
5 Risk
6 Regulatory framework for companies
7 Company stakeholders
8 Agency theory: the principal–agent problem
9 The audit
10 Corporate governance: financial aspects
11 Objectives of multinational companies
12 Objectives of public sector organisations
13 Charities

1 Financial decision-making

Financial decision-making covers a wide range of topics and functions within an organisation, a large number of which are covered in the syllabus. The main areas we will look at relate to answers to the following questions.

- Which investments should the firm undertake?
- How, where and when should finance be raised and how much?
- How should the firm's profits be used or distributed?
- What are the key principles in short-term financing?

These questions are more commonly referred to as:

- the investment decision
- the financing decision
- the dividend decision, and
- working capital management.

When making decisions in these areas, the firm must ensure that it achieves its objectives. The nature and importance of these decisions means that they are likely to involve the company secretary in an administrative role.

2 Types of company

A company is a separate legal entity, which means that its shareholders may take action against it, and vice versa. Most limited liability companies have their capital divided into shares. If a shareholder has paid in full for his or her shares, then liability is limited to the amount paid. This is the concept of limited liability. Its introduction in the nineteenth century was a major step forward in the funding of companies, as by limiting the liability of investors for the things done on their behalf by the managers of the company, it correspondingly made them more willing to accept the other risks associated with investing.

Features

The text is enhanced by a range of illustrative and self-testing features to assist understanding and to help you prepare for the examination. Each feature is presented in a standard format, so that you will become familiar with how to use them in your study.

The texts also include tables, figures and checklists and, where relevant, sample documents and forms.

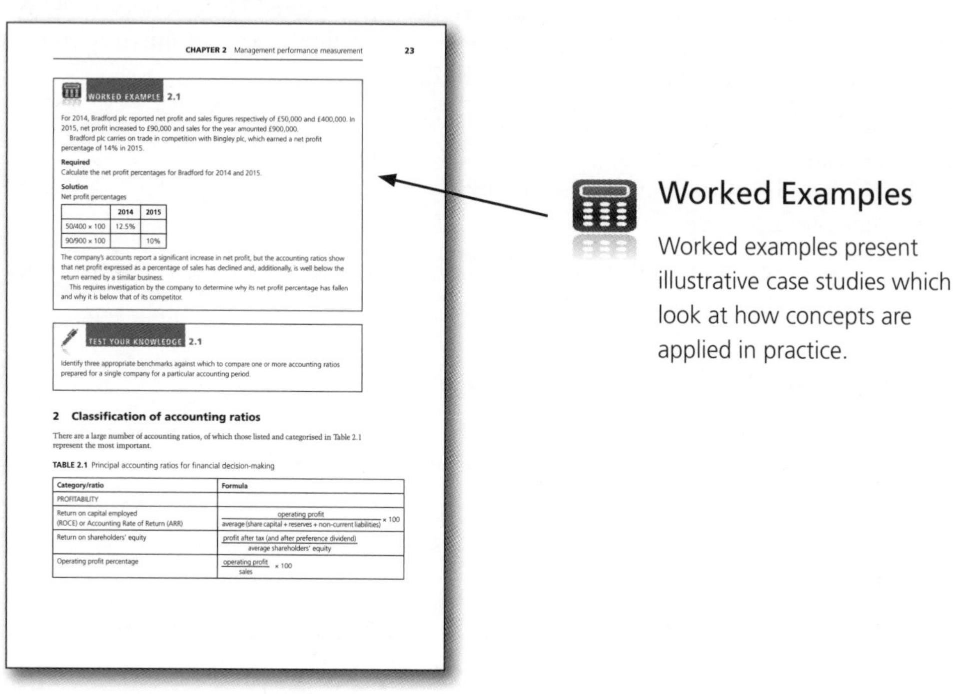

CHAPTER 2 Management performance measurement 23

WORKED EXAMPLE 2.1

For 2014, Bradford plc reported net profit and sales figures respectively of £50,000 and £400,000. In 2015, net profit increased to £90,000 and sales for the year amounted £900,000.

Bradford plc carries on trade in competition with Bingley plc, which earned a net profit percentage of 14% in 2015.

Required

Calculate the net profit percentages for Bradford for 2014 and 2015.

Solution

Net profit percentages

	2014	2015
50/400 × 100	12.5%	
90/900 × 100		10%

The company's accounts report a significant increase in net profit, but the accounting ratios show that net profit expressed as a percentage of sales has declined and, additionally, is well below the return earned by a similar business.

This requires investigation by the company to determine why its net profit percentage has fallen and why it is below that of its competitor.

TEST YOUR KNOWLEDGE 2.1

Identify three appropriate benchmarks against which to compare one or more accounting ratios prepared for a single company for a particular accounting period.

2 Classification of accounting ratios

There are a large number of accounting ratios, of which those listed and categorised in Table 2.1 represent the most important.

TABLE 2.1 Principal accounting ratios for financial decision-making

Category/ratio	Formula
PROFITABILITY	
Return on capital employed (ROCE) or Accounting Rate of Return (ARR)	$\frac{\text{operating profit}}{\text{average (share capital + reserves + non-current liabilities)}} \times 100$
Return on shareholders' equity	$\frac{\text{profit after tax (and after preference dividend)}}{\text{average shareholders' equity}}$
Operating profit percentage	$\frac{\text{operating profit}}{\text{sales}} \times 100$

Worked Examples

Worked examples present illustrative case studies which look at how concepts are applied in practice.

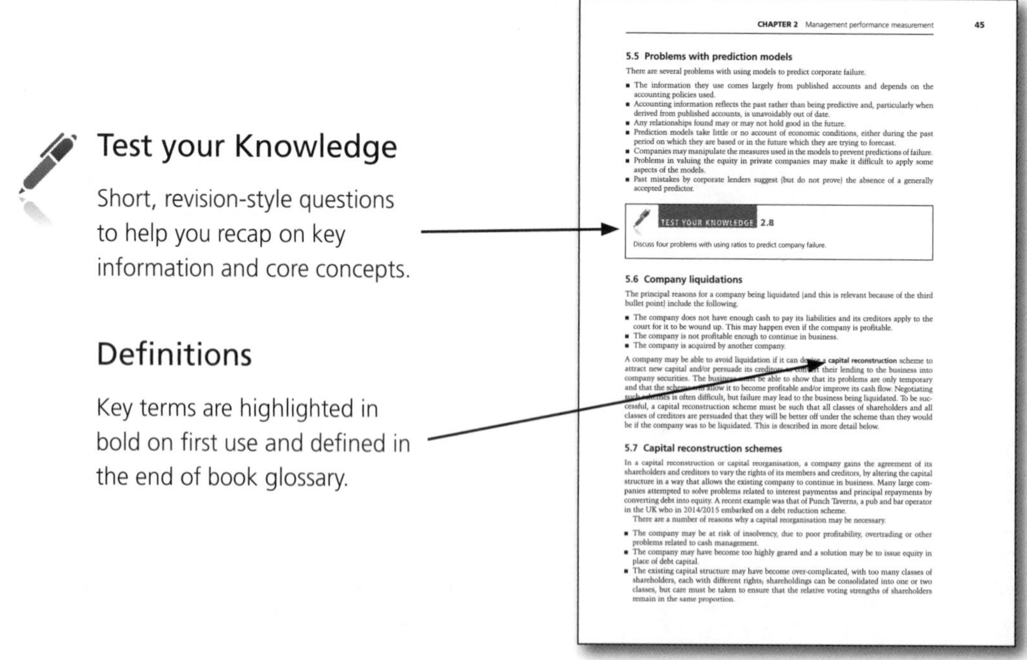

Test your Knowledge

Short, revision-style questions to help you recap on key information and core concepts.

Definitions

Key terms are highlighted in bold on first use and defined in the end of book glossary.

CHAPTER 2 Management performance measurement 45

5.5 Problems with prediction models

There are several problems with using models to predict corporate failure.

- The information they use comes largely from published accounts and depends on the accounting policies used.
- Accounting information reflects the past rather than being predictive and, particularly when derived from published accounts, is unavoidably out of date.
- Any relationships found may or may not hold good in the future.
- Prediction models take little or no account of economic conditions, either during the past period on which they are based or in the future which they are trying to forecast.
- Companies may manipulate the measures used in the models to prevent predictions of failure.
- Problems in valuing the equity in private companies may make it difficult to apply some aspects of the models.
- Past mistakes by corporate lenders suggest (but do not prove) the absence of a generally accepted predictor.

TEST YOUR KNOWLEDGE 2.8

Discuss four problems with using ratios to predict company failure.

5.6 Company liquidations

The principal reasons for a company being liquidated (and this is relevant because of the third bullet point) include the following.

- The company does not have enough cash to pay its liabilities and its creditors apply to the court for it to be wound up. This may happen even if the company is profitable.
- The company is not profitable enough to continue in business.
- The company is acquired by another company.

A company may be able to avoid liquidation if it can devise a **capital reconstruction** scheme to attract new capital and/or persuade its creditors to convert their lending to the business into company securities. The business must be able to show that its problems are only temporary and that the scheme will allow it to become profitable and/or improve its cash flow. Negotiating such schemes is often difficult, but failure may lead to the business being liquidated. To be successful, a capital reconstruction scheme must be such that all classes of shareholders and all classes of creditors are persuaded that they will be better off under the scheme than they would be if the company was to be liquidated. This is described in more detail below.

5.7 Capital reconstruction schemes

In a capital reconstruction or capital reorganisation, a company gains the agreement of its shareholders and creditors to vary the rights of its members and creditors, by altering the capital structure in a way that allows the existing company to continue in business. Many large companies attempted to solve problems related to interest paymentss and principal repayments by converting debt into equity. A recent example was that of Punch Taverns, a pub and bar operator in the UK who in 2014/2015 embarked on a debt reduction scheme.

There are a number of reasons why a capital reorganisation may be necessary.

- The company may be at risk of insolvency, due to poor profitability, overtrading or other problems related to cash management.
- The company may have become too highly geared and a solution may be to issue equity in place of debt capital.
- The existing capital structure may have become over-complicated, with too many classes of shareholders, each with different rights; shareholdings can be consolidated into one or two classes, but care must be taken to ensure that the relative voting strengths of shareholders remain in the same proportion.

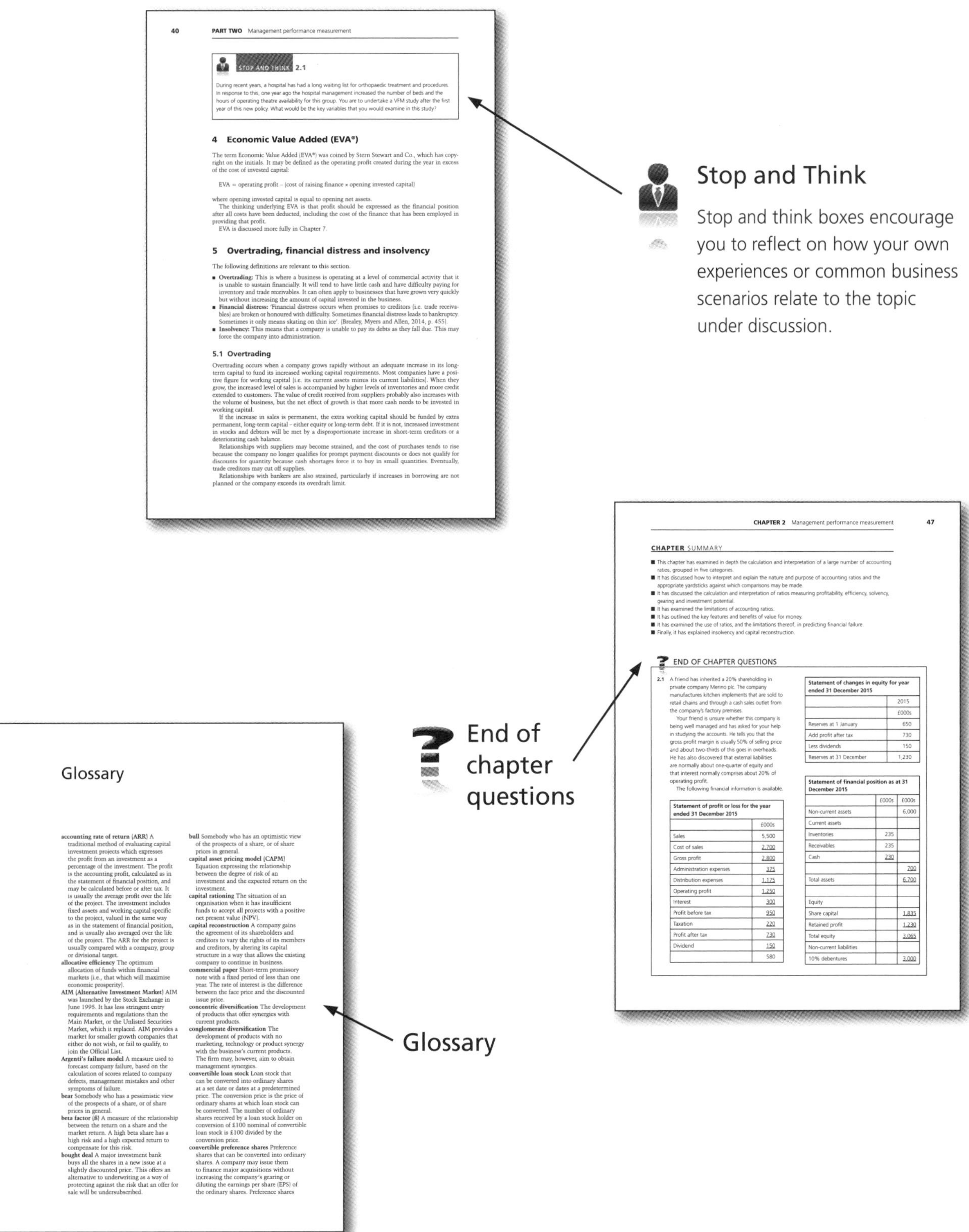

40 **PART TWO** Management performance measurement

STOP AND THINK 2.1

During recent years, a hospital has had a long waiting list for orthopaedic treatment and procedures. In response to this, one year ago the hospital management increased the number of beds and the hours of operating theatre availability for this group. You are to undertake a VFM study after the first year of this new policy. What would be the key variables that you would examine in this study?

4 Economic Value Added (EVA®)

The term Economic Value Added (EVA®) was coined by Stern Stewart and Co., which has copyright on the initials. It may be defined as the operating profit created during the year in excess of the cost of invested capital:

EVA = operating profit – (cost of raising finance × opening invested capital)

where opening invested capital is equal to opening net assets.

The thinking underlying EVA is that profit should be expressed as the financial position after all costs have been deducted, including the cost of the finance that has been employed in providing that profit.

EVA is discussed more fully in Chapter 7.

5 Overtrading, financial distress and insolvency

The following definitions are relevant to this section.

- **Overtrading:** This is where a business is operating at a level of commercial activity that it is unable to sustain financially. It will tend to have little cash and have difficulty paying for inventory and trade receivables. It can often apply to businesses that have grown very quickly but without increasing the amount of capital invested in the business.
- **Financial distress:** 'Financial distress occurs when promises to creditors (i.e. trade receivables) are broken or honoured with difficulty. Sometimes financial distress leads to bankruptcy. Sometimes it only means skating on thin ice'. (Brealey, Myers and Allen, 2014, p. 455).
- **Insolvency:** This means that a company is unable to pay its debts as they fall due. This may force the company into administration.

5.1 Overtrading

Overtrading occurs when a company grows rapidly without an adequate increase in its long-term capital to fund its increased working capital requirements. Most companies have a positive figure for working capital (i.e. its current assets minus its current liabilities). When they grow, the increased level of sales is accompanied by higher levels of inventories and more credit extended to customers. The value of credit received from suppliers probably also increases with the volume of business, but the net effect of growth is that more cash needs to be invested in working capital.

If the increase in sales is permanent, the extra working capital should be funded by extra permanent, long-term capital – either equity or long-term debt. If it is not, increased investment in stocks and debtors will be met by a disproportionate increase in short-term creditors or a deteriorating cash balance.

Relationships with suppliers may become strained, and the cost of purchases tends to rise because the company no longer qualifies for prompt payment discounts or does not qualify for discounts for quantity because cash shortages force it to buy in small quantities. Eventually, trade creditors may cut off supplies.

Relationships with bankers are also strained, particularly if increases in borrowing are not planned or the company exceeds its overdraft limit.

CHAPTER 2 Management performance measurement 47

CHAPTER SUMMARY

- This chapter has examined in depth the calculation and interpretation of a large number of accounting ratios, grouped in five categories.
- It has discussed how to interpret and explain the nature and purpose of accounting ratios and the appropriate yardsticks against which comparisons may be made.
- It has discussed the calculation and interpretation of ratios measuring profitability, efficiency, solvency, gearing and investment potential.
- It has examined the limitations of accounting ratios.
- It has outlined the key features and benefits of value for money.
- It has examined the use of ratios, and the limitations thereof, in predicting financial failure.
- Finally, it has explained insolvency and capital reconstruction.

END OF CHAPTER QUESTIONS

2.1 A friend has inherited a 20% shareholding in private company Merino plc. The company manufactures kitchen implements that are sold to retail chains and through a cash sales outlet from the company's factory premises.

Your friend is unsure whether this company is being well managed and has asked for your help in studying the accounts. He tells you that the gross profit margin is usually 50% of selling price and about two-thirds of this goes in overheads. He has also discovered that external liabilities are normally about one-quarter of equity and that interest normally comprises about 20% of operating profit.

The following financial information is available.

Statement of profit or loss for the year ended 31 December 2015	
	£000s
Sales	5,500
Cost of sales	2,700
Gross profit	2,800
Administration expenses	375
Distribution expenses	1,175
Operating profit	1,250
Interest	300
Profit before tax	950
Taxation	220
Profit after tax	730
Dividend	150
	580

Statement of changes in equity for year ended 31 December 2015	
	2015
	£000s
Reserves at 1 January	650
Add profit after tax	730
Less dividends	150
Reserves at 31 December	1,230

Statement of financial position as at 31 December 2015		
	£000s	£000s
Non-current assets		6,000
Current assets		
Inventories	235	
Receivables	235	
Cash	230	
		700
Total assets		6,700
Equity		
Share capital		1,835
Retained profit		1,230
Total equity		3,065
Non-current liabilities		
10% debentures		3,000

Glossary

accounting rate of return (ARR) A traditional method of evaluating capital investment projects which expresses the profit from an investment as a percentage of the investment. The profit is the accounting profit, calculated as in the statement of financial position, and may be calculated before or after tax. It is usually the average profit over the life of the project. The investment includes fixed assets and working capital specific to the project, valued in the same way as in the statement of financial position, and is usually also averaged over the life of the project. The ARR for the project is usually compared with a company, group or divisional target.

allocative efficiency The optimum allocation of funds within financial markets (i.e., that which will maximise economic prosperity).

AIM (Alternative Investment Market) AIM was launched by the Stock Exchange in June 1995. It has less stringent entry requirements and regulations than the Main Market, or the Unlisted Securities Market, which it replaced. AIM provides a market for smaller growth companies that either do not wish, or fail to qualify, to join the Official List.

Argenti's failure model A measure used to forecast company failure, based on the calculation of scores related to company defects, management mistakes and other symptoms of failure.

bear Somebody who has a pessimistic view of the prospects of a share, or of share prices in general.

beta factor (β) A measure of the relationship between the return on a share and the market return. A high beta share has a high risk and a high expected return to compensate for this risk.

bought deal A major investment bank buys all the shares in a new issue at a slightly discounted price. This offers an alternative to underwriting as a way of protecting against the risk that an offer for sale will be undersubscribed.

bull Somebody who has an optimistic view of the prospects of a share, or of share prices in general.

capital asset pricing model (CAPM) Equation expressing the relationship between the degree of risk of an investment and the expected return on the investment.

capital rationing The situation of an organisation when it has insufficient funds to accept all projects with a positive net present value (NPV).

capital reconstruction A company gains the agreement of its shareholders and creditors to vary the rights of its members and creditors, by altering its capital structure in a way that allows the existing company to continue in business.

commercial paper Short-term promissory note with a fixed period of less than one year. The rate of interest is the difference between the face price and the discounted issue price.

concentric diversification The development of products that offer synergies with current products.

conglomerate diversification The development of products with no marketing, technology or product synergy with the business's current products. The firm may, however, aim to obtain management synergies.

convertible loan stock Loan stock that can be converted into ordinary shares at a set date or dates at a predetermined price. The conversion price is the price of ordinary shares at which loan stock can be converted. The number of ordinary shares received by a loan stock holder on conversion of £100 nominal of convertible loan stock is £100 divided by the conversion price.

convertible preference shares Preference shares that can be converted into ordinary shares. A company may issue them to finance major acquisitions without increasing the company's gearing or diluting the earnings per share (EPS) of the ordinary shares. Preference shares

Reference material

The text ends with a range of additional guidance and reference material.

Most texts will include Appendices which comprise additional reference material specific to that module.

Other reference material includes a glossary of key terms, a directory of further reading and web resources and a comprehensive index.

Financial Decision Making syllabus

Module outline and aims

The Chartered Secretary has the responsibility of helping to ensure that decisions are properly made and implemented, and that appropriate risk management systems are in place, to maximise value for key stakeholders of the organisation. An understanding of how value is created or destroyed is therefore central to the governance of organisations in all sectors.

Although not always required to perform detailed treasury or finance functions, Chartered Secretaries need to have a clear understanding of how the process of creating and safeguarding value is managed in the organisation to assess the implications for shareholders and other stakeholders and the need for effective corporate governance. They are involved in the implementation of this process through activities such as processing board memoranda relating to investment or financing proposals, raising capital and other funding, managing profits or surpluses and ensuring both compliance with regulations and good financial administration.

The module aims to provide you with the knowledge and skills necessary to evaluate the impact of financial decisions on different constituencies of stakeholders. It will also enable you to participate in decision making and processes concerning the maximisation of value in investment, finance and risk management, and in the delivery of value for money in achieving the objectives of not-for-profit organisations.

Learning outcomes

On successful completion of this module, you will be able to:

- Explain how organisations make value-optimising financial decisions, and reflectively and critically assess the ethical issues arising from these decisions.
- Demonstrate a clear conceptual understanding of the fundamental financial theories relevant to financial decision making.
- Critically analyse and evaluate various financial models and decision making techniques and their impact on different constituencies of stakeholder.
- Apply financial analysis skills in the facilitation of strategic decision-making.
- Assess the features of alternative and diverse sources of finance and critically evaluate their appropriateness under different circumstances.
- Evaluate elements of risk, return and value in a range of strategic operational financial decisions and understand the implications in regulatory and governance terms of the consequences of doing so.
- Prepare reports to boards and senior managers setting out options for financial decision making.

Syllabus content

Financial governance: objectives and environment – weighting 10%

Objectives of financial decision making

The role of shareholder wealth maximisation in modern financial management
Shareholder versus stakeholder perspectives
Role of the finance function
Balancing risk and return

Shareholder wealth maximisation and ethical behaviour
Ethics and the finance function

Corporate governance

Corporate governance and the agency problem
Financial aspects of the UK Corporate Governance Code
New public management

Management performance measurement – weighting 5%

Measures of financial performance

Financial ratio analysis
Financial ratio analysis, including ratios relating to:

- profitability
- efficiency
- liquidity
- gearing
- investment performance

Value for money
Economic Value Added

Trading legitimacy

The nature of overtrading, including:

- the problems of overtrading
- the factors that may lead to overtrading
- financial ratios that may help to detect overtrading

Financial distress and insolvency, including the use of financial ratios based on univariate and multivariate analysis to predict financial failure

Making distributions to shareholders – weighting 10%

Dividend policy and shareholder wealth: traditional versus Modigliani and Miller arguments
Reasons for the importance of dividends
Factors determining the level of dividends
Scrip dividends
Special dividends and share buybacks

Long-term investment decisions – weighting 20%

Investment appraisal

The nature of investment decisions
Investment appraisal methods, including:

- payback period (including discounted payback period)
- accounting rate of return
- net present value
- internal rate of return
- advantages and disadvantages of the various investment appraisal methods

Practical issues in investment appraisal, including:

- cash flow estimation
- identifying relevant costs and benefits
- the impact of taxation
- the problem of inflation

Comparing investment opportunities with unequal lives
Single-period capital rationing and the profitability index
The process of approving, monitoring and controlling investment projects

Investment opportunities and risk

The problem of risk and the risk preferences of investors
Risk appraisal methods, including:
- sensitivity analysis
- scenario analysis
- simulations
- expected net present value
- event tree diagrams
- risk-adjusted discount rate

Portfolio effects and risk reduction

Shareholder value analysis

Shareholder value and the need for new forms of measurement
Shareholder value analysis and net present value
Comparison of shareholder value analysis and Economic Value Added
Total shareholder return and market value added
Evaluation of the shareholder value approach

Business combinations and share valuation – weighting 15%

Mergers and acquisitions

The economic rationale for mergers and acquisitions
Evaluation of the different forms of purchase consideration, including:
- cash
- shares
- loan capital

The motivation for mergers and acquisitions
The potential effect of a merger on the wealth of shareholders in each business
The main methods of resisting a proposed merger or acquisition
Regulatory and procedural issues concerning mergers and acquisitions
Valuation of potential business acquisitions, using:
- asset-based methods
- stock market methods
- cash flow and dividend-based methods

The advantages and disadvantages of each valuation method
The rationale for divestment and demerger activity and the potential effect of each form of restructuring on shareholder wealth

Capital markets and long-term financing decisions – weighting 20%

Financial markets and institutions

The role of the Stock Exchange
Advantages and disadvantages of a Stock Exchange listing
Stock market efficiency
The roles of AIM, private equity and business angels in helping smaller companies

Main sources of long-term finance

Ordinary shares
Preference shares
Share warrants
Raising equity through profit retention
Borrowings, including:
- term loans and mortgages
- loan notes and bonds
- Eurobonds (international bonds)

Finance leases (including sale and leaseback)
Hire purchase
Securitisation of assets
Government assistance

Raising long-term finance

Identification of financing needs through financial planning (projected financial statements)
Types of share issue, including:
- rights issues
- bonus issues
- offers for sale and public issues
- placings

Private Finance Initiative

Basic features
Issues and problems

Cost of capital and the capital structure decision

Cost of equity, including basic principles of the capital asset pricing model
Cost of loan capital
Weighted average cost of capital
Gearing, and its effect on risk and returns to shareholders
Factors influencing the level of gearing in practice
The capital structure debate: traditional versus Modigliani and Miller arguments

Working capital management and short-term financing – weighting 10%

Working capital management

The nature and purpose of working capital
The working capital cycle
Working capital needs of different forms of business
The interpretation of working capital ratios
The financial impact of changes to working capital policies
The management of inventories, including:
- forecasting future demand
- determining appropriate levels of inventory control
- methods of inventory recording and re-ordering
- inventory management methods such as economic order quantity model, materials requirement planning and just-in-time inventory management systems

The management of receivables, including:
- factors to be taken into account in determining which customers should receive credit and how much credit should be offered
- sources of information available when assessing creditworthiness
- policies to be adopted for efficient collections of outstanding receivables
- methods available for reducing risk of non-payment
- the financial impact of changes to receivables policies, such as changes to the credit period and changes to discount policies

The management of cash, including:
- factors affecting the amount of cash held
- cash management models
- the use of cash flow statements in managing cash
- the cash conversion cycle

The management of payables, including:
- the benefits of taking trade credit and the problems of taking excessive credit
- the policies to be adopted for the efficient management of trade payables
- the cost of discounts taken for prompt settlement

Short-term financing

External sources of short-term finance, including:
- bank overdrafts
- bills of exchange
- debt factoring
- invoice discounting

Internal sources of short-term finance, including:
- reducing inventories
- tighter credit control
- delaying payments to payables

Corporate risk management – weighting 10%

The nature of risk and risk policies

The nature of risk and the distinction between operating and financial risks
Key risk concepts, including:
- exposure
- volatility
- severity
- probability

Risk responses, including:
- risk transfer
- risk reduction
- risk avoidance
- risk retention

The relationship between risk and expected returns
Risk management policies and the risk appetite and values of a business
Frameworks for risk management policies, such as enterprise risk management

Managing financial risk

The main forms of financial risk:
- credit risk
- market risk

Methods for hedging financial risk, including:
- futures
- options
- forward rate agreements
- swaps
- money market hedges

Key areas of the syllabus

- Financial markets and institutions
- Dividend policy and alternatives to cash dividends
- Investment appraisal and the assessment of investment risk
- The rationale, financing and wealth effects of mergers and acquisitions
- Sources of long-term finance and their evaluation
- Cost of capital and the capital structure decision
- Working capital management and short-term financing

Acronyms and abbreviations

AEC	annual equivalent cost
AGM	annual general meeting
AIM	Alternative Investment Market (of the London Stock Exchange)
ANCF	annual net cash flow
ARR	accounting rate of return
ASB	Accounting Standards Board
β	beta
BACS	Bankers' Automated Clearing Services
BAN	business angel network
CA	Companies Act
CAPM	capital asset pricing model
CDO	collateralised debt obligation
CHAPS	Clearing House Automated Payments System
CMA	Competition and Markets Authority
DCF	discounted cash flow
EBIT	earnings before interest and tax (=PBIT)
EFG	Enterprise Finance Guarantee
EIS	Enterprise Investment Scheme
EMH	efficient market hypothesis
ENPV	expected net present value
EOQ	economic order quantity
EPS	earnings per share
ERM	enterprise risk management
EU	European Union
EV	expected value
EVA®	Economic Value Added
FIFO	first-in, first-out
FRA	forward rate agreement
FRC	Financial Reporting Council
FCA	Financial Conduct Authority
FV	future value
HMRC	Her Majesty's Revenue & Customs
HP	hire purchase
ICAEW	Institute of Chartered Accountants in England and Wales
IPO	initial public offering
IRR	internal rate of return
JIT	just-in-time
LIBOR	London Interbank Offered Rate
LIFFE	London International Financial Futures and Options Exchange
MBO	management buyout
MM	Modigliani and Miller
MNC	multinational company
MRP	material requirement planning
MV	market value
MVA	market value added
NCF	net cash flow
NHS	National Health Service
nomad	nominated adviser
NPV	net present value
Ofcom	Office of Communications (industry regulator)

Ofgem	Office of Gas and Electricity Markets (industry regulator)
Ofwat	The Water Services Regulation Authority
OTC	over-the-counter
PBIT	profit before interest and tax
P/E ratio	price–earnings ratio
PFI	Private Finance Initiative
PPP	Public Private Partnership
PSA	Public Service Agreement
PV	present value
RADR	risk-adjusted discount rate
RFR	risk-free rate
RM	return on the market
ROCE	return on capital employed
SD	standard deviation
SEAQ	Stock Exchange's Automated Quotations system
SMEs	small and medium-sized enterprises
SML	security market line
SPV	special purpose vehicle
SVA	shareholder value analysis
TSR	total shareholder return
UKLA	UK Listing Authority
USM	Unlisted Securities Market
VCT	venture capital trust
VFM	value for money
WACC	weighted average cost of capital
WDA	writing down allowance
WIP	work in progress

PART **ONE**

Financial governance: objectives and environment

LIST OF CHAPTERS

OVERVIEW

This part discusses the role of the finance function and the place of financial decision-making within a company. It goes on to examine corporate objectives, including that of shareholder wealth maximisation. It then discusses other objectives for companies and the role of stakeholders and reviews audit and corporate governance. This part ends with the objectives of public sector organisations and new public management.

LEARNING OUTCOMES

On successful completion of Part One, you will be able to:

- explain the conflicting pressures on corporate objectives and assess the ethical issues involved
- demonstrate a clear understanding of the impact of corporate objectives on different constituencies of stakeholder
- assess the key elements of the finance function, and
- understand the constraints imposed by regulation and governance.

1 Objectives and governance

■ **CONTENTS**

1 Financial decision-making

Financial decision-making covers a wide range of topics and functions within an organisation, a large number of which are covered in the syllabus. The main areas we will look at relate to answers to the following questions.

- Which investments should the firm undertake?
- How, where and when should finance be raised and how much?
- How should the firm's profits be used or distributed?
- What are the key principles in short-term financing?

These questions are more commonly referred to as:

- the investment decision
- the financing decision
- the dividend decision, and
- working capital management.

When making decisions in these areas, the firm must ensure that it achieves its objectives. The nature and importance of these decisions means that they are likely to involve the company secretary in an administrative role.

2 Types of company

A company is a separate legal entity, which means that its shareholders may take action against it, and vice versa. Most limited liability companies have their capital divided into shares. If a shareholder has paid in full for his or her shares, then liability is limited to the amount paid. This is the concept of limited liability. Its introduction in the nineteenth century was a major step forward in the funding of companies, as by limiting the liability of investors for the things done on their behalf by the managers of the company, it correspondingly made them more willing to accept the other risks associated with investing.

The two main classes of limited company are public and private companies. Company legislation defines a public company as one that has:

- an authorised share capital of at least £50,000
- a minimum membership of two (there is no maximum), and
- a name ending with 'public limited company' or 'plc'.

Not all public companies have their shares traded on the Stock Exchange. Those that do are known as 'quoted' or 'listed' companies.

A private company can be formed by one or more persons. They are often smaller or family-owned businesses. A private company:

- can have an authorised share capital of less than £50,000, and
- cannot offer its shares for sale to the general public.

There are well-known examples of private companies which became public companies and subsequently had their shares traded on the Stock Exchange: an example is the clothing retailer Laura Ashley, which started life as a family-owned private company.

Some companies have liability limited by guarantee. Each of the members undertakes, in the event of the company being wound up, to pay up to a small sum.

Companies with liability limited by guarantee do not have share capital. This form of incorporation is not suitable for companies whose purpose is to make and distribute profits. Companies with liability limited by guarantee include Network Rail, which owns and operates the British railway network (but not the trains), the charity Oxfam, and educational institutions such as universities whose main objective is to promote education and learning.

What are the differences between a public limited company and a private company?

3 Objectives of companies

3.1 Maximisation of shareholder wealth

The underlying assumption of the theory of finance is that a company's main objective is the maximisation of shareholder wealth in the long term. To achieve this objective, and since the shareholders own the company, the company's main objective should be to maximise its combined value, together with any returns paid out to shareholders in the form of dividends or returns of capital.

This should be done allowing for the time value of money (i.e. assuming that, all other things being equal, shareholders prefer returns earlier rather than later).

The amount returned in the form of dividends is the subject of a dividend policy (see Chapter 3). Dividend policy may be constrained by various factors, including the need to maintain adequate liquidity, the fact that many shareholders prefer dividend payments to be steady rather than erratic, and that the amount of a dividend may be read as a signal from the management about how well the company is doing. Subject to considerations of this kind, a company should aim to get a return on investment that is at least equal to the return required by shareholders, which is the cost of equity capital. If investments can be found that offer such a return, it is appropriate to invest shareholders' funds there. Investments that do not offer such a return are not an attractive use of shareholders' funds and the company should return money to the shareholders, to whom it belongs, as they can be expected to find a better use for it.

This means that the amount paid out as dividends will depend on the nature of the company and the sector in which it operates. Companies in growth sectors, or which have prospects of profitable growth in other sectors, are likely to reinvest more of their profits than companies that do not have good growth prospects.

Subject to considerations of the kind outlined above, which are discussed in greater detail below, the objective of a company should be to maximise its market value.

Depending on the nature of the company and its management, and the preferences of its shareholders, this objective may be pursued over a longer or shorter time period.

3.2 Alternative financial objectives

To demonstrate that the maximisation of shareholder wealth is the major objective of firms, it is helpful to consider other possible financial objectives.

The maximisation of company profits, or earnings, is often considered to be a major objective of firms. Clearly, profit is important, but changes in profits need not correspond directly to current or future shareholder wealth. For example, a company may obtain or provide capital by borrowing or issuing new shares or by investing profits that it has already made in new business developments. In the early stages, before it starts to generate returns, an investment may reduce profits.

Yet this need not affect shareholder wealth. If investors understand the company's capabilities and intentions and have confidence in its management, they may be willing to accept a short-term fall in profitability, confident that their investment will pay off in the longer term. If the company communicates effectively with existing and potential shareholders, the share price may even rise rather than fall. So, a short-term fall in profits can coincide with a rise in share price and shareholder wealth in both the short and long term. For example, United Utilities Group plc, a water and wastewater services provider, reported a 64% fall in profits in the year to March 2015. But other information caused the company's share price to increase by almost 19%.

Many companies target earnings per share (EPS): the earnings divided by the number of shares that qualify to receive dividends (this does not include **preference shares**). The arguments for and against using a company's profit as a measure of performance have been discussed. The value of EPS as a measure depends on the reasons for changes in the number of shares. If the number of shares is increased because the company has the prospect of earning the required return on an increased amount of capital, or if the number of shares is reduced because it does not expect to earn the required return, then the EPS gives a measure that has similar merits to earnings. If the amount of share capital and the number of shares are being changed for other reasons, in particular if the capital is being reduced to increase the EPS, this may not represent changes in the level of capital that increase shareholder wealth.

Some companies, and many investors, measure the performance of a company by the dividends that it pays and the rate at which they grow. The dividend growth model (see Chapter 12) shows how the value of a share can be calculated using these two variables, together with a discount rate that reflects the return required by shareholders.

There are two drawbacks to using this approach.

- The rate at which dividends grow will depend on the rate at which profits are reinvested. The optimal rate of reinvestment will depend on the availability of investments that give a rate of return at a level required by the shareholders. If dividends are determined taking account of this, the dividend growth model – giving the total present value of all future dividends, discounted at the shareholders' **cost of capital** – should give a correct and maximum value for the shares. If dividend policy is not set on this basis, it will not.
- The dividend growth model gives the value of a share to an investor who expects to receive a return, either in the form of future dividends or as proceeds from selling the share. As long as all investors take this view, the valuation can give a reasonable value (other payments received by shareholders as return of capital do not invalidate the principle). Some investors will view the shares of the company not as a portfolio investment, but as a means to gain control of the company. Even if they do gain control, they may be in a position to manage it so as to gain additional benefits (e.g. by combining it with other businesses or by disposing of under-utilised assets).

Another possible financial objective might be to maximise balance sheet or asset values (we saw above that the net value of the firm after meeting liabilities belongs to the shareholders). However, the net assets shown in the statement of financial position do not give a complete picture of the company's value. Most going concerns have market values far in excess of the book value of their assets, as this does not fully reflect a company's capacity to generate future business and profits. This is because intangible assets – which for many companies are the most valuable assets that they possess – are often not shown in the statement of financial position. While some may be (e.g. intellectual property rights), others may not. Perhaps the most important of these valuable but unrecognised assets are brands. Accounting standards do not allow brands to be shown in the statement of financial position unless they have been acquired. In more general terms, the value of the skills, experience, knowledge and contacts of a company's staff, with certain specific exceptions, do not appear in the statement of financial position.

3.3 Net present value maximisation

The market value of a company – which a company may be aiming to maximise in order to maximise shareholders' wealth – depends on the value that the market puts on the company's shares. This is subject to many influences, including economic and political factors outside the company's control. The company cannot control market sentiment, even though it may influence investors' perceptions of, and beliefs about, the company. Managers may well try to maximise a company's market valuation, particularly when they are rewarded by **share options** as the values of those options are directly linked to the share price. In addition, the timescale over which managers try to maximise market value may be driven by considerations such as the dates at which options can be exercised, as well as the market's expectations and preferences about when returns will be achieved.

In order to have a steadier target to aim for – one that is not influenced day-to-day by market variations, but which nevertheless is related to market expectations – companies can use another measure of value: the **present value** of the company's future cash flows.

The present value of a cash flow is simply the value of the future cash flow discounted to allow for the cost of capital over time. The cost of capital reflects the degree of **risk** of the company's business (this is discussed in Chapter 6). The present value of a future cash flow is the amount of money at today's date that would give the future amount if it were invested to earn compound interest. So, in terms of value, shareholders should be indifferent between a cash flow received in the future and a smaller sum (its present value) received today. The further ahead a cash flow is projected, the more it will be discounted; in other words, the smaller the sum today that will be equivalent to the future sum.

The total of the present values of all the company's future cash flows is the **net present value** (NPV) of the company. Other things being equal, managers should aim to maximise the NPV of the company. They can do this by investing funds in investment projects that have positive NPVs. Another way of putting this is that since the rate at which future cash flows are discounted to find an NPV is the return required by shareholders, the NPV of the company is maximised if managers invest in projects that increase shareholders' wealth (by giving discounted returns greater than the original investment) and in no others.

Shareholder value analysis (SVA) is based on the concept of NPV. It provides a simplified and standardised approach to the task of estimating a company's future cash flows and finding their present values. This approach is discussed in Chapter 7.

3.4 Other objectives

All of the objectives we have considered so far are financial. In addition, a company will have important non-financial objectives. These include:

- differentiating products and services so as to make them more attractive to customers than those of their competitors
- providing products and services of high quality
- innovation
- raising the skills of the workforce
- operating in compliance with the law
- sustainability, including maintaining a lower carbon footprint, and
- fair trade.

Financial and non-financial objectives are both important to a company. They may sometimes be in conflict, but often they are complementary. For example, training the workforce to increase their skills will increase costs in the short term, but should result in increased efficiency and improved quality, leading to additional business and profit in the longer term.

4 Role of the finance function

The role of the finance function within an organisation is considerable and includes the following aspects.

- Determination of the volume of financial resources required.
- Acquisition of the required financial resources, either internally through profit retention and dividend policy, or externally through share issues, debenture issues or loans.
- Maintenance of an optimum mix of funding, bearing in mind the potential impact of the capital structure on the level of risk and the value of the business.
- Consideration of the needs of the providers of finance, including the return they require on their investment in the form of dividends and capital growth. The financial manager should understand the effect of share price changes on the valuation of the business and on shareholders' wealth, and should understand and take account of the factors that determine share prices, particularly those over which they have control. The business should not only be maximising the wealth of its shareholders (subject to the other objectives outlined in section 3.4 above), but it should also be seen to be doing so, which requires the financial manager to understand and manage communication between the company and the providers of finance.
- Assessment and evaluation of investment opportunities, to ensure that resources are employed efficiently and profitably.
- Management of working capital and cash balances, so as to provide adequate but not excessive assets in the short and medium terms to maintain liquidity and allow efficient operations.
- Investment of surplus cash in short-term investments that offer a return with low risk and access to funds when needed. To do this, the financial manager must have a good understanding of the workings of the City and of financial markets generally.
- Setting up and operation of control systems to plan and authorise capital expenditure on fixed assets and to control the levels of current assets and liabilities, setting and implementing policies on stock holding and giving and taking trade credit.
- Auditing of control systems. In all but the smallest organisations, there should be an internal audit function to ensure that control systems are working properly and to help prevent and detect errors and fraud.
- Management of risk. The financial manager should play a major role in corporate risk management: identifying and, where possible, quantifying risks and taking action to deal with them commensurate with their nature and severity.
- Assurance of compliance with legislation. The business must comply with statutory requirements arising from parliamentary, central government and local government actions, including those giving force to EU directives and, for a listed company, the UK Listing Rules. This includes preparing financial statements that give investors and other users a true and fair view of the company's activities and of its financial position at the end of financial year.
- Handling of company reconstructions and combinations.

4.1 Areas of responsibility

The tendency to internalise corporate finance means that the financial manager of a major or multinational company must become an expert in a range of areas, including the responsibilities described above. The financial manager must also remain up to date in a worldwide market that is rapidly changing. It is a massive task and, to combat the resulting problems, larger companies have typically created specialist functions, each reporting to the financial director. They are senior roles and their functional responsibilities are discussed below. In the biggest organisations, responsibilities are further broken down and delegated. Smaller organisations may not require all the functions, so one person may take responsibility for more than one area of work. The job titles in different organisations may differ from those listed below, but the functions remain the same.

- **The controller:** This role encompasses capital budgeting and investment appraisal, stock and credit control, the selection of short-term investments and the internal and external audit functions.
- **The accountant:** The accountant is responsible for the records of financial data and for producing management reports and company accounts. The role is split into the disciplines of management and financial accounting.

- **The treasurer/cashier:** The role of the treasurer involves budgeting for cash flows, procuring adequate liquid funds and ensuring the physical security of cash resources. In a business that deals internationally, this function will also include foreign currency management.
- **Financial strategist:** This involves procuring and managing the correct volume and optimum mix of funds, while organising suitable channels of communication with external bodies, such as government and investors, and, as a member of general management, meeting the demands of fellow functional managers.
- **Corporate planner:** The responsibilities of this role include the development of strategic and business plans. In some organisations this may be the designated responsibility of a director.

Many smaller firms do not have a full-time financial manager. Instead, they rely on regular visits by a member of the firm's external audit staff. Some businesses lack an awareness of the degree of financial expertise required to enable their business to operate effectively. Even among firms that employ a financial manager, many limit their key responsibilities to the production of accounting information and recording of financial data.

When considering financial functions in organisations, remember that the financial manager must, to some extent, be concerned with the way in which finance interacts with the other activities in an organisation, such as production and personnel. The financial manager must ensure that the individual objectives of each function do not conflict with the overall corporate objective of the business. For example, the marketing manager who seeks to increase sales or market share must do so within budgetary constraints and profitably in the long term. Budgeting is a useful way of coordinating all functional activities.

5 Risk

Risk constitutes an aspect of financial management that is so important that it deserves to be considered in conjunction with the financial objectives discussed above. As we shall see when we discuss the cost of capital in Chapter 12 and capital structure in Chapter 13, risk needs to be balanced against return when making decisions about raising and investing capital. As we shall see in Chapter 6, risk may be interpreted and measured as variability in outcomes (typically variation in the return on investments).

As part of their strategic financial planning, companies determine what level of risk they are prepared to take in pursuit of profit.

This determination may be explicit or implicit. Chapter 17 discusses a framework for managing risk within companies. Multinational companies are aware that they are taking such risks. Companies in some industries where growth is slower, markets are more stable and the scope for innovation and change is limited, are often subject to fewer business risks arising from the nature of the markets and their method of operation. Companies using a large proportion of loan capital in relation to equity have a higher financial risk (see Chapter 13).

The most striking example in the recent past of risk as a factor having a bearing on financial management decisions has been that of banking. The global financial crisis that started in 2007 arose originally because of the risks taken by banks and other institutions in the USA who approved mortgage lending to individuals with a poor credit rating ('sub-prime lending'). Such risks, in themselves, might have been manageable, but were compounded when banks bundled loans together to create new financial instruments called 'collateralised debt obligations' (CDOs). These were designed to offer investors a range of different risk levels, with correspondingly varying rates of return. One problem with CDOs is that many investors, including professional investors, did not fully understand the nature and size of the risks involved. Neither did the banks that devised and marketed these instruments, nor the managers responsible for the traders that dealt in them. In the case of CDOs and other sophisticated financial investment instruments, companies were taking risks, as any trading institutions would, but they were not explicitly formulating what those risks were, or whether they were justified in relation to the returns that were being earned. As long as banks were making big and growing profits, they were not inclined to look too closely at the fine detail of the instruments that their researchers were devising and in which their traders were dealing. As a result, banks were exposed to risks arising not only from their own lending to individuals, but also from their lending to other institutions, which were far greater than they had realised. The sub-prime lending crisis led to a situation where banks could no longer be sure which, if any, other banks they could safely lend to. This led, in turn, to a failure of confidence in the banking system, not only on the part of banks but also on the part of individuals. During 2008, many banks throughout the world, but most importantly in the USA and the UK, had to be taken over by the state and/or supported by huge loans or injections of new equity capital.

Clearly, therefore, the assessment and management of risk is something that needs to be done in conjunction with setting financial objectives. The UK Corporate Governance Code (formerly the Combined Code on Corporate Governance) was first published by the Financial Reporting Council (FRC) (see below) in 2012. It sets out standards of good practice in relation to board leadership and relationships with shareholders. Companies are responsible for ensuring that the financial controls and systems of risk management are robust. In the case of banks, it seems apparent that, at that time, the Combined Code did not work.

6 Regulatory framework for companies

The main legislation regulating companies is the Companies Act (CA) 2006, which brought together the company law provisions of CA 1985 and CA 1989 and the Companies (Audit, Investigations and Community Enterprise) Act 2004. One of the controls required by law is that all medium-sized and large companies must have their financial statements audited (see section 9 below).

UK company law must incorporate Company Law Directives issued by the Council of the European Union (EU). For example, the Eighth Directive on company law requires more direct control of auditors, and therefore CA 1989 introduced the concept of supervision of auditors.

Companies are also regulated in other ways. For example, financial statements must be prepared in accordance with UK accounting standards, which are issued by the Accounting Standards Board (ASB), or international accounting standards. All listed companies in the EU now have to prepare their accounts to comply with accounting standards issued by the International Accounting Standards Board (IASB).

For utility companies, industry regulators were set up when publicly owned utilities were privatised to prevent the abuse of monopoly powers by newly privatised companies. (These regulatory bodies have evolved as the competitive situation in the industries for which they were set up has developed.)

Corporate governance is concerned with the way in which companies are run and how the interests of stakeholders, and most importantly shareholders, can be safeguarded, given that the shareholders, who are the owners of the company, are distinct from the management, which controls its assets. A consensus has developed in recent years about the importance of corporate governance and the need for companies to have systems in place to ensure good corporate governance, and to report to shareholders and others about what these systems are and how they are working. Many of the provisions of good practice in relation to corporate governance have regulatory and legal backing. Stakeholders and corporate governance are discussed in greater detail below.

7 Company stakeholders

In practice, companies often have multiple objectives (both financial and non-financial) involving various **stakeholder** groups, which prevent the maximisation of shareholder wealth. A stakeholder is a person or body that has made some kind of investment in the company and expects a return and, as a result, has some kind of interest in the success of the company. The nature of the investment and the return expected may be very explicit and specific, as in the case of shareholders. It may be less specific in, for example, the case of the community as a whole, where there is a more diffuse and generalised relationship between the company and the stakeholder. Nonetheless, there is some kind of compact, explicit or implicit, between the two parties, with obligations and expectations on both sides. The different stakeholder groups in an organisation were identified in 1975 by the Corporate Report (published by the Accounting Standards Committee), which identified stakeholders' objectives and specific requirements from accounting information. Different stakeholders will look at a company in different ways and have different objectives. The objectives of companies need to be formulated with an awareness of the identity and expectations of different stakeholder groups. We mention some of the stakeholder groups below and how a company can take account of them in formulating policy.

7.1 Shareholders and investors

Shareholders are an important stakeholder group, being the owners of the business.

To meet the needs of shareholders management must:

- maximise shareholder wealth (shown by the growth in share price and the payment of dividends)
- achieve a specific level of earnings, EPS and dividends per share (note that some shareholders prefer high dividends and some prefer capital gains (see Chapter 3), but the needs of the majority should be met as far as possible)
- stick to a pre-set target for operating profitability, represented by either a set return on capital employed or profit to sales ratio.
- expand the business when feasible – to be a worthwhile investment, growth, level of risk, return on investment and profitability in relation to competitor businesses and other investment opportunities will be expected to be at an appropriate level
- maintain the security (as far as is consistent with profit-making) of the shareholders' investment (the risk/return trade-off is discussed in more detail in Chapter 6) – this includes considering the fact that shareholders have different risk preferences and thus prefer different levels of borrowing by the company
- satisfy the investor that the company has sufficient cash flow to accommodate its plans and avoid future, potentially fatal, liquidity problems, and
- give details of political, charitable or social donations to allow shareholders to decide whether the convictions of the management are in line with their own views.

This is not an exhaustive list of management objectives with respect to shareholders.

You may be able to think of others. A company has to know (a) who its major shareholders are and (b) their objectives for the company, and concentrate on achieving these objectives. Such knowledge would also help to explain price movements when shareholdings change hands and might help the company fend off a takeover bid.

Companies may have only a few shareholders (e.g. a private family company) or they may have many small shareholders (e.g. some privatised utilities).

Advantages of having a large number of shareholders include:

- lower risk of one shareholder obtaining a controlling interest
- greater market activity in the company's shares (thus the likelihood of vast price movements caused by one shareholder selling all its shares is reduced), and
- takeover bids are easier to frustrate.

Against this, however, will be increased administration costs for covering statutory requirements for information to shareholders and it may be more difficult to meet all the conflicting objectives of shareholders.

7.2 Banks and other lenders

This group includes anyone who makes a loan or other financial accommodation available to an organisation. Examples are debenture holders, finance companies, building societies and venture capitalists.

The main concern of this group is the safety of their investment; lenders expect to get their money back within an agreed period and to make a profit. To maintain the safety of their investment, lenders want to ensure that the company's ratio of debt to equity does not become too high; an increase in the level of debt increases the risk of insolvency, with the company being unable to meet its required interest payments. Short-term lenders are especially concerned with 'corporate integrity' – the ability and willingness to pay interest and repay principal from cash generated by the business. Long-term lenders may impose a restrictive trust deed or set financial guidelines (e.g. a set proportion of working capital) to ensure the safety of their investment.

7.3 Business contact group

This group includes customers, suppliers, competitors and all other business affected by an organisation's activities. Their objectives include ensuring that the organisation deals honestly, does not misuse any monopoly or monopsony powers and adheres to the agreed terms of trade for delivery and payment. This group will be interested in developing long-term strategic relationships and in the continuity of trading opportunities with an organisation that is financially stable, with minimal administration.

Customers will want a reliable supplier who provides a product of consistent quality at a fair price and gives value for money. Customers will also be concerned with timely delivery, quality of service and the safety of the goods supplied.

Organisations in the business contact group will need information about the company, including its financial situation, to satisfy themselves on these issues. Some of this information will be available from published financial statements in the company's annual report and accounts. Considerations of commercial confidentiality will determine how much, if any, further information the company provides. In particular, some of the competitors in this group may be interested in acquiring the company as well as being business rivals.

7.4 Management

In the eyes of the law, the directors of a company are its managers. In practice, the management involves other people who are not directors. The management is the most powerful stakeholder group, as it is entrusted by the shareholders with the day-to-day running of the company. In practice, in most companies this control also extends to longer term strategic control. Provided the management retains the confidence of the shareholders, it has almost complete control over the company's business and assets. This uniquely powerful position justifies identifying it as a separate stakeholder group from the employees of a company.

If they achieve the company's objectives, the potential rewards for directors may be very large. There may also be balancing risks, including that they will lose their jobs if they fail to achieve their objectives. The relationship between the management of a company and its shareholders is dealt with in more detail in section 10.

7.5 Employees

Employees will be concerned with the remuneration they receive from the company, their working conditions and security of employment. They may also be concerned with:

- training and career development prospects within the company
- benefits in kind (e.g. company cars)
- pension and redundancy provisions, and
- the potential for future expansion of jobs – for themselves and friends and families.

7.6 Government

The government will want companies to obey the law, pay taxes and other public financial charges, and provide the statistical and other information that it needs to develop and implement economic and other policies. The government will also want companies to behave as good corporate citizens, for example in their relations with the community as a whole or in the effect they have on the environment.

In the case of privatised utilities, the government set up regulatory authorities to prevent the abuse of monopoly powers when British Telecom, British Gas, the electricity industry and the water supply industry were privatised in the 1980s and 1990s, including Oftel, Ofwat and Ofgas. These bodies had powers that included the authority to limit, and if necessary reverse, price increases.

These bodies have evolved as the competitive situation in these industries has developed. The main industry regulators are now: the Office of Communications (Ofcom), the regulator and competition authority for the UK communications industries; the Water Services Regulation Authority (Ofwat), which regulates water and wastewater operations in England and Wales; and the Office of Gas and Electricity Markets (Ofgem), which regulates electricity and gas markets in Great Britain.

7.7 The public

The needs of the general public can take many forms. For example, some may wish to see a restriction on contributions by organisations to political parties, charities or social groups or a restriction on business activities carried out with or in a particular country. Another example would be where local residents are interested in the amount of investment and degree of control that an entity has in their community and its ultimate effect on their local environment.

Where public financial support is provided, the public may wish to see a return in the form of jobs and services.

TEST YOUR KNOWLEDGE 1.2

(a) What is a stakeholder?

(b) Name nine possible different kinds of company stakeholder.

7.8 Stakeholder theory

We have seen how the interests of management and shareholders do not necessarily coincide, although they both have a general interest in the success and profitability of the company. In some cases the divergence of interests may be starker. Employees may have very different short-term interests from management and shareholders (e.g. during wage bargaining). In the longer term, all three groups could have a common interest in the long-term growth of a company, to which a well-rewarded, skilled and motivated workforce makes a major contribution. The interests of external stakeholder groups such as customers or suppliers may also be compatible with those of management and shareholders: customers have an interest in a company that is a reliable supplier; suppliers have an interest in a company that offers the prospects of continuing healthy demand for the products and services they supply.

Stakeholder theory provides a framework for analysing relationships of this kind. There are three main models, which set out different ways in which management – the most powerful stakeholder group – can resolve conflicts between the interests of other stakeholder groups.

The strong form

The strong form model states that management is answerable to all stakeholder groups and should take account of and try to satisfy the needs of all stakeholders. This involves balancing the demands – and possibly also the relative bargaining power – of different groups.

The minimalist version

This model of stakeholder relations asserts that management is answerable only to the shareholders, as owners. This clarifies things, although it may mean that other stakeholders get little of what they want.

The argument in support of this approach is not just a legal one. According to its proponents, if decisions are to be made about the competing claims of different stakeholder groups, they are made by management. If management is the arbiter between conflicting claims, it can play one group off against another. By being answerable to all stakeholders it is, in effect, answerable to none, so problems will be resolved in ways acceptable to and favoured by management.

The pragmatic view

According to this model, management is not formally answerable to all stakeholder groups, but should take account of their needs for reasons of commercial practicality. Even a single stakeholder group may have potentially conflicting objectives.

- Shareholders who want dividend income also want future growth; but future growth requires investment, which may limit the scope for dividends in the short term.
- Employees who feel that their interests are being disregarded will lose motivation and may leave. Investing in staff development, training and communication is, therefore, an investment in the future.
- Investment in customer service is also an investment in the future. Customers who do not get the service they expect may go elsewhere.

- Being a 'good corporate citizen' is not simply to indulge the whims of altruistic managers; it is an investment in the company's corporate reputation and enhances the value of its assets.

So, the task of satisfying stakeholder expectations is never simple. Pragmatic managers recognise the need to understand and cope with complexity. They know that taking pains to satisfy stakeholders is not idealistic but realistic and can offer commercial advantage.

7.9 Long-term versus short-term objectives

The UK stock market is often more concerned with short-term increases in share prices than with the maximisation of long-term profits. This may mean companies choosing investments that offer high profits in the first year in preference to projects that are more profitable but which take longer to provide a return. This preference is referred to as 'short-termism'. It has been quoted as a reason why managers in some companies have bought back most or all of the shares in their companies and given up their stock market share quotation. Emphasis on short-term results is particularly intense in the USA, where companies issue quarterly statements and where many pay quarterly dividends. The phenomenon is growing in other countries, as the pursuit of shareholder value gains momentum worldwide.

7.10 Management–shareholder relationship

The skills and experience of the senior management board, and to a lesser extent its subordinate management, are important to shareholders; they are employed to manage the shareholders' investment on their behalf. Shareholders must trust the integrity and ability of the managers; a dynamic board can make a significant difference to the performance of a business and to how the market views it.

8 Agency theory: the principal–agent problem

An agency relationship exists where one person (an agent) acts on the behalf of another (the principal).The management–shareholder relationship is an example of an agency relationship. **Goal congruence** occurs when the objectives of the agent match those of the principal. The principal–agent conflict arises in many companies when the separation of management and ownership leads to a lack of goal congruence. The financial and other rewards of managers (agents) may not be linked to the shareholders' (principals') financial return. In theory, management should not be able to act contrary to the wishes of shareholders because shareholders can dismiss the managers or sell their shares. Unfortunately, this is often not the case.

Small shareholders frequently have little knowledge about the running of the business and little power to alter its execution, while large institutional shareholders have often been passive and uninvolved. However, this is changing. Institutional shareholders are becoming more professional and better informed about the management of the companies in which they invest. They are increasingly willing to make their views known to companies' managers.

An example of the improvement in shareholder involvement has been the introduction of incentive schemes that attempt to encourage goal congruence between management and shareholders. The most popular is the **stock option scheme**. This gives senior managers the right to buy a certain number of the company's shares at a fixed price at a specified future date. The managers, therefore, have a financial incentive to act in ways that maximise the share price, which benefits all shareholders. However, such schemes have drawbacks: managers to whom options have been allotted are not obliged to buy shares if the price falls below the exercise price. The schemes can lead to volatility in the share price, which conflicts with the principle of a stable share price – something which many shareholders desire. In recent years, with less buoyant share prices, there have been moves by some company managers to rebase options (i.e. to set a new, lower exercise price, which is more likely to be exceeded). Such moves are increasingly being challenged by large institutional shareholders.

Another popular scheme involves profit-related incentives in which bonuses are based on the annual growth in EPS, measured against a pre-set target, such as the average performance of companies in the sector. However, it is possible to manipulate accounting figures and, as with any performance measure, EPS figures can also be affected by external factors, such as the economic or business cycle or tax regimes. Such measures may, therefore, give a misleading picture of management performance.

One way in which a lack of goal congruence may manifest itself is in **satisficing**. Since managers' objectives are not identical to those of shareholders, they may be tempted to do just enough to provide a return that shareholders consider adequate, rather than maximising shareholder returns.

The schemes described above offer one way of overcoming this behaviour, but there may be more general forces at work to discourage satisficing by managers. One is that markets for capital are competitive. If managers fail to maximise shareholder returns, their failure is reflected in a lower share price and a higher cost of equity capital. Companies that fail to exploit profit-maximising opportunities will be penalised. Another is that the market for management jobs and the rewards they offer is also competitive. If managers perceive that success in job preferment is related to the achievement of corporate objectives, including increasing shareholder wealth, they will not believe that they can afford to pass opportunities by.

9 The audit

As a company's ownership is separate from its management, some form of report is required to tell the owners (the shareholders) what use the managers (the directors) have made of the company's assets. This is provided by the company's annual report and accounts, which contains the following financial statements:

- statement of financial position
- statement of comprehensive income (or statement of profit or loss and other comprehensive income)
- statement of changes in equity, and
- statement of cash flows.

The annual report also contains the directors' report, together with notes on the accounts; the notes provide supporting information, including stating what accounting principles were used in their preparation.

The shareholders need to be confident that they can rely on the content of the annual report and accounts. The directors have a statutory duty to maintain accounting records, but the law requires an independent check of the statements produced. All UK companies with a turnover of more than £6.5 million or gross assets of more than £3.26 million are required to have their accounts audited. The annual general meeting (AGM) has to vote on the acceptance of the accounts and the appointment of the auditors.

The auditors are independent accountants who have to certify that the company's financial statements present a 'true and fair view' of the results for the year and the state of the company's affairs at the end of the year. What the shareholders hope and expect to see in the auditors' report, which is published as part of the annual report and accounts, is a statement of the following kind.

> In our opinion the consolidated financial statements:
>
> - give a true and fair view of the state of the Group's affairs as at 31 March 2015 and of its profit and cash flows for the year then ended;
> - have been properly prepared in accordance with the International Financial Reporting Standards (IFRS) as adopted by the European Union; and
> - have been prepared in accordance with the requirements of the Companies Act 2006 and Article 4 of the International Accounting Standards (IAS) Regulation.
>
> PricewaterhouseCoopers LLP
> Chartered Accountants and Statutory Auditors
> London
> United Kingdom
> 19 May 2015
> (Report of the independent auditors in the annual report of Vodafone Group plc for the year ended 31 March 2015.)

To prepare their report, the auditors obtain an explanation from the company of how the accounts were prepared, then make their own checks, including checking a sample of the accounting records of individual transactions. It is taken as a serious matter if the auditors are not able to endorse the financial statements and have to 'qualify' their report. They may, for example, point out that the accounts were prepared on a 'going concern' basis and suggest that this assumption may be open to doubt. One inference from this is that the company is in financial difficulty.

Even on a sample basis, an audit of a large company is an expensive undertaking. Some large UK companies have annual audit fees of tens of millions of pounds.

Despite this, there have been several instances where auditors have given favourable reports on accounting periods in which major irregularities have occurred. Examples have included Barings Bank, where a failure to apply internal controls allowed a trader to incur trading losses in derivatives markets that bankrupted the bank, and Enron, the US energy company, which filed for bankruptcy protection early in 2002 after receiving a clean audit report. In some cases, shareholders and bank depositors have taken action against audit firms on whose reports they had relied. Recent experience has led to:

- the reincorporation of many audit practices as limited partnerships in overseas jurisdictions and, since 2001, in the UK, limiting the personal liability of audit partners in the event of litigation by companies, shareholders, depositors and others
- much longer auditors' reports, which appear alongside statements by the directors on their role in providing the information on which the audit was based, setting out what the auditors did and did not do
- questions about the independence of auditors, particularly where an auditor provides consultancy services to the same client, often in return for very high fees
- demands that auditors should not also act as consultants to the same company, and
- a renewed impetus for the development of accounting standards to reduce or eliminate opportunities for directors to give misleading profit figures.

Clearly, the purpose of the audit – to provide credible assurances that outsiders can rely on what the financial statements say – is not always being achieved.

9.1 Internal audit and internal controls

Many companies, particularly large ones, have an internal audit function. Internal auditors are employees and work for the company throughout the year, not just during the annual audit. External and internal auditors cooperate; information provided by the internal audit department helps the external auditors in doing their job expeditiously and economically. Guidance on internal audits and on access by the head of the internal audit to the audit committee (a board committee independent of the company management) is provided in the Turnbull Report on internal control and in the UK Corporate Governance Code (see sections 10.4 and 10.7 below).

Even with an external audit and an internal audit function, mistakes can occur. Lapses in internal controls allowed large losses to be built up by traders working for Deutsche Bank and Société Générale. One of the problems for internal control systems, particularly in banks, is that some of the financial derivatives in which banks' traders deal are only imperfectly understood by the managers who are responsible for the traders. In addition, in the competitive pursuit of profit, managers may be willing to allow traders working under their control to take large risks. Sometimes, risky transactions turn out badly.

10 Corporate governance: financial aspects

Corporate governance consists of the processes by which companies are controlled and the systems that are put in place with the objective of protecting the interests of different stakeholder groups – most importantly, shareholders. The central reason why corporate governance is a problem, and why control systems are required, is the potential for conflicts of interest between directors and shareholders (see section 8 above). This has existed ever since joint stock companies were invented and has long been recognised. It is the reason why, with certain exceptions, companies' financial statements have to be audited. What has happened more recently – most importantly over the past 20 years (although the related development of accounting standards has been going on rather longer) – is that attention has focused on the reasons for specific cases of corporate governance failure. A consensus has developed that good practice should be formulated and systems set up to try to avoid these failures.

This section presents the reasons behind recent failures of corporate governance, the areas of company management that they involved and the corporate governance guidance that was developed as a result. Much of what follows repeats what is covered in the Corporate Governance module; it is included here because many of the issues are related to corporate financial management.

The section concludes with a brief exposition of the UK Corporate Governance Code, which is issued by the FRC. The Corporate Governance Code is intended for use by listed public companies (i.e. quoted on a recognised stock exchange) who are required to comply with it unless they give reasons for doing otherwise. It codifies good practice, which is also recommended for other companies as well as for quoted public companies. Other companies, which tend to be smaller, are not required to comply because, in certain respects, the requirements are not so relevant to them (e.g. the managers and owners of small companies, particularly if they are private, are often well known to each other – indeed they may well be the same people, so that some or all of the requirements concerning relationships between a company and its shareholders may be superfluous). In addition, for a small company, the costs of compliance may be disproportionate to any benefits in terms of improved corporate governance.

The first formulation of good corporate governance practice was published in 1992 by the Committee on the Financial Aspects of Corporate Governance (the Cadbury Committee, named after its chairman, Sir Adrian Cadbury). The Cadbury Committee was the first of a series of committees set up as a result of problems related to corporate governance. These problems were already recognised in principle as they had occurred in the past, but when they came to light as a result of a series of crises and scandals from about 1990 onwards there was a general view, which gathered support as time passed, that something ought to be done to prevent a repeat occurrence. Each successive problem raised issues that warranted consideration and action.

The following sub-sections describe briefly what each of the committees of enquiry has been concerned with.

10.1 Cadbury Committee and the Code of Best Practice

The Committee on the Financial Aspects of Corporate Governance (the 'Cadbury Committee') was set up in May 1991 by the Financial Reporting Council (FRC), the London Stock Exchange and the accounting profession in response to increasing public concern over the management of large companies and professional investors' low levels of confidence in financial reporting and auditing. Concerns included a lack of direction and control by companies' boards, failures of auditor and trustee independence and criminal behaviour by directors. These concerns arose from, and were increased by, a series of highly publicised company scandals and collapses, involving, among others, Guinness, Maxwell Communications Corporation, Blue Arrow and BCCI. In addition, shareholders and the general public were concerned about the financial rewards received by the directors of privatised utility companies, some of which were monopolies, even when company performance was deteriorating.

The Cadbury Committee considered the role of the board (including executive and non-executive directors) and the links between the board, auditors and shareholders.

In December 1992, the Committee published a Code of Best Practice, aimed primarily at UK public companies.

10.2 Greenbury Committee

The report of the Greenbury Committee, published in July 1995, focused on directors' pay. It included recommendations on the establishment of remuneration committees, made up solely of non-executive directors, to determine executive directors' remuneration, directors' service contracts and reporting directors' remuneration to shareholders.

Most of the Greenbury Code principles have been included in the Listing Rules of the Stock Exchange. In addition, the Company Accounts (Disclosure of Directors' Emoluments) Regulations 1997, which apply to all companies, listed and unlisted, require annual financial statements to disclose details of directors' remuneration, including:

- the aggregate amount of emoluments paid to or receivable by directors, including gains on the exercise of share options
- money and assets paid to or receivable by directors under long-term incentive schemes
- the net value of assets (other than money or share options) received or receivable by directors under these schemes, and
- pension contributions by the company.

10.3 Hampel Committee and the Code of Practice

The Hampel Committee extended the work of the Cadbury Committee.

In June 1998, the London Stock Exchange published the Hampel Committee Principles of Good Governance and the Code of Practice (the Combined Code), which incorporated the recommendations of the Cadbury, Greenbury and Hampel reports.

In summary, the Principles of Good Governance and the Code of Practice dealt with:

- the make-up and operation of the board
- directors' remuneration, and
- relations with shareholders (including dialogue on objectives with institutional shareholders), accountability, audit and internal control.

10.4 Turnbull Report: *Internal Control: Guidance for Directors of Listed Companies in the UK*

The Turnbull Report, published in September 1999 by the Institute of Chartered Accountants in England and Wales (ICAEW) with the support and endorsement of the London Stock Exchange, was designed to provide guidance for directors on the scope, extent and nature of the review of internal controls. Failures of internal controls in banks had permitted uncontrolled speculation by traders and led to large losses and, in the case of Barings, to the failure of the bank. The problem of internal controls is not a simple one to resolve, although part of the problem, in many cases, has been the failure to operate effectively the monitoring systems that are already in place. All companies' business involves some risk, and the nature of many trading transactions in financial markets is inherently speculative, uncertain and risky.

The Turnbull Report said that the board must regularly assure itself that systems are in place to monitor risks and must be effective in reducing these risks to an acceptable level. The board should prepare an annual statement to explain how the company has maintained a sound system of internal control. The guidance was reviewed in 2004 and updated in 2005.

10.5 The Higgs Review of the role and effectiveness of non-executive directors

Derek Higgs' report, written for HM Treasury and the (then) Department of Trade and Industry, was published in January 2003. It made proposals concerning the recruitment and appointment of non-executive directors, their induction and professional development, their tenure and remuneration, what should happen when they resign, their liability and their relationship with shareholders. In particular, it proposed the appointment of a senior independent director. This proposal was not generally welcomed by many companies, who felt that it was not consistent with effective management by executive directors, and in particular by the chief executive.

10.6 The Smith Report

The report of Sir Robert Smith's group was published in parallel with the Higgs Report and on the same day. It made recommendations on the composition and role of the audit committee and on its reporting to shareholders. These recommendations were designed to assist the audit committee in monitoring the independence, objectivity and effectiveness of the external auditors, including developing policies to control the provision of non-audit services by the external auditors. The Smith Guidance is now published as the FRC Guidance on Audit Committees.

10.7 The UK Corporate Governance Code

We have seen that the first code of good practice was issued in 1992 under its own authority by the Cadbury Committee, and the first version of the Combined Code was published in 1998 by the London Stock Exchange as a result of the work of the Hampel Committee. Since 1998, the Combined Code has been kept continuously under review; where appropriate, it has been modified and updated to take account of the findings and recommendations of committees of enquiry on corporate governance as each committee has issued its report. Modifications have also reflected the views of interest groups, such as directors and institutional shareholders. The Combined Code has been revised several times since 1998. The latest version of the UK Corporate Governance Code was published in 2014. The main principles of the Code are organised into five sections, as listed below. The summary of the 'Accountability' section is quoted in full as this is relevant to the risk management material in this module (Chapter 17), as is the 'Remuneration' section because it relates to material referred to earlier in this chapter.

The five sections of the UK Corporate Governance Code are:

Section A: Leadership

Section B: Effectiveness

Section C: Accountability
The board should present a balanced and understandable assessment of the company's position and prospects.
The board is responsible for determining the nature and extent of the principal risks it is willing to take in achieving its strategic objectives. The board should maintain sound risk management and internal control systems.
The board should establish formal and transparent arrangements for considering how they should apply the corporate reporting, risk management and internal control principles and for maintaining an appropriate relationship with the company's auditors.

Section D: Remuneration
Executive directors' remuneration should be designed to promote the long-term success of the company. Performance-related elements should be transparent, stretching and rigorously applied.
There should be a formal and transparent procedure for developing policy on executive remuneration and for fixing the remuneration packages of individual directors. No director should be involved in deciding his or her own remuneration.

Section E: Relations with shareholders

The UK Corporate Governance Code is issued by the FRC and reviewed every two years. Since the FRC is the regulator responsible for promoting high-quality corporate governance and reporting, the Corporate Governance Code is at the heart of the regulation of financial management.

TEST YOUR KNOWLEDGE 1.3

(a) Which committees have reported on corporate governance issues since 1990?
(b) Which aspect of corporate governance have these committees addressed?

11 Objectives of multinational companies

The objectives of multinational companies (MNCs) are similar to those of other organisations, but their formulation and achievement may be more complicated due to the different currencies in which business is conducted, exchange rate fluctuations, differences in costs of capital between countries and country-related risks.

Differences between capital markets in different countries may offer MNCs extra ways of achieving their financial objectives. The relative importance attached to share capital and debt capital varies in different countries. Other advanced countries place less emphasis on equity (share) capital than the USA and the UK. The reasons for these differences are historic and cultural. In this connection, the importance of different stakeholder groups also varies between countries. In Japan, the links between companies and banks are relatively closer than those with shareholders; cross-shareholdings between companies have an importance that is not matched in the USA or Europe. In Germany, relationships between companies and banks are also strong. This arises from traditional, cultural or legal approaches to funding, including the relative importance attached to both share and debt capital. MNCs that understand the capital markets in different countries, as well as having a trading presence, may have options for raising capital on favourable terms that are not available to companies operating in just one country.

12 Objectives of public sector organisations

The public sector includes central government departments, local authorities, the National Health Service (NHS), the police, public bodies which receive their principal financing from central or local government (e.g. the Arts Council, fire services) and nationalised industries. Many organisations in the public sector are not profit-making. Government may provide some or all of their funding and exercises some measure of control over their activities. Public sector organisations are funded either wholly or in part by money provided by government. Some public sector organisations are financed almost wholly by public money (e.g. the NHS) and some receive only grant aid for individual investment programmes.

Public sector organisations are created by Acts of Parliament, and some of the members of these organisations are appointed by government ministers. Ministers may have statutory powers to make other appointments, as in the case of nationalised industries, or administrative powers, as in appointments to advisory committees.

There are several possible differences between public bodies and commercial organisations.

- Public organisations may have monopolies in either a service or a geographical area.
- Although prices may be charged for some public services, they are rarely related to profit-making objectives and sometimes fail to cover the full economic cost. In general, the public sector does not use the price mechanism to test whether the public wants the services provided. Instead, the criteria applied tend to be based on the political judgement of elected representatives under the constraints of the political mechanism of elections, pressure groups and consultative processes.

The public sector exists to serve the community and, in the field of accounting, the stewardship of funds is often more important than the profit motive. However, the responsibilities of the financial manager and the need to exercise good financial public relations are as important as in commercial organisations.

12.1 New public management

Accountability is a very important issue in the public sector as the sector is responsible for delivering a range of statutory services. As has been indicated above, these are largely funded through taxation. This differs from the private sector, where individuals choose whether and how much to pay for goods and services.

The nature of accountability in the public sector has expanded significantly over the past 20 years. Traditionally, accountability has been as follows.

- **Parliamentary accountability:** Through a series of procedures and committees, Parliament ensures that expenditure has been in line with decisions made by Parliament.
- **Financial accountability:** This is the stewardship function and refers to the entrusting of assets to a steward. Stewardship accounting ensures that assets are extant and have only been used for those purposes specified by the organisation.
- **Legal accountability:** One must ensure that actions and expenditures are within the law.

To these, new public management, with its emphasis on importing private sector managerial practices into the public sector, has introduced managerial accountability. Managerial accountability requires public sector bodies to demonstrate that they have achieved their policy objectives while also achieving value for money from their expenditure, with clear emphasis on the 'three Es': economy, efficiency and effectiveness. (Value for money is discussed further in Chapter 2.) Managers who have responsibility delegated to them are required to demonstrate that tasks have been achieved, targets have been achieved and work has been carried out within budget.

This has resulted in many private sector practices being imported into the public sector under the standard of new public management. These include a range of management accounting techniques, including activity-based costing and the balanced scorecard.

Managerial tasks have been clarified and there has been enhanced transparency of responsibility, delivery, delivery outcomes and costs. Often this has been on an organisation-wide basis, so that schools and hospitals are required to demonstrate openness of outcomes and compare performance with other like organisations.

In an attempt to improve the performance of central government departments, the government has introduced more than 650 performance targets (Public Service Agreement (PSA) targets).

13 Charities

Charities are voluntary bodies; they are not part of the government or any other statutory body. Their prime objective is not to generate profits, although some charities do have subsidiaries whose purpose is to generate profits to provide funding for the charity's main purpose.

Charities are not allowed to distribute any profits they do generate but must use them in furtherance of their charitable purpose.

Charities can raise funds from donations, grants from government and other public sources and from endowment income if they have invested funds. They cannot raise equity capital, since they cannot pay dividends. It may be possible for charities to obtain funds by borrowing, though they would need to demonstrate that they had reliable sources of income to service debt. They may have investment decisions to make. They have different sources and uses of funds from commercial companies, and may aim to operate effectively, efficiently and economically, rather than profitably.

However, charities have an equal need for good husbandry in managing their financial affairs, and many of the financial management techniques that are relevant to companies are also relevant to charities.

1.4

What kinds of organisation do not have as their financial objective the maximisation of shareholder value?

CHAPTER SUMMARY

- This chapter started with an overview of corporate finance and the decisions it entails. We have looked at different kinds of business entity, and have seen that the purpose of most is to provide a financial return to shareholders. We have seen what objectives a company might set for itself to achieve this overarching goal.
- We have seen how the law, in particular CA 2006, regulates how companies operate. We have looked at the interests of different stakeholder groups and, in particular, how the relationship between a company's management (the directors) and the shareholders has come under scrutiny. In recent years, the Cadbury, Greenbury, Hampel and Turnbull committees have addressed different aspects of corporate governance.
- We have seen how multinational companies and not-for-profit, public sector and other organisations may have different financial objectives.
- You should now reflect on what you have learned so far and then attempt the practice questions.

END OF CHAPTER QUESTIONS

1.1 'Financial management relies on an organisation having well-defined financial objectives. During a general recession, objectives may change.' Discuss.

1.2 Why does a company need to communicate effectively with its shareholders? To what extent do UK companies do this?
What mechanisms or regulatory regimes exist to support and encourage such communication?

1.3 How might managers' objectives differ from those of other stakeholders? How may the achievement of management objectives affect the other stakeholders in the organisation?

PART **TWO**

Management performance measurement

■ LIST OF CHAPTERS

■ OVERVIEW

This part first discusses the principles of ratio analysis. It then goes on to list, explain and demonstrate the calculation of a range of accounting ratios, which relate to profitability, efficiency, short-term solvency, gearing and investment. From this it progresses to discuss value for money. It concludes by examining overtrading and financial distress.

■ LEARNING OUTCOMES

On successful completion of Part Two, you will be able to:

- explain the role and value of the different accounting ratios
- calculate accounting ratios and critically analyse the results of the calculations
- assess the features of value for money, and
- apply financial analysis skills to situations of overtrading and financial distress.

2 Management performance measurement

CONTENTS

1 Principles of ratio analysis

The accounts published annually by companies constitute an important source of information for external users. Their form and content are carefully regulated to ensure that they are a helpful and reliable guide to corporate progress. However, the amount of useful information that the figures give, considered in isolation, is limited.

Ratio analysis has been developed to help translate the information contained in the accounts into a form which is more helpful and readily understandable to users of financial accounts. The ratios do not appear in the accounts, however, and the user must calculate and interpret them.

Accounting ratios are calculated by expressing one figure as a ratio or percentage of another, with the objective of disclosing relationships and trends that are not immediately apparent from an examination of the accounts. The ratio that results from a comparison is only significant if an identifiable commercial relationship exists between the numerator and the denominator. For example, one would expect there to be a positive relationship between net profit and the level of sales; one would expect higher sales figures to show a profit. So the fact that net profit is £5 million is less informative than net profit expressed as a percentage of sales. If sales are £20 million, the net profit percentage could be calculated as follows:

$$\text{net profit percentage} = \frac{\text{net profit}}{\text{sales}} \times 100 = \frac{5}{20} = 25\%$$

To make an accounting ratio a useful yardstick of corporate performance it really needs to be compared with other values. The three sets of values against which ratios can be compared are:

- results achieved by the same company during previous accounting periods (trend analysis) – it is preferable that this is carried out using results from a number of years, rather than just one year (there is, of course, the problem that trading conditions might have changed over time)
- results achieved by other companies during the same period (cross-sectional analysis) – problems with cross-sectional analysis include the difficulty of finding a comparable company engaged in a similar range of business activities, while differences in accounting policies might detract from the significance of any findings
- predetermined standards or budgets – managers will certainly have developed forecasts and budgets for the forthcoming year, which will be particularly valuable in managing the company through the year. However, these will not be revealed to the outside world, so will not be available to external users of a company's accounts.

For 2014, Bradford plc reported net profit and sales figures respectively of £50,000 and £400,000. In 2015, net profit increased to £90,000 and sales for the year amounted £900,000.

Bradford plc carries on trade in competition with Bingley plc, which earned a net profit percentage of 14% in 2015.

Required
Calculate the net profit percentages for Bradford for 2014 and 2015.

Solution
Net profit percentages

	2014	**2015**
50/400 × 100	12.5%	
90/900 × 100		10%

The company's accounts report a significant increase in net profit, but the accounting ratios show that net profit expressed as a percentage of sales has declined and, additionally, is well below the return earned by a similar business.

This requires investigation by the company to determine why its net profit percentage has fallen and why it is below that of its competitor.

Identify three appropriate benchmarks against which to compare one or more accounting ratios prepared for a single company for a particular accounting period.

2 Classification of accounting ratios

There are a large number of accounting ratios, of which those listed and categorised in Table 2.1 represent the most important.

TABLE 2.1 Principal accounting ratios for financial decision-making

Category/ratio	**Formula**
PROFITABILITY	
Return on capital employed (ROCE) or accounting rate of return (ARR)	$\frac{\text{operating profit}}{\text{average (share capital + reserves + non-current liabilities)}} \times 100$
Return on shareholders' equity	$\frac{\text{profit after tax (and after preference dividend)}}{\text{average shareholders' equity}}$
Operating profit percentage	$\frac{\text{operating profit}}{\text{sales}} \times 100$

TABLE 2.1 Principal accounting ratios for financial decision-making *continued*

Category/ratio	Formula
Gross profit percentage	$\frac{\text{gross profit}}{\text{sales}} \times 100$
Note: operating profit = profit before interest and taxation	
EFFICIENCY	
Total asset turnover	$\frac{\text{sales}}{\text{average total assets}}$
Non-current asset turnover	$\frac{\text{sales}}{\text{average non-current assets}}$
Rate of inventories turnover	$\frac{\text{cost of goods sold}}{\text{average inventories level}}$
Rate of inventories turnover in days	$\frac{\text{average inventories}}{\text{cost of goods sold}} \times 365$
Rate of collection of trade receivables (in days)	$\frac{\text{average trade receivables}}{\text{credit sales}} \times 365$
Rate of payment of trade payables (in days)	$\frac{\text{average trade payables}}{\text{credit purchases}} \times 365$
SHORT-TERM SOLVENCY	
Working capital or current ratio	$\frac{\text{current assets}}{\text{current liabilities}}$
Liquidity or quick asset ratio	$\frac{\text{current assets} - \text{inventories}}{\text{current liabilities}}$
GEARING	
Gearing ratio (can use book values or market values)	$\frac{\text{non-current liabilities}}{\text{total equity plus non-current liabilities}}$
Interest cover ratio	$\frac{\text{profit before interest and tax}}{\text{annual interest payments}}$
INVESTMENT	
Dividend payout ratio	$\frac{\text{dividends for the year}}{\text{profits after tax and after preference dividend}} \times 100$
Dividend cover ratio	$\frac{\text{profits after tax and after preference dividend}}{\text{dividends for the year}}$
Dividend yield ratio	$\frac{\text{dividend per share}}{\text{market price per share}} \times 100$
Earnings per share (EPS)	$\frac{\text{profits after tax and after preference dividend}}{\text{number of ordinary shares}}$
Price–earnings ratio (P/E ratio)	$\frac{\text{market price per share}}{\text{EPS}}$

The procedure followed below is to use the detailed final accounts of Choir plc for 2015 (see Worked example 2.2) to illustrate the calculation and significance of the above ratios. Figures for 2014 are also provided and they will be used for comparative purposes. It is important that we do not attach too much importance to any one ratio but look at the extent it is supported or contradicted by other ratios.

WORKED EXAMPLE 2.2

The financial accounts for Choir plc, used in the following examples.

Statement of profit or loss for the year ended 31 December				
	2015		**2014**	
	£000s	£000s	£000s	£000s
Sales				
Credit		13,200		11,000
Cash		800		1,000
		14,000		12,000
Less				
Opening inventory	2,720		2,680	
Add credit purchases	11,340		9,400	
	14,060		12,080	
Less closing inventory	3,000		2,720	
Cost of sales		11,060		9,360
Gross profit		2,940		2,640
Expenses				
Administration	550		540	
Selling	800		790	
Distribution	650		560	
Depreciation	70	2,070	60	1,950
Operating profit		870		690
Less debenture interest		160		–
Profit before tax		710		690
Less corporation tax (30%)		213		207
Profit after tax		497		483

Statement of changes in equity (extract) for the year ended 31 December		
	2015	**2014**
	£000s	£000s
Reserves at 1 January	1,500	1,310
Add profit after tax	497	483
Less dividends	297	293
Reserves at 31 December	1,700	1,500

WORKED EXAMPLE 2.2 *continued*

Statement of financial position as at 31 December				
	2015		2014	
	£000s	£000s	£000s	£000s
Non-current assets				
Property, plant and equipment cost	1,800		1,400	
Accumulated depreciation	370		300	
Net book value		1,430		1,100
Current assets				
Inventory	3,000		2,720	
Trade receivables	3,120		1,920	
Cash at bank	240		40	
Total current assets		6,360		4,680
Total assets		7,790		5,780
Equity				
£1 ordinary shares	3,000		3,000	
Reserves	1,700		1,500	
Total equity		4,700		4,500
Non-current liabilities				
10% debentures		1,600		–
Current liabilities				
Trade payables	1,277		1,073	
Taxation	213		207	
Total current liabilities		1,490		1,280
Total equity and liabilities		7,790		5,780

The following additional information is provided.

- At 1 January 2014, trade receivables amounted to £1,600,000, gross assets to £5,420,000 and shareholders' equity to £4,310,000.
- The product range and buying prices were unchanged over the period 1 January 2014 to 31 December 2015.
- The debenture loan was received on 1 January 2015 and additional warehousing was acquired on that date at a cost of £400,000.
- No non-current assets were purchased during 2014.
- Dividends per share and the market value of an ordinary share at 31 December were:

Date	Dividend per share	Share price
31 December 2014	9.8 pence	£1.80
31 December 2015	9.9 pence	£1.76

2.1 Profitability ratios

Return on capital employed (ROCE)

$$= \frac{\text{operating profit}}{\text{average (share capital + reserves + non-current liabilities)}} \times 100$$

Note that 'average' refers to the average of the year end 31 December 2014 and the year end 31 December 2015 figures.

The calculation of ROCE for 2014 and 2015 is shown below:

2014 = (690/4,405) × 100 =	15.66%
2015 = (870/6,200) × 100 =	14.03%

Average capital employed was calculated as follows:

$$2014 = \frac{(£4{,}310{,}000 + £4{,}500{,}000)}{2} = £4{,}405{,}000$$

$$2015 = \frac{[(£4{,}500{,}000 + £1{,}600{,}000) + (£4{,}700{,}000 + £1{,}600{,}000)]}{2} = £6{,}200{,}000$$

The ROCE is called the primary ratio as it measures the overall pre-tax percentage return to those who provide funds or capital to the business. The profit figure used is the operating profit, before any deductions for loan interest or dividends.

In this case, although operating profit has increased from £690,000 to £870,000, the long-term capital has increased by the debenture loan of £1,600,000 and, as a consequence, the ROCE fell to 14.03% in 2015. The company raised £1.6 million of loans yet invested only £400,000 in new warehousing facilities.

Return on shareholders' equity

$$= \frac{\text{profit after tax (and after preference dividend)}}{\text{average shareholders' equity}}$$

The calculation of return on shareholders' equity is shown below:

2014 = 483/4,405 × 100 =	10.96%
2015 = 497/4,600 × 100 =	10.80%

In this case, average shareholders' equity was calculated as follows:

$$2014 = \frac{(£4{,}310{,}000 + £4{,}500{,}000)}{2} = £4{,}405{,}000$$

$$2015 = \frac{(£4{,}500{,}000 + £4{,}700{,}000)}{2} = £4{,}600{,}000$$

This ratio measures the return the company has earned on the funds invested by its ordinary shareholders: those funds include both issued share capital and reserves, which are owned by the ordinary shareholders. Therefore, it takes profit after tax and after preference dividend, as this is what is attributable to the ordinary shareholders of the company.

In this case the return on the shareholders' equity is just slightly higher than the interest rate on the debentures, and it has fallen slightly over the two-year period.

Operating profit percentage

$$= \frac{\text{operating profit}}{\text{sales}} \times 100$$

The calculation of the operating profit percentage is shown below:

2014 = 690/12,000 × 100 =	5.75%
2015 = 870/14,000 × 100 =	6.21%

This ratio measures the amount of profit obtained from each £1 of sales, before debenture interest and tax are deducted. It is a good initial indicator of company profitability and may help to explain changes in the ROCE and the return on shareholders' equity. In this case the percentage increased from 5.75% to 6.21%, which is associated with a growth in sales over the period. This indicates that the company has been more efficient in managing the costs in its profit and loss account.

Gross profit percentage

$$= \frac{\text{gross profit}}{\text{sales}} \times 100$$

The calculation of the gross profit percentage is shown below:

2014 = 2,640/12,000 × 100 =	22.00%
2015 = 2,940/14,000 × 100 =	21.00%

This ratio, which is often known as the 'gross margin', measures the relationship between sales and the cost of sales. This is of great importance to a company. Some corporate leaders look at two things before considering anything else: the growth in sales and the gross profit percentage. In this case, sales have grown by 16% but margins have fallen by 1% (from 22% to 21%). This is a concern as it will influence other measures of profit in the company, including the operating profit. The causes should be investigated; the notes to the statement of financial position above indicate that the company's prices were unchanged, so this must lead to an examination of the costs of inventory.

That the operating profit percentage has increased when the gross profit percentage has fallen indicates even more powerfully that management has done well to keep expenses under control.

WORKED EXAMPLE 2.3

A summary of the results of Briar plc shows the following figures. Note that average figures are unavailable.

	£000s
Credit sales	8,000
Cost of sales	5,800
Gross profit	2,200
Operating profit	1,300
Profit after tax	910
Equity	4,500
Capital employed	6,100

Required

Calculate:

1 return on capital employed
2 return on shareholders' equity
3 operating profit percentage
4 gross profit percentage.

Solution

1 ROCE = 1,300/6,100 × 100 = 21.3%
2 Return on shareholders' equity = 910/4,500 × 100 = 20.2%
3 Operating profit percentage = 1,300/8,000 × 100 = 16.3%
4 Gross profit percentage = 2,200/8,000 × 100 = 27.5%

2.2 Efficiency ratios

Total asset turnover

$$= \frac{\text{sales}}{\text{average total assets}}$$

The calculation of the total asset turnover is shown below:

2014 = 12,000/5,600 =	2.14
2015 = 14,000/7,585 =	1.85

Average total assets were calculated as follows:

$$2014 = \frac{(£5{,}420{,}000 + £5{,}780{,}000)}{2} = £5{,}600{,}000$$

$$2015 = \frac{[(£5{,}780{,}000 + £1{,}600{,}000^{*}) + £7{,}790{,}000]}{2} = £7{,}585{,}000$$

* The debenture was raised on 1 January 2015 and would have resulted in an increase in assets from that date, the start of the accounting year.

This ratio measures the amount of sales revenue raised per £1 of assets employed in the company. It indicates how efficiently management is in using its assets to generate sales. The ratio should be as high as possible, although if it is too high it may indicate that the company is overtrading – trying to manage on too small an asset base.

In this case, the ratio has dropped over the two years; although sales have increased over the period, assets have increased by a higher percentage. The company raised debenture loans of £1.6 million but the company's intentions with regard to this cash inflow are unclear.

Non-current asset turnover

$$= \frac{\text{sales}}{\text{average non-current assets}}$$

The calculation of the non-current asset turnover is shown below:

2014 = 12,000/1,100 =	10.91
2015 = 14,000/1,465 =	9.56

Average non-current assets were calculated as follows:

2014 = £1,100,000 (none were purchased during the year)

$$2015 = \frac{[(£1{,}100{,}000 + £400{,}000^{*}) + £1{,}430{,}000]}{2} = £1{,}465{,}000$$

* The warehouse was acquired on 1 January 2015.

This ratio measures the amount of sales revenue generated per £1 of the average non-current assets. Like the previous ratio, it indicates how efficiently management is using its assets to generate sales. It should be as high as possible, subject to the caveat mentioned above regarding overtrading. The ratio has fallen over the two-year period; non-current assets have increased more quickly than sales.

Rate of inventories turnover

$$= \frac{\text{cost of goods sold}}{\text{average inventories level}}$$

The calculation of the rate of inventories turnover is shown below:

2014 = 9,360/2,700 =	3.47
2015 = 11,060/2,860 =	3.87

Average inventories were calculated as follows:

$$2014 = \frac{(£2,680,000 + £2,720,000)}{2} = £2,700,000$$

$$2015 = \frac{(£2,720,000 + £3,000,000)}{2} = £2,860,000$$

This ratio measures the speed at which a company turns over its inventory. Two elements in the formula are worthy of a mention.

- **Cost basis:** Inventories (the denominator) are valued at cost for accounting purposes. Cost of goods sold (the numerator) must also be valued at cost for purposes of comparison.
- **Whole year comparison:** The cost of goods sold measures the goods invoiced to customers through the year, while the average inventories level measures the investment in inventory over the same period. This is why average inventories are used in the calculation.

This ratio can also be presented in terms of the number of days which elapse between the delivery of goods by suppliers and dispatch to customers, i.e. the stockholding period – the number of days that the goods are in stock. This is done by modifying the formula as follows:

$$\text{rate of inventories turnover, in days} = \frac{\text{average inventories}}{\text{cost of goods sold}} \times 365$$

Companies strive to keep the stockholding period as low as possible in order to minimise associated costs. An increase in the stockholding period from, say, 30 days to 60 days causes the investment in inventories to double. Extra finance then has to be raised, handling costs increase and the potential loss from damage to inventories and obsolescence is much greater. But, at the same time, management must ensure that there are sufficient raw materials available to meet production requirements (in the case of a manufacturer) and enough finished goods available to meet consumer demand. It is part of management's job to balance the conflicting objectives of stockholding.

The calculation of the rate of inventories turnover is shown below:

2014 = 2,700/9,360 × 365 =	105 days
2015 = 2,860/11,060 × 365 =	94 days

There has been a significant reduction in the average period for which inventories are held, which suggests that management has streamlined the purchasing, selling and distribution functions. Although sales have increased, the management has managed to restrain the growth in inventories and this means that resources which otherwise would be tied up in inventory may now be used elsewhere in the business.

TEST YOUR KNOWLEDGE 2.2

Why is it usual to use cost of sales rather than sales in order to calculate the rate of inventory turnover?

Rate of collection of trade receivables

$$= \frac{\text{average trade receivables}}{\text{credit sales}} \times 365 \text{ days}$$

The calculation of the rate of collection of trade receivables is shown below:

2014 = 1,760/11,000 × 365 =	58 days
2015 = 2,520/13,200 × 365 =	70 days

Average trade receivables were calculated as follows:

$$2014 = \frac{(£1{,}600{,}000 + £1{,}920{,}000)}{2} = £1{,}760{,}000$$

$$2015 = \frac{(£1{,}920{,}000 + £3{,}120{,}000)}{2} = £2{,}520{,}000$$

The denominator is confined to credit sales because only these give rise to debts outstanding. Where the split between cash and credit sales is not given, the total sales figure may be used to calculate a ratio; this will give useful information provided there is no significant change in the proportion of total sales made for cash.

It takes the company almost two weeks longer to collect its debts in 2015. The result is that a disproportionate amount of money is tied up in trade debts; these resources are yielding no return and are also losing value to the business during a period of inflation. The reasons for the change should be investigated: for example, it might be the result of a conscious policy decision to offer customers additional credit in order to make the company's products more attractive. This can be a sound business tactic, particularly when credit is tight, but management must make arrangements to finance the much higher level of trade receivables that results.

An alternative explanation for the slower rate of debt collection might be inefficiency in the credit-control department, whose functions include confirmation of new customers' creditworthiness before goods are supplied and following up overdue accounts. Failure to discharge both of these duties efficiently can result in an unduly large figure for trade receivables, increased financing costs and an increasing risk of bad debts.

TEST YOUR KNOWLEDGE 2.3

What are the possible reasons for an increase in a company's rate of collection of trade receivables?

Rate of payment of trade payables

$$= \frac{\text{average trade payables}}{\text{credit purchases}} \times 365 \text{ days}$$

The calculation of the rate of payment of trade payables is shown below:

2014 = 1,073/9,400 × 365 =	42 days
2015 = 1,277/11,340 × 365 =	41 days

The balance for trade receivables at the beginning of 2014 is not given in the financial figures, so we cannot make the above calculation for the year. We can make the calculation for 2015, but without a comparative figure for 2014 this is of little interpretative value. Comparable figures may be obtained, however, by basing each year's calculation on the closing figure for trade payables rather than on the average figure for the year. This tells us the number of days' purchases represented by the closing balance of trade receivables. It does not follow that a similar credit period was obtained throughout the year.

This measures the average period of time taken by companies to pay their suppliers. The results must be interpreted with particular care because not all suppliers grant similar periods of credit; provided there are no significant changes in the mix of trade creditors, the average payments period should remain stable.

A change in the rate of payment of suppliers may well reflect an improvement or decline in a company's liquidity. For instance, if a company is short of cash, it is likely that suppliers will have to wait longer for payment. This may be an acceptable short-term **strategy**, particularly where suppliers are aware of the customer's predicament. Management should take steps to raise additional finance otherwise supplies will eventually be curtailed. The figures calculated in this case show that there appears to be no such problem: the average period of credit taken from suppliers remains stable at about six weeks.

2.4

More information is now available about Briar plc, but average figures are again unavailable:

	£000s		£000s
Credit sales	8,000	Non-current assets	5,000
Cost of sales	5,800	Inventory	1,200
Gross profit	2,200	Trade receivables	500
Operating profit	1,300	Bank	100
Profit after tax	915	Trade payables	700
Equity	4,500	5% loan	1,600
Capital employed	6,100	Credit purchases	6,000

Required

Calculate:

1 Total asset turnover
2 Non-current asset turnover
3 Rate of inventories turnover
4 Rate of collection of trade receivables
5 Rate of payment of trade payables.

Solution

1 Total asset turnover = 8,000/6,800 = 1.18
2 Non-current asset turnover = 8,000/5,000 = 1.60
3 Rate of inventories turnover = 1,200/5,800 × 365 = 76 days
4 Rate of collection of trade receivables = 500/8,000 × 365 = 23 days
5 Rate of payment of trade payables = 700/6,000 × 365 = 43 days

2.3 Short-term solvency ratios

Working capital or current ratio

$$= \frac{\text{current assets}}{\text{current liabilities}}$$

The calculation of the working capital ratio is shown below:

2014 = 4,680/1,280 =	3.7
2015 = 6,360/1,490 =	4.3

Working capital is defined as the excess of current assets over current liabilities. An adequate surplus is normally interpreted as a reliable indication of the fact that the company is solvent. This ratio sheds further light on the short-term solvency of the company and on its ability to pay debts as they fall due by calculating the relationship between current assets and current liabilities. Textbooks frequently recommend a ratio of at least 2, but this is no more than a guideline. More important is the trend for the business and also the normal practice within the business sector in which the company operates. For example, a retailer who sells goods for cash normally operates with a much lower ratio than a manufacturer who sells goods on credit. Yet the manufacturing company may well hold inventories for a shorter period than a construction company; in the latter, inventory (partly completed buildings) may be built up over very many months while projects are under construction.

Choir plc is a firm of wholesale merchants. We can see from its accounts that most of its sales are made on credit and that the company also receives credit from its suppliers. The company therefore requires a working capital ratio sufficiently in excess of 1 to accommodate the large quantity of resources tied up in inventories. It is likely to allow customers roughly the same amount of credit that it receives from its suppliers, so resources tied up in inventories will not be converted into cash in time to pay trade debts as they fall due. A ratio of 1.5 is common in the wholesale sector, so the ratios calculated suggest that the company is financially stable. However, such high ratios may have unfavourable implications for profitability since resources tied up in current assets are not earning a return.

TEST YOUR KNOWLEDGE 2.4

(a) Why is it important to have an adequate balance of working capital?

(b) If the rate of inventory turnover improves, what will be the impact on the amount of resources tied up in inventory?

Liquidity or quick asset ratio

$$= \frac{\text{current assets} - \text{inventories}}{\text{current liabilities}}$$

The calculation of the liquidity ratio is shown below:

2014 = (4,680 – 2,720)/1,280 =	1.5
2015 = (6,360 – 3,000)/1,490 =	2.3

The purpose of the liquidity ratio is also to examine solvency. However, unlike the working capital ratio, it excludes inventory as this will not convert into cash as quickly as trade receivables. Inventory must first be sold; then the trade receivables paid.

A ratio of 1 is desirable; a ratio significantly below unity usually causes a company to encounter great difficulty in meeting its debts as they fall due, while a ratio in excess of unity indicates that the company has cash resources surplus to its requirements. While there is no doubt that Choir plc is solvent, there must be some doubt as to whether it is making the best use of its available resources.

Required

Using the figures given in Worked example 2.4, calculate:

1 working capital
2 working capital ratio
3 liquidity ratio.

Solution

1 Working capital = 1,800 – 700 = 1,100
2 Working capital ratio = 1,800/700 = 2.6:1
3 Liquidity ratio = 600/700 = 0.86:1

2.4 Gearing ratios

Gearing ratio

$$= \frac{\text{non-current liabilities}}{\text{total equity plus non-current liabilities}} \times 100$$

The calculation of the gearing ratio is shown below:

2014 = 0/4,500 =	0
2015 = 1,600/(4,700 + 1,600) × 100 =	25%

The gearing ratio indicates the extent to which long-term finance is provided by non-current liabilities rather than equity. Non-current liabilities: (a) require annual interest payments to be paid out; (b) have to be repaid at a certain future date; and (c) may be secured on the assets of the company. The higher the ratio, the more risky the company when judged by the stock market. A company with a high gearing ratio will find it difficult to raise further non-current liabilities. If it is successful, it will find that it faces high interest rates. Its equity cost of capital will also increase due to the increasing risk of the company.

This ratio may also be calculated using stock market values.

In this case there is no gearing in 2014, but in 2015 it is 25%. This is not considered to be particularly high.

Gearing is discussed in more detail in Chapter 13.

What is the purpose of the gearing ratio?

Interest cover ratio

$$= \frac{\text{profit before interest and tax}}{\text{annual interest payments}}$$

The calculation of interest cover ratio is shown below:

2014 = 690/0 =	0 (no interest payments)
2015 = 870/160 =	5.4

Interest payments are related to the level of gearing within a business. Interest payments are a business expense and must be met out of sales revenue if the company is to remain viable. The purpose of the interest cover calculation is to indicate the ease with which a company meets its fixed interest obligations out of operating profit. A low level of interest cover, following from a high level of gearing, indicates that the interest payable imposes a heavy burden on the company's finances, thereby increasing the risk of insolvency.

Interest cover is a ratio that receives a significant amount of attention from analysts and lenders. This is partly because it indicates the interest coverage provided by the company's profit-generating ability, but it is also of significance when service industries are considered. Loans are normally secured on land and buildings, but these may be absent in service-based industries, where tangible assets are at a low level. In these circumstances, it is particularly important to measure the ability of companies to generate enough revenue to cover finance charges and leave a sufficient balance for dividends and to finance eventual loan repayment.

The interest cover ratio for Choir plc appears adequate.

2.6

Required

Using the figures given in Worked example 2.4 calculate:

1. Gearing ratio
2. Interest cover ratio.

Solution

1. Gearing ratio = 1,600/(1,600 + 4,500) × 100 = 26%
2. Interest cover ratio = 1,300/80 = 16.25

2.5 Investment ratios

Dividend payout ratio

$$= \frac{\text{dividends for the year}}{\text{profits after tax and after preference dividend}} \times 100$$

The calculation of the dividend payout ratio is shown below:

2014 = 293/483 × 100 =	61%
2015 = 297/497 × 100 =	60%

This ratio measures the proportion of earnings attributable to shareholders that are paid out in the form of dividends. If 60% is paid out, then 40% may be retained in the company and used for future investment. In this case, the ratio is very consistent between the two years. In the UK, investors who receive dividends also receive a tax credit of 10% of the value of the dividend. Where the shareholder pays tax, the tax credit may be offset against the taxation liability due on the dividend.

Dividend cover ratio

$$= \frac{\text{profits after tax and after preference dividend}}{\text{dividends for the year}}$$

The calculation of the dividend cover ratio is shown below:

2014 = 483/293 =	1.6
2015 = 497/297 =	1.7

This ratio is the inverse of the dividend payout ratio. Like the interest cover ratio, it tells investors how 'safe' dividends are in the company.

Dividend yield ratio

$$= \frac{\text{dividend per share}}{\text{market price per share}} \times 100$$

The calculation of the dividend yield ratio is shown below:

2014 = 9.8/180 × 100 =	5.4%
2015 = 9.9/176 × 100 =	5.6%

This ratio relates the cash return from the share (the dividend) to its current market price. It permits the shareholder to compare the annual cash return with other investments. Of course, the return from equity is a combination of the annual dividend and capital growth.

Earnings per share (EPS)

$$= \frac{\text{profits after tax and after preference dividend}}{\text{number of issues ordinary shares}}$$

The calculation of EPS is shown below:

2014 = 483/3,000 =	16.1 pence
2015 = 497/3,000 =	16.6 pence

EPS is simply the profit attributable to each ordinary share. It is possible to compare the EPS with values from previous years (trend analysis), but it is not meaningful to compare those of different companies, because the figures are totally dependent on the number of shares each company has in issue, and different companies are likely to have different accounting policies.

However, EPS is widely used for the following reasons.

- It sets an upper limit for dividends, which some consider to be an important determinant of share price.
- By comparing earnings with dividends, a measure of potential future growth from the investment of **retained earnings** can be obtained.
- The popularity of the price–earnings ratio as an indicator of financial performance.

Price–earnings (P/E) ratio

$$= \frac{\text{market price per share}}{\text{EPS}}$$

The calculation of the P/E ratio is shown below:

2014 = 180/16.1 =	11.1
2015 = 176/16.6 =	10.6

The P/E ratio indicates the relationship between the market value of share capital and the profit for the year. The P/E ratio is also called the 'earnings multiple' of the company. There are three points that can be made about this ratio.

- The P/E ratio gives a stock market view of the quality of the underlying earnings. From this perspective, the higher the P/E ratio the better.
- The lower the P/E ratio, the 'better value' the holding, giving access to profit at a lower share price.
- The P/E ratio shows the number of years it would take to recoup an investment in the shares of a company from its share of the profits.

Choir plc's P/E ratio has deteriorated slightly over the two-year period.

WORKED EXAMPLE 2.7

Bridge Ltd and Pont Ltd are established companies engaged in similar lines of business. Turnover can fluctuate significantly from year to year. The results for the past year (2014/15) and excerpts from the financial statements for the year to 30 June 2015 are shown below:

	Bridge	Pont
	£000s	£000s
Results for 2014/15		
Operating profit for the year	840	840
Interest	400	100
Taxation (25%)	110	185
Dividends	300	500
Excerpt from statement of financial position		
Ordinary share capital (£1 shares)	1,500	3,200
Reserves	500	1,800
10% debentures	4,000	1,000
Assets employed	6,500	6,800
Share price at 30 June 2011	£2.00	£1.80

Required

For each company calculate:

1. ROCE
2. Return on shareholders' equity
3. Gearing ratio
4. Interest cover ratio
5. Dividend payout ratio
6. Dividend cover ratio
7. Dividend yield ratio
8. EPS
9. P/E ratio.

Solution

	Bridge	**Pont**
1 ROCE	840/6,000 × 100 = 14%	840/6,000 × 100 = 14%
2 Return on shareholders' equity	(840 – 510)/2000 × 100 = 16.5%	(840 – 285)/5,000 × 100 = 11.1%
3 Gearing ratio	4,000/6,000 = 66.7%	1,000/6,000 = 16.7%
4 Interest cover ratio	840/400 = 2.1	840/100 = 8.4
5 Dividend payout ratio	300/330 × 100 = 91%	500/555 × 100 = 90.1%
6 Dividend cover ratio	330/300 = 1.1	555/500 = 1.1
7 Dividend yield ratio	Dividend per share = 300/1,500 = 20 pence Yield = 20 pence/£2 = 10%	Dividend per share = 500/3,200 = 15.625 pence Yield = 15.625 pence/£1.80 = 8.7%
8 EPS	330/1,500 = 22 pence	555/3,200 = 17.3 pence
9 P/E ratio	200/22 = 9.1	180/17.3 = 10.4

2.6 Limitations of accounting ratios

The various calculations illustrated in this chapter suffer from a number of limitations which should be borne in mind by anyone attempting to interpret their significance. The main limitations are as follows.

- In isolation, ratios are of little use. In order to be useful there must be a comparison over time, between firms or against forecasts.

- Ratios will identify trends, but they rarely give definitive answers; they do not provide explanations. They are more likely to prompt further questions and a search for further information in order to find solutions. However, the external user's ability to obtain further information varies considerably. The shareholder may ask questions at the annual general meeting (AGM), a financial institution may demand extra information, but only management has direct access to the information.
- A deterioration in an accounting ratio cannot necessarily be interpreted as poor management. For example, a decline in the rate of inventories turnover may appear undesirable, but further investigation may reveal the accumulation of scarce raw materials that enables the factory to continue working when competitors are forced to suspend production.
- Too much significance should not be attached to individual ratios. For example, an ROCE of 30% might indicate that all is well, but this conclusion might be unjustified if further analysis reveals a working capital ratio of 0.3:1.
- Ratios are calculated from financial information included in company financial statements. These statements are usually based on historic costs, and the valuation of non-current assets purchased in the distant past may not be realistic. Accounting ratios based on these figures might be expected to improve during a period of rising prices, without any improvements in efficiency.
- Differences in accounting policies may detract from the value of inter-firm comparisons. For example, the valuation of inventories on the weighted average basis rather than the first-in, first-out (FIFO) basis would probably lead to lower inventory values and produce a lower working capital ratio.
- Where a company undertakes a mixture of activities, it is important to calculate separate ratios for each section where possible. For example, a multinational energy company may have businesses as diverse as oil prospecting, oil extraction, transportation, refining, petrol stations, coal mines and so on.
- The statement of financial position is a snapshot in time and particular care must be taken when interpreting accounting statements for a seasonal business. Where sales are high at a particular time during the year, such as at Christmas, stock might be expected to increase and cash to decline in the months leading up to the busy period. In these circumstances, deterioration in both the liquidity ratio and the rate of inventories turnover is not necessarily a cause for concern.

TEST YOUR KNOWLEDGE 2.6

Discuss four limitations of accounting ratios.

3 Value for money (VFM)

Within public sector organisations there is rarely a bottom line figure, such as profit, that can provide a single evaluative measure of performance. Many services are provided out of taxation, either central or local, and do not generate sales revenue, which can be the basis for generating profit or loss. Examples include primary and secondary education, defence and the NHS. As a consequence it has been necessary to derive other measures of performance; one of these is 'value for money' (VFM).

VFM may be defined as the ratio of benefits enjoyed to the net input of resources (i.e. the value of the output divided by the cost of the input). It is disaggregated into the three Es:

- **Economy:** Obtaining input resources at least cost. For example, in a school, a manager should be responsible for ensuring that teachers are on the correct grades of pay, and that the school is not overstaffed.
- **Efficiency**: This describes the 'intermediate' output of an organisation or its 'throughput'. Efficiency relates such outputs to the inputs used. In the school example, measurements of the efficiency of organisation of staff include:

  - the average number of students per teacher
  - the staff cost per student.
- **Effectiveness:** This attempts to measure how well a programme achieves its established goals. There are two complementary ways of approaching this:
  - by measuring outputs (i.e. the extent to which the programme meets its objectives). For a school, this could be the number of examination passes, the percentage of students who leave with five or more GCSE passes, the extent to which a school inspectorate indicates that non-academic objectives are met fully by the school, and
  - by adopting a managerial approach that specifies targets for the school and measures the extent to which those targets have been achieved. For example, the school has a target of at least 85% of its students leaving with five or more GCSE passes – to what extent is this achieved by the school?

Table 2.2 gives two other examples of how public sector programmes can be disaggregated into the three Es. In one, a health authority has identified a danger of acute influenza, which is likely to increase the number of deaths from influenza over the winter. The authority's response is to inoculate all those within susceptible groups. In the other illustration, a government body responds to a large number of destitute people by providing free mid-day meals to the group.

TABLE 2.2 Examples of the three Es

E	Influenza inoculations	Free meals
Economy	Obtaining the vaccines at least cost.	Obtaining the ingredients at least cost.
Efficiency	Organising the inoculation programme at least cost in staff and travel time. Providing a specific number of inoculations per hour.	Organising the production of the meals in a cost-effective fashion. To measure this, one could measure the overall cost per meal.
Effectiveness	*Output* Achieving a reduction in deaths from influenza from the expected high level to a 'normal' level. *Managerial* Achieving inoculation of 90% of the population of the at-risk groups in the first four weeks.	*Output* The extent to which the meals satisfy the needs of the target group. *Managerial* Providing meals for at least 80% of the target population.

VFM is important in not-for-profit organisations for the following reasons.

- It can be used to keep down spending. The expenditure department can be asked to provide efficiency savings to reduce its expenditure.
- It can be used to justify cuts in service provision, by highlighting those operations which provide low VFM.
- New public management judges that the achievement of VFM is part of managerial accountability for the expenditure of public funds and that external audit has been tasked with ensuring VFM is achieved.
- Resource allocation is assisted, allowing funds to be diverted to areas providing high levels of VFM; by doing this, the taxpayer gets more value per £1 of expenditure.

VFM has been codified and made operational in the government's 'Best Value' programme. This is defined as the duty to deliver services to clear standards, applying the three Es identified above. Furthermore, the concept of 'best value' embraces the desire to improve continuously the exercise of all functions undertaken by an organisation. Integral to this is benchmarking against other organisations.

STOP AND THINK 2.1

During recent years, a hospital has had a long waiting list for orthopaedic treatment and procedures. In response to this, one year ago the hospital management increased the number of beds and the hours of operating theatre availability for this group. You are to undertake a VFM study after the first year of this new policy. What would be the key variables that you would examine in this study?

4 Economic Value Added (EVA®)

The term Economic Value Added (EVA®) was coined by Stern Stewart and Co., which has copyright on the initials. It may be defined as the operating profit created during the year in excess of the cost of invested capital:

EVA = operating profit – (cost of raising finance × opening invested capital)

where opening invested capital is equal to opening net assets.

The thinking underlying EVA is that profit should be expressed as the financial position after all costs have been deducted, including the cost of the finance that has been employed in providing that profit.

EVA is discussed more fully in Chapter 7.

5 Overtrading, financial distress and insolvency

The following definitions are relevant to this section.

- **Overtrading:** This is where a business is operating at a level of commercial activity that it is unable to sustain financially. It will tend to have little cash and have difficulty paying for inventory and trade receivables. It can often apply to businesses that have grown very quickly but without increasing the amount of capital invested in the business.
- **Financial distress:** 'Financial distress occurs when promises to creditors (i.e. trade receivables) are broken or honoured with difficulty. Sometimes financial distress leads to bankruptcy. Sometimes it only means skating on thin ice' (Brealey, Myers and Allen, 2014, p. 455).
- **Insolvency:** This means that a company is unable to pay its debts as they fall due. This may force the company into administration.

5.1 Overtrading

Overtrading occurs when a company grows rapidly without an adequate increase in its long-term capital to fund its increased working capital requirements. Most companies have a positive figure for working capital (i.e. its current assets minus its current liabilities). When they grow, the increased level of sales is accompanied by higher levels of inventories and more credit extended to customers. The value of credit received from suppliers probably also increases with the volume of business, but the net effect of growth is that more cash needs to be invested in working capital.

If the increase in sales is permanent, the extra working capital should be funded by extra permanent, long-term capital – either equity or long-term debt. If it is not, increased investment in stocks and debtors will be met by a disproportionate increase in short-term creditors or a deteriorating cash balance.

Relationships with suppliers may become strained, and the cost of purchases tends to rise because the company no longer qualifies for prompt payment discounts or does not qualify for discounts for quantity because cash shortages force it to buy in small quantities. Eventually, trade creditors may cut off supplies.

Relationships with bankers are also strained, particularly if increases in borrowing are not planned or the company exceeds its overdraft limit.

Before this happens, relationships with customers may also be affected if the company fails to provide a full range of goods because it cannot afford adequate stock or presses customers for payment.

If the failure to manage cash efficiently is also matched by a failure to manage trade receivables and inventories, stocks and trade receivables may rise, possibly faster than any increase in turnover.

Profit margins may be reduced, either because of increased purchasing costs or because the company offers discounts to encourage its customers to pay early. But a company that is overtrading may still be trading profitably when it becomes insolvent.

If the bank limit is reached, no more trade credit is available and trade receivables are unwilling to pay more quickly, the firm could go out of business despite a full order book and the potential to be successful.

Actions to relieve the situation could include:

- faster debt collection, although too much pressure may lose customers
- more efficient inventory control
- slower payment to creditors, but there are limits that will be acceptable
- increased bank financing, although the bank will probably expect a capital injection from outside the business as well, and
- slowing down the rate of growth in turnover, to allow work in progress to be finished and stock sold, thereby reducing the amount of working capital needed.

Perhaps most importantly, a company needs to increase its permanent capital to match any increased investment in fixed assets and the increase in its working capital, which is likely to be permanent.

5.2 The causes of company failure

The main factor that causes a company to fail is inadequate management, which may misjudge costs, prices or markets, or base decisions on insufficient or out-of-date information. These shortcomings eventually cause the company to become insolvent and force it into administration. The causes of failure are therefore the factors that erode the liquidity of the company and leave it unable to attract further external finance or generate sufficient internal finance to continue in operation.

The causes of liquidity problems may be complex, but they can be sought in the following areas.

- **Finance costs:** Interest charges on debt represent a fixed cost. They do not vary with the rate of output. A company with a high proportion of debt finance has to meet substantial interest payments and it is possible for these to prove too great a burden, especially if there is a downturn in trading profit. Small companies often rely heavily on overdrafts for finance, and an increase in the rate of interest charged, particularly if it coincides with a fall in trading profits, can cause a great deal of difficulty.
- **Operating costs:** The high fixed costs associated with capital-intensive production methods can prove an excessive drain on resources, particularly if there is a fall in activity. Fixed costs do not respond to changes in the level of output and may be completely outside the control of management; for example, local authorities collect business rates from the occupiers of business premises, which must be paid by businesses, regardless of their profitability. Also, the variable cost per unit of output may rise due to a pay award or an increase in electricity costs. If a firm cannot increase its selling price to recover increased operating costs, its profit margins are eroded, or even converted into losses, thereby reducing the level of cash flowing into the business.
- **Overtrading:** A company may be profitable and growing quickly but management takes the unwise step of financing long-term developments with short-term funds. That is, they use money needed to meet operating costs to acquire non-current assets.
- **Unprofitable trading:** A company may fail, even if it is efficient and has the correct capital structure, if it cannot sell its products at a price high enough to cover its costs. This may be because competitors have lowered prices, or there is no longer a demand for that particular product.

- **Adverse currency movements:** When the value of the home currency of an exporter rises relative to other currencies, the value of its sales in overseas markets fall if the price list is in the overseas currency. For example, a Swiss manufacturer exports to the USA and the US customers pay a price in US dollars. In both 2014 and 2015 the company collected $100,000 from sales in the USA. However, the number of Swiss francs per US dollar in November 2015 was 0.88 whereas a year earlier it had been 0.98. When exchanged, the 2014 sales yielded 100,000 × 0.98 = 98,000 Swiss francs, while the 2015 sales produced 100,000 × 0.88 = 88,000 Swiss francs. The Swiss manufacturer has to pay its costs in Swiss francs and the reduced receipts might be insufficient for that purpose.

When symptoms such as those described above appear, a decision must be made on whether they can be rectified in sufficient time and at a small enough cost to enable the company to continue in existence. If it is fairly certain that the company is going to fail, commercial losses are minimised by injecting no further finance.

5.3 Ratios and company failure

As we have seen, ratio analysis can be used to assess several aspects of a company's performance, including its financial stability, return on investment and the efficiency and effectiveness of its management. Comparisons with past periods (time-series analysis) or with other companies or sector averages (cross-sectional analysis) can help to identify strengths and weaknesses. In particular, ratio analysis can help to predict corporate failure.

A business that depends heavily on one major customer or supplier should monitor that company's activities to detect any warning signs of potential trouble. This could cause serious problems for those who deal with it.

Corporate collapse is a serious problem; evidence shows that for every company in administration, there are three or four others with serious cash constraints.

Monitoring companies for signs of financial weakness can help to identify potential acquisition targets.

Ratios and other information for monitoring liquidity

Traditionally, the current ratio and the liquidity ratio (quick ratio), which are among the ratios described in this chapter, have been regarded as indicators of liquidity. A current ratio of less than 2:1 or a quick ratio of less than 1:1 have been said to indicate that a company is facing liquidity problems. Quoting figures that are supposed to apply for all companies is simplistic and unlikely to be useful. Ratios need to be viewed in the context of a company's business sector and the strength of its position in relation to trade payables and trade receivables. A large grocery retailer, for example, can have a current or quick ratio close to zero, since it has small stocks in relation to its turnover, almost no trade payables and trade receivables balances. It may have a large negative working capital figure, but its negotiating strength in relation to its suppliers means that it is at no risk of insolvency. A small retailer, with little negotiating strength in relation to its suppliers, could be at risk of insolvency with a much higher current or quick ratio.

Moreover, research (see Beaver, below) has found that these ratios and their trends give little or no indication of eventual business failure. Nevertheless, a worsening set of ratios could indicate that, whether satisfactory or not, the company's financial situation is deteriorating and needs to be watched.

Many companies, including banks, are making increasing use of liquidity measures based on cash flows. Examples include the ratio of cash flow to current liabilities and the ratio of cash flow to fixed costs. Such measures are based on the principle of relating the availability of the crucial resource (cash) to the causes of demand for cash that could cause shortages.

Other accounting information that may provide indications of financial difficulties includes:

- important post-balance sheet events
- large contingent liabilities, and
- large increases in intangible assets.

Non-accounting information contained in the annual report may also provide indications of company problems, as may changes in the composition of the board if able directors have left. In addition, the chairman's report, although generally optimistic (and not audited), and comments made by directors in analysts' briefings or when releasing preliminary results or at the annual general meeting, may reveal information about problems.

External events, such as legislation, political changes at home and abroad, competitors' actions and changes in economic variations (e.g. interest and exchange rates) may also give warning of potential problems. In addition, newspapers and journals may report on the financial and other difficulties a firm is, or may be, experiencing.

5.4 Predicting company failure

Some companies, such as Inter Company Comparisons, provide ratios based on published financial statements for all the companies in a sector, together with sector averages. These may be used, as we have seen, to spot potential liquidity problems.

There are a range of information sources and techniques that can help to warn of corporate failure. They include the following.

- **Performance Analysis Services:** The company was formed to collect and collate results of some 800 of the UK's largest, listed, industrial companies. From data collected, the company has developed ways of predicting which firms appear to be most at risk of receivership.
- **Dun and Bradstreet:** As a supplier of financial information and related services, Dun and Bradstreet has also developed an early warning system on possible company failures. The service is based on *Stubbs Gazette*, which is used as a key source, providing up-to-date information on compulsory winding-up orders, voluntary liquidations, court judgments, mortgages and charges.
- **Institute of Chartered Accountants in England and Wales (ICAEW):** ICAEW has produced an operational guideline on the continuity of business, which identifies a number of factors that put continuity into question:
  - loss of key management and staff
  - significantly higher stock levels, without the apparent source of finance to pay for them
  - regular work stoppages and labour disputes
  - dependence on a single product or project
  - dependence on a single supplier or large customer
  - outstanding legal proceedings
  - political risks
  - technical obsolescence
  - loss of a major franchise or patent, and
  - history of poor performance within the industry.

  What is important is the picture built up by the occurrence or reoccurrence of several factors, rather than one isolated event. If there is a build-up of such situations, then it can lead to managers having to deal with a series of crises, diverting their attention from the future needs of the business.

  In extreme circumstances, managers may have no option but to slim down the entity, resulting in a lower, but more manageable, operating capacity. Not all managers are willing to sacrifice the prestige of running a business of a certain size. Many problems stem from the failure of managers to react in time (if at all).
- **The Z score:** Financial ratios are designed in general to assess how effectively and efficiently a company deploys its resources. The **Z score** combines financial ratios in an attempt to measure a company's financial stability.

  An American, E. I. Altman, researched the relationship between ratios and business failure to find ways of predicting it (Altman, 1968). He related 22 accounting and non-accounting ratios to a selection of failed and continuing US companies. He concluded that there were five key indicators of impending failure and he used them to formulate the Z score.
  Altman's model emerged in 1968 as:

  $$Z = 1.2\,X_1 + 1.4\,X_2 + 3.3\,X_3 + 0.6\,X_4 + 1.0\,X_5$$

  where:
  X_1 = working capital/total assets
  X_2 = retained earnings/total assets
  X_3 = earnings before tax and interest/total assets
  X_4 = market value of equity/book value of total debt
  X_5 = sales/total assets.

Altman predicted that a score below 1.8 for a firm implied impending failure, and a score above 2.7 indicated a firm was unlikely to fail and should be considered safe. The range between 1.8 and 2.7 fell into a grey area in which the company's future was uncertain.

Using the data from Choir plc, the Z score for 2015 may be computed as follows:

X_1 = working capital/total assets = (6,360–1,490)/7,790 = 0.625
X_2 = retained earnings/total assets = 1,700/7,790 = 0.220
X_3 = earnings before tax and interest/total assets = 870/7,790 = 0.112
X_4 = market value of equity/book value of total debt = 5,280/3,090 = 1.790
X_5 = sales/total assets = 14,000/7,790 = 1.797
$Z = 1.2(0.625) + 1.4(0.218) + 3.3(0.112) + 0.6(1.709) + 1.0(1.797) = 4.25$

Therefore, according to Altman, Choir plc, with a score of 4.25, should be considered as unlikely to fail.

Altman's Z score has been criticised on the grounds that the sample size was small and applied only to US companies. Subsequent research has produced different results despite being based on similar principles.

Nonetheless, Altman's work represents an important effort to find a way to forecast business failure. The current view is that where a firm has failed, financial ratios can be identified that help to explain the reasons for the failure. The problem lies in making a forecast. The financial ratios of a failed firm can indicate to some degree why the failure occurs.

Although there has been no general acceptance of a single Z-score model, several variations of the original have been used with some success. Many banks use computer-based versions of Z scoring to monitor their corporate customers.

- **Argenti's model:** This model (also known as **Argenti's failure model**) is based on the calculation of scores related to company defects, management mistakes and other symptoms of failure (Argenti, 1976).

  Company defects include:
  - a passive board
  - an autocratic chief executive, and
  - weak budgetary control.

  Managerial mistakes include:
  - high levels of gearing
  - failure of a large project (in relation to the size of the company), and overtrading (the business expanding too quickly for its level of cash funding and thus having insufficient liquid funds to pay creditors).

  Symptoms of decline include:
  - deteriorating ratios, quality and staff morale, and
  - the use of window dressing when preparing financial statements.

  Argenti based his model on historical company data. As with the other models, its predictive ability is not proven.
- **Taffler:** Taffler (1982) has developed a model to predict business failure which is based on a series of ratios:
  - sales/total assets
  - the current ratio
  - the reciprocal of the current ratio, and
  - earnings before tax/current liabilities.
- **Beaver:** Empirical research conducted by Beaver (1966) found that the best predictor of corporate failure is a low cash flow to borrowings ratio, and the poorest measure for forecasting failure is the current ratio (current assets/current liabilities).

TEST YOUR KNOWLEDGE 2.7

Which organisations, researchers and measures offer ways of predicting corporate failure? What kinds of data do they use?

5.5 Problems with prediction models

There are several problems with using models to predict corporate failure.

- The information they use comes largely from published accounts and depends on the accounting policies used.
- Accounting information reflects the past rather than being predictive and, particularly when derived from published accounts, is unavoidably out of date.
- Any relationships found may or may not hold good in the future.
- Prediction models take little or no account of economic conditions, either during the past period on which they are based or in the future which they are trying to forecast.
- Companies may manipulate the measures used in the models to prevent predictions of failure.
- Problems in valuing the equity in private companies may make it difficult to apply some aspects of the models.
- Past mistakes by corporate lenders suggest (but do not prove) the absence of a generally accepted predictor.

TEST YOUR KNOWLEDGE 2.8

Discuss four problems with using ratios to predict company failure.

5.6 Company liquidations

The principal reasons for a company being liquidated (and this is relevant because of the third bullet point) include the following.

- The company does not have enough cash to pay its liabilities and its creditors apply to the court for it to be wound up. This may happen even if the company is profitable.
- The company is not profitable enough to continue in business.
- The company is acquired by another company.

A company may be able to avoid liquidation if it can devise a **capital reconstruction** scheme to attract new capital and/or persuade its creditors to convert their lending to the business into company securities. The business must be able to show that its problems are only temporary and that the scheme will allow it to become profitable and/or improve its cash flow. Negotiating such schemes is often difficult, but failure may lead to the business being liquidated. To be successful, a capital reconstruction scheme must be such that all classes of shareholders and all classes of creditors are persuaded that they will be better off under the scheme than they would be if the company was to be liquidated. This is described in more detail below.

5.7 Capital reconstruction schemes

In a capital reconstruction or capital reorganisation, a company gains the agreement of its shareholders and creditors to vary the rights of its members and creditors, by altering the capital structure in a way that allows the existing company to continue in business. Many large companies attempted to solve problems related to interest paymentss and principal repayments by converting debt into equity. A recent example was that of Punch Taverns, a pub and bar operator in the UK who in 2014/15 embarked on a debt reduction scheme.

There are a number of reasons why a capital reorganisation may be necessary.

- The company may be at risk of insolvency, due to poor profitability, overtrading or other problems related to cash management.
- The company may have become too highly geared and a solution may be to issue equity in place of debt capital.
- The existing capital structure may have become over-complicated, with too many classes of shareholders, each with different rights; shareholdings can be consolidated into one or two classes, but care must be taken to ensure that the relative voting strengths of shareholders remain in the same proportion.

- Capital with prior rights may carry a high fixed dividend, which then gives a misleading impression of the company, or preference shareholders may have control of the company. In such cases the structure should be reorganised into a more convenient form.
- The company may decide to replace preference shares with debentures to reduce corporation tax.

If a company needs to undertake a capital reconstruction because it is short of cash, it is likely to need to raise new capital and make changes in the capital structure that allow it to defer or reduce payments to lenders and creditors. Additional finance may come from existing shareholders or from a bank, generally in the form of equity finance, although some may be in the form of loan stock. Those providing such finance will require profit and cash flow forecasts to show how the business can be turned around and provide a good return for their additional money. In such cases, it is wise to maintain the income position of a particular class under the scheme as far as possible. Often, more income will be offered as an incentive to the holders of a particular security to agree to the capital restructuring.

Different classes of creditors are ranked in order of priority for payment in the event of liquidation. The order is:

1. the liquidator
2. creditors with fixed charges, e.g. bank loans secured on specific fixed assets
3. preferred creditors, including employees and tax creditors
4. creditors with floating charges over the assets (generally the current assets of the business) that crystallise on liquidation
5. unsecured creditors, including trade payables
6. shareholders.

Some creditors can have a fixed charge on an asset, with a floating charge over a group of assets for the balance of their loan. This is known as a 'fixed and floater'. A bank that has made a loan secured by shares or other financial securities which have fallen in value since the loan was made could be in this position.

Each class must have its claims satisfied completely before any money is available to pay the next class. Depending on the assets that are likely to be available, this may mean that some classes of creditors can expect nothing in the event of a liquidation and therefore have an interest in agreeing proposals that will keep the company in operation.

Different kinds of creditors have different income objectives and attitudes to risk.

It may be possible to devise changes in the capital structure that leave all classes better off than they would be in a liquidation. For example, loan stock holders may be willing to convert some of their loan stock into ordinary shares and have payment of interest deferred if the interest rate on their stock is increased. Trade creditors may be willing to wait for payment if they are paid interest, and may be prepared to exchange part of what they are owed for loan stock. Ordinary shareholders may be willing to have the nominal value of their shares reduced and to subscribe for new shares.

Secured lenders may have little to lose in pressing for a winding up (provided there are sufficient assets for them to be paid what they are owed) and may have to be paid in full as part of any reconstruction.

A reconstruction scheme must treat all parties fairly and not favour one group over others. The outcome of the scheme should be more beneficial to all classes of creditors than if the company goes into liquidation. If it is not, the class of creditors that does not stand to benefit from the reconstruction may press for the winding up of the company. The increased benefits to creditors (and investors) from the reconstruction scheme can be shown by comparing the liquidation value of the firm and the situation of different classes of creditors in a liquidation with the estimated future results arising from the reconstruction scheme.

Each class of creditors must agree to the reconstruction proposals by a 75% majority at a separate class meeting. Given this agreement, the company can apply to the court for approval, after which the reconstruction becomes binding on all parties.

CHAPTER SUMMARY

- This chapter has examined in depth the calculation and interpretation of a large number of accounting ratios, grouped in five categories.
- It has discussed how to interpret and explain the nature and purpose of accounting ratios and the appropriate yardsticks against which comparisons may be made.
- It has discussed the calculation and interpretation of ratios measuring profitability, efficiency, solvency, gearing and investment potential.
- It has examined the limitations of accounting ratios.
- It has outlined the key features and benefits of value for money.
- It has examined the use of ratios, and the limitations thereof, in predicting financial failure.
- Finally, it has explained insolvency and capital reconstruction.

END OF CHAPTER QUESTIONS

2.1 A friend has inherited a 20% shareholding in private company Merino plc. The company manufactures kitchen implements that are sold to retail chains and through a cash sales outlet from the company's factory premises.

Your friend is unsure whether this company is being well managed and has asked for your help in studying the accounts. He tells you that the gross profit margin is usually 50% of selling price and about two-thirds of this goes in overheads. He has also discovered that external liabilities are normally about one-quarter of equity and that interest normally comprises about 20% of operating profit.

The following financial information is available.

Statement of profit or loss for the year ended 31 December 2015	
	£000s
Sales	5,500
Cost of sales	2,700
Gross profit	2,800
Administration expenses	375
Distribution expenses	1,175
Operating profit	1,250
Interest	300
Profit before tax	950
Taxation	220
Profit after tax	730
Dividend	150
	580

Statement of changes in equity for year ended 31 December 2015	
	2015
	£000s
Reserves at 1 January	650
Add profit after tax	730
Less dividends	150
Reserves at 31 December	1,230

Statement of financial position as at 31 December 2015		
	£000s	£000s
Non-current assets		6,000
Current assets		
Inventories	235	
Receivables	235	
Cash	230	
		700
Total assets		6,700
Equity		
Share capital		1,835
Retained profit		1,230
Total equity		3,065
Non-current liabilities		
10% debentures		3,000

END OF CHAPTER QUESTIONS *continued*

Current liabilities		
Payables	405	
Taxation	230	
Total current liabilities		635
Total equity and liability		6,700

Required

(a) Calculate:

1. three ratios based on the above accounts which examine the management of working capital
2. three ratios based on the above accounts which examine the profitability of the company
3. two ratios based on the above accounts which examine the capital structure of the company.

Wherever possible, the ratios calculated should be those in respect of which comparative data are available.

(b) A discussion of the financial position and performance of Merino plc based on the results of your calculations under (a) and the information provided in the question.

2.2 The following information is provided by Ackworth plc and Cohn plc, which supply a similar range of products but are located in different geographical areas and are not in competition with one another.

	Ackworth	**Cohn**
	£000s	£000s
Operating profit	600	1,200
Turnover	7,200	9,000
Average investment in total assets	2,400	6,000

The following accounting ratios are provided by the trade association to which they each belong. The ratios are averages for members of the association.

Total asset turnover	1.5
Operating profit percentage	14%
Rate of return on total assets	21%

Required

(a) Separate calculations for the two companies of ratios equivalent to those provided by the trade association.

(b) An analysis of the performance of each company by comparison with members of the trade association and with each other.

2.3 Financial information is available for the following two companies in the same line of business. A client is considering investing in the equity in one of the companies and has approached you for advice on this.

Statement of financial position as at 31 December 2015

	Euro		**Dollar**	
	£000s	£000s	£000s	£000s
Non-current assets				
Land and buildings	381		286	
Fixtures and fittings	342		218	
Vehicles	62	785	59	563
Current assets				
Inventories	96		122	
Receivables	166		124	
Cash	9		6	
Total current assets		271		252
Total assets		1,056		815
Equity				
£1 ordinary shares		470		250
Reserves		35		65
Profit and loss		287		85
Total equity		792		400
Long-term liabilities				
Debentures		64		255

END OF CHAPTER QUESTIONS *continued*

Current liabilities				
Bank overdraft	20		21	
Payables	132		97	
Accrued expenses	48		42	
Total current liabilities		200		160
Total equity and liabilities		1,056		815
Current share price		3.50		4.65

Statement of profit or loss for the year ended 31 December 2015

	Euro		Dollar	
	£000s	£000s	£000s	£000s
Credit sales		570		747
Cost of sales				
Opening inventory	92		102	
Credit purchases	381		568	
	473		670	
Less closing inventory	96	377	122	548
Gross profit		193		199
Distribution costs	30		24	
Administrations costs	19		21	
Depreciation	40	89	50	95
Operating profit		104		104
Interest charges		7		27
Profit before tax		97		77
Taxation		46		36
Profit after tax		51		41
Dividends		37		30
Retained profit		14		11

Required

(a) Calculate a range of profitability, efficiency, solvency, gearing and investment ratios for both companies.

(b) Provide a reasoned recommendation to your client.

PART **THREE**

Making distributions to shareholders

■ LIST OF CHAPTERS

■ OVERVIEW

This part examines the relationship between dividend policy and shareholder wealth and provides different explanations of this relationship. It examines the importance of dividends and the different factors that determine the level of dividends. Finally, it examines scrip dividends, special dividends and share buy-backs.

■ LEARNING OUTCOMES

On successful completion of Part Three, you will be able to:

- demonstrate a clear understanding of the importance of dividends and factors that determine the level of dividends
- critically analyse and evaluate various models of dividend policy and shareholder wealth, and
- explain the role of diverse instruments, such as scrip dividends, special dividends and share buy-backs.

3 Distribution

■ **CONTENTS**

1 Dividend policy and shareholder wealth

Shareholders invest in a company in order to receive a return. The way the company pays that return to the shareholders is in the form of dividends. The amount of dividends paid to ordinary shareholders is a matter of company policy to be *decided by the board of directors* (and ratified by the shareholders). The issue to address here is whether the pattern of dividend payments over time can influence the wealth of the shareholders.

As indicated, the essence of corporate dividend policy is the choice between whether to pay dividends now or to invest funds to generate capital gains in the future. (Dividend decisions may also include decisions about scrip dividends, which pay dividends by issuing new shares.) There is a debate as to whether the market value of a company's shares (and thus the value of the firm) is affected by dividend policy.

This is illustrated in Worked example 3.1.

WORKED EXAMPLE 3.1

This example illustrates the impact of dividends on the statement of financial position and on shareholder wealth.

Company A has the following statement of financial position:

	£
Non-current assets	10,000
Current assets	
Trade receivables and inventory	3,000
Cash	600
Total assets	13,600
Loans	5,000
Net assets	8,600
Equity	
Ordinary share capital (£1 shares)	1,000
Reserves: profit and loss account	7,600
Total shareholders' funds	8,600

The directors of Company A pay a cash dividend to the ordinary shareholders of £0.50 per share, totalling £500. The company's share price prior to the dividend payment was £15.

We will examine the effect of this dividend on:

- the company's statement of financial position, and
- the company's share price.

WORKED EXAMPLE 3.1 *continued*

Effects on the statement of financial position

The dividend will have the following effects on the company's financial position.

Shareholders' funds:

- The dividend represents a distribution of profits so will reduce the profits retained in the business from £7,600 to £7,100, which reduces the value of shareholders' funds in the statement of financial position to £7,100 + £1,000 = £8,100.
- Therefore, a company must have sufficient distributable profits from which to take a dividend.

Cash balance:

- The cash payment will reduce the company's cash balance from £600 to £100.
- Therefore, a company must have sufficient cash to pay a dividend.
- If there is insufficient cash the company may have to:
  - issue more shares, or
  - borrow more money, or
  - cut back on the number of capital investments in order to pay the dividend.

Effects on the share price

The effect on the market price of the shares is more difficult to identify.

There are three possibilities:

	1	2	3
Share price prior to dividend (known as 'cum div')	£15	£15	£15
Dividend	£0.50	£0.50	£0.50
Share price after dividend is paid (known as 'ex div')	£14.50	> £14.50	< £14.50
Shareholder now has:			
Share worth	£14.50	> £14.50	< £14.50
Cash	£0.50	£0.50	£0.50
Total	£15	> £15	< £15
	Dividend has no effect on wealth	Dividend has increased wealth	Dividend has decreased wealth

Therefore, there are three theoretical conclusions.

- Dividends are irrelevant.
- Dividend payments may increase wealth.
- Dividend payments may decrease wealth.

1.1 Shareholders, dividends and taxation

Dividends affect the form in which shareholders receive their 'return'.

- For individual shareholders who are taxpayers, a cash dividend is treated as income for individuals and is therefore subject to income tax at the recipient's marginal rate of taxation. This may be as high as 50%. However, if cash is retained in the company, shareholders should benefit from a capital gain (they hope), which is subject to capital gains tax. The capital gains tax threshold is generous, in excess of £11,000 of capital gains per year.
- Non-taxpayers should be indifferent between capital gains and dividends, at least in terms of taxation (though they may have to go to the trouble of selling shares to generate income if dividends are reduced, leading them to prefer dividends).

- Corporate investors pay tax on income and capital gains at the corporation tax rate. Companies should therefore be indifferent between dividends and capital gains.

1.2 The traditional view of dividends

From a theoretical perspective, the traditional view of dividends was developed by Myron Gordon (1959). Dividends enhance shareholder wealth, so higher dividends would be preferred, hence the ex-div share price goes down by less than the amount of the dividend. The idea is that investors prefer a cash dividend now, which is certain, to a future capital gain or future dividends, which is uncertain. This is sometimes referred to as 'the bird-in-the-hand' theory.

There are two possible justifications for this:

- 'when valuing shares on the basis of earnings investors apply one multiplier to that proportion of earnings paid out as dividends and a much smaller multiplier (and therefore a lower value) to the undistributed balance' (Graham and Dodd, 1951).
- There is support for the view that companies carrying out riskier activities choose a lower payout policy. This is a safety-first policy designed to reduce the need for such companies to borrow, which would itself further increase the company's risk profile.

High dividend payouts reduce the risk that shareholders might lose their whole investment. In other words, the important factor is the difference in perceived risk between the current and future activities of the company. Immediate dividends are valued more highly than future dividends because of the perceived higher risk attached to the latter.

However, the traditional view has been criticised under what is referred to as the 'bird-in-the-hand fallacy'. It is argued that the risk of a company's dividends is derived from the risk of the business regardless of the time frame. Therefore, shareholders should be indifferent between the receipt of dividends now or later where the emphasis is on the effect of business risk in generating returns. Moreover, the fixation on earlier dividends tends to ignore the capital gains aspect of holding shares. Where companies are investing rather than paying dividends, shareholders may benefit from an increase in the share price in the future.

1.3 Modigliani and Miller's dividend irrelevance theory

According to a seminal 1961 paper by Modigliani and Miller (MM) on dividend irrelevance theory, the value of a company is determined by the net present value (NPV) of its investments, and not by its distribution policy. MM showed that, under the assumptions of perfect markets and rational investors, a company's cost of capital and the returns to investors are not affected by the dividends paid. If a company chooses to pay a dividend, then in perfect capital markets it can raise new capital in the market for investments at the same cost as the return earned by investors on the money paid out as dividends. If investors want cash for current expenditure, they can raise it in the absence of dividends by selling shares and creating 'home-made dividends'.

Worked example 3.2 demonstrates the MM theory at work.

WORKED EXAMPLE 3.2

An illustration of MM's dividend irrelevance theory.

- A company has a market value of £1 million with annual earnings of £100,000, or 10%. The company's cost of finance is 10% and it invests to obtain a 10% return.
- The company has to choose between distributing the £100,000 in dividends or, alternatively, investing the money within the business to earn a 10% return. MM shows that either course of action can lead to identical market values and earnings if the company replaces the dividend by raising a further £100,000 in the stock market at a cost of 10% per year and then reinvests that amount. The table below illustrates this.

WORKED EXAMPLE 3.2 *continued*

Distribute £100,000 in dividends	or	Retain £100,000 within the firm
The market value falls to £900,000 Cost of finance 10%		
Raise capital to invest Raise £100,000 at 10%		
Market value = £1 million Earnings 10% × £1 million = £100,000		Market value = £1 million Earnings 10% × £1 million = £100,000

However, the assumptions on which MM's dividend irrelevance theory is based can be challenged, lending support to the idea that the level of dividends can in fact have an effect on the value of the firm. The assumptions, with comments on their possible limitations, are as follows.

- There are no transaction costs or difficulties in borrowing.
  However, there often are transaction costs, and because of issue costs it may be considerably less expensive for the firm to retain its earnings and pay a lower dividend.
- Taxation can be ignored.
  In reality, taxation may have a bearing, as we have seen in section 1.1 above.
- In a perfect capital market all traders have equal and costless information about the share price. Similarly, shareholders receive all relevant information about the company's investment plans cost-free.
  However, imperfect information may mean that the NPVs of proposed projects are not immediately reflected in the firm's share price, although their effects will become apparent over time, while in an imperfect and uncertain market, dividend announcements can have a rapid impact on the share price.
- Individuals and companies can borrow at the same rate of interest.
  This is often not the case in practice.

In addition, empirical evidence suggests that investors prefer a dividend policy with either constant or steadily growing dividends, which help them to plan their finances, while uncertainty about the future can mean that shareholders may prefer a certain dividend now to an uncertain capital gain later.

1.4 Other theories relating to dividend policy

Information asymmetry

The directors of a company have access to all relevant 'inside' information relating to the company. However, the shareholders, unless they are also directors (which is unlikely), only have access to information that is released to them. The directors may use dividends as a signal of the future prospects of the business, with an increase in dividends reflecting their opinion of future growth expectations. It is argued that shareholders are more likely to pay attention to dividends than to the words of directors as dividends represent cash. Therefore, if cash is required for purposes of investment, the financial director is unlikely to cut dividends because of the signal that it sends to the market. Instead, the company is likely to go to the market to raise finance while maintaining dividend payments so that stated dividend policy and trend growth are not interrupted. This theory is often termed the 'signalling hypothesis'.

The share price at any time will reflect investors' opinions on future prospects of the firm, including their forecasts on future dividend payments. The announcement of the amount of the current dividend, which is decided by the directors, who have access to inside information, may cause investors to revise their forecasts. The current dividend gives evidence of future dividend growth prospects (or lack thereof!). In other words, the dividend acts as a signal from the directors to investors.

Agency costs

The directors of a company act as agents to the shareholders, who are the principals in the agency relationship. The directors should act in the best interests of the shareholders, and yet they may be tempted not to.

Agency costs arise because different interest groups are considered to be looking after their own interests. For example, when lenders provide loans to the company, they will ensure that their loans are secured on assets such as land and buildings; they may also insist on a minimum liquidity ratio and try to reduce growth in dividends to the growth in post-tax profit. These are designed to protect the interest of lenders. Thus, interest groups protect themselves and in the process impose costs or restraints on the behaviour of others. Similarly, shareholders will try to protect their interests against managers, who are commonly assumed to indulge in expensive cars, offices and bonuses. To try to forestall this, shareholders may insist that profits be distributed as dividends, thereby reducing the surplus cash in the company and the opportunity for managers to indulge any expensive tastes. Additionally, if the directors feel obligated to maintain dividend payments, this imposes on the directors the obligation to make decisions that will ensure that the company has sufficient cash resources to pay those dividends. This could be achieved by investing in projects with a positive NPV.

A possible consequence of the company continuing to pay dividends is that it may then be necessary to issue more shares to fund projects. This is inefficient in terms of transaction costs, and it could be argued that the shareholders benefit from stable dividend income and more information. If there was a share issue the directors would be obliged to justify why they want to obtain the extra funds.

Dividends as a residual

The idea of treating dividends as a residual of the investment decision is to take into account the high cost of undertaking a share issue. If we take the MM theorem above, the suggestion that the company could pay its dividend of £100,000 and simply raise the £100,000 by issuing more shares to the shareholders would, in reality, be very expensive. The company would incur the cost of administering the dividend payment and the significant cost of undertaking a share issue.

Hence, the proposition of treating dividends as a residual is that to increase the value of the company the directors should identify all positive NPV projects available and use the cash available to invest in those projects. Then, if there is any surplus cash this should be paid to the shareholders as a dividend. If they wish, the shareholders would then be able to invest this dividend in other firms, which have positive NPV projects available to them. The amount of dividends to shareholders is therefore the balancing figure and would fluctuate as the availability of positive NPV projects fluctuates.

This suggestion depends on shareholders being prepared to accept wide variations in the dividend payments they receive. There is also the issue of the information content of the dividend. If the directors cut the dividend, this might act as a negative signal to the market, which would adversely affect the share price.

Empirical evidence suggests that the stock market likes to see stable but growing dividends.

The clientele effect

The clientele effect refers to the fact that different shareholders have different needs.

- Some investors prefer companies with high payout policies. These include pension funds and trust funds, which are looking for regular income to pay out pensions etc., and retired people, who may require income to live on.
- Investors with high marginal rates of income tax might prefer low dividends and higher associated capital gains.

Thus, it is unlikely any distribution policy will meet the needs of all shareholders because of differences in the liability to taxation (most importantly through income tax, capital gains tax and corporation tax) of different shareholders and their different attitudes to risk. A company should adopt a dividend policy that maximises the wealth of one group of shareholders. Shareholders will then invest in companies that operate dividend policies in line with their needs – this is known as the 'clientele effect'. This implies that having adopted a particular dividend policy, a company should adhere to that policy and try to avoid future changes to such a policy.

Empirical work

Empirical work has mostly been carried out in the USA and the results imply that companies regard dividend policy as being important. The evidence seems to suggest that the stock market likes to see stable but growing dividends. Many companies engage in 'dividend smoothing', where the growth in dividends is related to the firm's expected long-term growth rate. Even when profits fluctuate, dividends continue to grow. Firms try to avoid cutting dividends. For example, a study of companies by Lintner (1956) found that many companies matched their dividend payments as a proportion of earnings. However, the growth in dividends tended to lag behind growth in earnings. Furthermore, increases in dividends were implemented only when managers were certain that the increased level of dividends could be sustained. Other studies on the signalling effect of dividends (Brav et al., 2005) confirm that managers try very hard to ensure that new levels of dividends can be maintained in the future. They are aware that if dividends have to be reduced, the market would interpret such a move with suspicion.

However, as Woolridge and Ghosh (1998) explain in their article 'Dividend cuts: Do they always signal bad news?' this is not necessarily the case for companies with many profitable investment opportunities but little cash. They found that when cuts are announced, the adverse effects outweigh the positive signal of investment, but all companies enjoy a recovery in share price in the next year, as long as they follow these key lessons:

- It is important that management communicates its investment strategy effectively.
- Signals that are costly (such as a stock repurchase) are more successful.
- Management must deliver on its promises or forfeit its credibility.

There is evidence to support the clientele effect. For example, Elton and Gruber (1970) find evidence of the existence of tax clienteles. Shareholders in companies paying high dividends have lower effective tax rates than shareholders in companies paying low or no dividends. This is explained by shareholders in the latter case preferring to receive their returns in the form of capital gains rather than dividends because as higher rate taxpayers they would wish to minimise their income tax payments. Other studies have identified other types of clienteles based on different investor preferences. For example, Becker et al. (2011) find that older investors prefer companies with high payout policies in order to provide them with a steady cash income.

Summary of dividend policy theories

Theories associated with 'dividends increasing shareholder wealth' are:

- agency theory
- information asymmetry
- some clientele effects
- traditional view: 'bird-in-the-hand' theory.

Theories associated with 'dividends decreasing shareholder wealth' are:

- dividends as a residual
- tax system
- some clientele effects.

TEST YOUR KNOWLEDGE 3.1

(a) Summarise the traditional view of dividends and the MM theory.
(b) Provide four arguments against the MM theory.
(c) Summarise three alternative theories relating to the impact of dividends on shareholder wealth.

2 The importance of dividends

Dividends are regarded as important within the business community for a variety of reasons:

- Dividends are recommended by the directors of the company and are subject to approval by a majority of shareholders at the annual general meeting of the company. So any decision regarding the amount of dividends has a high profile within corporate decision-making.
- Shareholders purchase shares for the potential returns that they will bring. Those returns manifest themselves as dividends, which represent the cash return to shareholders for bearing risk. Shareholders may also receive a further return when they sell their shares, but future share value will be influenced by the dividend policy of the company.
- Shareholders' expectations are extremely important and a company tries to meet and influence these expectations through its dividend policy. Many companies attempt to keep dividends growing over time at what they consider to be the company's growth rate, even though actual post-tax profits may fluctuate significantly. This policy is one of attempting to use dividends to signal the directors' expectations. Dividends are, therefore, an important signal to the stock market, and announcements of dividends by companies figure prominently in the business pages.
- Dividends can represent a significant outflow of cash for the company and so this is something that company management has to plan for. Management must ensure that the payment of dividends will not damage the liquidity and solvency of the company.
- For growth companies, there is a high-level choice to be made. What proportion of post-tax profits will be paid in dividends and what proportion will be used to finance capital expenditure. The company may be reluctant to seek external finance, due to the transaction costs of a share issue or because the company's gearing is already at a high level. If this company chooses to pay dividends, that decision may have a high opportunity cost in terms of the foregone capital expenditure.
- Dividends are important to many groups of shareholders, who will have expectations of a certain level of dividends. For this reason, many UK companies pay out an interim dividend, part way through the year, and a final dividend at the end of the year. British Petroleum plc pays out dividends quarterly.
- There is little doubt that sudden variations in dividend policy can lead to significant changes in the share price. It is important that management provides advanced explanations and forewarning in order to mitigate these fluctuations.

Identify five reasons for the importance of dividends.

3 Factors determining the levels of dividends

In practice, the directors of a company must bear several considerations in mind when determining dividend policy. These considerations include the following.

- **Shareholders' expectations:** The company should ensure its dividend policy is matched to the expectations of the company's shareholders, so as to avoid excessive turnover of shares.
- **Defence against takeover bids:** Dividends can be used by the company as part of a defence against an unwanted takeover bid. In such an event, the market may perceive an increased dividend as an indicator of improved future profitability, leading to an increase in the share price. This makes it more expensive for any potential bidder to gain control. In 2009, Cadbury, a UK confectionary manufacturer, issued a takeover defence document promising increased dividends as part of its defence against a hostile takeover bid from Kraft Foods, the world's second largest food company. However, the £11.5 billion deal was completed in January 2010.

- **Realistic attitude of the company to commercial pressures:** In 2014, the supermarket chain WM Morrison increased its dividend despite a fall in profits. The move was to appease shareholders at a time when the supermarket had been criticised for being late in extending its offering both online and to convenience store markets. The company defended the increase in dividend by arguing that it had ample cash to cover the payment. However, some commentators accused the supermarket of playing a risky game in terms of maintaining future dividends. In 2015/2016, it was announced that the dividend would be cut after the company posted its worst annual results in eight years.
- **Industry practice:** The market usually expects companies to follow industry practice. For example, the tobacco sector has traditionally had a policy of high dividends.
- **Investment demands:** The company may wish to restrict dividends so that it can finance as much investment as possible using retained earnings. This avoids incurring issue expenses and the possibility of diluting ownership (with an equity issue) or increased gearing (if the company issues debentures). Obviously, this depends on the business sector that the company is in and the scope for profitable investment. Up until 2003, Vodafone plc paid out a very low dividend as all its profits were reinvested in projects, such as new generations of networks and investment in other European markets. However, in 2004, it increased dividends significantly and embarked on a programme of repurchasing shares. In the UK, the majority of investment finance is provided from retained earnings.
- **Restrictive covenants:** These can restrict the amount paid out by the company in dividends. They are imposed by lenders to ensure that there is sufficient cash in the business to pay the annual interest and to provide for the eventual repayment of the loans. These covenants may restrict the growth in dividends to the growth in post-tax profits.
- **Return of surplus cash to shareholders:** The company may have a large amount of cash that it wishes to return to its shareholders, either because its future cash flow predictions are strong or it has no profitable opportunities for investing it. By 2004, Microsoft had accumulated a cash balance of $56 billion. This was increasing by $1 billion a month. In 2004, Microsoft paid a special dividend of $32 billion and doubled its regular quarterly dividends, increasing total regular dividend payments from $3.5 billion to $7 billion a year. It also announced a plan to buy back shares worth $30 billion over the following four years. Microsoft's action reflected the fact that it had become a mature company, and so its rate of growth and the scope for profitable investment of funds had fallen.
- **Company liquidity:** The liquidity of the company should be considered, together with the timing of cash flows (the company must remain solvent and have enough cash to pay any dividends it declares); the level of inflation affects the level of dividend that can be paid. The company must have sufficient capital to maintain its operating capability. For example, in November 2015, Amec Foster Wheeler (Amec), an oil and gas services engineer, announced a cut in dividends because of deteriorating performance as a result of the global economic slowdown and cutbacks in the oil and gas sector. The low oil prices had resulted in big oil companies cutting investment and demanding that clients such as Amec accept less attractive terms for the work which they have undertaken. With reduced profit margins, Amec sought to implement cost savings as well as halving the forthcoming dividend payment. The announcement of the dividend cut resulted in a fall in Amec's share price by almost a quarter.
- **Company gearing:** The company's gearing level can have an effect on its dividend policy, because any reduction in retained earnings will increase its gearing. The gearing ratio will further deteriorate if the company has to borrow to replace the cash lost through paying dividends.
- **Legal limitations:** The level of profits determines the level of dividends. The company will need to establish the legal position regarding the payment of dividends in the country or countries in which the company operates. For example, company law in the UK specifies that dividends can only be paid out of realised profits.

TEST YOUR KNOWLEDGE 3.3

Identify six factors that influence the levels of dividends paid by firms.

4 Scrip dividends

Scrip dividends are a conversion of profit reserves into issued share capital. These are offered to shareholders in lieu of a cash dividend. Enhanced scrip dividends are those where the value of shares is greater than the cash dividend offered as an alternative. Such dividends are of benefit to the company as they retain cash within the business. There may, however, be tax implications for individual investors. An advantage to shareholders is that they can increase their shareholdings without paying brokers' commission or stamp duty (currently 0.5% of the cost).

5 Special dividends and share buy-backs

If a company has surplus cash resources these can be returned to shareholders in three ways. The company can:

- increase the annual dividend and return to the 'normal' long-term dividend pattern in the following year
- pay a 'special' dividend, or
- repurchase or buy back shares.

5.1 Increased annual dividend

While this option is easy to implement, it is unlikely to be chosen because of the issue of signalling and because directors may be reluctant to cut the dividend in the year following the exceptional increase.

5.2 Special dividend

This is similar to a normal dividend but usually bigger and paid on a one-off basis. This will work as long as its special nature is clearly signalled to the shareholders.

5.3 Repurchase or buy-back of shares

An alternative to declaring a cash dividend is for a company to repurchase its own shares. Why buy back shares? There are various reasons for wanting to do this.

- It is a way of returning unwanted cash to shareholders; unwanted because the cash generated by the firm exceeds the amount of cash needed for good investment opportunities.
- It leads to **allocative efficiency**. Companies with cash but limited opportunities hand cash back to their shareholders, who can then invest in companies with little cash but many prospects.
- It is a way of changing a firm's capital structure. The directors can simply repurchase shares, which will reduce the shareholders' equity and therefore increase gearing. Alternatively, gearing may be increased further by replacing equity which is repaid with debt. This increase in gearing would enable the firm to benefit from the advantages of debt finance.
- Repurchasing shares will reduce the number of ordinary shares in circulation, which should offer the opportunity to enhance earnings per share (EPS) and dividends per share and should lead to a higher share price. It will increase future EPS as future profits will be earned by fewer shares.
- Individual shareholders choose whether they want their shares to be bought back, therefore letting individual investors decide whether they want the cash. (A special dividend goes to all shareholders.)
- It may prevent a takeover bid, because the control by the existing shareholder group will be increased.
- If the business is in decline, a share repurchase may give the firm's equity a more appropriate level.
- A quoted company may repurchase its shares to withdraw from the stock market.
- A firm may decide to go private, which happens when a small group purchases all the company's shares and the company is no longer quoted on the stock exchange. This may be done

to prevent a takeover bid, reduce the costs of meeting listing requirements or to limit the agency problem. In addition, because the company is no longer subject to volatility in share prices it can concentrate less on the short-term demands of the stock market and more on its own medium- and long-term requirements.

However, there are a number of disadvantages to a share buy-back.

- Repurchasing of shares may be viewed as a failure by the company to manage its funds profitably for shareholders.
- The company will require cash for the repurchase, so it is only an option for companies that have large cash balances.
- It may be difficult to fix a repurchase price that is to the advantage of all involved.
- A repurchase requires existing shareholder approval.
- Capital gains tax may be payable by those shareholders from whom the shares are purchased.
- It increases gearing by reducing equity while loans are left unchanged.

The conduct of any share repurchase scheme is also subject to regulation.

- A repurchase, or buy-back, of shares may be made by a company out of its distributable profits or out of the proceeds of a new issue of shares made especially for the purpose, provided the company is authorised to do so in its Articles of Association.
- A company may not, however, purchase its own shares where, as a result of the transaction, there would no longer be any member of the company holding other than redeemable shares unless they are fully paid up and the terms of the purchase provide for payment on repurchase.
- Purchases may be in the market or off-market. An off-market purchase is said to occur when the shares are purchased not subject to the marketing arrangements of the stock exchange, or other than on a recognised stock exchange. A buy-in of shares by a public company will be subject to the rules of the stock exchange and to the provisions of company law.

The change in the capital base will cause management to rethink its investment decisions, gearing, interest cover, earnings, etc. This is particularly important as the financial institutions focus their attention more towards income and gearing as indicators of financial risk.

TEST YOUR KNOWLEDGE 3.4

When might a company repurchase its shares?

CHAPTER SUMMARY

- The chapter first considers theories related to dividends and shareholder wealth. You must ensure that you understand these theories and can explain them.
- You should be aware of the importance of dividends.
- You should be familiar with factors determining the level of dividends and be able to relate some of these to other parts of this module.
- You must understand the differences between special dividends and share buy-backs and the advantages and disadvantages of share buy-back practices.

END OF CHAPTER QUESTIONS

3.1 Upton plc ('Upton') provides refuse disposal services for a large number of city councils. The company has been trading for five years and is currently owned by a large conglomerate. It has recently been decided to demerge the company and for Upton then to seek a listing on a leading stock market. The directors of Upton are currently preparing for the listing and are debating an appropriate dividend policy for the demerged company. Some directors take the view that the dividend policy adopted is critical to the success of the listing, whereas other directors believe that it is not important as the pattern of dividends has no effect on shareholder wealth.

Required

(a) Critically appraise the conflicting views of the directors and provide reasons why, in practice, the pattern of dividends is normally considered to be important. (15 marks)

(b) Assuming that the business decides to pay dividends, identify and discuss five factors influencing the amount of dividends that it may decide to pay. (10 marks)

3.2 Atherton plc is a well-established operator of up-market health clubs. It has grown strongly over the past ten years, benefiting from changing attitudes to health and exercise and a growing segment of well-paid people in their twenties and thirties, as well as a smaller, but still significant, group of prosperous and active people in their fifties and sixties.

However, Atherton's growth has slowed markedly in recent years, partly because of adverse economic developments, including higher interest rates, which have led to slower growth in consumer expenditure, and partly through increased competition from larger companies in the leisure sector. The senior management of Atherton is less confident than it was a few years ago about the company's future prospects. As a result, the directors have decided to review Atherton's traditional dividend policy of low payments and have asked the financial director to prepare a paper for discussion. The financial director has identified various options for the directors to consider and has asked you to comment on the financial management implications of each of them. The three options are:

1 to increase the dividend per share

2 to repurchase shares

3 to continue the existing policy.

Required

(a) Prepare a report for the financial director as requested.

(b) Comment on the actions that the company might take to stimulate business growth, with particular reference to their financial aspects.

ICSA FDM Pilot Paper

PART **FOUR**

Long-term investment decisions

■ LIST OF CHAPTERS

■ OVERVIEW

This part examines investment appraisal. It commences by looking at different methods of project appraisal. It examines payback, accounting rate of return and then discounted cash flow techniques. The role and impact of corporate taxation on investment appraisal is discussed. The part moves on to discuss the treatment of inflation, the problems posed by projects with unequal lives, capital rationing and the control of capital projects. Investment appraisal and risk is discussed at length, including the different methods employed by companies to deal with risk. The part moves on to a discussion of portfolio effect and risk reduction. Finally, it examines shareholder value analysis and value creation. It concludes by examining Economic Value Added, total shareholder return and market value added.

■ LEARNING OUTCOMES

On successful completion of Part Four, you will be able to:

- undertake investment appraisal using a range of different techniques
- demonstrate a clear conceptual understanding of a range of issues relating to investment appraisal
- evaluate elements of risk and return in a range of different risk assessment models, and
- assess the features of different aspects of value creation for shareholders.

4 Investment appraisal 1

■ **CONTENTS**

1 The need for investment appraisal techniques

Investment appraisal is the appraisal of expenditures incurred now in order to obtain a return in the future. Examples of investments or investment projects include a machine, a factory or a hospital. All require the investment of funds in the present in order to obtain returns in the future. Therefore, we can say that investments have three characteristics.

- The expenditure is often very significant within the business and can shape the future of the business.
- Investment involves time, as the benefits occur in the future.
- As the benefits occur in the future, there is an element of uncertainty about the timing and volume of these returns.

The term 'investment appraisal' is interchangeable with the term 'project appraisal'. Both terms are used in this chapter.

1.1 Types of investment decision

The main categories of investment decision for which managers need information are represented by the following questions.

- Should we launch a new product?
- Should we withdraw an existing product from the market?
- Should we expand capacity and, if so, by how much?
- Should we close down or cut back capacity and, if so, by how much?
- Should we invest in cost-saving activities and, if so, which of several alternatives should we choose?
- Should we replace existing equipment with a more productive alternative and, if so, when?
- How can we comply with environmental or health and safety regulations in the most efficient way?

1.2 Investment criteria

In making investment decisions, managers aim to maximise shareholder wealth by maximising long-term returns, taking account of the impact of factors such as risk and liquidity.

2 Relevant factors in project appraisal

Relevant factors are those factors that are significant to the decision under consideration. In the case of project appraisal, these include the following.

- Cash flows, as it is argued that cash gives one command over resources.
- Financing costs, specifically interest foregone. For example, if a company invests £100,000 in new computer-controlled machinery, the company loses the opportunity to invest that £100,000 in, say, a bank account.
- The timing of returns, because returns that happen sooner in a project's life are preferred to the same returns that occur later – because the early returns can be reinvested to become a greater sum at the later date.
- Incremental costs, because these represent future costs that occur as a result of a current decision.
- Working capital changes may be important because new projects often require additional investment in inventory and debtors and so these must be included in the analysis. Working capital is usually run down at the end of a project's life: inventory dwindles to zero and debtors pay up, with no further sales.
- Taxation may play an important role in the analysis. The capital cost of the project may attract tax breaks and the annual profits from the project will be subject to taxation.
- Future inflation will affect revenues and costs in different ways. If there are energy shortages, then oil, gas and electricity are likely to inflate more quickly than wages and salaries.

Non-relevant factors include the following.

- Past expenditure on the project, for example on a feasibility study, is regarded as a sunk cost; it cannot be influenced by the current decision and is regarded as a non-relevant cost.
- The apportionment of overheads, where these overhead costs would be incurred in any event. The overhead is only relevant to the extent that it actually increases in cash terms as a result of the project.
- Conventional financial reporting depreciation is regarded as non-relevant as it represents the apportionment of the net cost of the asset over the life of the asset. Depreciation is a book transfer, from one account to another, and does not consume or give command over resources. However, the cost of the asset and its residual value are both relevant to the decision, as is their timing.

3 Overview: methods of project appraisal

Table 4.1 identifies the five methods of project appraisal that we will be examining. The methods are classified according to whether they are **discounted cash flow** (DCF) methods or not.

TABLE 4.1 Project appraisal methods

Non-discounting methods	Discounted cash flow (DCF) methods
Payback period	Net present value (NPV)
Accounting rate of return (ARR)	Internal rate of return (IRR)
	Discounted payback

In order to illustrate these methods, we will make use of the data contained in Table 4.2.

TABLE 4.2 Example cash flow and annual profit figures for three projects

	Project A		**Project B**		**Project C**	
	Cash flows	**Annual profits**	**Cash flows**	**Annual profits**	**Cash flows**	**Annual profits**
	£000s	£000s	£000s	£000s	£000's	£000s
Year						
0	–1,000		–1,000		–2,000	
1	600	350	500	250	600	350
2	400	150	400	150	600	350
3	300	50	600	350	600	350
4	300	50	700	450	600	350
4					1,000	

The following additional information is provided for the examples in this chapter.

- Projects A and B have zero residual values. Project C has a residual value of £1 million and this is included in the cash flow for year 4.
- Annual depreciation is calculated on a straight-line basis and is as follows:
  - projects A and B: £1 million/4 years = £250,000 per year
  - project C: (costs £2 million – residual value £1 million)/4 years = £250,000 per year.
- Each annual profit is equal to the annual cash flow less annual depreciation of £250,000 per year.
- For each project the cash flow at year 0 is negative, but all other cash flows in these cases are positive.
- In the year column, year 0 is now.
- The projects are mutually exclusive. If we select one project, we cannot select either of the other two projects. The mutual exclusivity might, for example, be because we have a single area of land on which we can site only one of the projects.

4 Payback period

The payback period is the time it takes for the cash flows generated by a project to pay back the initial cash outflow (for capital investment, working capital and other start-up costs) at the start of the project. The payback period is based on cash flows rather than profits and ignores non-cash items such as depreciation. More generally, payback avoids dealing with accounting definitions.

The two decision rules for payback are as follows:

- A project is accepted if its payback period is within the company's target payback period.
- When comparing different mutually exclusive projects, the project with the shortest payback would be chosen, as long as it is within the company's target.

With reference to projects A, B and C above, the payback periods are as follows:

- Project A: two years.
  At the end of year 2, the cash inflows in years 1 and 2 sum to £1 million, the cost of the project in year 0.
- Project B: two years and two months.
  At the end of year 2, the cash inflows sum to £900,000 and a further £100,000 is needed. The cash inflows in year 3 amount to £600,000; if we assume that the cash inflows occur evenly through the year, it would take 1/6 of a year, or two months, to earn cash inflows of £100,000.
- Project C: three years and four months.

We are also informed that the company's target payback period is three years.

The decision regarding which project to select is therefore as follows.

- Both project A and project B meet the company's target as their payback period is within the three-year period specified.
- As the projects are mutually exclusive, project A should be selected as it has the shorter payback period.

When a payback problem results in part-year figures (as do projects B and C) you will have to decide whether to use decimal years, complete months or complete weeks in your answer. It is always advisable to round up partial months or weeks when calculating payback periods in order to:

- make the figures easier to assimilate and understand, as this is one of payback's strengths; and
- avoid giving managers a false impression as to the accuracy of your calculations.

You should never round down partial years, months or weeks as the asset will not have reached payback at the lower figure.

4.1 Advantages of payback period

- It is very easy to understand and to explain to others. It also has simple decision rules.
- It ranks investments; the quicker the payback the better.
- It focuses on cash and company liquidity, without which the company will find it difficult to survive.
- The longer the project continues into the future, the greater the risk. The sooner the cost of the investment is returned, the safer the project should be. So payback may be seen as a risk-reduction technique.

4.2 Disadvantages of payback period

- It ignores cash flows that are generated after the payback period and so ignores the total return of the project.
- It ignores the pattern of cash flows within the payback period; a project may have a slightly longer payback period but have cash inflows that are generated near the start of that period.

4.1

Required

For each project, what is the total cash inflow after the payback period that is ignored by the method?

Solution

Calculate the total return and post-payback return for each project:

	Project A	Project B	Project C
Payback period	2 years	2 years 2 months	3 years 4 months
	£000s	£000s	£000s
Capital cost	1,000	1,000	2,000
Total returns after the payback period	600	1,200	1,400
Post-payback returns as a percentage of total cash returns	37.5%	54.5%	41.2%

5 Accounting rate of return (ARR)

This method of project appraisal uses accounting profits to work out the average return that the owner of the business would get over the life of the investment. All figures are obtained from the financial accounts of the business.

Accounting rate of return (ARR), also known as the 'average return on investment' and the 'return on capital employed', is measured as:

$$\text{ARR (\%)} = \frac{\text{average annual profits over the life of the project}}{\text{average investment to earn that profit}} \times 100$$

Note that:

- the average annual profit is made up of the total annual profits over the life of the investment divided by the number of years involved; this can be before or after tax
- the average investment over the life of the project is given by:

$$\frac{\text{cost of asset + disposal value}}{2}$$

- there are several accepted ways of calculating the investment in the project.

The decision rules for ARR are as follows.

- If the ARR exceeds the target ARR for the company, the project should be accepted.
- If the projects are mutually exclusive, the project offering the higher ARR should be selected, provided that it meets the target ARR for the company.

In this case we are informed that the company's target ARR is 25%. The ARR for each of projects A, B and C is calculated below.

Project A (£000s):

Average annual profits = (350 + 150 + 50 + 50)/4 =	£150
Average investment = (1,000 + 0)/2 =	£500
ARR = (150/500) × 100 =	30%

Project B (£000s):

Average annual profits = (250 + 150 + 350 + 450)/4 =	£300
Average investment = (1,000 + 0)/2 =	£500
ARR = (300/500) × 100 =	60%

Project C (£000s):

Average annual profits = (350 + 350 + 350 + 350)/4 =	£350
Average investment = (2,000 + 1,000)/2	£1,500
ARR = (350/1,500) × 100 =	23%

The decision regarding which project to select is therefore as follows.

- Project A and project B meet the criteria as they both have an ARR of at least 25%.
- As they are mutually exclusive, project B should be accepted as it has the highest ARR of 60%.

5.1 Advantages of ARR

- It is widely accepted. It forms the basis of accounting reports because many managers readily recognise and understand the measure.
- It uses profits as its measure. As profit figures have been audited, one can place a degree of trust in the figures that are used.

- Profits are seen as the measure of business success. The technique focuses on the profits returned by projects.
- Managers' performance may be evaluated by shareholders using return on capital employed and so it would seem consistent to use the same technique in investment appraisal.

5.2 Disadvantages of ARR

- There are several ways of calculating both the numerator and denominator in the formula.
- While it does take account of all the profits earned over the period of the project, it treats £1 of profit in year 4 equally as the same amount in year 1, yet the latter would appear to be more valuable as it can be invested in the business. In other words, the method fails to recognise the time value of money. This is dealt with by the discounted cash flow methods of project appraisal, as we shall see below.
- The profit and capital values used to calculate ARR depend on the methods that the company chooses to use to, for example, value inventories and calculate depreciation. Different methods are possible and acceptable, leading to the possibility of ARR being calculated in different ways for similar – and apparently comparable – projects. Within one company or group of companies, accounting policies can be standardised, but if ARR is used to make comparisons between different companies, problems will arise in interpreting and comparing the figures.
- ARR is a relative measure, because the accounting profit is divided by the investment. This makes it possible to compare the profitability of projects of different sizes, but means that if ARR is used to choose between two projects, a large project may have a larger profit but lose out to a small project with a higher ARR.

WORKED EXAMPLE 4.2

An investment in a new machine costing £2,000 will generate profits (before depreciation) as follows:

Year	1	2	3	4	5
Profit before depreciation	£600	£550	£500	£450	£400

It is expected that at the end of year 5 the machine will have a realisable value of £1,000. Depreciation will be on a straight-line basis.

Required
Calculate the ARR for the project.

Solution
Average profits = (600 + 550 + 500 + 450 + 400)/5 = 500
Average investment = (2,000 + 1,000)/2 = 1,500
ARR = 500/1,500 × 100 = 33.3%

6 Discounted cash flow techniques

Discounted cash flow (DCF) techniques are based upon the concept of the 'time value of money'. It is argued that £1 now is always preferred to £1 some time in the future. Three reasons underpin this rationale.

- **Interest:** If you have £1 now you have the option to invest it and earn interest, so that it will be worth more than £1 in the future.
- **Uncertainty:** The present is certain but the future is uncertain, so £1 now is preferred to an uncertain £1 in the future.

- **Time preference:** The longer the period that we have to wait in the future, the greater the risk and uncertainty will be, and the greater the amount of interest that we will require to compensate us for the wait.

The time value of money finds its practical manifestation in the rate of interest. The rate of interest leads to two further concepts: compound interest and discounting.

6.1 Compound interest

Compound interest allows us to estimate the value that an investment will reach over time. For example:

- if we invest £1,000 for one year at 10%, it will grow to (£1,000 × 110/100) = £1,100
- if we then invest that sum for a further year, it will grow to (£1,100 × 110/100) = £1,210.

The formula that we can use to determine the future value of £1 using compound interest is:

$$FV = (1 + r)^n$$

where:
FV = future value
r = rate of interest
n = number of years
Table 4.3 shows an example of the calculation of compound interest.

TABLE 4.3 Compound interest

Principal	Interest rate	Years	Future value of £1 (FV)	Future value of principal
£	%		£	£
500	5	4	$= (1 + 0.05)^4 = 1.2155$	= 1.2155 × 500 = 607.75
500	2	4	$= (1 + 0.02)^4 = 1.0824$	= 1.0824 × 500 = 541.20
1,275	7	7	$= (1 + 0.07)^7 = 1.6058$	= 1.6058 × 1,275 = 2,047.40
9,430	9	5	$= (1 + 0.09)^5 = 1.5386$	= 1.5386 × 9,430 = 14,509.00

6.2 Discounting

Discounting is the process of finding the present value of a sum of money that we will pay or receive in the future. Like compounding (the application of compound interest) it makes use of the time value of money through the **discount rate**. Discounting can be regarded as the inverse of compounding.

The formula that we can use to find the present value of a sum of money is:

$$PV = 1/(1 + r)^n$$

where:
PV = present value (PV) factor
r = rate of interest
n = number of years
Table 4.4 shows the application of the present value formula.

TABLE 4.4 Discounting

Principal	Discount rate	Years	Present value of £1 (PV factor)	Present value of principal
£	%			£
3,000	5	3	$= 1/(1.05)^3 = 0.864$	= 0.864 × 3,000 = 2,592
2,500	8	5	$= 1/(1.08)^5 = 0.681$	= 0.681 × 2,500 = 1,702
2,000	3	7	$= 1/(1.03)^7 = 0.813$	= 0.813 × 2,000 = 1,626

6.3 Future value and present value

Table 4.5 shows the close relationship between future value and present value. It shows that, using a common interest rate and discount rate, the future value of an investment of £1 in year 0 always discounts to a present value of £1 at year 0.

TABLE 4.5 Future value and present value: the investment of £1 with a 10% interest rate

Years	Future value	PV factor	Present value at year 0
	£		£
0	1	1	1
1	1.1	1/1.1 = 0.909	1.1 × 0.909 = 1
2	1.21	1/1.21 = 0.826	1.21 × 0.826 = 1
3	1.331	1/1.331 = 0.751	1.331 × 0.751 = 1

In order to obtain the PV factors in the above case, we have made use of the formula given above. However, to avoid the need to calculate PV factors, a present value table is included in Appendix 1. The table shows the present value of £1 over a range of years (from 1 to 15) and for a range of discount rates (from 1% to 20%).

An excerpt from that table is shown below:

Years (n)	Discount rate (r)						
	1%	2%	3%	4%	5%	6%	7%
1	0.990	0.980	0.971	0.962	0.952	0.943	0.935
2	0.980	0.961	0.943	0.925	0.907	0.890	0.873
3	0.971	0.942	0.915	0.889	0.864	0.840	0.816
4	0.961	0.924	0.888	0.855	0.823	0.792	0.763
5	0.951	0.906	0.863	0.822	0.784	0.747	0.713

As you can see, the number of years is given running down the left-hand side and the discount rate is provided along the top row. You will see that, for any one year, the PV factor falls as the discount rate (i.e. interest rate) increases. As the interest rate increases, the future value increases and, as present value is its inverse, present value must fall as future value increases.

For any discount rate, you can see that the PV factor falls as we increase the number of years hence. Again, as the number of years increases, the future value increases and the present value falls.

From the table extract shown above, we can see that the PV factor of £1 at a 6% discount rate four years hence is 0.792. If a sum of £700 is offered in four years' time when the discount rate is 6%, the present value is £700 × 0.792 = £554.40.

So, when the rate of interest is 6%, a company would be indifferent between £554.40 payable now and £700 payable in four years' time. The £554.40 can be invested now to grow to £700 in four years' time.

Required

Use the present value table extract given above and find the present value of the following:

Future value	Discount rate	Years	Present value
£	%		£
650	5	4	
1,200	7	5	
5,430	4	3	
126	3	5	

Solution

Future value	Discount rate	Years	Present value
£	%		£
650	5	4	650 × 0.823 = 535
1,200	7	5	1,200 × 0.713 = 856
5,430	4	3	5,430 × 0.889 = 4,827
126	3	5	126 × 0.863 = 109

7 Net present value (NPV)

Net present value (NPV) is the first of the DCF methods of project appraisal that we shall consider. The technique makes use of the following concepts and techniques.

- It uses cash flows rather than accounting flows (or profits), because cash can be spent and has an opportunity cost whereas profits cannot be spent.
- It uses discounting.
- It nets off annual cash inflows and outflows to get the annual net cash flow (ANCF) for the year before applying discount rates.

The decision rules for NPV are as follows:

- Select only projects offering positive NPVs.
- When comparing different mutually exclusive projects, select the project with the highest positive NPV.

The illustration given in Table 4.6 refers to a company that has a 10% discount rate. The table uses the 10% discount factors from the present values table in Appendix 1 and data from Table 4.2 above.

A few points about the figures and calculations in Table 4.6:

- At year 0 (now) the present value of £1 is always £1, whatever the discount rate.
- In the ANCF and present value columns, annual net cash outflows are shown as negative figures (such as the investment in year 0) and the annual net cash inflows are shown as positive figures.
- The NPV is the algebraic sum of the annual present values, taking account of the positive and negative figures.
- Items such as depreciation are ignored as depreciation is not a cash flow. However, the initial cost of the project and any residual value are included.

TABLE 4.6 Example NPV calculations

		Project A		Project B		Project C	
Years	**10% discount factors**	**ANCF**	**PV**	**ANCF**	**PV**	**ANCF**	**PV**
		£000s	£000s	£000s	£000s	£000s	£000s
0	1.000	−1,000	−1,000.00	−1,000	−1,000.00	−2,000	−2,000.00
1	0.909	600	545.40	500	454.50	600	545.40
2	0.826	400	330.40	400	330.40	600	495.60
3	0.751	300	225.30	600	450.60	600	450.60
4	0.683	300	204.90	700	478.10	1600	1,092.80
NPV			306.00		713.60		584.40

- Interest and repayments of loan principal are not included in the cash flows because this would be double-counting (the sums have already been used in determining the discount rate for project appraisal). An exception is when finance is made available on special terms specifically for a particular project, so that the capital receipts and capital servicing costs are cash flows that are specifically part of the project. In this case the funding cash flows should be treated as project cash flows and the cost of capital determined in the same way as it would be for other comparable projects.

The decision regarding which project to select is therefore as follows.

- All projects have positive NPVs so they can all be accepted.
- As they are mutually exclusive, Project B should be chosen as it offers the highest NPV.

7.1 Advantages of NPV

- NPV takes account of the time value of money through the discount rate. These discount rates should relate to the company's costs of raising finance.
- NPV takes account of all the cash flows from year 0 to the end of the project's life.
- It provides a single NPV figure; a positive NPV figure ensures that all costs, including the costs of finance, are covered by the project and a surplus (NPV) is generated over and above the costs of finance. This is attributable to the ordinary shareholders and will serve to maximise shareholder wealth.

7.2 Disadvantages of NPV

- The calculation of discount rates can be challenging. (We will cover this in Chapter 12.)

7.3 Annuities

An annuity is defined as an equal annual payment or receipt. In the case of Table 4.2, the annual net cash flows of £600 in years 1, 2 and 3 for project C comprise a three-year annuity.

Appendix 1 sets out a table giving the present values of annuities. An excerpt from that table is shown below:

Annuity Table

Present value (in £) of a series of n equal annual payments of £1 a year, starting one year from now, discounted at a rate of r% per annum

Years (n)	Discount rate (r) 1%	2%	3%	4%	5%	6%	7%	8%	9%	10%
1	0.990	0.980	0.971	0.962	0.952	0.943	0.935	0.926	0.917	0.909
2	1.970	1.942	1.913	1.886	1.859	1.833	1.808	1.783	1.739	1.736
3	2.941	2.884	2.829	2.775	2.723	2.673	2.624	2.577	2.531	2.487
4	3.902	3.808	3.717	3.630	3.546	3.465	3.387	3.312	3.240	3.170
5	4.853	4.713	4.580	4.452	4.329	4.212	4.100	3.993	3.890	3.791

Looking at the 10% column and the three years row gives a factor of 2.487. This is the present value of £1 per year for each year from years 1 to 3 inclusive. In the above example, for project C, instead of calculating the present values in years 1 to 3 by multiplying each ANCF of £600 separately, we could carry out the appraisal as follows:

Years	10% discount factor	ANCF	Present value
		£000s	£000s
0	1.000	–2,000	–2,000.00
1–3	2.487	600	1,492.20
4	0.683	1,600	1,092.80
NPV			585.00

WORKED EXAMPLE 4.4

Here is an NPV exercise for you to try.

A company is considering the selection of one of two mutually exclusive machines. Each machine would last six years. Information about each acquisition is as follows.

- Machine 1 would generate ANFCs of £150,000; the machinery would cost £250,000 and have a scrap value of £80,000.
- Machine 2 would generate ANCFs of £180,000; the machinery would cost £350,000 and have a scrap value of £23,500.

The company's discount rate is 12%.

Required

Calculate the NPV of each machine. Which machine should the company choose and why?

Solution

Year	12% discount factor	Machine 1		Machine 2	
		ANCF	PV	ANCF	PV
		£000s	£000s	£000s	£000s
0	1.000	–250	–250.00	–350	–350.00
1–6	4.111	150	616.65	180	739.98
6	0.507	80	40.56	23.5	11.91
NPV			407.21		401.89

The company should choose machine 1 because it has a higher NPV than machine 2.

7.4 Perpetuities

When an investment yields the same cash flow for ever, that cash flow is known as a 'perpetuity' or an 'annuity in perpetuity'.

The present value of a perpetuity can be calculated as:

$$\text{present value} = \frac{\text{annual cash flow}}{\text{i}}$$

where:
i = the interest rate.

For example, if the rate of return is 30%, i = 0.3 and the present value of a perpetuity of £1 is:

$$\frac{£1}{0.3} = £3.333$$

7.5 NPV profile

For any project, the NPV can be calculated using a range of different values for the discount rate and the results drawn as a graph (Figure 4.1).

FIGURE 4.1 The impact of changes in discount rate on NPV

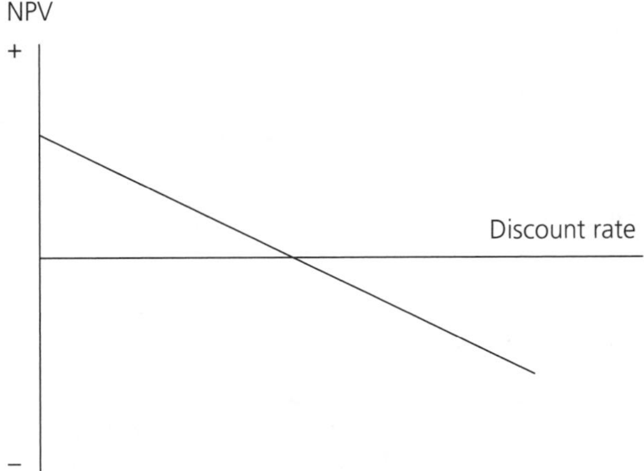

The relationship shown in Figure 4.1 means that in the case of a project in which there is investment early on followed by returns in the future, the project's NPV will fall as the discount rate increases. The NPV will reduce to zero, before falling into negative territory.

STOP AND THINK 4.1

The graph of NPV (Figure 4.1) slopes downwards because a higher discount rate (reflecting higher costs of raising finance) means a lower NPV. Why does this lead to lower NPVs?

8 Internal rate of return (IRR)

Internal rate of return (IRR) is the second of the DCF investment appraisal methods. It calculates the discount rate that provides an NPV of zero. In other words, it is the discount rate that allows the project to break even. It then compares this break-even discount rate with the company's cost of raising finance, termed the company's cost of capital.

IRR uses the same concepts as NPV:

- It uses cash flows rather than accounting flows (or profits), because cash can be spent and has an opportunity cost whereas profits cannot be spent.

- It uses discounting.
- It nets off annual cash inflows and outflows to get the ANCF for the year before applying discount rates.

The decision rules for IRR are as follows:

- If the IRR exceeds the cost of capital (the discount rate), it is worth undertaking the project as the additional return above the cost of capital will belong to the shareholders.
- If projects are mutually exclusive, then the project with the highest IRR is selected.

IRR is the most complex of all the investment appraisal techniques to calculate. Using a technique which is known as linear interpolation, it requires estimation by trial and error as follows:

1 Find a discount rate that gives a positive NPV.
2 Find a discount rate that gives a negative NPV. This would normally be a higher discount rate than that used in step 1.
3 Estimate a discount rate between these two rates that will produce a positive NPV.

The formula for calculating the IRR, giving effect to these steps, is:

$$IRR = DR_A + \left[\frac{NPV_A}{(NPV_A - NPV_B)} \times (DR_B - DR_A)\right]$$

where:
DR_A = the low discount rate used to appraise the project
DR_B = the high discount rate used to appraise the project
NPV_A = the NPV obtained with the low discount rate
NPV_B = the NPV obtained with the high discount rate.

To illustrate the calculation of IRR, we can use the cash flows and NPVs in Table 4.6 above to estimate the IRR for project A as follows:

1 NPV at 10% discount rate = £306,000.
2 NPV at 30% discount rate is calculated as below:

Years	30% discount factors	ANCF	Present value
		£000s	£000s
0	1.000	–1,000	–1,000.0
1	0.769	600	461.4
2	0.592	400	236.8
3	0.455	300	136.5
4	0.350	300	105.0
NPV			–60.3

3 Apply the formula:

$$IRR = 0.1 + \left[\frac{306}{306 - (-60)} \times (0.3 - 0.1)\right]$$

$$= 0.1 + [(306/366) \times 0.2] = 0.1 + 0.167 = 0.267$$
$$= 26.7\%$$

WORKED EXAMPLE 4.5

Required

For project B:

- NPV at 10% discount rate is £714,000 (rounded up to the nearest £000).
- NPV at 40% discount rate is –£38,000.

Calculate the IRR for this project.

For project C:

- NPV at 10% discount rate is £585,000 (rounded up to the nearest £000).

Calculate the NPV at 25% discount rate and then calculate the IRR.

- The PV factors for a 25% discount rate are as follows:
  - present value of £1 in year 4 = £0.41
  - present value of annuity of £1 for years 1 to 3 inclusive = £1.952

Solution

Project B:

$$\text{IRR} = 0.1 + \left[\frac{714}{714 - (-38)} \times (0.4 - 0.1)\right]$$

$$= 0.1 + (0.949 \times 0.3) = 0.3847$$
$$= 38.47\%$$

Project C:

NPV at 25%:

Years	Discount factor	ANCF	Present value
		£000s	£000s
0	1.000	–2,000	–2,000
1–3	1.952	600	1,171
4	0.410	1,600	656
NPV			–173

$$\text{IRR} = 0.1 + \left[\frac{585}{585 - (-173)} \times (0.25 - 0.1)\right]$$

$$= 0.1 + (0.7718 \times 0.15) = 0.2158$$
$$= 21.58\%$$

8.1 Advantages of IRR

- Like NPV, IRR takes account of cash flows and the time value of money.
- Business decision-makers appear to like dealing with a percentage rate that can be compared with the cost of capital. The percentage rate seems more intuitively acceptable than the more amorphous concept of NPV.
- The excess of a project's IRR over the cost of capital indicates the excess return for the risk contained within the project.
- It is argued that the IRR avoids disputes about which precise discount rate to use; it can be compared with a less precise ballpark discount rate.

8.2 Disadvantages of IRR

- IRR is a relative measure. A 30% return may sound excellent, but if the investment is small, the surplus return in terms of £s may not be large when the project's cash flows are discounted at the cost of capital. A larger project with a lower IRR may generate a larger surplus, as long as the IRR is in excess of the cost of capital.
- The IRR calculations assume that ANCFs are reinvested at the project's own IRR. However, suitable investment projects yielding this level of return may not be available at the times when the cash flows are generated by the project.
- If the project has large negative cash flows late in its life this can lead to more than one value for the IRR. Examples include nuclear power stations, which have very high decommissioning costs at the end of a station's life, or a chemical plant, where decontamination activity may need to be undertaken when the plant ceases production. Table 4.7 shows what can happen.

TABLE 4.7 Negative cash flows and multiple IRRs

Year	Annual cash flow	Discount rates							
	£ millions	7%	8%	9%	10%	11%	12%	13%	14%
0	–101	–101	–101	–101	–101	–101	–101	–101	–101
1–15	22	200.4	188.3	177.3	167.3	158.2	149.8	142.2	135.1
16	–300	–101.6	–87.6	–75.6	–65.3	–56.5	–48.9	–42.4	–36.9
NPV		–2.2	–0.3	0.7	1.0	0.7	–0.1	–1.2	–2.8

Table 4.7 shows that the NPV is zero with a discount rate of approximately 8%, and is also zero between 11% and 12%, indicating that the data contain two IRRs.

9 Discounted payback period

Discounted payback addresses one of the weaknesses of the payback period, in that it ignores the pattern or timing of returns within the payback period. It discounts the cash flows before calculating the payback period.

The two decision rules for discounted payback are as follows:

- A project is accepted if its discounted payback period is within a company's target discounted payback period.
- When comparing different mutually exclusive projects, the project with the shortest discounted payback period is chosen, as long as it is within the company's target.

The discounted payback period is calculated as follows:

1 Discount all net cash flows at the company's cost of capital.
2 Calculate the payback period using these discounted cash flows.

To illustrate the calculation of discounted payback period we will use the discounted cash flow data from Table 4.6, which are reproduced in Table 4.8.

For project A, after two years, the present value of total inflows is £875,800; after three years it is £1,101,100. The discounted payback period is between two and three years; more precisely, it is two years plus (124.20/225.30 × 12 months) = 2 years and 7 months (to the nearest month).

TABLE 4.8 Discounted cash flow data

		Project A		Project B		Project C	
Year	10% discount factor	ANCF	Present value	ANCF	Present value	ANCF	Present value
		£000s	£000s	£000s	£000s	£000s	£000s
0	1.000	–1,000	–1,000.00	–1,000	–1,000.00	–2,000	–2,000.00
1	0.909	600	545.40	500	454.50	600	545.40
2	0.826	400	330.40	400	330.40	600	495.60
3	0.751	300	225.30	600	450.60	600	450.60
4	0.683	300	204.90	700	478.10	1,600	1,092.80

WORKED EXAMPLE 4.6

Required

Using the figures given in Table 4.8, calculate the discounted payback periods for project B and project C.

Solution

Project B:

After two years, cumulative present value of cash flows (in £000s) = 784.90

Shortfall = (1,000 – 784.90) = 215.10

Discounted payback period = 2 years + [(215.1/450.6) × 12 months] = 2 years, 6 months.

Project C:

Note: The £1,000,000 residual value is an inflow that occurs at the end of year 4.

After three years, cumulative PV of cash flows (in £000s) = 1491.6

Shortfall = (2,000 – 1491.6) = 508.4

Discounted payback period = 3 years + [(508.4/409.8) × 12 months] = it does not payback in discounted terms until the end of year 4 when the residual value of £1,000,000 occurs.

9.1 Advantages and disadvantages

These are identical to those of payback period (see sections 4.1 and 4.2 above), with one exception. The disadvantage associated with failure to consider the pattern of cash flows within the payback period is no longer applicable.

10 Taxation and investment appraisal

Taxation complicates the project appraisal process. Expenditure on fixed assets is allowed as a deduction from taxable profits via a system of capital allowances. These are relevant to project appraisal as they determine the amount of taxation paid by the company. Taxation impacts on appraisal in the following ways:

- Accounting profit is not the same thing as taxable profit, on which taxation will be levied. With reference to project appraisal, a company's own depreciation calculations will need to be replaced by a system of capital allowances, called 'writing down allowances' (WDAs). These are imposed in order to standardise depreciation practices for the purposes of taxation. They are relevant because they will influence the amount of taxation that the company will pay over the life of a project. Capital allowances are determined by the government. At the time of writing, in the UK, the capital allowance on plant and machinery is 18% on a reducing balance basis. For investment appraisal purposes, we normally assume that the capital allowances given in the UK are based on a 25% annual WDA on a reducing balance basis.

- Companies pay corporation tax on taxable profits after the deduction of capital allowances. In the UK, the timing of the payment of corporation tax will vary according to the level of taxable profits. As a result, some companies pay corporation tax after the end of the accounting year. Other companies are required to pay corporation tax in instalments; consequently, they will pay most of their tax during and close to the end of the accounting year. To simplify things, we normally assume that corporation tax is payable a year in arrears, so there is a delay of about a year in cash-flow terms. Similarly, any reductions in tax, and consequently a reduction in cash outflows, as a result of capital allowances, are assumed to take effect the year after that in which the capital allowance was claimed.
- A further adjustment is made to the amount of taxation to be paid on disposal of assets or at the end of their lives, as follows:
  - if the asset's written-down value (using taxation rules) exceeds the asset's realisable value, then insufficient depreciation has been allowed by the tax authorities. In this case, an additional tax allowance is given. This is termed a 'balancing allowance' and may be offset against the profits for the year.
  - if the reverse occurs and the asset's written-down value is less than the realisable value, then too much depreciation has been allowed by the tax authorities. In this case, a further tax charge is made. This is termed a 'balancing charge' and will be added to the taxable profits for the year.
- The first year's capital allowance is called the 'initial allowance'. The initial allowance may be more than 25% (exceptionally it may be 100%) of the expenditure on acquiring a fixed asset. The initial allowances, the annual WDA and the rate of corporation tax will always be specified in the examination.

WORKED EXAMPLE 4.7

Resonate Ltd purchased a new lathe for £10,000, which it kept as a spare machine in case any of its other lathes broke down. The lathe was kept for four years before being disposed of for £2,000. The company claimed a 25% initial allowance and annual 25% WDAs. Resonate Ltd achieves taxable profits of £500,000 per annum and pays corporation tax at the rate of 30% on those profits. Its cost of capital is 7%.

Required

Prepare tables setting out the cash flows (to the nearest £) associated with the purchase and disposal of the spare lathe and calculate the NPV of the project.

Solution

As Resonate Ltd is profitable, the capital allowances on the lathe will result in a reduction in the company's tax payments.

Capital allowances are calculated as:

Year	Narrative	Capital allowance	Reducing balance
		£	£
1	Initial allowance 25% of £10,000	2,500	7,500
2	WDA 25% of reducing balance	1,875	5,625
3	WDA 25% of reducing balance	1,406	4,219
4	Balancing allowance = reducing balance less £2,000 disposal proceeds	2,219	0

WORKED EXAMPLE 4.7 *continued*

Tax saved and reduction in cash outflows as a result of the capital allowances are calculated as:

Year	Tax saved	Reduction in cash outflow
1	£2,500 × 30% = £750	0
2	£1,875 × 30% = £563	£750
3	£1,406 × 30% = £422	£563
4	£2,219 × 30% = £666	£422
5		£666

Cash flows associated with the purchase and disposal of the spare lathe are:

Year	0	1	2	3	4	5
	£	£	£	£	£	£
Initial cost	–10,000					
Tax saved			750	563	422	666
Disposal proceeds					2,000	
Net cash flow	–10,000	0	750	563	2,422	666

The NPV of spare lathe is:

Year	0	1	2	3	4	5	NPV
	£	£	£	£	£	£	£
Net cash flow	–10,000	0	750	563	2,422	666	
7% discount factor	1.000	0.935	0.873	0.816	0.763	0.713	
DCFs	–10,000	0	655	459	1,848	475	–6,563

Assume that the new lathe achieved cost savings that produced additional cash inflows of £5,000 per year in each of the four years it was owned by the company. In this case the NPV of the project will be as follows.

Year	0	1	2	3	4	5	NPV
Initial cost	–10,000						
Annual cash savings		5,000	5,000	5,000	5,000		
Tax @ 30% on annual cash savings			–1,500	–1,500	–1,500	–1,500	
Tax saved			750	563	422	666	
Disposal proceeds					2,000		
Net cash flow	–10,000	5,000	4,250	4,063	5,922	–834	
7% discount factor	1.000	0.935	0.873	0.816	0.763	0.713	
DCFs	–10,000	4,675	3,710	3,315	4,518	–595	5,623

WORKED EXAMPLE 4.8

Tortuity Ltd is considering investing £100,000 in extra equipment to provide a temporary expansion to its production capacity. The expansion will generate an additional annual contribution of £40,000 for the next three years. The extra equipment will be scrapped at the end of the third year and will have zero disposal value. The rate of corporation tax is 30%. The annual WDA (including the initial allowance) is 25%. Corporation tax is assumed to be paid a year after it is incurred; similarly, allowances are assumed to result in a reduction in taxation a year after they are claimed.

The company's cost of capital is 6%.

Required

Calculate the NPV of the project.

Solution

Capital allowance and tax saved on capital allowances:

Year	Narrative	Capital allowance	Reducing balance	Tax saved on capital allowances
		£	£	£
1	Initial allowance 25% of £100,000	25,000	75,000	
2	WDA 25% of reducing balance	18,750	56,250	= 30% × 25,000 = 7,500
3	Balancing allowance	56,250		= 30% × 18,750 = 5,625
4				= 30% × 56,250 = 16,875

NPV of investment:

Year	0	1	2	3	4	NPV
	£	£	£	£	£	£
Initial cost	–100,000					
ANCF		40,000	40,000	40,000		
Tax saved on capital allowances			7,500	5,625	16,875	
Tax on ANCF			–12,000	–12,000	–12,000	
Net cash flow	–100,000	40,000	35,500	33,625	4,875	
6% discount factor	1.000	0.943	0.890	0.840	0.792	
Present value	–100,000	37,720	31,595	28,245	3,861	1,421

CHAPTER SUMMARY

The chapter has:

- considered several of the most important concepts in project appraisal, such as cash flows and the time value of money
- examined two non-discounting approaches: payback and accounting rate of return (ARR)
- examined issues relating to compounding, discounting and the use of present value tables and present value of annuity tables
- considered the concept and calculation of net present value (NPV) and internal rate of return (IRR)
- returned to payback period to look at discounted payback, and finally
- examined the impact of taxation on project appraisal.

END OF CHAPTER QUESTIONS

4.1 Rowena Hull is the owner of the Bellevue Gymnasium and Health Club. Rowena is contemplating building a 25 metre swimming pool on some spare land attached to the club. The project is estimated to cost £500,000.

At present the club has a stable membership of 400 people, who each pay a membership fee of £250 per year. Rowena believes that having a swimming pool would cause the club's membership to increase by 100 members per year in each of the next three years until the club's capacity of 700 members is reached. It would also be possible to increase the annual membership fee by 80%. If the pool were built, the running costs of the club would immediately rise from £80,000 per year to £200,000.

Rowena plans to retire in five years' time, when she will sell the club. She believes that at that time the club would be worth £1,000,000 without a pool and £1,700,000 with the pool.

Rowena's cost of capital is 10%.

Required

(a) Calculate the payback period for the project.
(b) Calculate the NPV of the project.
(c) Comment on your results and advise Rowena.

4.2 Viernes Ltd has the option to rent or buy a machine.

- The machine would cost £125,000 and have a useful life of five years.
- The disposal value would be £50,000.
- If the machine were rented, it would cost Viernes Ltd £35,000 per year, payable in advance.
- The initial allowance is 25% and the annual WDA is 25% of the reducing balance.
- Corporation tax is charged on profits at 30%.
- Viernes Ltd is a profitable company.
- The company's cost of capital is 12%.

Required

(a) Calculate the NPV of the purchase decision.
(b) Calculate the NPV of the rental decision.
(c) Recommend the option that Viernes Ltd should choose. Justify your recommendation.

4.3 Pantile Communication plc is considering investing £200,000 to equip a recording studio. The project is expected to generate an annual contribution of £75,000 for each of the next four years. The equipment will be scrapped at the end of the fourth year and is expected to have a disposal value of £40,000.

The rate of corporation tax is 30%, and the initial allowance and annual WDAs are 25%.

The cost of capital is 8%.

Required

(a) Calculate the payback period and the discounted payback period for the project.
(b) Calculate the NPV of the project.
(c) Calculate the IRR of the project.
(d) Prepare a briefing note on the proposal for Pantile Communication's board of directors.

4.4 Windsor98 is a successful professional football club. The club plays in a small stadium, which is always full to capacity for its 25 home games. The capacity of the stadium is 10,000. The club's statement of profit or loss for the year ended 31 March 2014 is as follows:

END OF CHAPTER QUESTIONS *continued*

	£000s
Revenues	
Ticket sales (note 1)	7,125
Sponsorship	1,000
	8,125
Less expenses	
Players' wages	2,200
Management costs	1,000
Rent for ground	500
Other overheads	1,000
	4,700
Net profit	3,425
Less taxation (20%)	685
Net profit after tax	2,740

Note 1: Ticket sales were made up of 5,000 season tickets of £800 each and 5,000 match game tickets of £25 per game.

The rent for the ground was agreed five years ago and the annual rent is now up for re-negotiation. A new alternative stadium has become available which will seat 15,000. The leasehold stadium is on the market at £10 million, but the local authority's plans indicate that the stadium will need to be demolished in five years' time in order to construct a sports village on the site.

The club's marketing manager judges that advertising of £200,000 per year would produce the following sales for the new stadium.

- Season tickets: 6,000 at £800 each.
- Tickets per game: 7,000 at the following prices:
  - 25% at £30 each
  - 60% at £25 each
  - 15% at £15 each.

There would continue to be 25 home games per year. Sponsorship would increase to £1.25 million per year due to the increased capacity.

Additional security would be required and this, along with additional running costs, would increase 'other overheads' to £1.5 million.

At its current ground, there is a gymnasium that the club uses. The new stadium does not contain such a facility so the club would need to invest £250,000 in building and equipping a new gym at the commencement of the move.

The current ground also has an associated training ground but, if the move to the new stadium were to go ahead, the club would also have to lease a training ground for £100,000 per year.

The capital expenditure on the purchase of the stadium and the construction of the gym would all attract capital allowances at the rate of 25% per year on a reducing balance basis.

The club pays taxation at 20% on its taxable profits with annual taxation payable one year in arrears.

The club intends to appraise the project using NPV. Its discount rate is 15%.

Required

(a) Calculate Windsor98's annual pre-tax profit as a result of playing its home matches at the new stadium. In its accounts the company's policy is to depreciate all capital investments in the project over five years using straight-line depreciation assuming a zero residual value.

(b) Appraise the move to the new stadium using the NPV technique.

(c) The owners of the existing ground have indicated that they are prepared to renew the rental agreement to Windsor98 for a five-year period at a revised rent of £600,000 per year. You have calculated that this will produce an annual profit of £3,325,000 before taxation and also produce an after-tax NPV of £9,210,250 over the five-year period. Taking account of these figures and those that you have previously calculated with respect to the new stadium, provide a briefing note to management on the choice of stadium.

Investment appraisal 2

5

■ **CONTENTS**

1 Inflation

The rate of inflation can have a major impact on a project, and management must be made aware of any inflation assumptions made in NPV calculations. Remember that the rate of inflation can vary from year to year, and between different elements of cost and income, and that net cash flows may be very sensitive to variations in inflation rates between different factors. When this happens, it may be particularly important to allow for inflation when projecting cash flows. Cash flows that include different cost elements inflating at different rates may give a very different picture from those that ignore inflation.

The greater the rate of inflation, the greater the minimum rate of return required by investors, in order to compensate for loss of income due to a declining value of money.

When deciding what cost of capital to use in an investment appraisal we need to consider the difference between the real and money (or nominal) cost of capital. The real cost of capital is that in present value terms (in 'today's money'), whereas the **nominal cost of capital** or money cost of capital is that cash flow actually paid out, received or required by providers of capital. We normally deal with the money cost of capital.

The relationship between the money cost of capital and the real cost of capital is given by the following equation, referred to as the **Fisher equation**:

$$(1 + \text{money discount rate}) = (1 + \text{real discount rate}) \times (1 + \text{inflation rate})$$

or:

$$\text{money discount rate} = [(1 + \text{real discount rate}) \times (1 + \text{inflation rate})] - 1$$

or:

$$\text{real discount rate} = [(1 + \text{money discount rate})/(1 + \text{inflation rate})] - 1$$

For example, if a company's discount rate is 15% and inflation is 4%, the calculation of the real discount rate is:

$$\text{real discount rate} = (1.15/1.04) - 1 = 1.1058 - 1 = 10.58\%$$

Expectations about inflation are unlikely to be accurate and if they are significant to the outcome of the project, we should use the risk and uncertainty techniques discussed in Chapter 6.

Inflation may be treated in one of two ways in project appraisal:

- **Case 1:** All costs and revenues are expected to be affected equally by inflation. In this situation, all costs and revenues should be fixed in base year prices (i.e. prices at year 0). The cash flows should then be discounted using the real cost of capital. If, however, the relative prices of different inputs are expected to change, the real prices of inputs will not remain constant.
- **Case 2:** Costs and revenues are expected to be affected differentially by inflation. In this situation, relative prices are expected to move at different rates in the future. Historically, for example, at certain times labour costs have increased more quickly than general inflation. This is particularly the case in sectors where labour costs dominate, such as the service sector, or the NHS in the UK, where labour comprises 80% of total costs.

With differential inflation, one should use the money cost of capital and project cash flows in the money prices. One can also use this approach for case 1, but it does require some unnecessary calculations.

Surveys seem to show that companies are divided equally between these two approaches to dealing with inflation. Case 2 requires more long-winded calculations, but with computerised spreadsheets this should present no problem in practice.

5.1

An electricity business has a nominal cost of capital of 12%. It is to evaluate a new project that will require an investment of £200,000. It is estimated to have annual running costs of £55,000 and annual cash inflows of £120,000 at year 0. The project is expected to have a life of five years. Inflation is currently running at 4% per year and is expected to be at this level over the life of the project.

Required

Calculate the NPV of this project using both approaches to dealing with inflation.

Solution

Case 1:

Using the Fisher equation:

real cost of capital = (1.12/1.04) – 1 = 7.69%

Year	Discount factor (7.69%)		Cash flow	Present value
			£000s	£000s
0	1.000	Capital cost	–200	–200
1	0.929	Net cash flow	65	60.385
2	0.862	Do.	65	56.030
3	0.801	Do.	65	52.065
4	0.744	Do.	65	48.360
5	0.690	Do.	65	44.850
NPV				61.690

Case 2:

Year	Discount factor (12%)		Cash flow	Present value
			£000s	£000s
0	1.000	Capital cost	–200	–200
1	0.893	Net cash flow	67.6	60.367
2	0.797	Do.	70.3	56.029
3	0.712	Do.	73.1	52.047
4	0.636	Do.	76.0	48.336
5	0.567	Do.	79.0	44.793
NPV				61.572

Note:

- The annual net cash flow at year 0 = £120,000 – £55,000 = £65,000.
- This is inflated by 4% cumulatively for each 12-month period after year 0.
- The slight differences in the two NPVs reflect rounding in the discount factors and for all practical purposes they are identical.

A private health company is to invest a total of £500,000 in a pair of operating theatres. The annual estimated costs for each theatre at year 0 prices are as follows:

- salaries: £690,000
- running costs: £250,000.

Annual income for each theatre is estimated at £1,100,000.

Inflation is expected to influence costs and revenues differentially. Salaries are expected to increase by 7% a year and running costs by 5% per year. Income is expected to increase by only 4% per year due to increasing competition in the private healthcare market.

The operating theatres are expected to have a four-year life before major refurbishment is required. The company's nominal cost of capital is 14% per year.

Required

Calculate the NPV of the project, taking full account of inflation.

Solution

	Year 0	Year 1	Year 2	Year 3	Year 4
	£000	£000	£000	£000	£000
Cash inflows					
Income		1,144.00	1,189.76	1,237.35	1,286.84
Cash outflows					
Salaries		738.30	789.98	845.28	904.45
Running costs		262.50	275.63	289.41	303.88
Capital costs	500				
Total outflows	500	1,000.80	1065.61	1134.69	1208.33
Net cash flows	−500	143.20	124.15	102.66	78.52
Discount factors (14%)	1.000	0.877	0.769	0.675	0.592
Present value	−500	125.59	95.47	69.30	46.48
NPV	−163.16				

The project should be rejected as the NPV is negative.

2 Projects with unequal lives

This topic is concerned with evaluating projects with different costs and also different service lives. For example, in a new office block, two possible air conditioning systems can be installed. As well as having different costs, the two systems also have different expected lives.

Details for the two systems are as follows.

- **System A:** Capital costs are £130,000 with annual costs of £95,000. Life is anticipated to be 15 years.
- **System B:** Capital costs are £100,000 with annual costs of £110,000. Life is anticipated to be ten years.

The company's cost of capital is 10%.

A conventional analysis would be as follows.

System A

Year	10% discount factor	Cash flow	Present value
		£000s	£000s
0	1	–130	–130.00
1–15	7.606	–95	–722.57
NPV			–852.57

System B

Year	10% discount factor	Cash flow	Present value
		£000s	£000s
0	1	–100	–100.00
1–10	6.145	–110	–675.95
NPV			–775.95

In this case, system B is cheaper than system A over their respective lives. However, system B provides the air conditioning service for ten years whereas system A provides the service for 15 years.

One could divide system A's NPV by 15 to arrive at an annual cost and similarly divide system B's NPV by 10. However, this ignores the impact of discounting within the figures.

The recommended approach is to calculate the annual equivalent cost (AEC).

AEC is found as follows:

$$\frac{\text{project NPV}}{\text{present value of annuity over the life of the project}}$$

If we were to apply this to the preceding example:

- **System A:** AEC = £852,570/7.606 = £112,092 per year
- **System B:** AEC = £775,950/6.145 = £126,273 per year.

The AEC shows that on an annual cost basis, system A is cheaper than system B.

WORKED EXAMPLE 5.3

A refuse disposal company has to choose between two models of refuse disposal vehicle to add to its existing fleet. It needs to purchase another 20 vehicles.

Information about the two vehicle types is as follows:

	Vehicle type H12	Vehicle type K7
Expected life	6 years	8 years
Initial cost	£76,000	£85,000
Estimated residual value at end of life	£2,000	£1,500
Estimated annual costs		
Year 1 and 2 (per year)	£5,000	£4,500
Year 3	£7,000	£5,500
Years 4 and 5 (per year)	£6,000	£6,000
Years 6, 7 and 8	£7,000 (year 6)	£6,500

The company's cost of capital is 10%.

5.3 *continued*

Required

Calculate the annual equivalent cost of each model and recommend which vehicle type the company should select.

Solution

Year	10% discount factor	H12		K7	
		Cash flow	Present value	Cash flow	Present value
		£	£	£	£
0	1.000	76,000	76,000	85,000	85,000
1	0.909	5,000	4,545	4,500	4,090
2	0.826	5,000	4,130	4,500	3,717
3	0.751	7,000	5,257	5,500	4,130
4	0.683	6,000	4,098	6,000	4,098
5	0.621	6,000	3,726	6,000	3,726
6	0.564	5,000	2,820	6,500	3,666
7	0.513			6,500	3,334
8	0.467			5,000	2,335
NPV of costs			100,576		114,096

Note: For H12, year 6 cash flow = £7,000 – residual value £2,000 = £5,000.
For K7, year 8 cash flow = £6,500 – residual value £1,500 = £5,000.

In this case H12 costs less over its life than K7, but lasts for two years longer. To calculate the annual equivalent cost (AEC) of each project:

AEC of H12 = £100,576/4.355 = £23,094 per year

AEC of K7 = £114,096/5.335 = £21,386 per year.

On cost grounds, K7 is preferred to H12.

3 Capital rationing

An organisation is in a **capital rationing** situation when it has insufficient funds to undertake all projects with a positive NPV. A decision, therefore, must be made as to which project(s) to choose. The technique used depends on whether capital rationing applies only for the current period (i.e. single period) or for several periods, and whether the projects are **divisible projects** (i.e. can be undertaken in whole or in parts) or non-divisible (i.e. can only be undertaken as a whole or not at all). An example of a divisible project is a proposal to invest in a fleet of delivery vans: should the company invest in 20 vans, or in some smaller number up to 20?

In a situation where there is single-period capital rationing and divisible projects, management should choose the projects that give the highest NPV per £1 of capital invested (i.e. maximising the return from the limiting factor). This ratio is the **profitability index**. The profitability index, sometimes referred to as the benefit–cost ratio, is calculated by the formula:

$$= \frac{\text{net present value}}{\text{capital outlay at rationed time period}}$$

It follows that if capital is rationed at year 0 and that is when the capital outlay occurs, then the formula would be:

$$\frac{\text{net present value}}{\text{initial investment}}$$

The index is used to put capital investment projects in order of priority for the allocation of funds, since it shows how much surplus a project offers over the cost of capital per £ invested.

The decision rules are:

- a project with a positive or zero profitability index should be accepted, and
- where there are competing projects, they should be ranked in order of decreasing profitability index. Such ranking would start with the project with the largest index and working down the rankings so that as many projects as possible (with positive or zero indices) should be accepted until the available capital is used up.

If the projects are not divisible, the best method of solving such a problem is by trial and error, comparing the total NPV available from the different possible combinations of projects. The profitability index may be used as a starting point; it may not give the optimal decision and there is likely to be unused capital. This unused capital could be invested to earn interest. However, in the absence of suitable investment projects, it would be better to return any unused capital to the owners or shareholders.

WORKED EXAMPLE 5.4

The management of Rosie Ltd has found that for the following year the company has only £100,000 available for investment. The company's cost of capital is 20%. The management is currently considering four independent and divisible projects:

Project	Investment required	NPV at 20%
	£000s	£000s
W	100	48
X	20	16
Y	30	18
Z	45	21

Required

Advise Rosie Ltd on which of the four projects the company should implement.

Solution

First, we need to calculate the profitability index using the net present value per £1 of capital invested and rank the projects according to the results.

Project	Investment required	NPV at 20%	Profitability index	Rank
	£000s	£000s		
W	100	48	0.48	3
X	20	16	0.80	1
Y	30	18	0.60	2
Z	45	21	0.47	4

WORKED EXAMPLE 5.4 *continued*

The available £100,000 can now be allocated:

Project	Investment	NPV
	£000s	£000s
X	20	16
Y	30	18
W (1/2 of project W uses the remaining capital)	50	24
Total	100	58

This combination of projects gives the maximum return to the company and should be accepted by the management.

WORKED EXAMPLE 5.5

Candy plc is experiencing capital rationing in year 0, when only £60,000 of investment finance is available. No capital rationing is expected in future periods, but none of the three projects under consideration by the company can be postponed. The expected cash flows of the three projects are as follows.

Project	Year 0	Year 1	Year 2	Year 3	Year 4
	£000s	£000s	£000s	£000s	£000s
A	–50	–20	20	40	40
B	–28	–50	40	40	20
C	–30	–30	30	40	10

The cost of capital is 10%.

Required
Decide which projects should be undertaken in year 0, in view of the capital rationing, given that projects are divisible.

Solution
First, calculate the NPV of each project.

Year	10% Factor	Project A		Project B		Project C	
		Cash flow	Present value	Cash flow	Present value	Cash flow	Present value
		£000	£000	£000	£000	£000	£000
0	1.000	–50	–50.00	–28	–28.00	–30	–30.00
1	0.909	–20	–18.18	–50	–45.45	–30	–27.27
2	0.826	20	16.52	40	33.04	30	24.78
3	0.751	40	30.04	40	30.04	40	30.04
4	0.683	40	27.32	20	13.66	10	6.83
NPV			5.70		3.29		4.38

5.5 *continued*

Next, calculate the profitability index and the net present value per £1 of capital invested then rank the projects according to the results.

Project	Investment required in year 0	NPV at 10%	Profitability index	Rank
	£000s	£000s		
A	50	5.70	0.114	3
B	28	3.29	0.118	2
C	30	4.38	0.146	1

The available £60,000 in year 0 can now be allocated:

Project	Investment	NPV
	£	£
C	30,000	4,380
B	28,000	3,290
A (2/50 of project A using the remaining capital)	2,000	228
	60,000	7,898

This combination of projects gives the maximum return to the company and should be accepted by the management.

3.1 Mutually exclusive investments

The presence of mutually exclusive projects (if we invest in project A then we cannot invest in project B) means that we have to revisit the simple ranking by profitability index that we used in Worked example 5.4. If we now assume that projects X and Y are mutually exclusive, then both cannot be accepted. We must repeat the ranking exercise twice: once with project X in the list and once with project Y in the list, as follows.

Including project X:

Project	Investment	NPV
	£000s	£000s
X	20	16.0
W (8/10 of project W uses the remaining capital)	80	38.4
	100	54.4

Including project Y:

Project	Investment	NPV
	£000s	£000s
Y	30	18.0
W (7/10 of project W uses the remaining capital)	70	33.6
	100	51.6

As can be seen, the optimum solution when projects X and Y are mutually exclusive is to select project X and 8/10 of project W. As may be seen, the additional constraint decreases the overall NPV from £58,000 in Worked example 5.4 to £54,400.

3.2 Multi-period capital rationing

This is capital rationing that extends over more than one time period. This can make its solution quite complex, although management will again be trying to maximise NPV per £ of investment. Where there are divisible projects, linear programming can be used. Where projects are non-divisible, integer programming would be used. In both cases a computer program could be used to solve the problem.

3.3 Soft and hard capital rationing

Capital may be limited because a management decision is taken to limit investment funds or because of a lack of capital available from external sources.

If the availability of investment funds is limited by a management decision, this is called **soft rationing**. There are several possible reasons for this.

- Soft rationing may happen as part of a policy of devolving investment decisions to divisions. Rather than intervene in every divisional investment decision, the company may allow divisional managers discretion to make investments, subject to their own analysis and judgement, within a set capital investment budget.
- A company may limit the total amount of capital investment to control gearing or other financial measures or because of calculations about the cost of capital.
- A company may implement soft rationing in order to limit the amount of time spent on identification, evaluation and implementation of new investment projects.

If the availability of capital for investment is limited by a lack of sources outside the company, this is called **hard rationing**. With perfect capital markets this should not occur. Capital should be available at a cost that reflects the potential returns and risks of available projects. If imperfections occur, market perceptions of a company's prospects may be incomplete. This is more likely to occur in small, new companies operating in new markets with new technology than for large, well-established companies, whose business and prospects are well understood. This is certainly true in the UK at the time of writing as banks, still rebuilding their balance sheets after the 2008 recession, are unwilling to lend to small businesses.

4 Approving and controlling investment projects

Capital projects can mean a large investment of time and resources and, frequently, a delay before those resources start earning returns for the company. So the process leading to commencing work on a capital project can be long and detailed – to ensure that the correct projects are selected – and starts long before the financial investment appraisal process.

Initially, new projects must be generated within the firm, so it needs to have in place an organisation and culture that will generate new projects, such as a research and development department. New projects will initially be subject to scrutiny to ensure that they fit within the company's long-term strategy and that they appear to be realistic.

Many companies have multi-year capital budgets showing the planned expenditure on capital projects for the next three to five years, and usually a project must be approved for inclusion in the capital budget. Once in that budget, then provision may be made for the financing of the project, especially if it is large in scale, compared with the company's resources. Generally, the board of the company will approve the projects that are included in the capital budget, and, as has been indicated, will need to be convinced of how those projects fit into the company's strategy.

Once work on the project commences, it is very important that costs are kept within budget and that due completion dates are met. Individuals will be given responsibility for this and should report back to the company regularly on progress made against plan. If there is any delay, this pushes back the point at which returns start being earned. Cost control is really important.

An important aspect of capital investment appraisal should be a post-completion appraisal (or post-completion audit). Checking back on forecasts, when the actual facts become known, can help to bring discipline to the forecasting process. Over-optimistic projections may be brought to light, and issues identified that need attention when future investments are appraised. Of course, only those projects that have been implemented can be reviewed in this way. Rejected projects cannot be measured.

To keep the effort required in proportion to the benefits gained, a sample of projects may need to be selected for evaluation. For example, all projects above a threshold capital value can be audited, with a proportion of mid-range projects and a smaller proportion of smaller projects.

Post-completion appraisal needs to be carried out in an objective and dispassionate way. This is unlikely to happen if the objective of the appraisal is to apportion blame for any shortfall against target. Post-completion appraisal is most likely to be successful in companies that are 'learning organisations'.

CHAPTER SUMMARY

This chapter has continued looking at project appraisal and has built on the foundation laid in Chapter 4 by examining the following issues:

- the different ways that inflation can be treated in the appraisal process
- ways to deal with projects with unequal lives; projects which produce a service for different amounts of time and whose costs are different
- the problems faced in project appraisal when investment funds are rationed, and
- the approving and controlling of investment projects.

END OF CHAPTER QUESTIONS

5.1 The research department of Tolnedra plc, a multi product company, has developed four new products provisionally called Borune, Honeth, Rane and Vordue. The directors are now considering which, if any, of these products to manufacture and sell, and they have asked you for advice. You are provided with the following information:

1 Manufacture of the products will require an immediate outlay on plant and machinery, the costs of which are estimated as follows:

Borune	Honeth	Rane	Vordue
£1,200,000	£1,100,000	£840,000	£700,000

In all four cases the plant has a useful life of six years, at the end of which it will be valueless. Production of all four products is expected to cease after six years.

2 Annual cash flows (at current prices) are expected to be as follows:

Borune	Honeth	Rane	Vordue
£330,000	£290,000	£230,000	£200,000

3 The directors have decided that capital expenditure on the projects accepted must not exceed £1,600,000.

The company's monetary cost of capital is estimated to be 10%.

END OF CHAPTER QUESTIONS *continued*

Required

(a) Advise the directors of Tolnedra which of the new products, if any, to manufacture and sell on the assumption that all four products are independent of each other and the other activities of the firm. Your advice should indicate clearly your order of preference for the four products and what proportion you would take of any product whose manufacture is scaled down.

(b) Advise the directors of Tolnedra which of the new products, if any, to manufacture and sell on the assumption that Borune and Vordue are mutually exclusive. Your advice should indicate clearly your order of preference for the four products and what proportion you would take of any product whose manufacture is scaled down.

(c) Discuss the limitations of your advice in (a) and (b) above.

Notes:

For part (a) and (b) **only**, assume manufacture of any of the four products can take place on a reduced scale for a proportionate reduction in NPV.

Assume all cash flows arise at the end of each year unless otherwise stated.

5.2 Assume that two types of boiler for a heating system are available to you:

Gas boiler

Capital cost	£6,000
Annual energy cost	£3,000
Estimated lifespan	10 years

Electric boiler

Capital cost	£3,000
Annual energy cost	£4,000
Estimated lifespan	7 years

The cost of capital is 10%.

Required

From a financial point of view, which boiler is the most attractive?

5.3 (a) Explain the benefits of carrying out post-completion audits of capital investment projects. Suggest what issues ought to be considered before initiating procedures to do this.

(b) A company needs to replace its polishing machine. The polishing machine forms a part of the production process, and most products manufactured require polishing at various stages in their production. A polishing facility is expected to be required for as long as the factory remains in operation, and the company expects to continue operations in its existing factory for the foreseeable future.

Details of the two machines under consideration are set out below:

	Machine A	**Machine B**
Initial cost	£50,000	£90,000
Lifespan	4 years	7 years
Salvage value at end of:		
year 4	£5,000	
year 7		£7,000
Annual running costs (cash)	£10,000	£8,000

Both machines fulfil the same function and have equal capacities. The company's target rate of return for evaluating capital investment projects is 10%.

Required

(i) Determine which machine should be purchased. Explain your method and specify any assumptions made.

(ii) What would the initial cost of machine A have to be to make the two machines equally financially attractive?

5.4 Stamford Ltd specialises in the production of plastic sports equipment. The company has recently developed a new machine for automatically producing plastic cricket bats. The machine cost £150,000 to develop and install, and production is to commence at the beginning of next week. It is planned to depreciate

END OF CHAPTER QUESTIONS *continued*

the £150,000 cost evenly over four years, after which time production of plastic cricket bats will cease. Production and sales will amount to 30,000 bats each year. Annual revenues and operating costs, at current prices, are estimated as follows:

Sales (£9.60 each)	£288,000
Variable manufacturing costs	£200,000

This morning, a salesman has called and described to the directors of Stamford Ltd a new machine, ideally suited to the production of plastic cricket bats. This item of equipment is distinctly superior to Stamford's own machine, reducing variable costs by 30% and producing an identical product. The cost of the machine, which is also capable of producing 30,000 cricket bats per annum, is £190,000.

Assume that:

- annual revenues and operating costs arise at the year-end
- the general rate of inflation is 10% per annum
- the company's money cost of capital is 21%
- the existing machine could be sold immediately for £12,000
- if purchased, the new machine could be installed immediately
- either machine would have a zero residual value at the end of four years.

Required

(a) Calculate the NPVs of the two options, using the real cost of capital.

(b) Advise the management as to which course of action should be followed, providing an explanation of the significance of your calculations in (a).

Ignore taxation.

Project appraisal and risk

6

■ **CONTENTS**

1 Introduction

Risk has particular importance for investment decisions because large sums of money are often involved. If things do not turn out as expected, the effect on shareholder wealth and the fortunes of the business can be profound. In addition, investment projects often involve long timescales. This means that there is plenty of time for unexpected changes to occur.

In financial management, risk usually refers to volatility of returns. Returns that can be denoted by a horizontal straight line demonstrate no volatility and may be described as risk free. However, returns that fluctuate and can be unpredictable are risky returns. Later in this chapter we will examine how to measure the amount of risk in a series of returns.

2 Risk preference

This refers to the attitude of investors to risk. There are three categories of risk preference:

- **Risk-seeking investors:** These are investors who actively seek risk. Given the choice between a safe investment and a risky investment, they will choose the latter. In evaluating investments, they will be deterred less by risk than other investors and, in consequence, will require a lower return from the investment for any additional risk. Risk-seeking investors may be characterised as gamblers!
- **Risk-averse investors:** The attitude of these investors is the opposite to those in the risk-seeking category. They will tend to avoid risk. If risk has to be taken, they will ensure that the additional return for the risk being taken on will compensate them adequately. Evidence suggests that most investors, and most managers, are risk-averse, requiring significantly additional returns to compensate for any additional risk.
- **Risk-neutral investors:** These investors neither seek nor avoid risk. Risk-neutral is a definition of an investor who purposely overlooks risk when deciding between investments. In other words, a risk-neutral investor is only concerned with an investment's estimated return.

3 Sensitivity analysis

Sensitivity analysis is a non-probabilistic approach to project appraisal. It examines how sensitive the returns on a project are to changes in key variables, such as:

- any increase in capital costs
- any increase or decrease in projected sales volumes
- any increase or decrease in variable costs.

The methodology is as follows.

1 Specify a base case situation.
2 Ask a series of 'what if' questions; for example, what if projected sales were to be changed by –10%, –5%, +5% and +10%?
3 Calculate the NPV under each of these assumptions.
4 Combine questions:
   – selectively, or
   – randomly.
5 Evaluate the project's sensitivity to changes in the key variables (look at the percentage change in NPV generated by a percentage change in a variable).
6 Make a decision.

WORKED EXAMPLE 6.1

To illustrate the use of sensitivity analysis, we consider the following example.

Market assumptions are:

Market size	£3,750 million
Market share	10%

Cash flow projections (£ million) are:

Investment (year 0)	–150
Revenue items (years 1–10)	
sales	375
variable cost	300
fixed cost	30
depreciation	15
Pre-tax profit	30
Tax (50%)	15
Post-tax profit	15
(ANCF	30)

Note: ANCF = post tax profit (15) + depreciation (15)

The cost of capital is 10% (ten-year present value of annuity = 6.145).

The NPV is therefore: (30 × 6.145) – 150 = £34.35 million.

Calculation and presentation of sensitivity analysis

A computer-based spreadsheet is essential. As shown in Table 6.1, each variable is changed in isolation, i.e. with all other variables unchanged.

TABLE 6.1 Sensitivity analysis

Variable	Three states			NPV (£ million)		
	Lower assumption	Market assumption	Higher assumption	Lower assumption	Market assumption	Higher assumption
Market size	£3,375m	£3,750m	£4,125m	+26	+34	+57
Market share	4%	10%	16%	–94	+34	+172
Sales	350m	375m	380m	–42	+34	+50
Variable cost	360m	300m	275m	–150	+34	+111
Fixed cost	£40m	£30m	£20m	+4	+34	+65

WORKED EXAMPLE **6.1** *continued*

One-way table

A one-way table is used to test for a range of values in any one variable. For example, in Table 6.2 we see what happens to NPV as market size changes.

TABLE 6.2 One-way table

Market size	**NPV**
£ million	£ million
3,375	26
3,750	34
4,125	57

Two-way table

A two-way table is used to test for a range of values in two variables. For example, Table 6.3 shows what happens to NPV when both market size and market share change.

TABLE 6.3 Two-way table

NPV	**Market share 4%**	**Market share 10%**	**Market share 16%**
Market size £3,375m	–113	+26	+135
Market size £3,750m	–94	+34	+172
Market size £4,125m	–76	+57	+209

Note: The underlying calculations for the NPVs given in the table are not shown.

WORKED EXAMPLE **6.2**

A new swimming pool will cost £150,000 and then have annual running costs of £77,000. Demand is based upon the following factors:

- entry fee is £5
- target population is 50,000 people
- estimated percentage of target who will use the swimming pool is 5%
- average number of uses per user per year is 10.

The estimated life of the swimming pool is five years.

The discount rate is 10%.

Required

(a) Calculate the NPV of the project.

(b) Conduct sensitivity analysis on the entry fee and the number of uses per year by preparing one-way tables.

WORKED EXAMPLE **6.2** *continued*

Solution

(a) NPV

Year	Narrative	10% discount factor	ANCF £000s	Present value £000s
0	Capital cost	1.000	–150	–150
1–5	ANCF	3.791	48*	181.97
	NPV			31.97

* ANCF = (50,000 × 5% × 10 uses × £5) = £125,000 – £77,000 = £48,000.

(b) Sensitivity analysis

(i) Population: 50,000. Target: 5%. Uses/year: 10.

Entry fee	NPV
£	£000s
6	126.74
5	31.97
4	–62.81

Notes:

£6 × 0.05 × 50,000 × 10 = £150,000 per year. Annual NCF = £150,000 – £77,000 = £73,000 × 3.791 = £276,743 – £150,00 = £126,743.

£4 × 0.05 × 50,000 × 10 = £100,000 per year. Annual NCF = £100,000 – £77,000 = £23,000 × 3.791 = £87,193 – £150,000 = –£62,807.

(ii) Population: 50,000. Fee: £5. Target: 5%.

Uses per year	NPV
	£000s
11	79.36
10	31.97
9	–15.42

Notes:

£5 × 0.05 × 50,000 × 11 = £137,500 – £77,000 = £60,500 × 3.791 = £229,356 – £150,000 = £79,356.

£5 × 0.05 × 50,000 × 9 = £112,500 – £77,000 = £35,500 × 3.791 = £134,581 – £150,000 = –£15,419

3.1 A commentary on sensitivity analysis

- Sensitivity analysis increases the amount of information available to the decision-maker, but it does not give a single-figure signal as to whether the project is acceptable or not.
- The technique is transparent and easily understood.
- It changes one variable at a time, which may limit its usefulness.

- No use is made of the probability of each of the assumptions tested; they are all weighted equally.
- There is a danger that the amount of information may overwhelm the decision-maker.
- The sensitivity information may have operational value in allowing managers to resource those variables which are seen to be most critical.
- The technique is used by a range of organisations; for example, the NHS requires this to be used for all capital appraisals.
- It is ideally suited to a computerised spreadsheet package, which takes the cost and drudgery out of the constant recalculations.

3.2 The pivot approach to sensitivity analysis

A complementary approach, termed the 'pivot approach', is to ask the question: By how much must a variable change before the NPV becomes zero? In other words, what level of change can a project sustain and still break even? Alternatively, what level of change is necessary to turn an acceptable project into an unacceptable project?

The procedure for undertaking this approach is as follows:

1. Find the NPV of the project using the original estimates for the variables (capital cost, revenues, operating costs, discount rate etc.).
2. For each variable in the NPV calculation, calculate by how much the variable must change before the NPV becomes zero. This is done independently for each variable.
3. Present the results in a table, as shown in Table 6.4.

TABLE 6.4 Sensitivity table

Variable	Original estimate	Maximum or minimum value	% change	Notes
Capital cost	£150m	£184m (max.)	23	1
Revenues	£375m	£369.5m (min.)	−2	2
Variable costs	£300m	£305.5m (max.)	1.8	3
Fixed costs	£30m	£35.5m (max.)	18	4
Market share	10%	9.8% (min.)	−2	5

Notes:

1. In order to calculate by how much the capital cost can increase before the project breaks even and the NPV becomes zero, we add the projected NPV to the capital cost. If capital cost increases by the amount of the NPV, the NPV will become zero (i.e. 150 + 34 (NPV) = 184). The increase in capital cost is therefore 34/150 = 23%.
2. In order to calculate how much revenue can decrease before NPV becomes zero, we divide the NPV by the present value of annuity factor to give the annual equivalent of the NPV. This amount can then be subtracted from annual revenues to give a break-even NPV (i.e. 34/6.145 = 5.5). Therefore, revenue can fall by only £5.5 million per year to £369.5 million. As a result, the fall in annual revenue = 5.5/375 = 2%.
3. In order to calculate by how much variable costs can increase before NPV becomes zero, we again divide the NPV by the present value of annuity factor to give the annual equivalent of the NPV. This amount can then be added to annual variable costs to give a break-even NPV (i.e. 300 + 5.5 = 305.5). The increase in annual variable costs is then 5.5/300 = 1.8%.
4. In order to calculate by how much fixed costs can increase before NPV becomes zero, we again divide the NPV by the present value of annuity factor to give the annual equivalent of the NPV. This amount can then be added to annual fixed costs to give a break-even NPV (i.e. 30 + 5.5 = 35.5). The increase in fixed costs is therefore 5.5/30 = 18% per year.
5. Market share must be like revenues (i.e. the market share that gives a zero NPV is 98% of 10% = 9.8%).

The sensitivity table indicates which variables the project is most sensitive to.

This approach provides more information for the decision-maker about an important area. From an operational perspective, it indicates those variables on which more management time may be worth spending. For example, if the project is particularly sensitive to the capital cost, then greater importance may be placed upon the management of the construction phase to ensure that it is completed within budget.

6.3

Apply the pivot approach to the data in Worked example 6.2, applying it to capital cost, annual revenues and annual variable costs.

Solution

Variable	**Original**	**Maximum/ minimum**	**%**	**Workings**
Capital cost	£150,000	£181.970 (max.)	21	Capital cost + NPV
Revenues	£125,000	£116.567 (min.)	6.7	NPV/3.791 = £31,970/3.791 = £8,433 per year £125,000 – £8,433 = £116,567 £8,433/£125,000 = 6.7%
Variable costs	£77,000	£85,433 (max.)	11	£77,000 + £8,433 = £85,433 £8,433 /£77,000 = 11%

4 Scenario analysis

Scenario analysis involves preparing NPV calculations according to different possible states of the world. A common form of scenario analysis is to present three possible states of the world: a most likely view, an optimistic view and a pessimistic view. The three states in Table 6.1 above could be categorised as pessimistic, most likely and optimistic.

Unlike sensitivity analysis, scenario analysis involves changing a number of key variables simultaneously in order to replicate each particular state of the world.

By examining each possible outcome, decision-makers may gain a better feel for the 'downside' risk and 'upside' potential of a project, as well as the most likely outcome.

This approach has a number of weaknesses:

- it does not indicate the probability of each state of the world occurring, which is important when evaluating the possible outcomes
- as the number of variables that are changed increases, the model becomes increasingly difficult and time-consuming to interpret and to act upon, and
- it does not identify other possible scenarios that may occur.

5 Simulations

Another way of dealing with variable factors is to use a **simulation model**.

Simulation models are programmed and run on computers using random numbers. A model of the cash flows is constructed and values are assigned at random, within their ranges of possible values, for those factors (such as capital costs, volumes, selling prices, cost prices, rates of use of labour and materials, and wages) the values of which can vary. The randomly selected values of all the variable factors are used to calculate the project NPV. The process is repeated many times, and a different NPV is calculated each time. The resulting set of NPVs can be used to show how the NPV varies under the influence of all the variable factors.

This approach, known as 'Monte Carlo simulation', can be used to answer questions about, for example, the probability of a project making a loss or the probability of one project having a greater NPV than another. It can also be used to test the vulnerability of outcomes to possible variations in uncontrolled factors, or to evaluate possible changes in the project specification.

6 Expected net present value (ENPV)

Unlike the methods that have already been described, this approach makes use of probabilities. An example of the use of probabilities is given in Table 6.5.

TABLE 6.5 Probability of rain tomorrow

Outcomes	Probability
Rain	0.6
No rain	0.4
	1.0

Table 6.5 contains a probability distribution and it tells us that there is a 60% chance of rain and a 40% chance of no rain. The following are key points about using probabilities and probability distributions.

- Probabilities should always sum to 1, as they do in Table 6.5.
- A 60% chance of rain is more informative than just 'I think it's likely to rain'.
- Ideally, the probabilities should be derived by looking at statistics for the number of times things have happened before.
- In practice, there will also be expert input into the derivation of probabilities, so that a meteorological expert will have looked at statistics and, more importantly, looked at incoming weather systems before stating the probabilities. Another type of expert input is a market research study.
- The probabilities may be subjective and provided by managers; but if they are backed up by experience, understanding and good judgement then we should accept them.

In financial decision-making, probabilities are used in two types of summary measure:

- expected value and expected NPV (ENPV) – these measure the returns
- **standard deviation** of returns – this measures risk or **volatility**.

6.1 Expected value and ENPV

In both of these techniques, the outcomes are weighted by probabilities to provide an expected value of returns.

For example, there is a 0.2 probability that monthly sales will be £10,000, a 0.5 probability that they will be £12,000 and a 0.3 probability that they will be £15,000.

The expected value of monthly sales is calculated as follows:

Sales	Probability	Sales × probability
£10,000	0.2	£2,000
£12,000	0.5	£6,000
£15,000	0.3	£4,500
Expected value	1.0	£12,500

In this case, the expected value of monthly sales is £12,500. This is a summary measure of the expected returns. As can be seen, the sales are weighted by the probabilities. The figure of £12,500 does not appear among any of the outcomes, but it is the expected figure based on the probabilities of the different outcomes.

The application of ENPV can be explained using an example of a project for which the following information is provided.

- Capital cost: a 70% probability that capital cost will be £300,000 and a 30% probability that it will be £400,000.
- Annual net cash flow (ANCF): a 30% probability that it will be £50,000 per year, a 60% probability that it will be £75,000 per year and a 10% probability that it will be £100,000 per year.
- The project life is expected to be ten years.
- The cost of capital is 10%.

The ENPV is calculated as shown in Table 6.6.

TABLE 6.6 Example ENPV calculation

Year		p*	Outcome	p × outcome	10% discount factor	
			£000s	£000s		
0	Capital cost	0.7	300	210		
		0.3	400	120		
	Expected cost			330	1.000	–330.00
0–10	ANCF	0.3	50	15		
		0.6	75	45		
		0.1	100	10		
	Expected ANCF			70	6.145	430.15
	ENPV					100.15

*p = probability

It is important to understand that expected value and ENPV are nothing to do with risk but are summary measures of return.

To illustrate this point, consider the two projects shown in Table 6.7, which have identical ENPVs.

TABLE 6.7 Project ENPV calculations

Project A			Project B		
p	NPV	p × NPV	p	NPV	p × NPV
	£000s	£000s		£000s	£000s
0.2	50	10	0.2	120	24
0.7	30	21	0.2	60	12
0.1	20	2	0.6	–5	–3
		33			33

Although both projects have identical ENPVs, project B looks much riskier than project A as its cash flows include a 60% probability of making a loss of £5,000. A risk-averse investor would certainly avoid project B!

WORKED EXAMPLE 6.4

An opportunity has arisen for your company to acquire the specialist product stocks of a bankrupt business for £50,000. The net proceeds from the sale of these stocks will be influenced by a number of factors originating from outside the company. The range of possibilities appears to be as follows:

Year	Possible amounts of net sales proceeds	Probability
1	£24,000	0.6
	£20,000	0.3
	£16,000	0.1
		1.0
2	£60,000	0.5
	£48,000	0.3
	£20,000	0.2
		1.0

The estimates for year 2 are independent of those for year 1. The company's required rate of return is 20%.

Required

Calculate the ENPV and state whether on this basis the company should go ahead with the project.

Solution

Year	Cash flow (CF)	Prob (p)	p × CF	20% discount factor	Present value
	£		£		£
0	–50,000			1.000	–50,000
1	24,000	0.6	14,400		
	20,000	0.3	6,000		
	16,000	0.1	1,600		
			22,000	0.833	18,326
2	60,000	0.5	30,000		
	48,000	0.3	14,400		
	20,000	0.2	4,000		
			48,400	0.694	33,590
	ENPV				1,916

As the expected net present value is positive, the company should go ahead with the project.

6.2 A commentary on ENPV

- ENPV provides a clear decision rule: a positive ENPV should be accepted as it will increase shareholder wealth if it proceeds and outcomes follow expectations.
- It is simple to calculate and takes account of all the probabilities.
- Probabilities are difficult to estimate and one may have to rely on subjective probabilities.

- The average outcome may not be one that is forecast to be realised. For example, in Table 6.6 above, the expected capital cost is £330,000, yet the forecasts of capital cost are either £300,000 or £400,000.
- It is a good idea to report individual outcomes as well as expected outcome.
- The degree of variability of the possible returns around the average (expected) return is not taken into account. For example, consider projects A and B:

Project A		**Project B**	
p	NPV	p	NPV
0.3	400	0.3	1,500
0.4	1,600	0.4	1,600
0.3	2,800	0.3	1,700
ENPV	1,600	ENPV	1,600

Both projects have the same ENPV, but project A is clearly more risky than project B because its returns are more widely distributed. ENPV does not take account of differences in variability as it is a measure of return; variability or dispersion is measured by standard deviation.

6.3 Standard deviation of returns

This is a measure of risk or volatility. The standard deviation measures dispersion around the expected value. Like expected value, it is a summary measure. One should always look at the probability distribution as well as the summary measures because a significant amount of information may be lost in the process of summarisation.

You should understand the meaning and significance of standard deviation. To help with this, using the data for project A in Table 6.7, the standard deviation is calculated as follows:

	1	**2**	**3**	**4**	**5**	**6**
	p	**NPV**	**p × NPV**	**d**	**d²**	**pd²**
		£000s	£000s	£000s	£000s	£000s
	0.2	50	10	17	289	57.8
	0.7	30	21	−3	9	6.3
	0.1	20	2	−13	169	16.9
EV			33	Variance		81
				SD		9

Notes:

Column 4: d (deviation) = NPV – EV, so 50 – 33 = 17, 30 – 33 = −3 and 20 – 33 = −13.

Column 5: d^2 = 17 × 17 = 289 etc. By squaring the deviations, the negative numbers are removed.

Column 6: pd^2 = probability × squared deviations, so 0.2 × 289 = 57.8 etc.

EV = expected value

Variance: this is the sum of column 6.

SD = standard deviation; this is the square root of the variance. In this case, the standard deviation is £9,000.

The standard deviation is a measure of spread or volatility, so the higher the standard deviation, the greater the volatility or risk of the project.

6.4 The coefficient of variation

The standard deviation is an absolute figure, and so the larger the cash flows, the larger the standard deviation. However, the risk for project X, with a standard deviation of £2,000 and an

ENPV of £8,000, is the same in relative terms as the risk for project Y, with a standard deviation of £20,000 and an ENPV of £80,000. In order to be able to compare standard deviations from projects of different sizes, the coefficient of variation may be calculated. This is simply:

$$\text{coefficient of variation} = \frac{\text{standard deviation}}{\text{expected value or ENPV}}$$

The coefficients of variation for project X and project Y are:

Project	Standard deviation/ENPV	Coefficient of variation
X	2,000/8,000	0.25
Y	20,000/80,000	0.25

WORKED EXAMPLE 6.5

The following two competing projects have been subject to appraisal:

	Project A			Project B		
		£000s	£000s		£000s	£000s
Capital cost		500			270	
	p	NPV*	ENPV	p	NPV*	ENPV
Expected returns	0.3	138.83	41.65	0.2	89.34	17.87
	0.6	119.05	71.43	0.6	49.41	29.65
	0.1	–45.52	–4.55	0.2	9.49	0.95
ENPV			108.53			48.47
Standard deviation			52.10			25.26

Note: *At the level of expected returns, ignoring the probability of return.

Required

(a) Calculate the coefficient of variation.

(b) Outline the main risk/return issues that management should consider in choosing between these two projects.

Solution

(a) Coefficient of variation:

A = 52.1/108.53 = 0.48

B = 25.26/48.47 = 0.52

(b) The main issues are as follows.

1 Project A appears more risky than project B as it has a much higher standard deviation. However, in relative terms, taking account of the size of the ENPV, project B is marginally riskier than project A, which has a slightly higher coefficient of variation.

2 However, project A has a 0.1 probability of a negative NPV of £45,520. All project B's NPVs are positive, with no probability of a loss.

3 In terms of return, project A has a higher ENPV of £108,530 and will increase shareholder wealth by £60,060 more than Project B.

7 Event tree diagrams

Where a range of possible outcomes arise from an investment, it may be helpful to organise the information in an event tree diagram, where each branch represents one possible outcome of the project. A probability is usually assigned to each outcome.

The following example illustrates this approach.

A company that carries out oil exploration has commenced work in a new area. The cost of transporting and setting up the testing equipment is £500,000. The project is planned to last two years and the company has estimated the following probabilities of returns in each year:

Year 1		Year 2	
P	ANCF	P	ANCF
	£000s		£000s
0.3	900	0.4	700
0.7	500	0.6	450

The annual returns for each year are independent of the other year's returns.

The possible outcomes are as follows:

Outcome	Year 1 £000s	Year 2 £000s	Joint probabilities*	
1	900	700	= 0.3 × 0.4 =	0.12
2	900	450	= 0.3 × 0.6 =	0.18
3	500	700	= 0.7 × 0.4 =	0.28
4	500	450	= 0.7 × 0.6 =	0.42
				1.00

*The overall probability of that event occurring by multiplying each year 1 probability by each year 2 probability.

The event tree is constructed as follows:

			Probability	Cash flow £000s	Joint probability
	Outcome 1	Year 1	0.3	900	
		Year 2	0.4	700	0.12
	Outcome 2	Year 1	0.3	900	
		Year 2	0.6	450	0.18
Outlay £500,000					
	Outcome 3	Year 1	0.7	500	
		Year 2	0.4	700	0.28
	Outcome 4	Year 1	0.7	500	
		Year 2	0.6	450	0.42
					1.00

8 Risk-adjusted discount rate (RADR)

The risk-adjusted discount rate (RADR) increases or decreases the discount rate according to how risky the project is. A more risky project would be discounted at a higher rate, making it more difficult to achieve a positive NPV. The relationship between risk and discount rate is shown in Figure 6.1.

FIGURE 6.1 Risk-adjusted discount rate

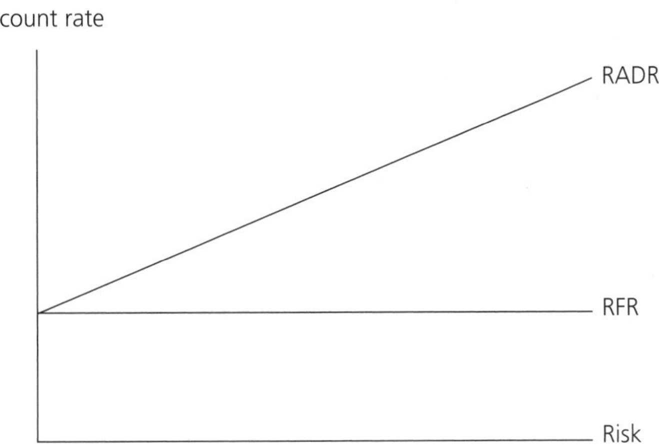

Figure 6.1 indicates that as a project becomes riskier (horizontal axis), the discount rate increases. When risk is zero, the discount rate is equal to the risk-free rate (RFR). As risk increases, the premium or additional return required for bearing risk also increases, as shown by the diagonal line representing the discount rate.

However, although we have found out how to measure the risk of projects (by measuring the standard deviation of returns), the link between an increase in the standard deviation (or coefficient of variation) and the percentage increase in the discount rate is unclear (e.g. if the coefficient of variation increases by 5%, how much should the discount rate increase?).

This can lead to the application of judgement by managers although several researchers have established a link between stock market risk and required returns on equity. This is discussed in Chapter 12 in the section on the capital asset pricing model (CAPM).

9 Portfolio effect and risk reduction

A portfolio is a collection of investments held by an individual or a company. A company may make external financial investments when it has surplus funds available and will also have a portfolio of its own projects. To manage this portfolio effectively and to understand investor behaviour in the management of the firm's own share price, the financial manager needs to have a good working knowledge of both financial markets and sources of finance (see Chapter 11) and of portfolio theory.

Portfolio theory provides investors with insights into the required rates of return on investments in relation to their risks. Portfolio theory is based on a range of assumptions. While these assumptions may not all hold true in the real world, portfolio theory helps investment managers to construct portfolios that best meet the requirements of investors in terms of risk and return.

When determining the composition of the portfolio, the investor or company will consider:

- the return received from the investment – obviously higher returns are more desirable than low or negative returns; in general, the better the growth prospects of the firm, the better the expected returns
- risk and security – investors will wish to minimise their risk in relation to the levels of return obtained, and

- the liquidity of the investments – it may be important that they are only to be held for a short term.

9.1 Portfolio risk and return

A portfolio can reduce overall risks to an investor. This is achieved by diversification. By including several investments in a portfolio, an investor can reduce the level of risk, because the factors that cause variations in performance are not the same for all investments. An example is a unit trust, which spreads its funds among a large number of investments.

Portfolio theory is concerned with the relationship between the risks and returns of the individual investments in a portfolio and how the combination of individual investments determines the overall risk and return of the portfolio. To investigate this in more detail, we need to consider correlation – the relationship between the returns on different investments. We will look at three aspects of correlation.

- **Positive correlation:** Positive correlation can arise when two investments are in the same industry or related industries. If one investment is successful and rises in value, then the other may also do well. Similarly, if the first does badly, then the second is likely to follow. For example, if there is a boom in the domestic property market, the shares of a house building company will probably rise in price; at the same time, the shares in another house builder or a builders' merchant will also rise in value.
- **Negative correlation:** This happens when, if one investment performs well, another tends to perform poorly, and vice versa. For example, when the price of oil rises, the price of an oil company's shares is likely to rise, but the shares of companies such as airlines, whose costs are affected by the price of oil, will be likely to fall in value. Note that we say 'likely'. Other factors, such as the buoyancy of the world economy, may encourage rises in the prices of both oil companies' and airlines' shares, while terrorist attacks will probably cause falls for both of them. So, we are unlikely to find two investments that are exactly out of step, just as we are unlikely to find investment with perfect positive correlation, where prices are exactly in step.
- **Nil correlation:** Here, the performance of an investment is unrelated to that of another. Something like this situation could arise, for example, with an engineering firm and a clothing manufacturer. Many of the environmental factors and most or all of the internal organisational factors that influence the success of the engineering firm may be quite separate and independent from those that affect the success of the clothing manufacturer. So their share prices are likely to vary to a large extent independently. However, general economic conditions and stock market sentiment are likely to affect both companies in similar ways. So, while the correlation between the two share prices is likely to be small, it may not be zero.

From the above, we can see that an investment manager can reduce portfolio risk by choosing investments whose performance is negatively correlated or, where this cannot be achieved, by seeking investments whose correlation is low.

STOP AND THINK 6.1

Can you think of further examples of investments with positive, negative and nil correlation?

Worked example 6.7 shows how the return of a portfolio can be measured and how standard deviation can be used to give a measure of the risk of a portfolio under different assumptions about the correlation between the performance of the constituent investments.

WORKED EXAMPLE 6.7

The following data relate to security A and security B:

Economic conditions	Probability	Return	
		A	B
		%	%
Boom	0.25	24	–3
Normal	0.50	11	10
Recession	0.25	–6	18

As can be seen, there is a negative correlation between the returns from A and from B because when A's returns increase, B's returns fall, and vice versa.

Security A: expected return

Probability (p)	Return (x)	px
	%	%
0.25	24	6
0.50	11	5.5
0.25	–6	–1.5
Expected return (ER)		10

Security A: standard deviation

Return	ER	d (= return – ER)	d^2	Probability (p)	pd^2
24	10	14	196	0.25	49
11	10	1	1	0.50	0.5
–6	10	–16	256	0.25	64
Variance					113.5
Standard deviation					10.65

Security B: expected return

Probability (p)	Return (x)	px
	%	%
0.25	–3	–0.75
0.50	10	5
0.25	18	4.5
Expected return (ER)		8.75

WORKED EXAMPLE **6.7** *continued*

Security B: standard deviation

Return	ER	d (= return – ER)	d^2	Probability (p)	pd^2
–3	8.75	–11.75	138.06	.25	34.52
10	8.75	1.25	1.56	.50	0.78
18	8.75	9.25	85.56	.25	21.39
Variance					56.69
Standard deviation					7.53

A portfolio of A and B shares

If you wanted to calculate a portfolio consisting of 50% of your investment (whatever the amount of money involved is) in share A and 50% in share B, then you would get equal proportions of whatever the return might be.

50% of A and 50% of B: expected return

expected return = (0.5 × 10%) + (0.5 × 8.75%) = 9.38%

The following table shows the calculation of the standard deviation of returns in this portfolio.

The first column shows the return from holding 50% of A and 50% of B. The figures are calculated as follows:

Probability (p)	Average returns from A and B	
0.25	(24 – 3)/2 =	10.5
0.5	(11 + 10)/2 =	10.5
0.25	(–6 + 18)/2 =	6

50% of A and 50% of B: standard deviation

Return 0.5A + 0.5B	ER 0.5A + 0.5B	d (= return – ER)	d^2	Prob (p)	pd^2
10.5	9.375	1.125	1.26	0.25	0.31
10.5	9.375	1.125	1.26	0.50	0.63
6	9.375	–3.375	11.39	0.25	2.85
Variance					3.79
Standard deviation					1.95

To summarise:

	A	B	Portfolio
Expected return	10%	8.75%	9.38%
Standard deviation	10.65%	7.53%	1.95%

Therefore, the overall risk/return situation can be improved by taking a portfolio approach. In this case, the very high negative correlation between the securities' returns gives a great benefit in reducing the standard deviation to 1.95%, which is significantly below the standard deviations of A and B individually. However, the dramatic improvement seen here is an exceptional case; one usually sees marginal changes.

WORKED EXAMPLE 6.7 *continued*

If, however, the returns of A and B were positively correlated, the portfolio standard deviation would be rather different.

If they were positively correlated, the returns from A and B would be as follows, with both increasing in boom and decreasing in recession.

Economic conditions	**Probability**	**Return %**	
		A	B
Boom	0.25	24	18
Normal	0.50	11	10
Recession	0.25	–6	–3

The expected return and standard deviation of each share would be unchanged. The expected return of the portfolio would also be unchanged as it is simply an average of A's returns plus B's returns. The standard deviation of the portfolio would be calculated as follows:

50% of A and 50% of B: standard deviation

0.5A + 0.5B	**ER 0.5A + 0.5B**	**d (= return – ER)**	**d^2**	**Prob (p)**	**pd^2**
12 + 9 = 21	9.375	11.625	135.14	0.25	33.79
5.5 + 5 = 10.5	9.375	1.125	1.26	0.50	0.63
–3 + –1.5 = –4.5	9.375	–13.875	192.52	0.25	48.13
Variance					82.55
Standard deviation					9.09

To summarise

	A	**B**	**Portfolio**
Expected return	10%	8.75%	9.38%
Standard deviation	10.65%	7.35%	9.09%

As can be seen, the portfolio, in this case, does not reduce risk as the standard deviation of the portfolio is 9.09%. This result is due to the positive correlation between the returns of A and B.

WORKED EXAMPLE 6.8

The following data relate to security X and security Y. You are required to advise a potential investor on their acquisition.

Economic conditions	**Probability**	**Return %**	
		X	Y
Boom	0.30	21	–3
Normal	0.40	12	10
Recession	0.30	–4	25

6.8 *continued*

Required

(a) Calculate the expected return and standard deviation of both securities and of a portfolio made up of 50% of security X and 50% of security Y.

(b) Prepare a briefing note to the investor, explaining your results and including a recommendation on the acquisition of the two securities.

Solution

(a) Expected returns (ER) and standard deviations (SD)

Security X:

Probability (p)	Return (x)	px	d	d²	pd²
0.30	21	6.3	11.1	123.21	36.96
0.40	12	4.8	2.1	4.41	1.76
0.30	–4	–1.2	–13.9	193.21	57.96
	ER	9.9		Variance	99.68
				SD	9.98

Security Y:

Probability (p)	Return (x)	px	d	d²	pd²
0.30	–3	–0.9	–13.0	169.00	50.70
0.40	10	4.0	–0.6	0.36	0.14
0.30	25	7.5	14.4	207.36	62.21
	ER	10.6		Variance	113.05
				SD	10.63

Expected return of portfolio is 0.5(9.9) + 0.5(10.6) = 10.25%

Return 0.5(X + Y)	ER	d	d²	pd²
(10.5 – 1.5) = 9	10.25	–1.25	1.56	0.47
(6 + 5) = 11	10.25	0.75	0.56	0.22
(–2 + 12.5) = 10.5	10.25	0.25	0.06	0.02
			Variance	0.71
			SD	0.84

(b) Briefing note

Summary of calculations

	X	Y	Portfolio
Expected return	9.90%	10.60%	10.25%
Standard deviation	9.98%	10.63%	0.84%

The table shows the expected return from each security. The returns are very similar. The standard deviation indicates the riskiness or volatility of the returns of each security. Security Y is slightly more risky than security X.

WORKED EXAMPLE 6.8 *continued*

The portfolio column indicates the returns and risk of a portfolio made up of 50% of security X and 50% of security Y. The return from the portfolio is simply an average of the returns from the two securities. However, the risk of the portfolio shows a significant reduction compared with the risk of each individual security, with volatility of 0.84% compared with volatility of 9.98% and 10.63% for the two securities if held independently, as measured by the standard deviation.

The portfolio's risk reduction occurs because the two securities, X and Y, are negatively correlated; the returns move in opposite ways. When X's returns are high, Y's returns are low and vice versa.

The portfolio is recommended as it offers similar returns but significantly reduced risk.

9.2 The application of portfolio theory

Portfolio theory is concerned with selecting and optimising a set of investments by considering the returns on those investments and the variability of such returns. A portfolio is usually a collection of shares, but it could also comprise other investment opportunities.

Relevance to practical financial planning

Portfolio theory demonstrates that risk can be diversified away with a carefully selected type and number of securities. If an investor such as a company is obliged to diversify (say, by legislation or similar restrictions), portfolio theory can show that risk will actually increase. Such investment in larger-than-optimum numbers of securities is called 'naïve diversification'.

The use of mathematically based portfolio models is not widespread, despite the availability of software programs to perform the calculations. Probably the most common reason for this is that managers are sceptical about analysts' forecasting abilities and prefer to rely on their own judgement.

However, several comparative studies have shown that there is no legal way to consistently outperform the market. Indeed, some randomly selected portfolios have performed better than optimum selected portfolios, at least for a short time. This has encouraged some fund managers to believe that they can outperform the optimum portfolios by a number of short-term wins.

We saw above that portfolio theory can be applied to investments other than stocks and shares, including its use by companies choosing a selection of projects and business ventures to invest in. Companies will be able to reduce risk and stabilise profits by investing in businesses with a negative or weak positive correlation between them; for example, a company that produces central heating systems would reduce its risk by a greater amount by diversifying into paints than by diversifying into winter coats.

The advantages of diversification are:

- a reduced risk of corporate failure, due to lower total company risk (and thus lower potential costs of redundancy)
- more stable internal cash flows, which should help increase debt capacity, thus reducing the cost of capital and, in turn, increasing shareholder wealth
- a reduction in systematic risk, if companies invest in foreign markets generally protected by barriers to trade, thus increasing the risk/return combinations available to investors.

A company may, however, over-diversify and thus experience the following problems:

- Conglomerates often have indifferent returns, leaving them vulnerable to takeover. The stock market often values the price–earnings (P/E) ratios of individual companies within the group higher than that of the conglomerate, thus providing an incentive for the buyer of the group to 'unbundle' and sell off parts of the group.
- There will be difficulties in becoming familiar with all the parts of the group and this lack of knowledge could lead to missed opportunities.
- Companies may lack the skills and expertise to manage all the elements of the group, and indeed may lack the skills to manage a diversified group.
- Empirical evidence has found that investors can diversify more efficiently than companies.

Companies considering diversification should assess the above points (tailored to their particular industry). However, in general, some diversification does help to protect against short-term profit fluctuations, but too much can create severe problems for the group.

9.3 Limitations of portfolio theory

The assumptions on which portfolio theory is based, and the way in which it is formulated, mean that there are limitations to the theory and its applicability.

Portfolio theory is:

- concerned with a single-period framework; it is not a dynamic model and therefore can only be revised as the anticipated performance of securities alters or new ones become available (in this respect, it has no predictive qualities)
- concerned with guesswork to estimate the probabilities of different outcomes, which may be a particular problem when the model is being used to assess diversification by the firm into new uncharted markets or products
- subject to investor attitudes; these may be difficult to determine and reflect on when making decisions, and investors' perceptions or propensity for risk may well change over time
- not the most convenient method for considering physical investment in fixed assets or those generating irregular cash flows; a mix of 'paper' and 'physical' investments is best handled using techniques centred on risk/reward probability theory
- based on simplifying assumptions:
  - that investors behave rationally and are risk-averse
  - the agency problem is ignored; managers may be more risk-averse than shareholders as they may be concerned about job security
  - legal and administrative constraints are also ignored
- not suited to considering taxation; taxation in particular can give rise to very complex models and so its effects are often ignored
- not able to cope with investment policies, such as selling short and other leverage devices
- based on the assumption of constant returns to scale and divisible projects, neither of which may occur in practice.

Portfolio theory also ignores various other aspects of risk, e.g. the risk of bankruptcy.

The volume and type of information required can also be a disadvantage, although this is now more widely available than used to be the case (at a cost).The quality of information, however, is still somewhat variable, and in any case, portfolios have to be updated and revised regularly. Each revision will carry administrative, transaction and switching costs.

CHAPTER SUMMARY

This chapter considers the impact of risk on project appraisal and also its impact in portfolio management.

It started by discussing non-probabilistic approaches to project appraisal, such as sensitivity analysis, scenario analysis and simulations. It then progressed to the explicit use of probabilistic information to calculate expected value and expected NPV. The strengths and limitations of this approach were examined and it was found that it failed to consider the variability of returns, which led on to a discussion of standard deviation and the coefficient of variation. The chapter then went on to discuss event tree diagrams and the risk-adjusted discount rate.

The section on portfolio effects and risk reduction demonstrated the importance of negative correlation in reducing overall portfolio risk. Whereas portfolio return is simply a weighted average of returns for elements in the portfolio, portfolio risk can be reduced where the returns from its component securities move in opposite ways in boom or slump conditions.

END OF CHAPTER QUESTIONS

6.1 A company is considering adding a new cruise liner to its existing fleet. The ship is estimated to cost £40 million and has an expected life, before major refurbishment, of 20 years. Annual running costs are estimated as follows.

Variable costs: £500 per passenger
Fixed costs: £15 million per year

The best estimate of the annual number of passengers is 32,000. However, it is accepted that numbers may be as low as 15,000 per year or as high as 40,000 per year.
Each passenger is expected to bring in revenues amounting to £1,200, but this might be as low as £800 or as high as £2,000.
The company's cost of capital is 10%. The 20-year present value annuity factor at 10% is 8.514.

Required

(a) Calculate the NPV of the project using the 'best estimate' figures.
(b) Prepare a two-way sensitivity analysis table, using annual number of passengers and revenue per passenger.
(c) Prepare a sensitivity table, using the pivot approach, focusing on:
- capital costs
- fixed costs
- annual number of passengers.

(d) Prepare a briefing note to the board of the company outlining the key results and providing a recommendation to the board.

6.2 The directors of Timetree plc are considering which one of two investments to add to their portfolio of projects. The following information is available:

Environment:	Recession	Stable	Boom
Probabilities:	0.3	0.5	0.2
Returns (%):			
Existing portfolio	17	18	23
Project B	25	20	15
Treasury bills (risk free)	5	5	5

The additional investment will comprise 10% of the new portfolio.

Required

Carry out appropriate calculations to determine which of the two investments should be added to the existing portfolio. Outline the principles which are employed in your calculations.

6.3 A company is considering investing in a new machine. The machine is expected to reduce operating costs in the company's factory. Research costing £5,000 has already been incurred in determining which machine to purchase and it has recommended the CSS5, which will have a purchase cost of £63,000 and installation costs of £3,000.

The machine is expected to produce annual net savings each year for the next ten years. The manufacturing manager and the chief engineer have estimated the following probabilities of annual savings:

Probabilities	Annual net savings
0.2	£15,000
0.5	£12,000
0.3	£10,000

The company's cost of capital is 10%.

Required

Calculate the ENPV of the project, its standard deviation and its coefficient of variation.

7 Shareholder value analysis

■ **CONTENTS**

1 Shareholder value analysis (SVA)

In this chapter a central theme is shareholder wealth creation. Some of the decision models used for capital investment appraisal, for example NPV and IRR, are based on this concept of wealth. A high NPV indicates that a project will increase future net cash flows of a company sufficiently to cover all costs, including the cost of capital, which is allowed for by discounting future cash flows.

The cash flows of the company as a whole will, therefore, be higher. This higher cash flow should result in higher dividends; the expectation of these higher dividends will increase the price of ordinary shares of the company.

When the directors of a company report to the shareholders on their performance the main reporting mechanism is the annual report and accounts. The reporting model used has traditionally been accounting profit with a focus on earnings per share and return on capital employed, with the capital employed shown in the statement of financial position used for the calculation. Consequently, when directors evaluate the performance of the company, and its various divisions, the focus may also be on accounting profit and return on capital employed. This can lead to decisions being made that will not increase shareholder wealth. This topic studies various attempts to design a reporting model that is consistent with the objective of increasing shareholder wealth.

Shareholder value analysis (SVA) is based on the concept of NPV. It provides a simplified and standardised approach to the task of estimating a company's future cash flows and finding their present values. SVA states that managers should concentrate on the **value drivers**, which are the factors that increase shareholder value. These include:

- growth in sales
- profit margins
- investment in fixed assets
- investment in working capital
- the cost of capital
- the tax rate.

SVA sets out a number of steps using these value drivers to make approximate estimates of future cash flows and to discount them to give present values. The estimates are only approximations as they are based on profit figures that are not, in fact, cash flows and because they use assumptions about growth, capital investment requirements and how far ahead results can be projected. All of these assumptions and estimates may involve large errors.

Managers using SVA aim to control the profit margins, growth rates, capital requirements and other factors corresponding to the value drivers so as to maximise shareholder value (which is an approximation to the NPV of returns to shareholders) in the long term. This approach is used for example by the Disney Corporation and Pepsi Cola Inc. Partly because of the uncertainties associated with many of the estimates, it does not have universal appeal.

1.1 Free cash flow

The concept of free cash flow is central to the idea of SVA. Free cash flow may be defined as cash flow in excess of the amount needed to fund all projects that have positive NPVs. Free cash flow represents surplus cash.

Firms should retain within the business money that can be invested in any project which will give a return in excess of the cost of capital (i.e. a positive NPV at the cost of capital). It can be argued that any cash flow surplus to this should be returned to the shareholders. It is called 'free' cash flow as it is free to be distributed to equity investors.

7.1

Why might companies not return free cash to the shareholders?

Handing back cash has the following implications for managers of a company.

- It reduces their power, because they have a smaller 'empire'.
- It reduces their flexibility to take investment opportunities quickly, as there will be no free cash within the firm.
- It reduces their flexibility to react to an economic downturn, as free cash can be used to absorb losses. Retention of free cash within the firm could increase the likelihood of a company surviving and avoiding administration or liquidation and the associated costs.

Definition of free cash flow

Free cash flow may be calculated as follows:

Free cash flow
Sales
Less operating costs
= Net operating profit
Less tax
Less incremental investment in non-current assets
Less incremental investment in working capital
= Free cash flow from operations

Investment in fixed assets and depreciation

Investment in fixed assets can be of two types:

- Investment to replace existing assets. This type of investment does not add to the stock of assets. A simplifying assumption is made in free cash flow that the annual depreciation equals this replacement investment. This saves adding back depreciation (as it is a non-cash expense) and also deducting replacement capital investment.
- Investment in additional non-current or fixed assets. This is investment in new projects and allows the company to grow. This is termed 'incremental investment in non-current assets'.

HDA plc's financial statements for 2010 and 2011 give the following figures.

Statements of profit or loss for the year ended 31 May		
	2015	**2014**
	£000s	£000s
Turnover	6,952.2	6,034.0
Less cost of sales	5,910.3	5,135.6
Gross profit	1,041.9	898.4
Less operating expenses	730.1	606.1
Operating profit	311.8	292.3
Tax	96.9	83.2
Profit after tax	214.9	209.1
Dividends	90.4	32.6
Retained profit for the financial year	124.5	176.5

	2015	**2014**
	£000s	£000s
Reserves at 1 June	1,308.4	1,131.9
Add profit after tax	214.9	209.1
Less dividends	90.4	32.6
Reserves at 31 May	1,432.9	1,308.4

Statements of financial position as at 31 May				
	2015		**2014**	
	£000s	£000s	£000s	£000s
Non-current assets		2,536.6		2,716.1
Current assets				
Inventory	307.4		301.8	
Accounts receivable	390.4		454.5	
Cash	43.4		50.4	
		741.2		806.7
Current liabilities				
Accounts payable		974.1		1,125.7
Net current liabilities		232.9		319.0
Total assets less current liabilities		2,303.7		2,397.1
Non-current liabilities		646.8		864.7
Total assets less liabilities		1,656.9		1,532.4

WORKED EXAMPLE 7.1 *continued*

Equity				
Share capital		224.0		224.0
Reserves		1,432.9		1,308.4
		1,656.9		1,532.4

Note: Investment in additional non-current assets for the year ended 31 May 2015 amounted to £119,500.

Required
Calculate the company's free cash flow for the year ended 31 May 2015.

Solution

Free cash flow for year ended 31 May 2015		
	£000s	£000s
Sales		6,952.2
Less operating costs (5,910.3 + 730.1)		–6,640.4
Net operating profit		311.8
Less tax		–96.9
		214.9
Less incremental investment in non-current assets		–119.5
		95.4
Less incremental investment in working capital		
Inventory	+5.6	
Accounts receivable	-64.1	
Accounts payable	+151.6	93.1
Free cash flow		2.3

WORKED EXAMPLE 7.2

Trick plc generated sales of £180 million during the year and has an operating profit margin of 20% of sales. The tax rate was 20% of operating profit. During the year £10.8 million was invested in net working capital and £8.6 million was invested in additional non-current assets.

Required
Calculate the free cash flow.

Solution

	£ million	**£ million**
Sales		180.0
Profit margin		36.0
Taxation		7.2
Profit after tax		28.8
Less net working capital	10.8	
Less additional non-current assets	8.6	19.4
Free cash flow		9.4

1.2 Steps in SVA

Shareholder value analysis involves carrying out the following calculations for a company or a division within the company:

1 Use the value drivers as a basis for estimating the free cash flows that are expected to arise in the planning horizon.
2 Calculate the NPVs of those free cash flows.
3 Estimate the value attributable to the period after the planning period, termed the 'residual' or 'terminal period'. This can be calculated by calculating the value of a perpetuity in the last year of the planning period. The value in the last year is usually based on a constant level of sales and operating profit arising in the future. This approach assumes that the constant cash flow will flow indefinitely.

However, it should be noted that there are alternative ways of calculating the value arising after the planning period. For example, the value can be based on a growing level of sales and operating profit, which may incorporate continuing incremental investment in non-current assets and working capital. Alternatively, the value of future cash flows may be based on the net book value of assets that is expected at the end of the planning period.

If the steps above are applied to the company as a whole, this gives 'corporate value'. Total 'shareholder value' is then corporate value less the market value of total loan capital.

The following data are available:

Branham plc	
Sales for year 0	£4,000
Annual sales growth rate	15%
Operating profit margin (% of sales)	10%
Tax rate	20%
Incremental non-current asset investment rate (% of incremental sales)	15%
Incremental working capital investment rate (% of incremental sales)	10%
The planning horizon (years 1–3)	
The required rate of return	11%
Market value of debt	£250

Required

Estimate free cash flows and calculate the shareholder value.

Solution

	Year 1	Year 2	Year 3
	£	£	£
Sales	4,600	5,290	6,084
Operating profit (10%)	460	529	608
Less taxation (20%)	92	106	122
	368	423	486
Less incremental non-current asset investments	90	104	119
	278	319	367

WORKED EXAMPLE 7.3 *continued*

Less incremental working capital investment	60	69	79
Free cash flow	218	250	288
Discount factor	0.9009	0.8116	0.7312
Present value	196.40	202.90	210.59
Present value of planning horizon	£610		

Notes:
Sales: year 1 = 4,000 × 1.15 = 4,600; year 2 = 4,600 × 1.15 = 5,290; year 3 = 5,290 × 1.15 = 6,084.
Incremental non-current investments: year 1 = 600 × 15% = 90; year 2 = 690 × 0.15 = 104; year 3 = 793 × 0.15 = 119.
Incremental working capital: year 1 = 600 × 0.1 = 60; year 2 = 690 × 0.1 = 69; year 3 = 793 × 0.1 = 79.
The present value of the terminal value is the free cash flow in year 3 discounted in perpetuity at 11% and then discounted back to year 0.The free cash flow amount is £486 assuming a constant level of sales after year 3.

present value in perpetuity = 486/0.11 = £4,418
present value at year 0 = 4,418 × 0.7312 = £3,230

Corporate value is:

= present value of free cash flows + present value of the terminal period
= 610 + 3,230 = £3,840

Shareholder value is:

= corporate value – market value of debt
= 3,840 – 250 = £3,590

WORKED EXAMPLE 7.4

Required
Apply SVA to a firm with the following value drivers, assuming that the last reported annual sales were £40 million.

Sales growth rate	10%
Operating profit margin	12%
Tax rate	20%
Incremental non-current asset investment (% of the change in sales)	10%
Incremental working capital investment (% of the change in sales)	5%
Planning horizon	4 years
Required rate of return	12%
Market value of debt	£7 million

WORKED EXAMPLE 7.4 *continued*

Solution

	Year 1	Year 2	Year 3	Year 4
	£000s	£000s	£000s	£000s
Sales	44,000	48,400	53,240	58,564
Operating profit	5,280	5,808	6,388	7,028
Tax	1,056	1,162	1,278	1,406
	4,224	4,646	5,110	5,622

	Year 1	Year 2	Year 3	Year 4
Less				
Incremental non-current asset investment	400	440	484	532
Incremental working capital investment	200	220	242	266
Free cash flow	3,624	3,986	4,384	4,824
Discount factor	0.8928	0.7972	0.7118	0.6355
Present value	3,235	3,178	3,120	3,066
Present value of planning horizon	12,599			

Present value of planning horizon		12,599
Present value of terminal value	(5,622/0.12) × 0.6355	29,773
Corporate value		42,372
Less market value of debt		7,000
Shareholder value		35,372

1.3 Strengths and weaknesses of SVA

The strengths of SVA are as follows:

- SVA can be used at a variety of different levels (e.g. for product lines, for individual projects, at divisional level or at whole-firm level).
- It is relatively easy to understand and apply. One reason why it is easy to apply is that it uses accounting values.
- It is consistent with the valuation of shares on the basis of discounted cash flow.
- It makes explicit the value drivers for managerial attention.
- The value drivers may be used to benchmark the firm against its competition.

The weaknesses of SVA are as follows:

- SVA assumes a constant change in the various cash flow elements and that they are related to the level of sales. This may not be the case. The value after the planning period is difficult to calculate with any accuracy and various approaches can be used.
- The assumption of a constant percentage increase in value drivers lacks realism.
- The accounting system might be unable to provide the required information, e.g. the value drivers.

1.4 SVA and conventional measures of shareholder wealth

SVA would determine the increase in shareholder wealth over a one-year period by subtracting the shareholder value at the start of the year from the shareholder value at the end of the year. The figure would then reflect the increase in shareholder wealth resulting from the actions of managers running the company for that period. This is clearly very different from the conventional use of earnings to measure business performance.

1.5 What's wrong with using earnings for performance evaluation?

Earnings per share may be used for evaluating the performance of a business and is used in the calculation of the price–earnings (P/E) ratio. A refinement on earnings per share is return on capital employed, which takes into account the value of capital employed in the statement of financial position. Earnings-based measures of performance do have their limitations, including the following.

- Accounting profit is subject to distortion. When profit is calculated, a judgement has to be made regarding, for example, which depreciation method to use. The choice of method will have a direct impact on the profit figure reported, and therefore on earnings per share and return on capital employed.
- The value of the capital investment is often understated. Some assets, such as goodwill, may be excluded from the statement of financial position and tangible assets may be stated below their true value.
- The cost of capital and discounting are not taken into account.
- Risk is not considered. Taking on more risky projects may enhance returns. These projects could destroy value if the additional return does not compensate for the additional risk. A focus on earnings fails to take into account risk.

The P/E ratio is based on earnings and is subject to the same limitations.

2 Value creation

The following changes can be made to a company's existing businesses in order to create additional value.

- Increase the return on existing capital.
- Raise the amount invested in those parts of the business which generate positive returns in excess of the cost of capital.
- Divest assets from parts of the business where returns are below the cost of capital.
- Extend the length of the planning horizon over which the positive returns are achieved.
- Reduce the required rate of return. This may be achieved by, for example, changing the capital structure so as to reduce the cost of capital – assuming that is possible!

3 Economic Value Added (EVA®)

Economic Value Added (EVA®) is an alternative to SVA. The term was coined by Stern Stewart and Co., which has copyright on the acronym and may be defined as the operating profit created during the year in excess of the cost of invested capital:

EVA = operating profit – (WACC × opening invested capital)

where WACC is **weighted average cost of capital**, and opening invested capital is equal to opening net assets. (WACC is the average cost of long-term finance to the company; this is discussed in Chapter 12.)

The thinking underlying EVA is that profit should be after all costs, including the cost of the finance that has been employed in providing that profit.

7.5

A firm has a weighted average cost of capital of 15%. Its operating profit is £3 million. The firm had invested capital of £12 million at the start of the financial year.

Required

Calculate the firm's EVA for the year.

Solution

EVA = £3 million – (15% × £12 million)
= £3 million – £1.8 million
= £1.2 million

3.1 Advantages and disadvantages of using EVA®

EVA has the following advantages:

- It uses accounting concepts, such as profits, that are familiar to managers. It sits far more closely with accounting figures than does SVA.
- It reduces the need to overhaul data collection and reporting procedures.
- It makes the cost of capital visible to managers.

EVA has the following disadvantages:

- It does not concern itself with present value. It is a function of this year's earnings figures and may lead to the pursuit of short-term projects by managers.
- The balance sheet does not necessarily reflect invested capital. For example, some assets such as the value of brands or intellectual capital, created by investing in training, may be excluded from the balance sheet and understate the value of invested capital required for EVA.
- As it is based on accounting earnings, the subjective nature of the earnings calculation limits its reliability.

4 Measuring value creation: total shareholder return (TSR)

Total shareholder return (TSR) is made up of the capital gain (or loss) on a share plus the dividend income:

$$\text{TSR} = \frac{(\text{selling price} + \text{all dividends received}) - \text{purchase price}}{\text{purchase price}}$$

TSR directly measures the return actually achieved by shareholders. However, there are limitations to this approach. Being a function of the market price of the share, TSR will be subject to:

- market-wide factors, which will affect all shares to a greater or lesser extent, and
- the risk characteristics of the company's particular industry sector.

For a full understanding it would be necessary to compare the TSR against an appropriate benchmark, for example the performance of other companies in the same sector, which will tend to have the same level of risk.

TSR is also dependent on the time period chosen.

5 Measuring value creation: market value added (MVA)

Market value added (MVA), which was developed by Stern Stewart and Co., is the difference between the current value of the company and the funds invested by shareholders and long-term debt holders. It is the value added to the business since it was formed, over and above the money invested by shareholders and debt providers:

MVA = market value – capital

where market value is the current market value of debt, preference shares and ordinary shares, and capital is all the cash raised from finance providers or retained from earnings to finance new investment in the business, since the company was founded.

5.1 What if the company pays a dividend?

According to Stern Stewart and Co., if a company pays a dividend, both the market value and the capital parts of the equation are reduced by the same amount, therefore the MVA is unaffected. When a company pays a dividend:

- the share price falls by the amount of the dividend payment, and
- the shareholders' funds balance on the statement of financial position, included in the capital part of MVA, will be reduced by the amount of the dividend.

This makes the assumption that the pattern of dividends has no effect on shareholder wealth, an issue we discussed when we studied dividend policy in Chapter 3.

WORKED EXAMPLE 7.6

A plc was formed 20 years ago with £12 million of equity finance. The company has retained profits of £3 million. The company has no debt or preference shares and the market value of the company is now £26 million. The company is planning to have a rights issue to raise a further £4 million, which will be invested in a project that has a positive NPV of £2 million.

Required

(a) What is the MVA before the rights issue?

(b) By how much will the market value of the firm increase after the rights issue? Consider whether the rights issue is successful.

Solution

(a) Before the rights issue:

Market value:

	equity	£26 million
Capital:	ordinary shares	£12 million
	retained profits	£3 million
	total capital	£15 million

MVA = 26 – 15 = £11 million

(b) After the rights issue:

With the rights issue, the £4 million represents the money raised that would then be used as the initial investment in the capital project. The key question the shareholders ask when there is a rights issue is what is the money going to be used for and does that use (which might be an identifiable investment project, or it might be, for example, to repay part of the company's debt) have a positive NPV? If it does have a positive NPV, as in this case of £2 million, then the market value of the company will increase by the £4 million funds raised plus the NPV of £2 million, a total of £6 million.

Hence the MVA becomes:

= 26 + 6 – (15 + 4) = £13 million.

The rights issue could therefore increase MVA by:

= 13 – 11 = £2 million

the NPV of the project financed by the rights issue.

5.2 Stock market influences

It is important to note that in Worked example 7.6, the **rights issue** will only be successful if the shareholders are informed of the use to which the funds are to be put and if that use has a positive NPV. It is not certain that the shareholders would be given sufficient information to identify the amount of value the project will add to the company. Two concepts are relevant here.

- **Market efficiency:** How efficient is the market? How quickly will the information be reflected in the price of the share and therefore in the market value of the company?
- **Competitive advantage:** Value is created by being able to generate a return in excess of the required return for the period of the planning horizon. When information is published in relation to value-creating opportunities there is a risk that it will inform competitors, whose response may reduce or even remove that value. Whether this happens depends on issues such as the presence of barriers to limit the entry of competitors into the market. For example, a drug patent is one way in which the positive performance spread can be protected.

WORKED EXAMPLE 7.7

Tricko plc began trading five years ago. It has five million £1 ordinary shares in issue which have a market value of £1.55 each. The business also has £3 million 5% debentures, which have a market value of £98. In addition the business has retained earnings of £1.5 million.

Required

Calculate the MVA.

Solution

	£ million	£ million
Market value		
Ordinary shares (5 million × £1.55)	7.75	
Debentures (£3 million × 0.98)	2.94	
		10.69
Total amount invested		
Ordinary shares	5.0	
Retained earnings	1.5	
Debentures	3.0	9.5
MVA		1.19

5.3 Weaknesses of MVA

There are several areas of weaknesses in the MVA approach.

- Estimation of the amount of capital invested. Since the 'capital' part of the formula for MVA is based on values given in the statement of financial position, if any items are omitted from 'capital' then the MVA will be overstated. Stern Stewart and Co. makes a number of rather arbitrary and complex adjustments to capital in an attempt to address this issue.
- When was the value created? This could have been a long time ago and therefore as a result of the efforts of directors who no longer work for the company.
- MVA is an absolute measure. The absolute level of MVA is perhaps less useful for judging performance than the change in MVA over a period.
- Is the rate of return high enough? Since the timing of creation of the MVA is unclear, it is difficult to identify whether the implicit return that has been achieved is sufficient to compensate for the risk.

CHAPTER SUMMARY

This chapter has examined the objective of shareholder wealth creation. It has looked at a range of different valuation concepts and approaches, including free cash flow, EVA, TSR and MVA. It has emphasised the disadvantages of conventional earnings approaches, but has also taken a critical view of the alternatives.

END OF CHAPTER QUESTIONS

7.1 Tynant plc

The company is a long-established trading concern.

Statements of profit or loss for the year ended 31 March		
	2015	2014
	£000	£000
Turnover	10,000	9,000
Less cost of sales	8,000	7,200
Gross profit	2,000	1,800
Less operating expenses	900	800
Operating profit	1,100	1,000
Tax	220	200
Profit after tax	880	800

Statements of financial position as at 31 March				
	2015		2014	
	£000	£000	£000	£000
Non-current assets		2,700		2,500
Current assets				
Inventory	600		300	
Trade receivables	600		400	
Cash	320		100	
		1,520		800
Current liabilities				
Accounts payable		1,300		1,100
Net current assets (liabilities)		220		(300)
Total assets less current liabilities		2,920		2,200
Non-current liabilities		600		700
Total assets less liabilities		2,320		1,500
Equity				
Share capital		200		200
Reserves		2,120		1,300
		2,320		1,500

Note: Investment in additional non-current assets for the year ended 31 March 2015 amounted to £200,000.

END OF CHAPTER QUESTIONS

Required

Calculate the company's free cash flow for the year ended 31 March 2015.

7.2 Dwr plc is considering entering a new market. Estimates of sales for each year of the next four-year planning horizon are as follows:

Year	£ million
1	40
2	44
3	49
4	55

After year 4, sales are expected to stabilise at the year 4 level.

The following information is available:

- Operating profit margin is expected to be 12%.
- Tax rate is 20% of operating profits.
- Additional non-current asset investment each year will be 20% of sales growth.
- Additional working capital investment each year will be 10% of sales growth.

The business has a cost of capital of 14%.

Required

(a) Using an SVA approach, calculate the effect of entering the market on shareholder value.

(b) Prepare a briefing paper on the advantages and disadvantages of SVA.

PART **FIVE**

Business combinations and share valuation

LIST OF CHAPTERS

OVERVIEW

This part examines the rationale for mergers and acquisition. It then evaluates methods of purchase consideration and goes on to investigate the relationship between mergers and shareholder wealth. It discusses resistance, regulatory and procedural issues related to mergers. It then examines different methods of valuing a takeover target, namely, stock market methods, cash- and dividend-based approaches and asset-based methods. The part ends by considering divestment and de-merger activity.

LEARNING OUTCOMES

On successful completion of Part Five, you will be able to:

- apply skills of financial analysis in valuing a takeover target
- assess the different methods of purchase consideration, and
- demonstrate a clear understanding of resistance, regulatory and procedural issues.

8 Business combinations 1

■ **CONTENTS**

1 Rationale for mergers and acquisitions

1.1 Strategies for growth

Strategy means the ways in which a company commits its resources in furtherance of its objectives. It is likely to involve decisions about products, markets, customers, competitive positioning and organisation, together with corporate finance decisions. Most companies' objectives involve growth. The three main strategies that a firm may adopt for growth are: expansion, integration and diversification.

Expansion

This is the growth or development of existing or new markets or products in response to changes in technology, customer taste or simply to exploit an opportunity in the market.

Integration

One form of expansion is integration, which may take either of the following forms.

- **Horizontal integration:** This applies where a firm adds new markets for its existing products or introduces new products to its current markets. It may be done so that the firm can benefit from economies of scale or scope.
- **Vertical integration:** This applies where a firm expands along the supply chain. This can be backwards (to integrate the supply of components or raw materials) or forwards (taking in processes which bring it one step closer to the end customer). It allows a firm to have greater control over the industry, including quality, quantity, price and share of the profits, although it will make the company more prone to falls in demand within the industry as a whole.

Diversification

This policy is also a form of expansion. Integration is sometimes referred to as 'related diversification'. 'Unrelated diversification' comprises **concentric** and **conglomerate diversification**.

- **Concentric diversification:** This is the development of products that offer **synergy** with current products. (The term 'synergy' comes from the Greek meaning 'working together'.) Its business significance is the idea that, by combining activities, it is possible to achieve more than would be possible if the activities remained separate, or to achieve what was achieved before with fewer resources or at lower cost.
- **Conglomerate diversification:** This is the development of products with no marketing, technology or product synergy with the business's current products. The firm may, however, expect to attain management synergies.

Advantages of diversification include the following:

- The firm can move quickly into a high-profit area by acquiring a firm in that market.
- The resultant larger firm may have better access to funds.
- A larger firm may have greater influence in the market and in the political environment.
- Operating in different markets may spread risk.
- Profitability may improve as a result of the diversification.
- The acquisition of new businesses may facilitate withdrawal from existing markets.
- There may be cash synergy if cash surpluses from one business can be used to provide cash for others; however, the takeover of firms in the same industry may be referred to the Competition and Markets Authority (CMA) because they increase market share and reduce competition. Conglomerate and concentric diversification are not likely to be referred to, because they do not change the competitive situation.

However, there are several problems associated with conglomerate diversification:

- Profits from one subsidiary may be used to cross-subsidise other loss-making subsidiaries; this may deprive successful businesses of resources and allow inefficiencies to persist elsewhere.
- Empirical evidence has shown that earnings per share (EPS) are diluted when companies with high price – earnings (P/E) ratios are acquired and that risk may be increased rather than reduced.
- Empirical evidence has also shown that anticipated management synergies are often not realised in practice.

2 Economic justification for growth by acquisition

Internal or organic growth is one method of growth. Another method is by acquiring or merging with another company (known as 'external growth').The purchase of a controlling interest in one company by another is known as an acquisition or takeover. A merger or amalgamation is the combination of two separate companies into one single entity. It is often difficult to determine in practice whether a takeover or merger has occurred, especially when there is a difference in size between the organisations. While many such combinations are called mergers – and the two terms are often used interchangeably – in reality there are very few true mergers. These tend to occur in industries with histories of poor growth and returns.

Note: you should take care not to confuse acquisitions and mergers with joint ventures. In a joint venture, the managers of two or more businesses decide to establish a new company under their common ownership and management for the purposes of exploiting an opportunity which neither of them has the resources to exploit individually.

There are several reasons why mergers and acquisitions may be worthwhile. One is that they offer some kind of synergy. A firm must consider the cost and value of the merger or acquisition and the relationship between the two.

Common reasons for companies to undertake acquisitions and mergers are to:

- reduce competition (in the UK, the CMA exists to prevent this)
- acquire a new product range or move into a new market
- obtain tax advantages (possibly by acquiring a loss-making company, whose past losses can be set against future profits of the combined entity)
- spread risk by diversifying into countercyclical markets or products, so as to stabilise total sales or profits
- obtain resources more quickly or cheaply than may be possible through internal growth – these could include assets that are undervalued or can be sold off ('asset stripping')
- acquire cash (if the target company is very liquid), access to finance, expert staff, management expertise, technology, access to supplies or production facilities
- achieve economies of scale in production, purchasing or marketing
- act as a defence against being acquired itself, either by purchasing the predator company or by making itself bigger and thus harder to take over, and
- use shares as consideration for a purchase rather than cash, which a policy of organic growth would require.

There are also major problems inherent in acquisitions and mergers.

- Many takeover bids are contested, with the directors of the target company doing their best to prevent the takeover.
- Shareholders of the target company may be unwilling to sell their shares or agree to the acquisition.
- Problems may arise in integrating the workforces and large-scale redundancies may be necessary.
- The difficulties involved in integrating new products, markets, customers, suppliers, management and systems can lead to management overload.
- There may be problems in unifying dividend policies affecting the shareholders of both companies.
- Anticipated economies of scale, especially in head office functions, often do not materialise or, indeed, may become diseconomies of scale.
- Logistical problems can arise when the acquired sites are geographically separate from existing sites.
- Public relations problems may be encountered, with customers and the general public boycotting the firm because they disagree with the takeover.
- Regulatory intervention (see below) may be triggered.
- The acquiring company may pay over the market value for the company it acquires and, in so doing, may stretch its financial resources and even risk administration then liquidation.

A bidder needs to consider the views of its own shareholders, as well as the shareholders of the target company, and of the market. The company must also determine how it will pay for the company – will it be with cash, share exchange, via loan stock or by some combination of these methods? Unless the transaction is purely financed by cash, the target company's shareholders will have an interest in the new merged firm.

Reasons why a company's shareholders and the market may not approve of a takeover or merger include the following:

- there may be social or moral disapproval of the target company, e.g. it may produce arms or deal with a country with an unpopular regime
- the merger may result in a fall in the EPS or net asset backing per share, and
- the merger may result in an increase in risk due to the nature of the industry or financial profile of the target company.

A company may not need shareholder approval, but a lack of shareholder and market backing can lead to a fall in the market price of the company's shares. This means that the company is failing to achieve its primary objective of maximising shareholder wealth.

Moreover, when a takeover is to be paid for by issuing new shares in the acquiring company, shareholder approval at an annual general meeting or emergency general meeting will be required.

TEST YOUR KNOWLEDGE 8.1

(a) Give six reasons why a company would undertake an acquisition or merger.
(b) List six potential problems with acquisitions and mergers.

3 Methods of purchase consideration

Acquisitions may be financed by cash, shares, debentures or a mixture of the three methods. The choice of payment will be determined by individual circumstances. When a merger takes place, a share-for-share exchange occurs.

The factors to be considered when deciding the form that the consideration for acquiring a firm will take are as follows.

- A potential capital gains tax liability may arise when shareholders dispose of their shares for cash.

- The issue of new shares by the acquiring company may lead to a change in shareholder control.
- The issue of new shares will affect the purchasers' EPS.
- It may be cheaper to fund the takeover with debt rather than with equity because interest is an allowable expense that reduces taxable profit and, in consequence, reduces the taxation charge.
- Increases in borrowing or share capital may have to be formally approved by shareholders as such increases will affect the level of gearing.
- The views of the shareholders in the target company should be considered. They may wish to maintain an investment in the firm and therefore prefer shares, and they will want to ensure that the return from their investment does not fall – a fall in dividends will need to be matched by a capital gain.

The price paid for the target company will reflect market forces and will tend to be higher when there are several interested parties in competition. The package can be negotiated in such a way as to benefit both parties. This could involve staggering the purchase over a period of time to aid the purchaser's cash flow, or offering shareholders in the target company the option of payments in loan notes instead of cash to enable them to determine the timing of any capital gains tax liability.

The cost of the acquisition or merger will be the purchase price (including the legal fees etc.), plus any amounts to be invested in the target company, less the sale proceeds of any surplus assets in the target company.

When considering the cost of the investment, the projected returns and profits must be considered along with existing figures to ensure that the merger or acquisition is in the company's best interests.

3.1 Shares

A share (or paper) purchase involves the exchange of shares in the purchaser company for shares in the target company. The shareholders of both companies are now shareholders in the purchaser company. For example, when bookmakers Ladbrokes merged with Gala Coral in 2015, the Gala Coral shareholders received 93 million Ladbroke shares representing 48.25% of the issued share capital of the combined entity.

This practice has the advantage of allowing the target company's shareholders to continue to own equity and giving them a stake in the new company. There may be some dilution of control, but this will depend on the size of the target company. There should be no dilution of earnings; if the aim is to increase shareholder wealth, as it should be, EPS should exceed the total EPS of the two individual companies.

3.2 Cash

In a cash purchase, the purchaser pays cash for the shares in the target company. For example, in October 2015, Belgium-based brewer AB InBev concluded a £68 billion merger with rival brewer SAB Miller by making a cash offer of £44 per share to SAB shareholders. The cash offer represented a premium of 50% on SAB Miller's share price. The purchaser may either have cash available or may raise it from a stock market issue of shares or loan stock. For example, in early 2015, BT Group acquired EE, Britain's largest mobile phone network operator, for £12.5 billion in cash. At that time, BT announced that it had various options for raising cash including a rights issue.

A proportion of the cash may be generated by:

- sale and leaseback of equipment or premises
- staff share purchase schemes or rights issues to existing shareholders
- disposal of surplus assets
- bank borrowing, and
- increasing working capital (e.g. by improving credit control). Long-term assets should not normally be funded using short-term finance. (However, in some instances this is not an imprudent step: supermarket companies, which have steady sales income and receive substantial credit from their suppliers, while making almost all their sales on a cash basis, may invest in new stores using the credit extended by their suppliers as capital.)

A cash purchase effectively ends the involvement of the target's shareholders, although they can still purchase shares in the merged company on the stock market. The target shareholders will be subject to capital gains tax (if they exceed the annual allowance) as they are disposing of their shares.

3.3 Vendor placing

This is a mixture of the two approaches detailed above. New shares in the acquiring company are placed with buyers by the company's stockbrokers to raise the cash to pay the target company's shareholders.

3.4 Loan capital

This would require the acquiring company to raise loans (e.g. by a debenture issue). The proceeds would then be used to pay for shares in the target company. As far as the target company is concerned, the impact is the same as paying cash. Alternatively, the shareholders of the target company could be offered loans or convertible loans. This may be an attractive proposition as they will provide a return, but with lower risk, and could convert to equity in the future.

There are three implications for the acquiring company.

- The loan interest will reduce corporation tax in the acquiring company, making this the most tax-efficient method of acquisition.
- The loan increases the amount of debt in the acquiring company's capital structure. This is known as increasing the company's gearing (see Chapter 13), making investment in the company a riskier proposition.
- Acquisition by loan capital will not lead to dilution of control or earnings in the acquiring company.

TEST YOUR KNOWLEDGE 8.2

What are the main factors that determine the form of purchase consideration used by a company?

4 Mergers and shareholder wealth

Following a merger or takeover, the anticipated advantages may not materialise. Expected sales increases or cost savings may not be achieved, and increased administration costs and duplication of effort may outweigh benefits gained elsewhere.

Thorough research and preparation will help to reduce such risks. Selection of a target company with the following characteristics will help:

- a well-defined market niche
- a balanced customer portfolio
- a position within a growth industry
- a stable and motivated workforce
- high added value
- good technical know-how
- a short production cycle
- a location near the acquirer's business
- a close match with the corporate strategic plan, and
- provision of something the firm does not already have.

Issues that need to be addressed in the months following a merger include:

- achieving cost savings
- harmonising working practices and systems
- implementing organisational change, and
- changing corporate culture if the cultures of the merging companies are different.

Some mergers have failed because senior managers have not given sufficient attention to such matters. This may be a particular problem if the purpose of a merger is to achieve market power by increasing size and reducing competition.

Two measures of increase in shareholder wealth are the EPS and the share price. We have seen that the shareholders of the company making an acquisition may be concerned about changes in their EPS. The effect of a merger on EPS depends on the relative P/E ratios of the two companies. If the acquiring company has a higher P/E ratio than the target, then EPS will rise. This is known as the 'boot strap' effect. This may be accentuated if the projected synergy and profit growth benefits are achieved. However, sometimes the effect of a merger or takeover on the EPS and the share price may be misleading, particularly where the method of financing involves a share exchange. This is known as the 'boot strap game'.

WORKED EXAMPLE 8.1

Brick plc and Tile plc have agreed to a merger to form House plc. Details of the companies are as follows:

	Brick plc	**Tile plc**
Number of ordinary shares	100,000	100,000
Market price per share	£40	£20
Current earnings	£200,000	£200,000
EPS	£2	£2
P/E ratio	20	10

The terms of the merger are that Brick plc will exchange one of its shares for every two of Tile plc. The result is as follows:

	House plc
Number of ordinary shares	150,000
Market price per share	£40
Current earnings	£400,000
EPS	£2.67
P/E ratio	15

The number of ordinary shares comprises 100,000 in Brick plc and 50,000 shares arising from the one-for-two share exchange with Tile plc. The 150,000 shares have a price of £40 each. However, under the combination, the EPS has increased to £2.67 which is a rise of one-third. This may appear to be advantageous to both sets of shareholders, but the gain may be illusory. Such an increase in EPS will only arise if there is higher earnings growth in the future due to synergy and increased efficiency. Such growth might also be expected to increase the market value of House plc. Moreover, the total market value of the combined entity is £6 million which reflects the individual market values of Brick (£4 million) and Tile (£2 million). For shareholder wealth to increase, the market value would need to increase and this, in turn, would be reflected in a higher EPS. Thus, by playing the boot strap game, too much emphasis is being placed on EPS. In reality, it is the difference in the P/E ratios of the two companies with Brick's P/E ratio being higher than Tile's and, in particular, the combined P/E ratio of 15 which may be misleading. The assumption is that the P/E ratio of 15 is appropriate after the combination has taken place. This may be questionable given that Tile's P/E ratio was lower before the merger.

List seven characteristics of a target company that are instrumental in the successful outcome of a merger.

5 Resistance devices

The City Code on Takeovers and Mergers (known as the Takeover Code) requires directors to act in the best interests of the shareholders, employees and creditors. There may be circumstances when they consider that it is in the best interests of these parties to contest the bid. The directors can contest an offer if they feel that the terms offered are too low, that there is no advantage to the merger or because employees or shareholders are opposed to the bid. If the former is the case, the acquiring company may offer a higher price. The relative price of the two companies' shares is a very important issue during a takeover or merger bid that uses shares as part of the consideration. A significant rise in the target's shares or a fall in those of the predator can jeopardise the takeover by reducing the value of the consideration offered to the shareholders of the target firm.

To defend against an unwelcome takeover bid, the directors have to plan and take action as early as possible. They should keep a careful watch on dealings in the company's shares to spot if an individual (or group of individuals) is building up a significant holding. They must constantly review the market price of their shares in relation to their earnings and asset values, to determine whether the company is undervalued by the market and therefore susceptible to a takeover. In addition, directors should assess the company's position within its industry in terms of its technological resources, size, etc., to see whether it is uncompetitive and likely to attract a takeover bid by a major player in the industry. A further tactic is to maintain contact with a range of stockbrokers, analysts and investment bankers, who are the most likely to hear about rumours of any takeover strategies at an early stage.

The majority of mergers and bids are masterminded and engineered by investment banking firms; a defending company will almost invariably have to appoint its own investment bank to act in its defence.

The appointment of an investment bank is just one of the substantial costs which may be incurred in contesting a takeover bid; others include advertising, public relations and underwriting costs. The predator company will also incur these costs. There is also the possibility of capital gains or losses on the sale and repurchase of shares in the target company.

5.1 Resistance tactics

For a takeover bid to succeed enough shareholders must be willing to sell; this will happen when they are attracted by the potential capital gain due to the high offer price or when they are unhappy with the current share price performance.

The tactics that may be adopted by the directors to contest a bid may include any or all of the following.

- Convincing the shareholders that the shares are valued too low and they should therefore not sell them, usually by circulating profit and dividend forecasts. They can also suggest that a change of management might prove risky to the company's share forecast by the issue of 'defence documents' and press releases.
- Revaluing the company's assets (using independent expert valuers) to increase the asset backing and encourage upward movement in the share price.
- Launching a strong publicity campaign, aimed at highlighting present strengths and potential, including commitments to improvements, such as efficiency.
- Using additional shares, either by issuing a block of shares to a friendly party, who will act in the directors' interests making it almost impossible for the bidder to acquire 100% control, or by issuing 'A' shares, so as to maintain shareholder control but increasing the funds required by the predator to purchase the company.

- Inviting a bid from another company (a 'white knight') which the directors believe would be friendlier than the initial offeror. This is called a 'defensive merger'.
- Arranging a management buyout.
- If the companies are of a similar size, then the target company could make a counter-bid for the predator.
- Launching an advertising campaign against the predator, its accounts and methods of operation.
- Asking to have the bid referred to the Competition and Markets Authority.
- The target company could introduce a 'poison pill', making the business unattractive to a bidder by selling some of its more attractive assets.

It is important to remember that, just as bids must follow the City Code on Takeovers and Mergers, so must the actions taken by directors defending a company against a takeover bid.

If a takeover of an unquoted company is resisted then the bid may simply fail.

However, with a quoted company, some or all of the shareholders may wish to sell and there is a greater chance that the takeover will succeed.

8.4

Why might the directors of a target company be likely to oppose a bid? What actions might they take to try to prevent it succeeding?

6 Regulatory and procedural issues

6.1 Takeover procedure and the Takeover Code

The Takeover Code specifies how companies are expected to behave during a takeover or merger. The Code is issued by the City Panel on Takeovers and Mergers (the Panel).The purpose of both the Panel and the Code is to ensure that all shareholders receive fair and equal treatment. The Code has been regularly updated.

6.2 Extent of coverage of the Code

The Code applies to offers for all listed and unlisted public companies as well as statutory and chartered companies considered by the Panel to be resident in the UK, the Channel Islands or the Isle of Man. It also applies to an offer in respect of a private company of the same residency, where at some time during the ten-year period prior to the announcement of the offer:

- its equity capital has been listed on the Stock Exchange
- dealings in its shares have been advertised in a newspaper on a regular basis, or
- it has filed a prospectus for the issue of equity share capital at Companies House.

The Code is concerned with takeovers and mergers for all companies defined above and includes partial offers and offers by a parent company wishing to acquire shares in its subsidiary. Generally, the Code excludes offers for non-voting, non-equity capital.

As explained below, the Code now has statutory backing. Those who fail to conduct themselves in accordance with its rules may, by way of sanction, have the facilities of the securities markets withdrawn.

The Code is made up of a number of general principles, which are statements of good commercial conduct, together with 38 Rules, supported by substantial notes. The Rules are not written in technical language and should be interpreted in terms of their underlying spirit and purpose rather than as a legal framework.

Note: the code refers to 'offeror' and 'offeree' but to maintain consistency with the terms previously used in this chapter, 'offeror' has been replaced with 'predator' and 'offeree' with 'target'.

6.3 General principles

The six general principles that make up the Code are detailed below.

1 All holders of the securities of a target company of the same class must be afforded equivalent treatment; moreover, if a person acquires control of a company, the other holders of securities must be protected.
2 The holders of the securities of a target company must be allowed sufficient time and information to enable them to reach a properly informed decision on the bid; where it advises the holders of securities, the board of the target company must give its view on the effects of implementation of the bid on employment, conditions of employment and the locations of the company's places of business.
3 The board of a target company must act in the interests of the company as a whole and must not deny the holders of securities the opportunity to decide on the merits of the bid.
4 False markets must not be created in the securities of the target company, the predator company or any other company concerned with the bid in such a way that the rise or fall of the prices of the securities becomes artificial and the normal functioning of the markets is distorted.
5 A predator must announce a bid only after ensuring that it can fulfil in full any cash consideration, if such is offered, and after taking all reasonable measures to secure the implementation of any other type of consideration.
6 A target company must not be hindered in the conduct of its affairs by a bid for its securities for longer than is reasonable.

From time to time, conflicts of interest may arise for the financial advisers involved. This may happen where material confidential information is available to them or where the adviser is a part of a multi-service organisation. In the first situation, conflict may be resolved by the adviser declining to act; in the second, a careful segregation of the business will be necessary to prevent conflict occurring within the Rules – this is sometimes referred to as 'building a Chinese wall'.

6.4 Rules of the Code

The Code contains 38 rules which are supported by detailed notes.

While you do not have to memorise individual rules, you should have a thorough understanding of their nature and the way they impact on the parties to a takeover. We will consider the rules of the Code under the following headings:

- the approach, announcements and independent advice
- dealings and restrictions on the acquisition of shares and rights over shares
- the mandatory offer and its terms
- conduct during an offer, and
- substantial acquisition of shares.

The approach, announcements and independent advice

An offer should be proposed to the board in the first instance. The identity of the predator or, in an approach with a view to an offer being made, the potential predator, must be disclosed at the outset. The board must be satisfied that the predator has the resources to implement the offer (Rule 1).

An announcement should be made as soon as sufficient details have been decided.

Any announcement of a firm intention to make an offer must disclose:

- the terms of the offer
- the identity of the predator and details of any existing shareholding
- the conditions to which the offer is subject, and
- details of any arrangements which may be an inducement either to deal, or not to deal, in the shares.

Promptly after the start of the offer period, the board of the predator company must send a copy of the announcement to its shareholders and to the Panel.

Any person stating that they do not intend to formulate an offer for a company will normally be bound by the terms of that statement. All statements should be as clear and unambiguous as possible (Rule 2).

Rule 3 requires that the board of the target company must obtain competent independent advice on any offer, and the substance of that advice must be communicated to the shareholders. This is especially important in cases such as management buyouts. The Panel considers that it is inappropriate for independent financial advice to be given to the predator by a person who is either in the same group as the financial adviser or who has a substantial interest in either the predator or the target.

Dealings and restrictions on the acquisition of shares and rights over shares

Rule 4.1 restricts dealing in the securities of the target company by any person other than the predator, where such a person has access to confidential, price-sensitive information, from the time when there is reason to believe an offer is imminent to the time of its determination (or lapse). Additionally, dealing will not be permitted in the securities of the predator company where the offer is price-sensitive in terms of its effect on the predator's securities.

Rule 4.2 restricts the sale of securities in the target company by the predator during the period of the offer, unless the Panel has given its approval and at least 24 hours' public notice has been given. After such consent and notice, the predator may make no further purchases.

Rule 4.3 limits the opportunity for persons to contact private or small corporate shareholders with a view to seeking irrevocable commitments to accept (or to refrain from accepting) an offer, or a contemplated offer, without the prior approval of the Panel.

When a person or group acquires interests in shares carrying 30% or more of the voting rights of a company, they must make a cash offer to all other shareholders at the highest price paid in the 12 months before the offer was announced.

When an offer is contemplated and the predator (or person acting in concert) acquires shares in the target during the three months prior to the offer, subsequent general offers must not be on less favourable terms without the consent of the Panel.

If, while the offer is open, the predator purchases shares at a higher price than the offer price, then the offer price must be increased to not less than the highest price paid for the shares so acquired (Rule 6).

Immediate announcements may be required should the terms of the offer require amendment under Rules 6, 9 or 11. Rule 7.1 requires immediate disclosure relating to the number of shares acquired and the price paid, as soon as an acquisition at a price higher than the offer price has been agreed.

Any dealings by the parties to a takeover or their associates must be disclosed to the Stock Exchange daily by noon on the business day following the transaction, and that information will then be made available to the Panel and to the press. Additionally, disclosure (excluding to the financial press) will be required where purchases or sales of relevant securities in the target or the predator companies are made by associates for the account of non-discretionary clients, who are themselves not associated.

Intermediaries may be required to disclose the name(s) of their client(s) (Rule 8).

The mandatory offer and its terms

Various rules lay down the requirements and mechanics of a formal offer, providing time limits in respect of acceptances, counter-offers, etc. The various options available to both the predator and the target are also laid down and reflect the percentage of shareholders accepting or rejecting the offer. While you do not have to remember detailed prescriptions for your examination, they do exist and must be adhered to by all parties concerned.

Conduct during an offer

The Rules lay down the requirements of the Code relating to the conduct of the parties to an offer while it is progressing, as summarised below.

- All shareholders must have equality of information.
- Advertisements must be cleared by the Panel before their publication
- Details of all documents and announcements must be lodged with the Panel.
- Generally, no action is to be taken that would mislead shareholders or the markets.
- Transfers by the target must be promptly registered.

- Special care must be exercised with all documents, and the terms of the bid must be carefully detailed in writing, including conflicting views, and so forth. Offer documents should always be available and on display.
- Specific rules govern the way in which profit forecasts are stated and assets valued.
- The offer document should normally be posted within 28 days of the announcement of a firm intention to make an offer. An offer must be open for at least 21 days after it is posted; this period of time may be extended by further notice.

Substantial acquisition of shares

The rules regulate the speed at which a person, or persons acting in concert (a concert party), may increase shareholdings between 15% and 30% of the voting rights of the company. They also invoke the accelerated disclosure of acquisitions of shares or rights over shares relating to such holdings.

6.5 Statutory backing

The first merger law in the UK was the Monopolies and Mergers Act 1965, which introduced the test to determine whether a merger was 'in the public interest'. The principle currently underlying UK merger law, as codified in the Enterprise Act 2002, is that mergers shall be judged by whether they 'substantially lessen competition'. Mergers are investigated by the Competition and Markets Authority (CMA) which was established under the Enterprise and Regulatory Reform Act 2013. This Act merged the Office of Fair Trading and the Competition Commission and the CMA began operating in April 2014. The CMA has a statutory duty to investigate any merger that could potentially give rise to a substantial decline in competition.

The EU has had a role in competition law since 1962 and, in 1990, the EC Merger Regulation set turnover thresholds to determine whether a merger had a 'Community dimension' and was therefore subject to the EC Merger Regulation. It set the test of whether a merger was acceptable in terms of market dominance. Under the current EC Merger Regulation, introduced in 2004, the test is now whether a merger 'significantly impedes effective competition'.

Long-standing legislation has a bearing on specific aspects of mergers: the insider dealing provisions of the Criminal Justice Act 1993 apply to the part of the Code that deals with prohibited dealings. The Companies Act 2006, like the Companies Act 1985, also has a bearing: section 552 prohibits a company from giving financial assistance for the purchase of its own shares, and sections 979–982 allow a company which holds 90% of the shares of another company following a bid to compulsorily purchase the remaining shares on the same terms, while allowing the remaining shareholders to insist on their shares being bought.

In recent years, the regulation of the processes involved in mergers and acquisitions has been put on a statutory, rather than a self-regulating, basis. The Panel on Takeovers and Mergers has been designated as the supervisory authority in relation to takeovers, pursuant to the 2004 European Union Directive on Takeover Bids. The statutory functions of the Panel are set out in Part 28 of the Companies Act 2006 and the Takeovers Directive (Interim Implementation) Regulations 2006 give statutory authority to the Takeover Code.

TEST YOUR KNOWLEDGE 8.5

What are the main areas covered by the City Code on Takeovers and Mergers?

CHAPTER SUMMARY

The chapter initially discussed the rationale for mergers and acquisitions. It dealt with the reasons for these and expanded on ideas of integration and diversification. It then progressed to methods of purchase consideration, including shares, loans and cash, and the relative advantages of the different types of consideration. It then dealt with the factors that are likely to lead to a successful outcome to a merger, and those which would be detrimental. It considered why directors in a target company may wish to resist a bid and the various resistance devices that are available. Finally, it discussed regulation, specifically the City Code on Takeovers and Mergers and the statutory backing to regulation.

END OF CHAPTER QUESTIONS

8.1 (a) What advantages are derived from a successful takeover bid?

(b) What steps would you take to defend your company from a hostile takeover bid?

8.2 (a) What codes, legal requirements or regulations govern the conduct of a company that makes a takeover bid?

(b) Blue plc and Yellow plc have entered into negotiations to merge and form Green plc. Details of the companies are as follows:

	Blue plc	**Yellow plc**
Ordinary share capital	£50,000 in 10p ordinary shares	£300,000 in £1 ordinary shares
Estimated maintainable future earnings	£200,000	£92,280
Agreed P/E ratio for amalgamation	15	13

Discuss possible ways in which new shares in Green plc may be allocated between the shareholders of Blue plc and Yellow plc.

9 Business combinations 2

■ CONTENTS

1 Valuation of a takeover target

Before a company makes an offer, it needs to decide how much it is willing to pay.

There are a number of ways of valuing companies. Some are aimed at estimating a market price for the shares when there is no market price because the shares are not traded. An important example of this is for initial public offerings of shares (methods that are appropriate in this situation are described in Chapter 11). In the case of an acquisition, the purchaser needs to know what the target company is worth so that it can judge whether it is likely to be able to acquire it at an acceptable price. In this situation, a target is most likely to be valued on the basis of one or more of the following:

- stock market methods
- cash flow and dividend-based methods
- asset-based methods.

2 Stock market methods

2.1 Price–earnings (P/E) ratio approach

A method that may be used to value shares in an acquisition (as well as for an initial public offering; see Worked example 11.10 in Chapter 11) is to use the following relationship:

market share price = EPS × P/E ratio

The current value of EPS (earnings per share) is known, based on the company's latest results, and future values may be estimated on the basis of earnings projections.

What P/E ratio to use is a matter of judgement, and depends on such factors as:

- the business sector and its prospects
- P/E ratios of comparable companies in the same sector
- whether the company is currently quoted
- company business and prospects
- company size
- asset backing
- reputation of the company and its management
  - security of cash flows and earnings, which are affected by:
  - business risk
  - financial risk, related to financial structure, i.e. the level of gearing, and degree of dependence on a small number of key individuals
- economic conditions

- market sentiment
- make-up of shareholdings and financial standing of main shareholders.

This approach has a number of advantages.

- It uses information that is readily available.
- Profit is one of the objectives of business and this approach incorporates profits (earnings) per share.
- The terminology involved is one with which managers are accustomed to dealing.

The disadvantages are as follows.

- EPS-based estimates have a special disadvantage in connection with acquisitions: they are estimates of how the shares are valued, or might be valued, by the market, rather than what the shares are worth to the acquirer. This may be useful information for negotiating purposes, and may help the acquirer judge how much it may need to pay, particularly if the target company's shares are not quoted, but may not tell it much about whether the acquisition is worthwhile.
- Acquiring companies often value potential acquisition targets in terms of earnings, and calculate the effect of the acquisition on their own EPS (see Worked example 9.1). An acquisition that increases the EPS of the acquirer is described as 'earnings enhancing'. The estimated earnings of the new acquisition will take account of any improvements in profitability that the new management believes it can achieve by better operational and financial management or by achieving synergies from the combined businesses. Whether the projected improvements in earnings will benefit the acquirer depends on whether it can achieve the same rates of growth in the earnings of the acquired company as it has done for itself before making the acquisition, and it is partly a matter of judgement whether or not this will happen (see the 'boot strap' effect in Chapter 8).
- There is a potential weakness in the use of EPS to evaluate targets, which we have come across in discussing capital investment appraisal: the calculation of earnings depends on the accounting principles applied and the judgements exercised in preparing financial statements, so that earnings is not an absolute figure. Future profits can be discounted to find a value for the target company. The drawbacks of using profits rather than cash flows are the same as those for EPS referred to above.
- In the case of the target company, it will be necessary to find similar listed businesses in order to undertake the valuation.

Some of these issues are highlighted in Worked example 9.1.

WORKED EXAMPLE 9.1

Company A acquires Company B to form New A. The following data are used to determine the share exchange:

	Company A	Company B
Total earnings	£270,000	£270,000
No. of shares	1,000,000	1,200,000
EPS	27p	22.5p
Share market price	£4.05	£2.25
Market value of company	£4,050,000	£2,700,000
P/E ratio	15	10
Dividend per share	20p	15p

Company A has a higher P/E ratio than Company B because it is seen by the market to be better managed and have better growth prospects.

Company A would need to issue £2,700,000/£4.05 = 666,667 new shares to exchange for the 1,200,000 shares in Company B.

After the merger, the position of the new merged company would be as follows.

New A plc

Total earnings	£540,000
No. of shares	1,666,667
EPS	32.4p
Share market price	£4.05
Market value of company	£6,750,000
P/E ratio	12.5

- On the basis of the pre-merger values of the companies and the number of shares in issue, the new share price after the issue is still £4.05 and the P/E ratio is 12.5, the average of the P/E ratios of Company A and Company B before the merger.
- This may not turn out to be the case. Generally, the market will tend to place a higher P/E ratio on the combined company than would be expected from the result of averaging.
- The P/E ratio of the combined company New A may turn out to be higher than 12.5; it may even be something close to Company A's P/E ratio of 15 before the merger. Using the figure of EPS for the combined company New A of 32.4p, a P/E ratio maintained at 15 would give a share price for New A of £4.86. This would reflect market expectations that the assets of Company B will be managed similarly to those of Company A (including the achievement of synergies and cost savings that Company A will have claimed in its offer documents).
- The shareholder profile and, possibly, the balance of voting control will change after a merger, as a result of the new shares in Company A issued as consideration to acquire the shares of Company B. The make-up of shareholdings often changes after an acquisition, especially in the case of a reverse takeover (when a smaller company acquires a larger one and may need to more than double its equity capital in order to fund the purchase).

Company A has found a similar company to Company B, in the same line of business and with similar growth prospects. However, its P/E ratio is 14. If Company A were to use this P/E ratio to value Company B, then:

- the valuation of Company B would be 14 × £270,000 = £3,780,000
- the number of shares offered by Company A would then be £3,780,000/£4.05 = 933,334 shares.

After the merger, the position of the new merged company would be as follows.

New A plc

Total earnings	£540,000
No. of shares	1,933,334
EPS	27.9
Share market price	£4.05
Market value of company	£7,830,000
P/E ratio	14.5

As can be seen, the P/E ratio is 14.5, the average of the pre-merger P/E ratios of Company A and Company B.

9.2

Smith plc is considering acquiring Jones plc, whose current post-tax earnings are £5 million. It has 10 million ordinary shares on issue. The board of Smith plc believes that it could reduce operating costs significantly in Jones plc, which would increase earnings by £0.5 million. The increased size of the firm would mean that its current loans could be renegotiated at a lower level of interest, saving £0.25 million per annum, and the level of remuneration paid to directors would be cut by £0.15 million. The P/E ratio of Smith plc is 13 and this will be used to value Jones plc.

Required
Calculate the value of Jones plc.

Solution
First, calculate the estimated future profits:

Current earnings	£5.00 million
Operating savings	£0.50 million
Savings in interest costs	£0.25 million
Savings in directors' remuneration	£0.15 million
Estimated future profits	£5.90 million

EPS = £5.90 million/10 million = 59p
Share price = 59p × 13 = £7.67
Value of the company = £7.67 × 10 million = £76.7 million. (This is the same as: estimated future profits × P/E ratio; i.e. £5.9 million × 13 = £76.7 million.)

2.2 Dividend yield approach

This approach values a potential takeover target's shares as follows:

$$\text{share price} = \frac{\text{target dividend per share}}{\text{dividend yield}}$$

The advantages of this method are that:

- it uses cash rather than earnings; cash is less influenced by accounting policies than are earnings.
- it makes use of a stock market ratio (i.e. it relates valuation to the market), and
- as we have indicated in Chapter 3, dividends are of great importance to shareholders.

The disadvantages are that:

- dividends are only a part of the shareholder return (i.e. post-tax profits). The amounts of dividends depend on dividend policy, and
- like the P/E ratio, we must find similar listed businesses in order to provide the dividend yield for the valuation of unlisted companies.

WORKED EXAMPLE 9.3

There is another company, Company C, that Company A wishes to acquire. It has demonstrated high growth and high levels of profitability. It is an unquoted company and the following information is available with respect to it:

Total earnings	£500,000
Total dividends	£300,000
Total ordinary shares	1,000,000
Dividend per share	30p

Company A has found a listed company in the same line of business as Company C and which has a similar growth rate and dividend payout rate. The comparator company's dividend yield is 8%.

We can now derive an approximate market value for Company C's shares and the market value of the company and determine how many of Company A's shares have to be issued to purchase the company:

Market value of each share =	30p/0.08 = £3.75
Market value of Company C =	£3.75 × 1,000,000 = £3,750,000
The number of Company A's shares required =	£3,750,000/£4.05 = 925,926 shares

After the merger, the position of the new merged company would be as follows.

New A plc

Total earnings	£770,000
No. of shares	1,925,926
EPS	40p
Share market price	£4.05
Market value of company	£7,800,000
P/E ratio	10.1

However, it would be expected that a P/E ratio close to 15 would be obtained for the combined company and if this were achieved, the position of the new merged company would be as follows.

New A plc

Total earnings	£770,000
No. of shares	1,925,926
EPS	40p
Share market price	£6
Market value of company	£11,555,556
P/E ratio	15

TEST YOUR KNOWLEDGE 9.1

What are the advantages and disadvantages of the dividend yield approach to company valuation?

3 Cash flow and dividend-based methods

3.1 Free cash flows and SVA

Because of the problems associated with the use of accounting profits, potential target companies may often be valued on the basis of free cash flows. Free cash flows represent the surplus cash generated by a company after payment of interest, dividends and tax, and also after allowing for capital investment needed to maintain the fixed assets and to increase investment (fixed or current) to support the growth of the business. Estimates of future free cash flows will be based on estimates of the rate of growth of the target's business and the scope for efficiency improvements.

The acquiring company views the target as simply a machine for generating cash, and the value of the target is the present value of the projected future cash flows. The present values of projected future cash flows are calculated using the target company's weighted average cost of capital, on the grounds that this represents the cost of capital incorporating a level of risk appropriate for the target company's business. (See Chapter 4 for discounted cash flow calculations, and Chapter 12 for weighted average cost of capital.)

The accuracy of an estimated value of a target company produced in this way will depend on the accuracy of the cash flow projections and the value of the discount rate used. The valuation may depend heavily on the level of cash flows some years ahead, and because the uncertainty in projecting cash flows is likely to increase with the time ahead, cash flows after some cut-off point may be given a defined value. If the new owners have a different capital structure from the present one, the discount rate may need to be adjusted. This is covered in Chapter 7.

Shareholder value analysis

We have seen in Chapter 7 how shareholder value analysis (SVA) can be used to value a company, and may be used in connection with a company's objective of maximising the present value of the company. When SVA is used in this way, by focusing on optimising value drivers (sales growth, profit margins, investment in fixed assets and working capital, the cost of capital and tax rates) it provides a stimulus to financial managers to take actions designed to maximise shareholder value. It also provides a way of estimating the value of the company, taking account of future prospects, quickly and simply. In principle, therefore, SVA offers a way for outsiders to value companies. It has the advantage that much of the information needed can be obtained or estimated from published financial statements. It requires judgements about what improvements the bidder might be able to make in value drivers if they were to gain control. Potential bidders are likely to feel that they can make such judgements. If they did not, they would not be likely to bid.

However, the use of SVA by a potential bidder suffers from the same weaknesses as those it suffers from when used by the management of the company: it is subject to uncertainty and error. This can occur, for example, in determining the time horizon up to which growth in cash flows can be projected, and in the vulnerability of estimates of the business value to variations or errors in the estimated values of this time horizon and the cost of capital. In addition, SVA does not produce a net present value (NPV) based on cash flow projections, since the starting point of the calculations is the profit margin, not cash flows. The method of calculation also has further inherent errors, since the separate inclusion of depreciation and fixed asset investment cash flows involves some double-counting.

WORKED EXAMPLE 9.4

Company A is considering acquiring Company D. The following information is available about Company D.

- Free cash flows are expected to be £100,000 per year for each of the first four years.
- The terminal value after year 5 has a present value of £350,000.
- The company has long-term loans amounting to £240,000.

Company A's cost of capital is 10%.

Year	10% discount factor	ANCF £000s	Present value £000s
1	0.909	100	90.90
2	0.826	100	82.60
3	0.751	100	75.10
4	0.683	100	68.30
5+	0.621	350	217.35
	NPV		534.25

The present value of free cash flow is therefore calculated as:

= £534,250 – £240,000 = £294,250

Using a SVA/free cash flow approach, the price that Company A should pay for Company D is £294,250.

TEST YOUR KNOWLEDGE 9.2

What are the principal advantages and disadvantages of using SVA as a method of valuing takeover targets?

3.2 Use of the dividend valuation model

This model is examined more fully in Chapter 12. It is based on the proposition that the value of a share equals the present value of dividends expected to be received from the share. To calculate the present value of expected future dividends we need to know the current dividend, the expected rate of growth of the dividend and the appropriate discount rate. The discount rate used should reflect the risk of the business. The market price of the shares (if they are quoted) will reflect the market's assessment of this risk.

This method has the following advantages.

- It is clear and is cash-based.
- The degree of risk in the target shares can be incorporated into the discount rate used in the valuation process.
- It could be appropriate if the purchaser of shares in the target does not aim to gain management control. It is also appropriate if the person acquiring the shares expects the generation of earnings and the dividend policy of the target company will be unchanged. This is likely to be the case if the acquirer is a portfolio investor who is not in a position to change the management or policies of the target company.
- If, for any reason, an investor believes that the risk associated with a company's shares, or the rate at which dividends can be expected to grow, is different from what the market is

assuming, then the investor's valuation of the shares will be different from the market price. This will indicate that, so far as the investor is concerned, the shares are undervalued or overvalued, suggesting that the shares should be bought or sold.

The method also has the following disadvantages.

- It is difficult to forecast future dividend payments. These can rarely be forecast with any confidence more than a year or two ahead.
- Calculating the required rate of return (i.e. the discount rate) is also problematic as this should relate to the risk implicit in the target's business and financial structure.
- Although dividends represent the annual cash returns to the shareholder, it can be argued that they understate the total returns. These are provided by the after-tax earnings per share, which will also be reflected in the share price and are part of the total shareholder wealth.

In simple terms, the valuation of the future dividend stream is given by:

$$\text{present value} = \frac{d_1}{(1+k)} + \frac{d_2}{(1+k)^2} + \frac{d_3}{(1+k)^3} + \frac{d_4}{(1+k)^4} + \cdots \frac{d_n}{(1+k)^n}$$

where:
$d_1, d_2 \ldots$ = dividend for next year, the year after and so on
n = number of years, and
k = the discount rate used in the valuation.

WORKED EXAMPLE 9.5

Xtra plc wishes to value a potential takeover target. The target's current dividends amount to 24p per share and these are expected to grow by 1p per share per year for the next five years, after which they are expected to stabilise at 30p a share. The target has issued a total of 200,000 shares. Xtra has identified an appropriate discount rate of 14% and this is to be used in the valuation process.

Year	14% discount factor	Cash flow	Present value
		Pence	Pence
1	0.877	25	21.92
2	0.769	26	19.99
3	0.675	27	18.23
4	0.592	28	16.58
5	0.519	29	15.05
6+	0.519/0.14 = 3.707 (see note)	30	111.21
	Value of one share		202.98

The target company is valued at £2.0298 × 200,000 = £405,960

Note: The year 6 discount factor has to reflect the following points:

- The 30p dividend per share is constant in perpetuity, the present value of which is 30/0.14 = 214.29p.
- This is received at the end of year 5, so it has to be discounted using the 0.519 factor = 214.29 × 0.519 = 111.21p.
- The factor of 3.707 is obtained by 0.519/0.14 = 3.707, a shortcut approach, which gives the same answer of 3.707 × 30 = 111.21p.

Alxa plc wishes to value a potential takeover target. The target's current dividends amount to 35p per share and these are expected to grow by 1p per share per year for the next four years, after which they are expected to stabilise at 40p a share. The target has issued a total of 500,000 shares. Alxa has identified an appropriate discount rate of 16% and this is to be used in the valuation process.

Required

Calculate the current market value of the takeover target.

Solution

Year	16% discount factor	Cash flow	Present value
		Pence	Pence
1	0.862	36	31.03
2	0.743	37	27.49
3	0.641	38	24.36
4	0.552	39	21.53
5+	0.552/0.16 = 3.45	40	138.00
	PV		242.41

The value of the company = £2.4241 × 500,000 shares = £1,212,050.

4 Asset-based methods

There are two asset-based methods of valuing a potential takeover target:

- historic cost approach, and
- market value approach.

4.1 Historic cost approach

This approach values a company using figures from the statement of financial position as follows:

company value = value of assets – value of liabilities

We have the following information about a target company:

- statement of financial position value of assets: £485,000
- statement of financial position value of liabilities: £120,000
- number of ordinary shares: 250,000.

From this information we can calculate:

- the value of the company:
  = £485,000 – £120,000 = £365,000
- net asset value per share:
  = £365,000/250,000 = £1.46

The advantages of this approach are as follows.

- The information is readily available from the published statement of financial position and the net asset value is easily calculated.

- The share valuation figure provides a floor price for the value of the company. This is the price that does not consider earning potential but just looks at the net asset value.
- The assets may act as collateral for additional borrowing by the merged company.

However, it does have disadvantages.

- Most companies are worth more than the assets shown in the statement of financial position, partly because intangible assets, including brands and goodwill, are not usually shown (goodwill is only shown if it results from the acquisition of a company).
- Some assets, such as land and buildings, may have been revalued, but their revalued cost might be less than their realisable value and therefore understate the value of the assets.
- The primary reason for holding net assets is to earn profits, which this method totally ignores.

It may be appropriate for a potential purchaser to value a takeover target on the basis of assets if it has identified undervalued assets which it believes it can realise at a price higher than the value of the business as a going concern. In the 1960s, asset-strippers such as Slater-Walker would acquire a company whose assets – usually land and buildings – were undervalued in the balance sheet, sell those assets, and then either run the business with minimal assets or close it down.

4.2 Market value approach

The asset-stripping experience referred to above led companies to be more careful about showing assets at realistic values in their balance sheet. As a result, share prices took account of the realisable values of assets and corporate predators were less likely to be able to gain control at prices that made asset-stripping worthwhile. In the 1980s and 1990s, corporate predators such as Hanson valued targets on the basis of asset values in a slightly different context.

They identified undervalued conglomerates – diversified businesses where the corporate management was not getting the best results from a range of often unrelated businesses. The predators acquired the shares of the conglomerate and sold the separate businesses as going concerns to other companies operating in the same industries. These purchasers possessed relevant business expertise that allowed them to get a better return from the business than the previous management of the diversified conglomerate. One of the key skills of acquisitive companies like Hanson has been their ability to value companies.

In consequence, a purchaser that wishes to value a company using a market value approach would have to ensure all assets are properly considered.

- Non-current assets have to be valued on a realisable value basis. This is preferable to the historic cost approach as it does give a current market value for the asset, but this is very much a break-up value as it does not consider the value of the business as a going concern.
- A value has to be placed on any intangible assets, such as brands, that do not appear in the balance sheet. This will help a purchaser which wants to incorporate the target company as a going concern in its own business to improve its asset valuation. Methods for valuing brands are usually based on identifying the present values of the cash flows attributable to the brands, and are essentially the same as those described above for free cash flows.

WORKED EXAMPLE 9.7

A target company has a net asset value of £875,000 and there are 150,000 ordinary shares. The target's fixed assets include land valued at £150,000, but which has a current realisable value of £230,000. Additionally the target has brands that have been valued at £125,000.
In this situation, the net asset value is given by:

= £875,000 – £150,000 + £230,000 + £125,000 = £1,080,000

The net asset value per share is therefore:

= £1,080,000/150,000 = £7.20

5 Divestment and de-merger activity

In Chapter 8 we discussed mergers and acquisitions and the reasons why companies may undertake them. Sometimes, a company chooses to become smaller rather than bigger; there are many possible reasons for this.

- A company may find that a growth strategy has been a mistake. It may wish to sell an unprofitable subsidiary, or a profitable subsidiary to finance expansion elsewhere or perhaps to reduce borrowing.
- A firm may wish to dispose of businesses that no longer fit its core business. For example, Bass, once the largest brewer in the UK, sold its breweries and changed its name to Six Continents as it refocused its strategy on its pubs and restaurants and hotels and resorts businesses.
- Some companies specialise in buying companies and either turning around loss-making operations or stripping their assets then selling them on.
- The owners of a private company might wish to reorganise their assets for inheritance tax-planning purposes.

Divestment can take the form of management buyouts, management buy-ins, spin-offs, sell-offs, de-mergers and going private.

It is not always easy to move out of a market – perhaps due to a reluctance to admit to failure. Management may feel they are safer continuing in the market and may want (mistakenly) to attempt to recover sunk costs. There may also be economic costs: it might be easier to sell a going concern; there might be large redundancy costs; or the withdrawal of a product might have a detrimental impact on the sales of the company's other products. In certain countries, legislation or government intervention may hinder or even prevent withdrawal from a market.

TEST YOUR KNOWLEDGE 9.3

Why might a company decide to withdraw from a business?

5.1 Management buyouts

A management buyout (MBO) is the acquisition by existing management of all or part of a business from the owners. The owners may be the shareholders, an owner-proprietor or the parent company, although it is generally the directors who make the divestment decision. In general, MBOs have been of profitable subsidiaries that do not match the group's strategic plans.

The advantages of MBOs are as follows.

- For the vendor, an MBO provides an alternative to the closure of the business or part of it and prevents its sale to a third party, who could be a competitor. The employees are more likely to be cooperative in an MBO than in a sale to a third party.
- The sale of the going concern may well achieve more money for the vendors.
- For the management team, the buyout allows them to purchase an operation of which they already have full operational knowledge. They must be certain, however, that they can turn the business around to obtain a better return once they are released from the constraints of the current ownership.
- An MBO will also allow the management team to be owners rather than employees; if the business is threatened with closure, it will prevent them from losing their jobs.
- For the financiers who may be invited to participate, there is a reduced risk compared with a new venture, which has no track record to be evaluated.

There are also potential problems with management buyouts.

- Technical managers, who are good at managing processes, might not have the financial or legal knowledge required to conduct an MBO. They will have to rely on expert advisers, who can be costly, for the tax and legal complications that can arise from an MBO.

- Redundancies often follow an MBO, as a way to cut costs. In addition, there might be problems convincing employees of the need to change working practices or the company could lose key employees. There might also be previous employment and pension rights to be maintained, which could be a drain on resources.
- Individual managers will be required to be financially committed to the venture. This might include borrowing from the bank, which could have negative implications for the managers' personal financial affairs.
- Problems might arise with regard to the continuity of relationships with suppliers and customers.
- It might be difficult to decide on a fair price to be paid for the business.
- Management could resent the board representation required by suppliers of finance, who might use their position to influence the way in which the business is run.
- Cash flow problems can arise, especially if fixed assets need to be replaced.

Financing MBOs

The management team's personal financial resources, which they are willing to invest, will generally be insufficient to buy the business and they will have to find financial backers. To convince the backers of the viability of their proposal, the management team should prepare a business plan. This should include cash flow, sales and profit forecasts and planned efficiency savings. This will probably be relatively straightforward – management should have access to a lot of this information, especially if the vendor agrees to the sale.

Financial backers include banks, accepting houses and venture capitalists; in general, they view their investment as long-term. There will often be several financiers providing venture capital for an MBO and they may require an equity stake in the business because of the risk they are taking – indeed, often the management has only a minority of the shares in the business. Some backers may insist that some of their capital be in the form of redeemable **convertible preference shares** with voting rights should dividends become in arrears. This form of security allows them to capitalise on the business if it is successful and to cover themselves if the business fails. The purchasing company will usually be financed by bank and subordinated debt, together with the management's and financiers' equity.

The resultant business will often have a **financial gearing** level which is far higher than that accepted in general trading circumstances. This is made possible partly by the nature of subordinated debt (also known as 'intermediate debt', or 'mezzanine finance'). Subordinated debt ranks after other debt capital and before equity for payment; it often has conversion rights or equity **warrants** attached. These allow for conversion from debt to equity at some predetermined point in the future. The rate of interest is higher than that for other debt, but lower than the cost of equity.

We noted above that the financiers' money is at risk in such an investment, and should be assessed in relation to:

- the expertise, motivation and ability of the management team (including the mix and range of management skills) and the amount they are willing to invest from their own funds
- the management team's relationships with suppliers and customers
- the projections contained in the business plan
- whether the projected return from their investment is sufficient to offset the risk they are taking
- why the business is being sold and what is being bought
- whether additional capital is required to replace or improve the assets of the business
- what the price is and whether it been set at the correct level.

These risks will be considered against projected returns before the financiers agree to back the buyout. More capital will often be needed to finance growth. Raising it might be difficult because of the high existing ratio of debt to equity. Financiers may commit to the provision of further capital at the start, but will apply stringent performance conditions before allowing a further release of funding.

An alternative form of funding for expansion is for the management to float the company, perhaps on **AIM** (the Alternative Investment Market). This, too, will require careful thought as it will involve relinquishing at least some control over the business, but it does allow financiers a means to realise their investment.

The long-term viability of a typical MBO in its initial form is a question of very careful risk assessment. It is the ability of the management to plan and develop the business which determines its success. There have been a number of great successes in the past – National Freight is an example. Empirical evidence has found a number of possible reasons for success, including reduced overheads, higher levels of managerial motivation, quicker and more flexible decision-making, more austere action on pricing and debt collection and the MBO having acquired the business for a good price.

9.1

How can a financial backer in an MBO attempt to protect his investment?

5.2 Buy-ins

A management buy-in is similar to an MBO, except that it is a team of outside managers who mount a takeover bid to run the company.

5.3 Spin-offs

A spin-off is the creation of one or more new companies, with shares being held by the shareholders of the old company in the same proportion as before. The assets of the business, having been separated, will be transferred to the new company, which will usually be under different management from the old company.

5.4 Sell-offs

A sell-off is the sale of part of the company, generally for cash, to a third party. An extreme form of sell-off is the liquidation of the entire company.

5.5 De-mergers

A de-merger is the opposite of a merger. A de-merger can be achieved either by selling part or parts of the business to a third party or by offering the shareholders shares in the de-merged parts of the business in place of their current shares in the 'merged' company. A famous example of a de-merger is the split of BT and O_2.

De-mergers have both advantages and disadvantages, mainly arising from their smaller size (e.g. if there were diseconomies of scale before the de-merger, these should be reduced). Similarly, any economies of scale will also be reduced. There may also be an increased risk of takeover or, if the attractive parts of the company have been divested, there may be a reduced takeover risk. Other advantages include an ability to concentrate on fewer areas; this should improve efficiency, overcome control problems and increase cash and earnings. Disadvantages include the reduction in the ability to raise finance, lower turnover, lower status and fewer profits.

The stock market's reaction to the de-merger will depend on why it has happened and the view on the future profitability of the demerged components, but generally they are viewed favourably. This may be because the visibility of individual parts of the business has improved and there is a greater choice of shares for investors.

5.6 Going private

A listed company may decide to go private. This occurs when a small group purchases all of a company's shares and the company is no longer quoted on the stock exchange. The reasons for such a move may be to prevent takeover bids, reduce the costs of meeting listing requirements and limit the agency problem. In addition, because the firm is not subject to volatility in its share price, it can concentrate less on the short-term needs of the stock market and more on its medium- and long-term requirements.

CHAPTER SUMMARY

This chapter has considered the following methods of share valuation:

- P/E ratio
- dividend yield
- free cash flow
- dividend valuation model
- historic cost, and
- realisable market value

and has discussed the advantages and disadvantages of each of these methods.

The chapter has also explained why companies divest, discussed the difficulties of so doing and outlined the alternative methods of divestment:

- MBOs
- buy-ins
- spin-offs
- sell-offs
- demergers, and
- going private.

END OF CHAPTER QUESTIONS

9.1 (a) What actions can a company take in order to avoid liquidation?

(b) What factors influence the success of an MBO?

9.2 The board of directors of Fortunate plc is undertaking a review of the group's operations. Concern has been expressed regarding the performance of the light manufacturing division and the board is considering its disposal.

Fortunate has received an informal offer of £6.5 million for the operation. Profits of the subsidiary have been estimated after the allocation of some central costs and a charge for depreciation. The losses incurred during the past two years are as follows.

Statement of profit or loss	**Year 1**	**Year 2**
	£000s	£000s
Turnover	13,500	12,900
Direct production costs	9,500	9,600
Allocation of central overhead	2,320	2,400
Finance charges	1,250	1,600
Depreciation	600	500
Loss before tax	(170)	(1,200)
Tax	–	–
Loss after tax	(170)	(1,200)

Statement of financial position	**Year 1**	**Year 2**
	£000s	30002
Land and buildings	2,100	2,100
Plant and machinery (net)	3,800	3,650
	5,900	5,750
Current assets		
Inventories	2,300	2,550
Trade receivables	1,700	1,900
Cash	40	20
	4,040	4,470
Less current liabilities		
Trade creditors	3,200	3,750
Trade payables	400	600
	3,600	4,350
Net current assets	440	120
Total assets	6,340	5,870
Finance from central funds	6,340	5,870

The divisional accountant estimates that 65% of the allocated central overhead has been incurred by the division, which would be saved if the division were closed. The depreciation charge is believed to be realistic and can be expected to remain at this level. For tax purposes, depreciation is the same as the accounting charge.

END OF CHAPTER QUESTIONS *continued*

All finance has been provided by the group's central treasury. This is charged at a composite rate representing Fortunate's weighted average cost of capital. It is currently 14% per year in money terms and 7% per year in real terms.

The division is believed to be riskier than Fortunate's other activities and this additional risk would justify adding 3% per year to both Fortunate's money and the real discount rate.

Turnover of the light engineering division is expected to grow by 4% per year for each of the next five years.

Direct costs are expected to increase by 8% per year and central overhead by 10% per year. The central finance charge should remain fairly constant.

At the end of the five years, the division is expected to have a net of tax disposal value equal to the value of land and buildings at the end of year 5, plus £1 million. Land and buildings have an estimated current market value of 80% of their book value and the plant and machinery a market value which is 75% of their book value. Both are expected to grow in value at a rate of 8% each year.

Were divestment of the division to occur, Fortunate would take responsibility for redundancy payments, with an immediate post-tax cost of £1.5 million. Should divestment not occur, estimated redundancy costs of £0.5 million after tax are expected in two years' time.

Assume corporation tax is charged at 30% and is payable in the year that it arises.

It is now December in year 2.

Required

(a) Evaluate whether, on financial grounds, Fortunate should accept the offer of £6.5 million for the light engineering division. Your evaluation should include a DCF analysis, stating clearly the assumptions you make.

(b) Discuss possible reasons for a company undertaking a divestment.

(c) Discuss and illustrate how the City Code might influence the behaviour of a financial manager defending a company against an unwelcome takeover bid.

9.3 ABC Ltd, which is investigating the possible acquisition of XYZ Ltd, for diversification purposes, has asked you to advise the firm on the basis of the following information:

	£000
Assets	
Non-current assets	
Land and buildings	900
Plant (net of depreciation)	600
Investments	450
	1,950
Current assets	
Inventories	600
Trade receivables	600
Cash	300
	1,500
Total assets	3,450
Equity and liabilities	
Ordinary shares	1,500
Reserves	900
	2,400
Non-current liabilities	
10% debentures	750
Current liabilities	
Trade payables	300
Total equity and liabilities	3,450

Profits for the last three years are:

2013: £350,000
2014: £300,000
2015: £450,000.

You are also told the following:

- It is estimated that the investments have a market value of £675,000, and that the inventories could be sold for £750,000. The other assets have values as stated in the statement of financial position.
- ABC Ltd will not require some of the existing investments or plant to the value of £225,000 in total.
- The investments have produced annual income of £45,000 per annum for the past five years, and are expected to continue to do so.

END OF CHAPTER QUESTIONS *continued*

- ABC Ltd would repay the debentures at par, immediately after acquisition.
- ABC Ltd requires a return on capital of 10%.

Required

Calculate the maximum price which ABC Ltd should be prepared to pay for XYZ Ltd on each of the following bases.

(a) Break-up value.

(b) Discounted cash flow, assuming that the operating cash flows to be discounted are as follows:

2016:	£450,000
2017:	£600,000
2018:	£450,000
2019 onwards:	£570,000.

PART **SIX**

Capital markets and long-term financing decisions

■ LIST OF CHAPTERS

■ OVERVIEW

This part starts by examining the role of stock markets and then considers other institutional sources of long-term finance. It then considers the main sources of long-term finance available to a limited company. It also examines the role of the Public Finance Initiative in providing funds for government projects. The costs of raising funds from different sources are examined, as are different models for calculating the cost of equity finance. This part ends by examining the capital structure decision from theoretical and practical perspectives. It analyses the benefits and risks associated with raising debt finance.

■ LEARNING OUTCOMES

On successful completion of Part Six, you will be able to:

- explain the role that the primary financial markets and institutions play in providing finance for companies
- assess the main features of long-term finance for companies
- demonstrate a clear conceptual understanding of the fundamental financial theories related to the costs of capital, and
- critically analyse and evaluate various financial models related to the capital structure decision.

10 Financial markets and institutions

■ CONTENTS

1 Why do we have stock markets?

All advanced, and many developing, countries have some form of stock market. One important function of stock markets is to provide a primary market: a mechanism that brings together organisations wishing to raise capital and investors with capital to invest. Companies need to issue shares to come into existence. A common way of achieving this is for a public limited company to issue shares on a stock market.

A company may issue shares:

- to raise funds for investment
- in a stock exchange flotation – in the UK, a minimum proportion of shares must be made available to the public unless the shares are already widely held
- to shareholders in another company in the process of a takeover bid – this is really only feasible when shares that are offered have an identifiable market value and can be easily traded on a recognised stock exchange.

In a primary market the issuer of shares or other financial instruments receives money from investors, but in most stock exchange transactions the company that has issued securities is not involved and neither receives nor pays money. A typical stock exchange transaction has the net effect of transferring shares from one shareholder (through a broker or market-maker) to another investor. The market-maker buys shares from the seller and supplies shares to the buyer. Brokers act as agents and intermediaries between sellers or buyers and market-makers, but do not own, buy or sell shares (although they may trade separately on their own account). The company whose shares are being traded is not involved until the company or its registrar records the transfer of shares and updates the shareholder register.

2 Financial markets

There are several different stock markets in the world, of differing levels of sophistication, the three major ones being London, New York and Tokyo. The London Stock Exchange is the primary focus of this book. The London Stock Exchange functions as both a primary and a secondary market. A primary market (or 'new issues market') is one in which organisations can raise 'new' funds by issuing shares or loan stock, while a secondary market deals in existing securities. The existence of a secondary market permits the primary market to operate more efficiently. In addition to acting as primary and secondary markets for corporate shares and loan stock, the London Stock Exchange also functions as the market for dealing in **gilts** (government securities).

2.1 The main market

Any company that wishes to be floated on the main market must comply with the Stock Exchange rules and regulations. You may also see flotation on the Stock Exchange referred to as 'going public' or 'getting a listing on the Stock Exchange'. The list of quoted companies constituting the main market is known as the 'Official List'. The Financial Conduct Authority (FCA) regulates admission of securities to the Official List. The Stock Exchange provides the infrastructure to allow trading in the shares of listed companies. It is regulated by the UK Listing Authority (UKLA) a division of the FCA, which is responsible for approving applications for listing and compliance with the FCA Listing Rules.

The Listing Rules for an official listing, issued by the UKLA, include the following requirements:

- applications for listing must be of at least a minimum size
- the market capitalisation must be at least £700,000; 25% of the shares should normally be held by persons unconnected with the company
- the company must have a successful audited track record of at least three years
- the company must have sufficient working capital for at least 12 months
- a sufficient number of shares of a tradeable value (i.e. the share price should not be too high) must be made available to the general investing public to allow a free market in the company's shares
- directors and senior management must be shown to be suitably experienced, and
- the company must be able to act independently of any one controlling shareholder (i.e. one holding 30% or more of voting shares).

The principal advantages and disadvantages of a full Stock Exchange listing are summarised in Table 10.1.

TABLE 10.1 Advantages and disadvantages of listing a company on the Stock Exchange

Advantages	Disadvantages
Once a listing is obtained, a company will generally find it easier to borrow funds because its credit rating will be enhanced.	Publicity may not always be advantageous. An unquoted company will be able to conceal its activities because of its lower profile in the community at large.
Additional long-term funding can be raised by a new issue of securities.	The costs of entry are high.
Shares can be traded easily, facilitating expansion of the capital base.	A measure of control will be lost when shares are made available to the general public.
Future acquisitions will generally be easier because the company will have the ability to issue securities as consideration for the transaction.	The requirements of the UKLA Listing Rules are onerous and compliance is mandatory.
Share option schemes can be put in place to attract the highest calibre employees. The profile of the business and its management team will be raised considerably.	The company may be more exposed to a hostile takeover.

2.2 AIM

AIM (the Alternative Investment Market) was launched by the Stock Exchange in June 1995 to replace the Unlisted Securities Market (USM). Like the USM, it is a market for smaller-growth companies that either do not wish to join the Official List or fail to qualify. It has less stringent entry requirements and regulations than the main market.

Fast-growing businesses, with turnover levels between £4 million and £20 million, are often keen to be listed on AIM, which is growing strongly. In particular, many computer and high-tech companies feel that an AIM listing can give them a higher profile in the City and better access to funds. However, many small and medium-sized companies still find that the costs of entry into the AIM, though lower than those for the main market, reduce its accessibility.

Companies wishing to enter the AIM must, with certain exceptions, issue a prospectus. This must comply with the Prospectus Rules issued by the FCA. The company's directors are responsible for the document, as it is not examined by the Stock Exchange.

The exemptions from the Prospectus Rules include:

- small offers to raise less than £100,000 (or equivalent) in total
- subsequent offers when a prospectus (or equivalent) has already been issued
- restricted offers to a small number of investors or to knowledgeable investors, and
- offers with a minimum subscription of £50,000 (or equivalent) per subscriber.

Companies trading on the AIM must publish details of directors' dealings and interim reports and release any price-sensitive information promptly.

Every company trading on the AIM must choose a nominated adviser from an official list; this is a permanent post which involves advising the company's directors of their obligations under the AIM rules. The nominated adviser ('nomad') warrants that the company is suitable for inclusion on the AIM. Each company must also select a nominated broker from the member firms of the Stock Exchange, who will support trading when there is no market-maker and deal with investors.

In common with all quoted companies, AIM companies are subject to the Exchange's Market Supervision and Surveillance Department and can be fined for breaches of AIM rules.

Unlike the Official List, there are no requirements governing size, profitability, track record, number of shareholders or ratio of shares in public hands for AIM companies. The only restriction on the types of security that can be traded is the requirement that they are fully transferable.

HM Revenue & Customs (HMRC) treats AIM shares as unquoted. This distinction gives investors a number of tax benefits, which helps in raising finance.

Amihud and Mendelson (1988) explain that, in some markets, certain shares experience 'thin trading' – a situation where shares are traded very infrequently. There is no hour-by-hour update of the share price; a share may be traded one day and next traded in three months' time. As well as providing little evidence of current market price, these shares may also be difficult to sell. These are known as 'less liquid' securities. Such securities provide investors with a higher return than more liquid securities to compensate for bearing the added trading costs of less liquid securities. For corporate management, the requirement to offer a higher return significantly increases the costs of raising finance.

TEST YOUR KNOWLEDGE 10.1

On which markets can a company's shares be traded? What would determine the market on which a company would choose to seek a listing?

2.3 Over-the-counter markets

It is possible to buy shares and other financial instruments in the **over-the-counter (OTC) markets**. These are neither regulated nor supervised by the Stock Market so there is less protection for the investor, although the costs of dealing on the OTC market are less than those of dealing on the main or secondary markets. Some of the largest transactions in shares and bonds are OTC transactions.

2.4 Market participants

Following the 'Big Bang' in 1986, which abolished the requirement for member firms to trade in a single capacity, firms now act as agents of the investor (previously the responsibility of the broker, who arranged transactions between investor and jobber and received a commission) while also acting as principal in their own right in buying and selling shares (previously the role of the jobber). Some firms act only as agency brokers, working solely as agents on behalf of clients in return for commission, and do not deal as principals for themselves.

Traders acting in a dual capacity are called 'market-makers'. Market-makers must be members of the Stock Exchange. They must register to deal in certain types of security and agree to quote two-way prices (for buying and selling) for the shares in which they trade.

Firms that deal as market-makers have to set up 'Chinese walls' to separate the broker and dealer functions. This is to prevent unscrupulous market-makers from making profits at the expense of the investor (and the firm) and also helps to provide some protection for market-makers and firms against allegations of this type of practice.

2.5 Some other commonly used market terms

The Stock Market (and its related activities) is full of terms peculiar to it, such as the 'Chinese walls' noted above. A few of the more common terms are mentioned below. As you read the financial press you will undoubtedly come across them.

Bull markets are those with rising prices at times of strong investment demand and **bear** markets are ones where prices fall as investors sell shares. Optimistic people are described as bullish, expecting increases in share prices, whereas bearish people are more pessimistic about market prospects.

A **stag** is someone who applies for shares in a new issue, intending to sell them straightaway. The opportunity to do this arises when new issues are priced low to ensure that all the shares are sold, with the result that trading can start at a substantially higher price.

3 Other sources of finance

The markets discussed above are not the only sources of finance. Other major sources are detailed below.

3.1 Commercial or clearing banks

Commercial banks are a major source of short-term (and recently medium-term) corporate financing. Long-term loans from banks are in the form of mortgages. The banks will expect the customer to provide a reasonable proportion of the required funding from its own resources (e.g. from equity). Clearing banks prefer to lend against security (e.g. assets). The rate of interest charged to larger companies on medium-term bank loans will be set at the London Interbank Offered Rate (LIBOR) plus a margin, which depends on the credit rating of the borrower and the riskiness of the borrowing. For smaller companies, the interest rate will be the bank's base rate plus a margin, again depending on the riskiness and credit rating of the firm applying for the loan. The rate of interest in both cases can be fixed or variable. A fixed rate of interest is adjusted every quarter, half-yearly, three-quarterly or yearly in line with changes in LIBOR.

3.2 Investment banks

These banks provide a range of investment services, generally for corporate clients, including:

- helping in issuing and underwriting of share issues and share registration
- providing venture capital and large-scale medium-term loans to companies
- taking wholesale deposits in all currencies
- dealing in foreign exchange and the bullion markets and, through subsidiaries, in stocks and shares
- providing advice during takeovers and mergers
- granting acceptance credits
- managing client investments and acting as trustees, and
- providing general investment and deposit advice to corporate clients.

3.3 Institutional investors

These are institutions with large funds to invest in assets that provide sufficient returns and security to satisfy their stakeholders. Their investments include those in company stocks and shares. The UK's main institutional investors are listed below.

Unit trusts

Unit trusts were developed to allow small investors to hold a diversified portfolio of investments (see Chapter 6). The portfolio is managed on behalf of investors by a unit trust company which deducts management expenses from the income of the portfolio before paying the investors their share of the income. Each investor holds a sub-unit or stake in the portfolio. The sub-units are tradable; their price being determined by the underlying value of the securities included within them.

Investment trusts

Investment trusts invest in a wide range of securities, though they are generally concerned with quoted and larger unquoted companies. They are interested in both returns and securities, wishing to maintain a steady growth in income to pay their shareholders' dividends.

Hedge funds

Hedge funds invest capital in potentially high-risk investments. Investment funds are usually restricted by regulators to investing in particular kinds of investment. No such restrictions apply to hedge funds, which may invest in shares, sovereign debt, bonds, currencies, commodities and other assets. They may invest in financial derivatives (whose values depend on the value of other financial assets), including options and futures. The name derives from the fact that the effects of factors such as political or economic developments or market sentiment can be mitigated by short selling (or by the use of financial instruments such as options and futures). If a fund buys some investments and sells others short (selling assets that it does not yet own with the intention of buying them later at a lower price), the overall effects of variations that affect all investments tend to be cancelled out (or 'hedged'). Short selling is inherently risky. If the price of a security rises, and the short-seller has to replace the security that it has sold, the short-seller may make a potentially unlimited loss. Hedge funds do not necessarily hedge (i.e. reduce the potential risk of changes in prices). They may use financial instruments in a way that can increase rather than decrease risk, and do so with the intention of generating profits.

Hedge funds have a range of different strategies for seeking profit, involving different methods for finding and exploiting undervalued assets and market imperfections.

The net asset value of a hedge fund may be many billions of pounds. Hedge funds often increase the size of the investments that they can make, and thereby the financial risks that they take, by borrowing heavily.

The managers of hedge funds can earn substantial rewards in the form of salaries, annual fees that may amount to approximately 4% of the total value of the fund and performance fees up to 40% or even more of the annual fund profit.

Because of the high risks that hedge funds run in the pursuit of profit and the high fees that they charge, they cannot be marketed to all investors. They are not advertised generally and are sold only to the more sophisticated investors, including professional investors, who have large sums to invest and who are willing and able to incur greater risks than other investors.

Venture capital organisations

Venture capital is capital invested in a new or expanding business, or in a management buyout, generally in exchange for an equity stake in the business and a seat on the board.

Several organisations offer venture capital. The biggest and oldest venture capital provider is the 3i Group.

Venture capital is a high-risk, high-return investment, which is generally short term, being between five and seven years' duration. Venture capitalists often aim to realise their investment and take profits when the businesses in which they have invested are floated on the AIM.

To qualify for venture capital, a company must be able to show the venture capitalist that it has the ability to succeed; that the product or service is viable and meets a need in the market; that sufficient levels of the correct form of finance are available; and that there is, or will be, a good management team in place.

Venture capital trusts (VCTs) are investment trusts that invest in the new shares of approved unquoted smaller companies. Financial companies and some property-related businesses do not qualify, nor do companies with gross assets of more than £8 million. VCTs spread risk by holding portfolios of shares in several companies. No single holding can represent more than 15%

of a VCT's investments. Individual investors receive tax relief at 30% of the amount subscribed for new VCT shares (up to £200,000 a year since the tax year 2004/2005), provided that the shares are held for five years. Investors in VCT shares pay no income tax on dividends and can also receive capital gains tax relief.

Enterprise Investment Scheme

The Enterprise Investment Scheme gives tax relief up to 30% of the amounts invested by individuals – up to a maximum investment of £1 million in each tax year – in qualifying companies with assets of less than £15 million. It also offers exemptions from capital gains tax and inheritance tax.

Private equity

Private equity is an unquoted equity investment. While this description applies to venture capital and to the equity capital of long-established unquoted companies, the most frequent and characteristic use of this name is to denote investment in large, established companies by investment funds using a small number of private investors. The investors may be individuals (e.g. those who have acquired controlling stakes in UK football clubs such as Manchester United, Manchester City and Chelsea) or entities such as pension funds (e.g. the Ontario Public Pension Fund acquired Associated British Ports).The individual investors may be the managers of a company who acquire control of their company in a management buyout. If this involves heavy borrowing to provide the finance, a management buyout may be called a 'leveraged buyout'. Private equity investors are often willing to take greater risks than the management of a public company, in particular by gearing – borrowing heavily to help finance their acquisition.

Business angels

These are private individuals who invest part of their estate in start-ups in the form of venture capital and also contribute their personal managerial expertise. Business developers must be aware that angels will own a stake in their company.

Business angels are generally experienced entrepreneurs who invest their money, skills and time in newly created businesses in exchange for a share of their capital. Typical business angel investments range between £25,000 and £250,000. Many famous companies, including Apple, Amazon.com and Body Shop, achieved their initial growth thanks to the contribution of one or more business angels.

More recently, business angel networks (BANs) have emerged at regional level to recruit angels and match them with local entrepreneurs looking for finance and advice. The number of such BANs in Europe has grown significantly since 1999. In the USA, more than 170 such networks have been identified. The total number in Europe is closer to 200.

As they mature, the range of services provided by BANs becomes increasingly sophisticated, including:

- angel syndication, so that angels with specific skills and experience can invest outside their local area
- setting up dedicated funds to invest in collaboration with angels
- providing easier exit routes for angels once the business is up and running
- establishing academies for business angels
- creating programmes for the development of entrepreneurs, and
- providing integrated financial packages from different sources.

For entrepreneurs, this funding source provides the following advantages:

- investment opportunities below the usual minimum level offered by formal venture capitalists
- speedy decision-making on investment
- investment that does not necessarily require collateral
- investment in newly created businesses without evidence of a positive track-record being a prerequisite
- investment decisions tend to be made on a more subjective basis, such as personal chemistry between angel and entrepreneur, than is the case with formal venture capitalists, and
- angels are geographically closer to entrepreneurs, who can therefore also benefit from the angel's personal advice and networks. This proximity often attracts other funding sources.

Pension funds

Pension funds hold large amounts of money which will provide retirement benefits for their members. In most pension funds there is a surplus of incoming funds from contributions over outgoings as pension payments. The surplus must be invested to achieve the best possible return, while maintaining the security of the funds. The pension fund manager often spreads the investment between gilts, equity and property. Pension funds may provide substantial finance for major investment schemes, such as commercial property development.

Insurance companies

These, along with pension funds, provide the majority of funds for investment in the UK. They have similar investment policies, seeking secure returns and steady growth to meet their commitments.

10.2

Can you identify the main sources of finance in addition to share issues?

4 Efficient market hypothesis (EMH)

The EMH originates in the work of two researchers in the 1950s: Kendall (1953), working in the UK, and Roberts (1959), working in the USA, who found that successive share price changes are independent over time and that share prices follow a 'random walk'. They held that share prices react to new information about a company as it becomes available. Since new information arises randomly, share prices move randomly, so it is not possible to predict future price movements by studying past price movements. Research into this 'random walk' led to the formulation of the EMH. The American economist Eugene Fama (1965) defined an efficient capital market as 'one where security prices reflect all available information'.

The EMH relies on stock markets being efficient and displaying perfect market characteristics. The principles underlying the hypothesis are listed below:

1 The market price of a security represents the market's consensus as to the valuation of that security.
2 Public information – about the economy, financial markets, the individual company, its results and prospects – is widely available to investors.
3 Market prices adjust readily and quickly to new situations (e.g. changes in interest rates or decisions – good or bad – taken by the company).
4 No investor is large enough alone to influence the market price of the share.
5 Transaction costs are low or zero.
6 There are negligible restrictions on investment.
7 No individual dominates the market.
8 Costs of buying and selling are at a level that does not discourage trading to any significant extent.
9 Share prices change quickly in response to new information available to buyers and sellers.

To understand the EMH fully we shall look first at three interrelated measures or types of efficiency: allocative, operational and information processing.

- **Allocative efficiency** is the optimum allocation of funds within the financial markets, i.e. that which will maximise economic prosperity.
- **Operational efficiency** is the lowest level of transaction costs possible and is present when there is open and free competition within the market.
- **Information processing efficiency** is the quick and accurate pricing of securities, preventing speculation driving prices up to unrealistic levels. In finance, a distinction is made between three potential levels of information processing efficiency according to the type of information

that is reflected in share prices. Fama (1970) identified the three forms of efficiency as the weak form, the semi-strong form and the strong form.

- *The weak form* – the information available to investors is historical, based on past share prices and company results. Share prices change as and when this information becomes available. Share prices reflect all information contained in past price movements. This implies that it is futile to try and use trading rules based on past share price movements in order to try to predict future share prices.
- *The semi-strong form* – the investor has access to all publicly available information about a company, including press releases. Share prices react not only to released information, but also to the expectation of changes in the company's fortunes. Thus, share prices reflect all relevant publicly available information (as well as past information under the weak form). Investors will be able to see beyond the creative accounting or 'window dressing' that companies use in an attempt to overstate profits. Therefore, there is no point in analysing publicly available information after it has been released because it is already reflected in the share price.
- *The strong form* – the share price reflects all available relevant information, including insider information. This implies that even insiders are unable to make abnormal returns because the share price reflects all information, both public and private. Acting on insider information is illegal, so it is very difficult to get an accurate picture of the practice and the evidence for the existence or otherwise of the strong form. However, it is widely acknowledged that most markets appear to be inefficient at this level.

There has been a large amount of empirical research on this theory in the UK and USA, including that of Fama (1991). The overwhelming evidence is that security markets are efficient in a semi-strong form (and therefore also in a weak form) in that share prices reflect all publicly available information and react to the release of information according to the random walk.

Testing the hypothesis depends on the form. With regard to the weak form, testing involves trying to establish whether or not it is possible to predict future share prices by studying past share prices and movements. As stated above, share prices will change as new information is randomly released in the market. Evidence suggests that the movement of share prices follows a random walk and, therefore, successive share price movements cannot be accurately predicted, which supports markets being weak-form efficient.

Other tests of weak-form efficiency include runs tests and filter tests. Studies of runs tests (Fama, 1965) examine the sign of price changes over time and try to identify a pattern from the length of runs of price changes with the same sign. The findings indicate that the sign of price changes over time is random and such daily changes are independent, which provides further support for weak-form efficiency. Filter tests (Alexander, 1961) study movements between an upper and lower limit (the filter) for a given share price and attempt to use the information in order to create trading rules. For example, when the share price reaches the upper limit, the rule would be to sell the share. At the lower limit, the share would be bought. Studies have found that although it is possible to make abnormal returns compared with a 'buy and hold' strategy, transaction costs have the effect of wiping out such gains. Therefore, the results of empirical studies support the weak form of market efficiency.

With regard to semi-strong-form efficiency, testing looks at the speed and direction of share price changes in response to new information. If the semi-strong form holds, then the release of new information should cause the share price to change instantaneously and in the right direction. Most empirical work has been carried out in the form of event studies and, in general, the evidence supports the semi-strong form. For example, studies show that the release of accounting information is rapidly incorporated into the share price well before the annual reports are published (Ball and Brown, 1968). A study of stock splits (see Chapter 11, section 11.9) by US firms found that share prices reacted speedily and in the right direction (Fama et al., 1969). A stock split involves splitting existing shares into smaller shares; for example, an ordinary share of £10 could be split into ten shares of £1. After the split, the total market value should not be affected. However, the study found that share prices rose after stock splits. This was because those companies involved in stock splits tended to be performing well and, as a result, the expectation of better future prospects and potentially higher dividends resulted in an increase in share prices.

Strong-form tests examine whether individuals or groups have access to information and are able to make gains. The few so-called direct tests which have been carried out on the use of such information show that insiders are able to make abnormal gains (Finnerty, 1976; Jaffe,

1974). Therefore, it can be argued that markets are not strong-form efficient. Further evidence is provided by indirect testing (e.g. whether fund or portfolio managers are able to make excess returns using their specialist knowledge of firms with which they are involved). A seminal study of several mutual funds found that although some managers were able to make abnormal gains, such returns were neutral when management fees were taken into account (Jensen, 1968).

There are times when the theory does not appear to hold. For example, in October 1987 the value of shares on the London Stock Exchange fell by one-quarter during the course of the month (losing about 10% of their value in a single day), although there was no specific new information that could be identified as the cause of the fall. In contrast, the steep fall in share prices in 2008 (when share prices in the UK, as measured by the FTSE 100, fell by about one-third over the course of the year) could be attributed to accumulating evidence of economic and financial problems, particularly associated with the global credit crisis that started with sub-prime lending failures in the USA in 2007. In the years just before and just after 2000, an apparently irrational series of events occurred with the 'dot.com' boom and subsequent crash. A largely unfounded belief that high-tech companies related to the computer industry and the internet would displace more conventional companies as the leaders of industry and commerce drove up the prices of these companies' shares. For a time, in stock market valuation terms, these companies were, in fact, dominant. Microsoft had the highest market capitalisation in the world; Bill Gates, its founder and chairman, was the richest man in the world. A market reappraisal – based partly on the insolvency of some high-flying internet companies, but also on a re-evaluation of information that had long been publicly available – drove down the prices of many 'dot.com' shares to a fraction of their peak values.

You may wonder how the 1987 crash – and the 'dot.com' boom and the crash that followed it in 2001 – can be explained. One theory is that the EMH holds best when the market is stable, but during a bull phase or a bear phase the market is driven by speculation and uncertainties. This irrationality can also be seen when there is an overreaction in the short term to company and/or economic events, an overemphasis placed on large companies and when the cause of price movements is related to the time of day, week, month or year.

4.1 The implication of the EMH

The EMH and the empirical evidence noted above indicating its validity have implications for companies, investors and analysts as detailed below.

- The current market price is the best available indicator of a share's intrinsic value. Therefore, to search for undervalued shares using publicly available information is a waste of time and share analysts should instead concentrate on efficient diversification of investment for clients.
- Individual investors should not worry about investment analysis, but should instead choose a well-diversified portfolio consistent with their risk preferences.
- NPV techniques (see Chapter 4) should be used to evaluate projects, because this is the method by which the market will evaluate the company.
- The market value of the firm will only be as good an estimate of intrinsic value as the quality of public information available concerning the company permits.
- If EMH holds, creative accounting can be seen by the market.
- The timing of new issues is deemed to be unimportant and there is no merit in substantially discounting them as they will be correctly priced by the market.
- Large premiums paid above the market price on takeover are difficult to justify.
- The EMH does not imply perfect forecasting ability, but states that the market makes a correct evaluation of uncertain future events. Nor does it imply that portfolio managers are incompetent, even though, on average, the experts do no better than the general investor, or that share prices cannot represent fair value because they are consistently moving up and down – indeed, it is the working of the EMH that is reflected in fluctuating share prices and which prevents investors and portfolio managers alike from consistently outperforming the market.

You may wonder why, if the EMH shows that fundamental analysis does not produce excess returns, so many people are employed in carrying out fundamental analysis. First, some people distrust the EMH and believe they can outperform the bull market during a bull phase. Second, some investors will be more successful than average while others will not (due to chance rather than making effective use of publicly available information) and therefore investors regard gambling on the markets as a 'fair game'. There is also evidence that unit trusts, while performing no better in bull markets, do tend to do better in falling markets.

Finally, and ironically, it is the continual search for company information by share analysts that ensures there is an efficient flow of information in the market, which is essential for the EMH to function.

5 Alternatives to the EMH

Over the past two decades there have been several financial scandals involving the use of (illegal) insider information. This has led to some experts dismissing the EMH, except in its weakest form, and deriving alternative theories of market behaviour.

5.1 Speculative bubble theory

This theory states that the price of securities moves above their true value, creating a bull market, because investors believe they will rise in future. However, eventually the bubble will burst when investors consider all previously available economic and company information and a crash will occur. Thus, rises and falls in the market do not reflect economic conditions. The South Sea Bubble of 1722 was an early example of a speculative stock market bubble where investors followed a herd instinct and drove up prices above their rational valuation. More recent examples have been the internet bubble in the late 1990s and the house price bubble of the 2000s.

There is some empirical research to support this, including evidence that investors are risk-seeking in a bear market in an attempt to minimise their losses.

5.2 Catastrophe theory

This theory developed from the speculative bubble theory and argues that capital markets have the following characteristics:

- they are dynamic
- they use feedback mechanisms with 'critical' levels – when activity reaches certain levels the equilibrium prices of the market no longer apply, and
- prices in capital markets are not based on economic forecasts, and small changes in the events affecting a company can lead to disproportionately large changes in the prices of its securities.

This last point results in large-scale chaos or instability, making predictions of prices impossible except in the short term. The chaos is made worse if a number of speculators amplify price movements by their attempts to maximise their own profit. This, it is argued, is one reason for the phenomenon of short-termism, discussed in Chapter 1.

TEST YOUR KNOWLEDGE 10.3

(a) What are the three types of market efficiency?
(b) What are the three forms of information processing efficiency?

CHAPTER SUMMARY

This chapter began by explaining the function of stock markets and then examined the main London stock market. It identified the advantages and disadvantages of a stock exchange listing. It then considered the AIM and OTC markets.

The chapter has identified a range of alternative providers of capital, including unit and investment trusts, hedge funds, venture capital and business angels. It then considered the more theoretical topic – the EMH, exploring the important issues relating to the principles underpinning the EMH, forms of efficiency and the implications of the EMH in general.

END OF CHAPTER QUESTIONS

10.1 (a) What are the choices available to a company that wishes to have its shares traded in London?

(b) Discuss the advantages and disadvantages of a full listing on the London Stock Exchange.

10.2 Explain why directors may want to 'take a company private'.

10.3 (a) Describe the characteristics of capital markets and the types of efficiency.

(b) Describe the three forms of market efficiency according to the EMH.

11

Main sources of long-term finance

■ CONTENTS

1 Ordinary share capital (or equity)

The key features of ordinary shares are as follows.

- Shares are described as permanent capital because the funds supplied for their acquisition are non-returnable to the investor who provided them in most circumstances, other than in the event of liquidation.
- The ordinary shareholders collectively own the company, but stand last in line for rewards on investment and in the event of liquidation. They do, however, have ownership of the remaining funds in either a trading period or in the event of liquidation.
- Ownership means that the ordinary shareholders bear the greatest risk. In return for their acceptance of the risk they are equity shareholders, each share carrying a vote in the management of the business, although managerial control may be limited.
- In the case of a limited company, the Articles of Association will include details of each class of shares, which comprise the capital structure of the company.

STOP AND THINK 11.1

If you were averse to taking risks, why would you avoid buying ordinary shares?

1.1 Nominal value of ordinary shares

We have already determined that the owners of the ordinary shares of a company are the shareholders. To show their ownership they have shares issued to them. Shares are issued in the UK at a nominal, authorised, par or face value, generally of £1, 50p, 25p, 10p or 5p. Be careful not to confuse nominal value with market price, to which it bears no relation. The market price is the price that shares are sold for. (If the market value and the nominal value are the same, the shares are said to be at par value.) The only exception to this rule of no relationship is when the shares are first issued and the nominal value is the minimum at which the market price would be set. Established companies issuing new shares to the market, with existing shares that have a market value in excess of the nominal value, may issue the new shares at a premium (i.e. at a value greater than their nominal value).

Not all countries have company shares with nominal value; it would be a useful exercise for you to find out if countries which you deal with at work have shares with nominal values.

1.2 Authorised share capital

The maximum amount of share capital that a company may issue (detailed in the company's Memorandum of Association) is known as the 'authorised capital'. Do not confuse this with a company's issued capital.

1.3 Issued share capital

The issued share capital is the nominal value of share capital allotted (also referred to as issued) to shareholders. The maximum amount of capital that can be issued is an amount equal to the authorised share capital. The rights and voting powers of shares and the differentials between the different classes of shares are listed in the Articles of Association.

1.4 Types of ordinary shares

The issue of different classes of ordinary (equity) shares is strongly discouraged by the stock market and is only allowed in exceptional cases. In the following section, we look at some of the different types of share capital but, unless stated otherwise, we shall generally be considering ordinary share capital.

2 Other types of share

2.1 Preference shares

Unlike ordinary shares, preference shares are entitled to a fixed percentage dividend, which is paid before any profits are distributed to ordinary shareholders. Like an ordinary share dividend it can only be paid if there are sufficient distributable profits available. Preference shareholders may be entitled to receive the nominal value of their shares in the event of a company winding up before any distribution is made to ordinary shareholders – in which case the rules underlying it will be stated in the company's Articles of Association.

Cumulative preference shares

With cumulative preference shares, however, unpaid dividends on the shares are carried forward and must be paid before any dividends can be paid to ordinary shareholders.

Participating preference shares

Participating preference shares may be entitled to some extra dividend, over and above their fixed dividend entitlement, but it may only be paid after the ordinary shareholders have received an agreed amount in dividend.

Convertible preference shares

Convertible preference shares are preference shares that can be converted into ordinary shares. A company may issue them to finance major acquisitions. Preference shares potentially offer the investor a reasonable degree of safety with the chance to make profits as a result of conversion to ordinary shares if the company prospers.

Redeemable preference shares

A limited company may, if authorised by its Articles of Association, issue shares which are to be redeemed or repaid at some date in the future. Therefore, redeemable preference shares may be issued provided the Articles permit the company to do so. The shares will be redeemable either at some future date or within a range of dates. At that time, the shareholder's investment will be returned to the shareholder.

Preference shares constitute a small proportion of companies' finance, especially in recent times – investors prefer loan stock, where the returns and security are greater. From a company's point of view, the dividend on preference shares, unlike interest on loan stock, is not allowable against corporation tax.

2.2 Deferred shares

These are the last in line for dividends and the proceeds of liquidation. In rare circumstances, a founder's ordinary share may be authorised and held by the founders of the company. Where it exists, it will rank behind all other shares for dividends.

2.3 Non-voting shares

A company may issue non-voting shares, which still carry the risk of **equity shares** but do not allow the shareholder any say in the running of the company. For this reason they are not very popular except in takeover bids (see Chapter 8).

2.4 Retained profits (part of equity)

Retained profits are part of shareholders' funds. They represent part of the shareholders' investment in the company and provide the largest source of new funding for UK companies.

2.5 Dividend payable

Dividends are paid on ordinary shares as a percentage return on their nominal value. For example, the holders of a £1 nominal ordinary share in a company which declares a dividend of 20% will receive 20p per share, regardless of the price they paid for the share. The dividend yield on a share equals the dividend divided by the market price of the share.

If the dividend is reduced, the dividend yield falls and the shares become less attractive compared with similar risk investments. Demand for the shares therefore falls and some investors will wish to sell, increasing the supply of those shares. The market price of the shares falls until the yield is in equilibrium with returns received elsewhere for similar levels of risk. This is, of course, a highly simplified explanation, but it does underpin the basic rationale behind the workings of the stock market.

Dividends are generally dependent on the results of the company. This benefits the company as ordinary shares have a fluctuating service cost, which only increases (in theory at least) during periods in which the company is successful.

2.6 Newspaper information on shares

Many of the broadsheet newspapers include a section showing security prices and related information, including:

- the highest and lowest prices during the year
- the closing price the previous day
- the change in price over the previous trading day
- dividends net of tax
- dividend cover
- gross yield, and
- the price–earnings (P/E) ratio.

You should 'read' such information on a regular basis and ensure that you understand the information contained in the different columns.

2.7 Shares categorised by volume of trading

Shares are categorised according to the company type and trading frequency.

- **Alphas:** These are the shares of the most prestigious companies, which are generally heavily traded and dealt in by a large number of market-makers. Prices are posted immediately on the Stock Exchange's Automated Quotations system (SEAQ).
- **Betas:** These are also large companies' securities, but they are not as heavily traded as alphas. They must have at least four market-makers dealing in them and prices quoted on SEAQ are those at which firm deals can be made.
- **Gammas:** These securities are traded less frequently than betas and the prices quoted for them are merely indicative.

3 Share warrants

Warrants are rights given to lenders allowing them to buy new shares in a company at a future date at a fixed, given price. This is known as the 'exercise price' and the time at which warrants can be used to obtain shares is known as the 'exercise period'. While warrants are generally issued alongside unsecured debt, they are detachable from the debt and can be traded up to the end of the exercise period.

The value of the warrant depends on the market's view of the future price of the shares that it can be used to purchase. Its theoretical value is the difference between the current share price and the exercise price multiplied by the number of shares that can be purchased with each warrant. If the share price is less than the exercise price, the theoretical value is zero, since the investor will be better off buying the shares in the market than buying warrants and using them to buy shares at the exercise price.

The market value of the warrant may be greater or less than the theoretical price, depending on whether investors believe that the share price will rise or fall between now and the date when the warrant can be exercised. During the exercise period the value of the warrant will not fall below the theoretical price, because if it does, it will offer a lower-cost way of buying shares than buying them in the market.

The price of warrants and their attached premiums depends on the length of time until the end of the exercise period, the exercise price, the current share price and the future prospects of the company. Generally, if the company has good prospects, then the warrants will be quoted at the warrant conversion premium. This is calculated by comparing the cost of purchasing a share using the warrant and the current share price. The premium will reduce the closer it is to the exercise period, because if there were a premium during the exercise period, it would be cheaper to purchase the shares directly rather than via a warrant.

WORKED EXAMPLE 11.1

Ella plc issued 50p warrants which entitle the holder to purchase one share at £1.75 at a specified time in the future. The current share price is £1.50.

Required

Calculate the conversion premium.

Solution

	£
Cost of the warrant	0.50
Exercise price	1.75
	2.25
Current share price	1.50
Premium	0.75

The premium is quoted as a percentage of the current share price – in Ella plc's case the premium is 50%.

WORKED EXAMPLE 11.2

Aldo plc issued 75p warrants which entitled the holder to purchase one share at £2.00 at a specified time in the future. The current share price is £1.80.

Required
Calculate the conversion premium.

Solution

	£
Cost of the warrant	0.75
Exercise price	2.00
	2.75
Current share price	1.80
Premium	0.95

The conversion premium is 53%.

3.1 Advantages of share warrants

For investors, there are several advantages in purchasing warrants.

- Initially, they have to spend less than they would if they were purchasing shares and, because of this lower outlay, the potential loss is much smaller (the value of the warrant compared with the value of the share).
- Conversely, because the initial outlay is less than for shares, any increase in the share price (and thus in the warrant's price) will result in a greater percentage increase in the wealth of the warrant-holder than of the shareholder. For example, a 25p increase in the value of Ella plc's shares (see Worked example 11.1) would give shareholders an increase in their wealth of 25/150 or 16.67%, but warrant-holders would have an increase in wealth of 25/50 or 50% – this is known as the 'gearing effect' of warrants.
- A final advantage for taxpayers is that profits from warrants are classed as capital gains rather than income.

Companies often issue warrants to make debt issues more attractive, and even sometimes to make them viable. In addition, they may be able to offer a lower rate of interest on the debt if warrants are attached to the issue. Warrants are a potential future source of equity which do not require dividends immediately or cause a dilution of the EPS or current shareholder control.

TEST YOUR KNOWLEDGE 11.1

When will the market price of a warrant be zero?

4 Raising equity via retentions

As we have seen, retained earnings are the most important source of investment funds for many businesses and are usually the managers' first choice. **Internally generated funds** include retained earnings and cash generated by the business other than profit. An example is provisions for depreciation: non-cash costs that are deducted in calculating the profits, but which do not involve payments by the company, with the result that the amount of cash available for investment is greater than the profits.

One reason why many businesses choose internally generated funds as a source of investment funds first is that this avoids the expenses associated with new equity issues. Other reasons for preferring to use internally generated funds to other sources of capital include the following.

- All equity-based capital growth usually has lower immediate costs than borrowing, as dividend yields are usually much less than interest on debt capital; retained profits have no immediate additional dividend costs.
- Increased profits arising from new investments raise the EPS, and present and prospective profit growth may also increase the P/E ratio. With rising share prices, shareholders may be content to see part or all of their return in the form of a rising share price rather than increased dividends. This conserves cash.
- There is only limited need for authorisation by non-management stakeholders. If managers retain the confidence of shareholders, they remain free to make many decisions on investments and funding and can rely on shareholder support for larger decisions that need to be approved by general meetings of the company.
- No change is involved in the balance of equity control. New equity issues can lead to dilution of the control exercised by existing shareholders.
- Bank borrowing, including overdrafts, brings with it third-party scrutiny; this may be salutary, but is often not welcomed by managers.
- Fixed-interest borrowing raises gearing, and with it the possibility that operating cash flows may not cover interest payments if profits come under pressure.

There are some factors that limit the use of internally generated funds.

- There might not be enough internally generated funds. Particular cases are new companies, which might need a lot of cash for investment but might not yet be making profits – or even generating any revenue! Examples of the latter include fledgling biotechnology or e-commerce companies.
- The flow of funds might not match the timing of investment requirements.
- Interest on debt attracts corporation tax relief. Dividends do not.
- It may be possible to determine an ideal mix of equity and debt in the capital structure. (This is discussed in Chapter 13.)
- Although the immediate cash cost of new equity may be low and that of retained funds nil, the total cost of equity includes capital growth as well as income (growth in the share price as well as dividends). Investments should be limited to those that give a rate of return that justifies this cost, plus a margin for risk. (This is discussed in Chapter 6.) If no suitable investments are available, shareholders are incurring an opportunity cost by having their money kept in the company and may be able to use it more profitably elsewhere. The money should be paid out to them. In recent years, several large companies (including privatised utilities and demutualised building societies) have made special dividend payments for this reason.

TEST YOUR KNOWLEDGE 11.2

Why would companies choose to provide capital from internally generated funds?

5 Borrowings: debt and other forms of loan capital

5.1 Bonds and debentures

A bond is a general term for various types of long-term loans to companies. Companies often raise long-term, interest-paying **debt**, which is known as 'loan stock'. Its holders are long-term creditors of the company. Debt capital is attractive to companies because the interest charges on it are allowable against corporation tax and the status quo of shareholder control is also maintained. In addition, we will see in Chapter 13 that an increase in the gearing ratio may be beneficial to shareholders by improving their EPS.

There are, however, limits to the amount a firm will borrow, including restrictions in the Articles of Association, debenture trust deeds (see below) and market attitudes.

In addition, interest rates can make high levels of borrowing impractical and there can be insufficient security to cover new loans. We shall discuss in detail the optimal amount of gearing a company should have in Chapter 13.

Loan stock is often issued at its nominal value or face value (i.e. at par). The nominal value represents the amount the company owes and the 'coupon rate' (or interest rate) is based on the nominal value. The coupon rate set depends on the company, its credit rating and the market conditions when the debt is issued. The market value of the stock will, however, fluctuate with changes in interest rates and in response to the company's results and prospects.

A debenture is a multiple loan to the company in the sense that it is contributed by several people as opposed to just one. Debentures attract a fixed rate of interest and debenture-holders are creditors, not members, of the company. Therefore, their interest ranks for payment above shareholders' dividends and must be paid even if the company has made a loss.

Debentures may be redeemable or permanent; holders of permanent debentures can obtain a return of their original investment by disposing of their holding to a third party. Companies may repurchase permanent debt.

Most debentures are redeemable, with typical issue periods being 10 to 30 years. The debentures often have two redemption dates, such as 2030/31, giving the company the choice of redeeming in 2030 or 2031. The company's choice of redemption date will depend on:

- whether the company has sufficient liquid funds to redeem the debentures, and
- the current levels of interest rates compared with the rate being paid on the debentures.

Debentures tend to be issued in times of low inflation and low interest rates. The redemption will be financed by cash reserves or by raising fresh debt or equity capital. A company and potential investors will compare the finance a company has available with the planned repayment of its debt shown by the repayment dates of its loan stock and debentures.

Debentures may be issued at par, at a premium or at a discount. Debentures issued at large discounts and redeemable at par or above are known as 'deep discount bonds'. They are generally issued at low rates of interest which can be attractive to companies with cash-flow problems. The true rate of interest will be shown as an expense in the income statement, and in the statement of financial position the debenture liability will grow by the amount of unpaid discount. There is a high cost of redemption. The investor may be attracted by the capital gain at maturity, but you should note that it is taxed as income (less notional interest not paid).

Security

Debentures are generally secured by a trust deed setting out the terms of the contract between the company and the debenture holders. The deed may include security given in the form of:

- a specific or fixed charge over particular asset(s) in the form of a mortgage debenture, restricting the alteration and disposal of the asset by the company, or
- a general or floating charge on assets, giving a general lien to the debenture holders, but not restricting the company in its utilisation of assets.

The trust deed may also contain provisions for a trustee (e.g. a bank) acting on the behalf of debenture-holders to intercede if the terms of the trust deed or Articles of Association in relation to the debentures were breached, such as a failing to pay the correct amount of interest or exceeding prearranged borrowing limits. A receiver may be appointed if the company is unable to honour its debts.

A well-established company may occasionally issue an unsecured or naked debenture. Naked debentures generally have interest rates at least 1% higher than secured debt to compensate investors for the additional risk they are bearing.

Registration

Mortgages and debentures must be registered in the company's own register of charges and with the Registrar of Companies to record their existence.

Purchase of own debentures

A company may enter the market and buy up its own debentures without needing to seek the approval of shareholders. It may do this if the current market price of the debentures makes this an attractive way of investing surplus funds, or if covenants require it to repay existing borrowings before making new capital issues.

Types of interest

The great majority of debentures are issued at fixed rates of interest. There are two possible variations.

- **Floating rates:** The interest rate will vary as it will be linked to current market interest rates. For the issuing company, floating rates afford protection in periods of volatile interest rates as it will benefit when rates fall. Investors benefit, as they should obtain a fair return whatever happens to interest rates generally. For example, the interest rate might be set at the London Inter Bank Offer Rate (LIBOR) plus a percentage. The market value of the debentures depends on the coupon rate of interest compared with general market rates. The value should remain stable as the interest payable on the debentures will follow that of the market.
- **Zero coupon:** These are debentures that are issued with no rate of interest attached. Instead, they are issued at a discount. Thus there is an implied rate of interest in the level of the discount. The advantage to the borrower is that there is no cash outlay until redemption. For the lender, there may be tax advantages in not receiving income in the short term.

Return for investors

To determine whether an investor will receive a certain rate of return by investing in a particular debenture, you need to calculate the present values of all the cash flows involved by discounting at the market required rate of return.

WORKED EXAMPLE 11.3

The required rate of return on the market is 15% and an investor is considering investing in 12% debentures redeemable at par in three years' time.

The investor will receive 12% of £100 (i.e. £12) in interest each year for three years and at the end of three years the debentures will be redeemed at their nominal value. The cash flows received and their present values are as follows (we assume interest is paid at the end of the year and ignore taxation).

Year	Narrative	Cash flow	Discount factor	Present value
		£	15%	£
1	Interest	12	0.870	10.44
2	Interest	12	0.756	9.07
3	Interest	12	0.658	7.90
3	Redemption	100	0.658	65.80
				93.21

The total of the present values of the cash flows received is £93.21.

This means that an investment in the debenture will give the 15% return the market requires if the market price of the debenture today is £93.21. If it is more than this, the investor will not get the required return and s/he will not be interested in buying.

TEST YOUR KNOWLEDGE 11.3

(a) What is a variable rate bond?
(b) What is a zero rate bond?

5.2 Reverse yield gap

Generally, the investor will expect to be compensated for increased risk of loss by an enhanced return, and vice versa. Consequently, ordinary shareholders expect a higher return than debenture holders, as debenture interest will be paid each year whatever the financial results, whereas payment of dividends is not guaranteed. If the company is unable to pay interest, debenture holders have a prior claim on its assets.

When the return from equities exceeds that available from fixed-interest stocks, there is said to be a yield gap. When fixed-interest returns are higher than those from equities, there is said to be a reverse yield gap. The expressions 'yield gap' and 'reverse yield gap' usually refer to differences between the interest yield on debentures and the dividend yield on shares.

For most shares, it is variation in the share price and not dividends that has the greatest effect on shareholders' wealth. The main risk for shareholders is the possibility of a fall in the share price and not a cut in the dividend, though the two are often related. The capital value of debentures can also vary, though the price of loan stock usually varies less than the share price. For most equities, the most important component of the return to investors is in the form of capital appreciation rather than dividends, though when share prices fall the capital growth component is negative, and when share prices remain depressed the dividend yield often rises. In general, with a widespread and enduring expectation – if not always a reality – of rising share prices, the yield gap is a reverse yield gap: the running return on debentures in the form of interest is higher than the dividend yield on equities.

5.3 Mortgages

A mortgage is a form of secured loan placing the title deeds of freehold or long leasehold property with a lender as security for a cash loan, usually up to two-thirds the value of the property. The cash is generally repayable over a prearranged period and interest (at either a fixed or floating rate) is payable on the amount borrowed.

TEST YOUR KNOWLEDGE 11.4

(a) If you were very averse to taking risks, why might you be more likely to buy loan stock than ordinary shares?
(b) Which kind of loan stock would you prefer?
(c) What risks would you still be taking?

5.4 Convertible loan stock

Convertible loan stock has proved to be a particularly attractive form of capital instrument during recent years. Usually this class of stock is sold as fixed interest loan stock initially, but there will be an option to convert the loan into equity shares at a given price and during a specified period. The conversion price often increases over time in line with growing expectations as to the share price and returns from the shares. The conversion value (the current market value of a unit of stock converted into shares) will be below the loan stock value on issue, but is expected to rise as conversion approaches.

From the investors' point of view, they will stand to gain a stake in the company while maintaining the status of creditors and will receive the security of fixed interest during the potentially risky period when their funds are being used. At a later date and without extra outlay, they may exercise the right to convert to equity, by which time the investment, it is hoped, will have begun successfully to contribute to the company's profits.

The company benefits by securing funds at fixed interest rates, lower than the rates payable on non-convertible stock, supplemented by tax relief on its interest payments, at a time when it might not be able to support the burden of dividend payments. As the intention is to convert into equities, funds do not have to be repaid. There should be a realistic chance that the future increased dividend payments can be met from profits generated by successful utilisation of the invested money.

There is no specific requirement for loans to be converted into shares on every occasion. There may be an option not to convert, but simply to redeem the original investment.

The following calculations are used in relation to convertible loan stock.

- **Conversion ratio:** This shows the number of ordinary shares that will be obtained from each unit of loan stock. For example, if a company has 8% convertible loan stock standing at par and £10 of loan stock can be converted into three ordinary shares, the conversion ratio is:

  $$\frac{3}{£10} = 0.3$$

  i.e. 0.3 shares will be obtained for every £1 of loan stock converted.

- **Conversion price:** This is the amount of stock necessary to obtain each ordinary share. In the example above this would be:

  $$\frac{£10}{3} = £3.33$$

  i.e. £3.33 of stock is required for each share.

- **Conversion premium:** This is the difference between the market value of the stock and the conversion value of that stock on the date of issue. Let us assume that the 8% convertible loan stock has a market value of £120 per £100 nominal and the market price of ordinary shares on the day the loan stock is issued is £3. A £100 nominal of loan stock can be converted into 0.3/100 = 30 ordinary shares, so its conversion value on the day of issue is 30 × £3 = £90. The conversion premium is:

  $$\frac{£120 - £90}{£90} = 33.33\%$$

  The premium per share is calculated as:

  $$= \frac{\text{market value of convertible loan stock}}{\text{no. of shares at conversion date}}$$

- **Current price:** In our example we have:

  (£120/30) – £3 = £4 – £3 = £1 per share.

From the point of view of the issuing company, the greater the amount of conversion premium the better, because they will have to issue fewer shares for the amount of original loan stock. For the investor, the level of conversion premium that is judged acceptable will depend on future expectations for the company.

The investor may, for instance, expect that the value of each share will rise between the date of purchase and the date of conversion. In our example, if the price has risen to £5, the value of the conversion will then be (30 × £5) = £150 for an original investment of £120.

The attractiveness of convertible loan stock will depend on a combination of factors, such as:

- the cost of the stock at the time of purchase
- the period of time to conversion, and
- stockholders' future expectations for the company.

Convertible loan stock will tend to have a lower coupon rate of interest than normal stock. The lower interest rate represents the price the investor is prepared to pay for conversion rights.

The market value of the convertible stock should always be higher than the market value of non-convertible loan stock with the same coupon rate and redemption date. If the two prices are equal, it means the market does not expect it to be worthwhile to convert the stock into ordinary shares.

The advantages of convertible loan stock to the respective parties are shown in Table 11.1.

TABLE 11.1 Advantages of convertible loan stock

Issuing company	Investors
Stock can be issued at a lower coupon rate, which is useful in times of high interest rates.	The market value of the stock cannot fall below that for similar ordinary stock of the same coupon rate.
Interest on loan stock should be tax-deductible, unlike dividends on equity.	Increases in share prices will cause the value of the conversion to rise because this is the amount the investor will eventually receive.
As it is a form of deferred equity, there will be no cash outlay on redemption.	Stockholders will be paid before shareholders in the event of liquidation.
Under International Accounting Standards, convertible loan stock has to be split into an equity element and a liability element. The liability element will increase gearing but the equity element will reduce gearing.	
If share prices are depressed, it may be easier to issue loan stock instead of equity.	

WORKED EXAMPLE 11.4

A company issues 10% convertible loan stock, which can be converted into ordinary shares in five years' time at the rate of 20 shares per £100 nominal of loan stock. The share price at the time of issue is £4.20.

Required

Calculate:

1 the conversion ratio
2 the conversion price
3 the conversion premium.

Solution

1 Conversion ratio = 20 shares/£100 = 0.2 share/£1 of loan stock
2 Conversion price = £100/20 = £5.00
3 Conversion premium = £5.00 – £4.20 = £0.80

5.5 Debt credit rating

The risk for an investor of investing in debentures and other loans is less than the risk of investing in shares, but, in principle, there is still a risk of default. This risk affects the return required by investors, and therefore both lenders and borrowers have an interest in knowing what that risk is, and in particular how it is seen by the market – which means how it is assessed by rating agencies. Since the bond market (for large issues) is global, the main bond rating agencies operate globally, although they are usually based in the countries where the value of bonds in issue is greatest. The largest bond rating agencies are based in the USA: Standard & Poor's, Moody's and Fitch. Other important rating agencies include AM Best in the USA, DBRS (Dun & Bradstreet) based in Canada, and the Japan Credit Rating Agency. Agencies assess the creditworthiness of bond issues, using elaborate scales with grades to indicate the degree of creditworthiness. Standard & Poor's, Moody's and Fitch use ten grades – reflecting different degrees of creditworthiness – for investment-grade bonds and a similar number of grades for non-investment-grade bonds. Investment-grade bonds are considered to be the safest, and are the bonds that banks are allowed to invest in. For short-term bonds, a slightly simplified set of grades is used. The ratings given by Standard & Poor's for investment-grade bonds range from AAA (the highest) to BBB;

by Moody's from Aaa to Baa3; and by Fitch from AAA to BBB–. Non-investment-grade bonds are popularly known as 'junk bonds'. Junk bonds are frequently used in high-risk transactions. Such transactions include funding for management buyouts and acquisitions by organisations that are prepared to take high risks and aim to realise their investment and take profits quickly, including private equity groups and hedge funds.

Credit rating agencies grade the issuers of bonds (companies, governments and other public bodies) as well as bonds. At the time of writing, an international financial crisis has occurred in the Euro area due to the downgrading of bonds issued by Greece and other countries. Established companies value their good standing with rating agencies, because any damage to their credit rating will potentially have a large adverse effect on their cost of capital. Rating agencies, for their part, tend to be cautious about changing ratings, and a reduction in the credit rating of a large company is a newsworthy event. The major rating agencies were slow to reduce the ratings of major US car manufacturers, well after it became clear that they were facing serious problems of efficiency, market competitiveness and profitability. The major rating agencies were criticised by the Securities and Exchange Commission, the US financial regulator, in the middle of 2008 for giving top credit ratings to lending instruments linked to sub-prime mortgage lending, which had been proved to be unsafe investments. It has been argued that the capacity of agencies to carry out risk assessments was not sufficient to cope with the number and variety of loan-based derivative instruments that had been developed in the preceding years, many of which had been so elaborate and arcane that they had not always been fully understood by the banks that issued and traded them.

There has been a further, longer-term, problem with the standing of credit rating agencies as assessors of risk: the agencies that provide assessments of the creditworthiness of companies and the bonds that they issue are often earning substantial income from the same companies by providing other forms of financial information. This creates a potential conflict of interest.

6 Leasing

The legal distinctions between leasing, hire purchase and rental are well defined, but it is often, in practice, difficult to distinguish between them. The company secretary needs to know about leases for equipment – common ones in the UK include those for office equipment and cars.

6.1 Leasing agreements

A leasing agreement is formed between two parties – a lessor and a lessee.

A financier (the lessor), generally a finance house subsidiary of a bank, purchases the asset and provides it for use by the company (the lessee). The lessor is considered to be the legal owner and can claim capital allowances for the asset. The lessee makes payments to the lessor for the use of the asset. There are two forms of leases.

- **Finance leases:** These are leases in which the lessor (the owner) will expect to recoup the whole (or most) of its cost of performing the contract during the initial period of rental, referred to as the 'basic lease period' (or 'primary term'). At the end of the period the asset is generally leased for a further period for a peppercorn rent, sold by the lessor or sold by the lessee for the lessor for a large amount of the proceeds. The servicing and maintenance of the asset is the lessee's responsibility. Finance leases are reported on the face of the statement of financial position (meaning that both the asset and the liability appear). Finance leases give the lessee the rights and obligations of ownership and are a form of borrowing that increases capital gearing.
- **Operating leases:** These are leases other than finance leases and do not currently have to be reported on the face of the statement of financial position, although there are proposals to require this in the future. Common examples include short-term rental contracts for office equipment and contract hire agreements for the provision of vehicles. Operating leases do not cover the economic life of the asset: at the end of one contract the equipment is leased to someone else. This is especially useful for the lessee in the case of high-tech products which quickly become obsolete, the risk being borne by the lessor. The servicing and maintenance of the asset are the lessor's responsibility. As operating leases are currently not reported on the statement of financial position, they will not be included in gearing calculations.

However, liability for payment of future rentals under the terms of contract will be reported as a note to the accounts and will thus be considered when the company's accounts are analysed, e.g. by potential lenders.

Leases are popular with lessors, lessees and suppliers: suppliers like them because they are paid fully for the asset at the start of the contract; lessors are able to make profits from leasing equipment and obtain tax relief on the purchase; while a lessee may find this option cheaper and easier to secure than arranging a bank loan to purchase the asset. A lessee may also have insufficient cash to purchase the asset outright.

11.5

What are the differences between a finance lease and an operating lease?

6.2 Sale and leaseback

This is a financing arrangement whereby a company sells its building to an investment company or other specialist in the field. The purchasing company (lessor) takes an interest in the freehold land on which the property stands and the selling company becomes the lessee, which then rents the building which it previously owned, generally for a minimum of 50 years. The rent is reviewed every few years. Boots and British Telecom have both used this method of finance.

The lessor will wish to obtain a good investment, which could be rented to another company if for some reason the original lessee no longer wishes, or is unable, to rent the property. Thus the lessor would prefer the building to be in good repair, non-specialised and in an area which is, or is likely to be, experiencing rising commercial property prices.

The main advantage of this method of financing is that the company can raise more money than would be the case if the property is used as security for a mortgage.

The main disadvantages are that fewer assets remain to support future borrowing, and the removal of a significant asset from the statement of financial position could cause an adverse reaction by financial commentators and the market in general.

Other disadvantages are that:

- the company loses the flexibility to move or to sell the property
- the real cost can often be very high, especially if rents are increasing rapidly, and
- the company loses future capital gains on the property.

7 Hire purchase

Hire purchase (HP) is in many respects a hybrid between lending and renting. The facility may be simply defined as hiring with the option to purchase. The HP payments consist partly of capital and partly of interest payments. On payment of the final instalment, ownership of the asset passes to the customer. By concession, HMRC will generally permit the customer to claim and retain tax relief on capital allowances provided that the option-to-purchase fee is less than the market value at the end of the contract term.

The common procedure is for the finance house to buy the good from the supplier who delivers it to the customer. The finance house and the customer set up an HP agreement, which includes the payment of an initial deposit, the size of which depends upon the finance company's policy and the creditworthiness of the customer.

For the customer, the advantages of HP are that the interest part of each payment is allowable against tax and capital allowances can be claimed on the asset.

8 Securitisation of assets

This is the practice whereby, instead of lending money to a company, a bank raises finance for it by setting up a special purpose vehicle (SPV) to acquire the company's securities, such as **commercial paper** or the rights to future income. The SPV will then arrange to sell bonds to investors. The company obtains the receipts from the bond issue and the rate of interest will be lower as it will be partly offset by the income obtained from the securitised paper etc. Therefore, the advantage for a company is that the interest rates that it has to pay under this arrangement are often lower than the bank's lending rates.

9 Government assistance

9.1 Enterprise Investment Scheme (EIS)

The EIS allows individual investors (who are unconnected with the company) to subscribe for shares in unquoted companies and to obtain tax relief at 30% on the amount subscribed (up to a maximum of £1 million in each tax year), provided they keep their shares for at least three years. The shares must be paid up in full. The company must not have assets greater than £15 million. Individuals can obtain exemption from capital gains tax when they sell their shares and claim income tax relief for capital losses. The scheme also permits business angels to become directors of companies they invest in and to obtain tax relief.

9.2 Enterprise Finance Guarantee (EFG) scheme

The EFG is a loan guarantee scheme intended to facilitate additional bank lending to viable small and medium-sized enterprises (SMEs) with insufficient or no security with which to secure a normal commercial loan.

EFG was launched in January 2009 to help viable SMEs obtain the working capital and investment that they need during a time of unprecedented tightened credit conditions. It now aims to help such SMEs seeking finance for investment and growth as the economy recovers.

EFG is a targeted measure to be used by lenders on a discretionary basis. It is not designed for the majority of viable businesses to whom banks should lend. It is also not a mechanism through which businesses or their owners can choose to withhold security that a lender would normally lend against. It is not intended to facilitate lending to businesses that are not viable and that banks have declined to lend to on that basis. The lenders are provided with a government-backed guarantee for 75% of the value of each individual loan. Thus, the guarantee provides protection to the lender in the event of default by the borrower.

EFG supports lending to viable businesses with an annual turnover of up to £41 million, seeking loans of between £1,000 and £1 million and repayable over a period of three months to ten years. The British Business Bank oversees and administers the EFG on behalf of the Department for Business, Innovation and Skills.

9.3 Grants

Grants may be available for business projects that create new jobs but cannot proceed without financial assistance. Grants are available from a range of institutions, including governmental bodies and the Prince's Trust.

10 Raising long-term finance: identification of financing needs

In order to identify total financing needs, the company will need to project its requirements for several years ahead. Table 11.2 shows how a company can project its financing needs over a three-year horizon.

TABLE 11.2 Financing requirements: three-year programme

Year	Year 1	Year 2	Year 3
	£ million	£ million	£ million
Non-current asset increases (decreases)	5.0	5.0	7.0
Permanent working capital increases (decreases)	1.5	1.0	1.0
Cyclical current asset increases (decreases)	0.2	(0.1)	
Total additional finance required	6.7	5.9	8.0

More detailed information would be prepared for year 1, being organised to show monthly cash flows. Once year 1 is completed, it is replaced in the programme by a more detailed year 2 and a new year 3 is added.

The non-current assets would relate to planned research and development, planned land acquisition or planned plant and machinery acquisition. The permanent working capital increases would relate to long-term permanent trends in trading activity. The cyclical current asset changes relate to short-term increases and decreases in trading activity.

10.1 Financing of the identified needs

Different levels and types of long-term and short-term sources of finance can be used to fund the non-current assets and the working capital of the business. The method chosen will have an impact on the cash flow of the organisation.

- **Aggressive:** An aggressive approach to the financing of working capital is to finance all fluctuating current assets and some more permanent working capital from short-term sources. Non-current assets should be financed by long-term sources of finance. This may be beneficial to the company if the short-term funds are cheaper than the equivalent long-term ones, but increases the likelihood of liquidity and cash flow problems.
- **Conservative:** A conservative approach would be to use long-term financing to fund all non-current assets and permanent working capital and the fluctuating current assets. In fact, it is only when current assets are large that short-term financing is necessary; at other times there may be surplus cash to invest. The company would probably invest this in marketable short-term securities, especially if the amount is significant.
- **Balanced:** A balanced approach is to fund non-current assets and permanent working capital from long-term sources and fluctuating current assets from short-term sources.

The method used will be a choice for senior management and will reflect their overall policy and plans for the organisation. However, a business may be forced to adopt a sub-optimal approach (from the management's viewpoint) due to restrictions in their ability to raise the 'correct' type of funds. As in all areas, the policy adopted by the firm should match the expectations of the shareholders.

Moreover, the market's view of the company's prospects and abilities will determine the level of debt investors will be willing to lend the company. The nature of the industry that the company operates in will also affect the level of debt and short-term finance that the market will consider prudent – the more volatile the sector, the lower the level of debt and short-term finance which would be advisable.

11 Raising long-term finance: methods of issuing shares

One way in which a firm can finance expansion is to issue additional equity – usually on the main stock exchange or second-tier market – either by a quoted company issuing additional shares or by an unquoted company obtaining a quotation. An unquoted company may also wish to issue shares without being floated.

We discuss below various methods of issuing shares. The factors which help to determine the best approach to adopt are the amount to be raised, the cost of raising it and the state of the market and economic conditions generally.

11.1 Offer for sale

Offers for sale are popular with companies being floated for the first time and undertaking a large issue – for example, an unquoted company may sell some of its existing shares on the market. An unquoted company can also issue new shares and market all (new and existing) shares. This is also referred to as an 'initial public offering' (IPO). The selling of existing shares provides a wider market for finance (and shares) in a company and allows shareholders a chance to sell their shares. A company will only receive additional funds if new shares are issued.

An unquoted company applying for quotation has to be sponsored by a stock exchange member firm and an issuing firm. The responsibility of the former is to ensure that the company fulfils the requirements for listing; the issuing house has to ensure that the issue is successful both in price set and take-up of shares.

In an offer for sale, the company must publish a prospectus giving details of its business and the capital that is to be raised, on the basis of which investors are invited to subscribe for shares. The issue price of shares is often set at a discount to what might be obtained to create enough demand for all the shares to be issued and encourage strong demand and a premium above the issue price in trading immediately after the issue. If the issue is undersubscribed, any shares left unsold are taken up by the **underwriters**.

11.2 Sale by tender

Sales by tender are occasionally used for large, first-time issues, but are less common than offers for sale because of uncertainties as to how much finance will be raised and the possibility that they may give the impression that the issuing house is unable to set a price for the shares.

The issuing house (or the company) invites members of the public – also through a prospectus – to subscribe by tender, stating how many shares they wish to buy and at up to what price. Sometimes there is a minimum price below which tenders will not be accepted. Applications may be dealt with in a number of ways. The most common methods are explained in Worked example 11.5.

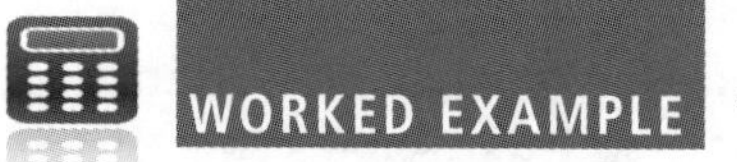

11.5

ABC plc is to make an issue of two million ordinary shares by tender. The minimum tender price has been fixed at 50p. Applications are received as shown below.

Tender price	Number of shares applied for	Value of applications	Cumulative number of applications	Cumulative value of applications
£	000s	£000s	000s	£000s
2.00	100	200	100	200
1.75	200	350	300	550
1.50	300	450	600	1,000
1.25	400	500	1,000	1,500
1.00	450	450	1,450	1,950
0.75	550	412	2,000	2,362.5
0.50	1,000	500	3,000	2,862.5

11.5 *continued*

Different methods of dealing with the scenario depicted above are as follows.

1 Applications are accepted in full at the prices tendered, starting with those offering the highest prices and working downwards until the new issue has been allotted in full. Therefore, in the example above, the issue is fully subscribed at a price between £0.75 and £2.00, which yields an overall value of £2,362,500 for the two million shares. This method is unsuitable for most public issues as it tends to frighten away the private investor and the issue is spread over relatively few applications.
2 Shares are allotted in full, starting with the applications offering the highest prices and working downwards until all the issue has been fully allotted. However, here, the price fixed is that of the lowest tender to be accepted and all applications pay this price. In our example, the issue price is the point where the full two million shares are allotted, namely at £0.75. As everyone will pay this price, the issue will raise 2 million × £0.75 = £1,500,000. While the approach is fair for the small shareholder, the issue is not usually spread among many applicants.
3 A further improvement results from a method whereby two prices are fixed. Applications at prices between them are scaled down. Applications at lower prices are rejected and those above the higher price are accepted in full, up to a certain maximum number, or scaled down slightly.

There are, of course, a number of variations to the methods outlined in Worked example 11.5, and issuing houses are continually researching to make improvements. Although small investors tend to avoid tenders as they have difficulty in deciding on a fair price, recent experiences suggest that the fixing price is usually not much different from the ensuing market price, reflecting the influence of the institutional investors.

Advantages of sales by tender

For the company issuing shares, a sale by tender offers two main advantages.

- The paperwork is reduced, as the number of applications is lower.
- The fixing price in recent years has usually been higher than would be necessary in an offer for sale. In an offer for sale, the price is kept low to ensure that the offer is accepted, but in a tender, the forces of supply and demand have improved the price.

11.6

What uncertainties is an investor subject to if tendering for shares?

11.3 Placing or selective marketing

This method is often used for a small first-time issue, or when a quoted company wishes to raise additional finance. The shares are acquired by a market-maker, who passes them on to a small number of investors.

The method is common because it is relatively cheap, with the sponsoring firm approaching selected institutional investors privately. However, it does limit the number of shares available for trading on the market.

A variant of this is the **bought deal**, where a major investment bank will buy all the shares in a (possibly larger) new issue at a slightly discounted price. This offers an alternative to underwriting as a way of avoiding the risk that an offer for sale will be undersubscribed. It may be chosen because the cost of the discount can be less than the underwriter's fees.

11.4 Stock exchange introduction

This is the introduction of the shares on the stock exchange so that a quotation (i.e. a price) can be fixed, rather than the issue of shares. An introduction cannot be made unless sufficient shares are available to establish a market and thus a price. This method therefore tends to be restricted to larger firms.

11.5 Rights issue

A rights issue is an issue of additional shares to existing shareholders to raise further capital. Shareholders can choose whether or not to accept the offer to subscribe for new shares. The rights of existing shareholders to buy the new shares are known as 'pre-emptive rights' – they have the right of first refusal. The new shares are offered at a discount (with a price below the existing market price), because if the rights issue price is higher than the market price, shareholders who want to buy more shares can do so more cheaply in the market. In order to minimise the risk that a general fall in share prices will reduce the market price of the shares to below the rights issue price, the rights issue price is usually set 20% or 30% (or even more) below the market price.

When offering shares in a rights issue, the company sends an explanatory letter to each shareholder detailing the price, accompanied by a provisional allotment letter indicating the number of shares for which the member is entitled to subscribe. For example, a '1 for 5 rights issue at 120p per share' means that for every five shares a shareholder holds, the shareholder can purchase an additional share for 120p. The offer must be on a 'rights basis': the number of shares for which the shareholder is entitled to subscribe is in the same proportion to the member's existing holding for all members eligible to receive the offer.

Forms of acceptance or renunciation accompany the offer. The member has three options.

- If the member accepts the offer, and exercises their rights, they lodge their acceptance and cheque with the company.
- A member who chooses not to accept the offer may renounce their rights in favour of someone else. The member can sell the rights for some or all of their shares in the market.
- If shareholders do not either take up the rights or sell them, the company must, under the rules, sell the new shares in the market for the best price available and, if there is any surplus over the rights issue price, pay over the surplus (after deducting any selling expenses) to those shareholders who have neither subscribed nor sold their rights. There is no guarantee that any surplus will be available.

Advantages of rights issues

Rights issues offer advantages to both the company and existing shareholders. For the company, there is less administration and no prospectus is required, both of which reduce the costs.

Shareholders obtain shares at what appears to be a discount – although the share price after the rights issue will, in theory, fall to a level that leaves them no better and no worse off.

A shareholder who takes up their rights maintains their proportion of the (increased) ordinary share capital and makes a further investment in the company, without the dealing costs that would be incurred in buying shares in the market. If they do not wish to take up their rights, they can sell them in the market, allowing the purchaser to buy the new shares at the rights issue price.

Calculation of issue price

The issue price is the amount that the company wishes to raise from the issue divided by the number of new shares. The number of shares will be such that the issue price is below the current market price. A discount of approximately 20% to 40% is usual. At the time of writing, recent rights issues have been made by Standard Chartered Bank, RSA Group, Deutsche Bank, Serco and Mothercare. The number of shares issued will also take account of the number currently in issue (issuing too many new shares in relation to the business to be financed would dilute the EPS too much).

Calculation of ex-rights price

The ex-rights price (the theoretical price after issue) is a weighted average based on the total value of the company after the rights issue, including the money subscribed for new shares.

WORKED EXAMPLE 11.6

A company is making a 1 for 3 rights issue, with each new share costing £2. The current market price of the shares is £3.

Required
Calculate the ex-rights price.

Solution
The ex-rights price is calculated as:

	£
Rights value of three shares (3 × £3)	9.00
Amount subscribed for one new share	2.00
Total (value of four shares after the rights issue)	11.00
Theoretical ex-rights price of one share (£11/4)	2.75

The ex-rights price could also be shown in terms of the total value of the issued shares divided by the total number of shares after the rights issue.

Actual price after issue

The actual price after a rights issue often differs from the theoretical price, due to changes in expectations concerning future earnings. The actual price may be higher than the ex-rights price because the market interprets the rights issue as evidence that the company is taking action, either to exploit profit opportunities or to deal with problems. On the other hand, the actual price may be lower than the ex-rights price due to uncertainty about the company's prospects or concern that the rights were needed to pay off debts to avoid insolvency.

WORKED EXAMPLE 11.7

	£
Rights value of three shares (3 × £3)	9.00
Amount subscribed for one new share	2.00
Total (value of four shares after the rights issue)	11.00
Theoretical ex-rights price of one share (£11/4)	2.75

Here the shares can be valued on a price to earnings basis.

Required
Consider the situation where the money invested in the new shares is expected to yield the same return in terms of earnings as the existing shares. Then look at what happens if expected earnings on the additional capital investment are higher or lower. The current P/E ratio is 10.

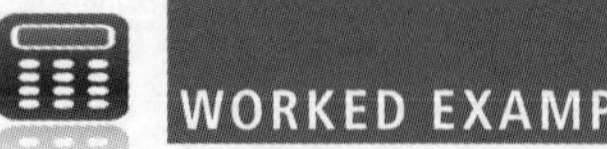

WORKED EXAMPLE 11.7 *continued*

Solution

A P/E ratio of 10 means that the earnings are currently 10% of the market value, i.e. £3/10 = 30p. If three million shares are currently in issue, earnings will equal £900,000 in total.

- If expected earnings from the money invested in new shares also earn 10%, the total earnings will yield £1.1 million, because: £2.75 × 4,000,000 × 10% = £1,100,000.
  Monetary value of the shares (× P/E ratio of 10) = £11,000,000.
  The share value is therefore £11,000,000/4,000,000 or £2.75, i.e. the same as the theoretical ex-rights price.
- If the new shares are expected to yield 15%:
  Total earnings (£900,000 + (1,000,000 × £2 × 15%)) = £1,200,000
  Monetary value of shares = (10 × £1,200,000) = £12,000,000
  Value per share = £12,000,000/4,000,000 = £3.00
- If the new shares are expected to yield 5%.
  Total earnings (£900,000 + (1,000,000 × £2 × 5%)) = £1,000,000
  Monetary value of shares = (10 × £1,000,000) = £10,000,000
  Value per share = £10,000,000/4,000,000 = £2.50

As can be seen, the actual impact on shareholder wealth will depend on the earnings generated compared with the existing earning rates – if lower, the market value will fall; if higher, it will rise.

Value of rights

We noted earlier that shareholders can sell their rights, in which case they receive the value of the rights less any dealing expenses. The value of the rights is the difference between the market price after the issue and the issue price of the new shares. In Worked example 11.6, the shares are issued in the rights issue at a price of £2. We calculated a theoretical ex-rights share price of £2.75. So the right to buy one new share in the rights issue is worth £2.75 – £2 or 75p. Since one new share is issued for every three shares held before the issue, the value of rights for each share held before the issue is 75p/3 shares, or 25p per share.

WORKED EXAMPLE 11.8

AB Telecom has two billion issued ordinary shares. The share price is £2.60. It announces a 1 for 2 rights issue at a price of £2.00.

Required

Calculate the impact on the wealth of a shareholder who holds 1,000 shares and who:

(a) takes up the rights issue
(b) sells the rights
(c) ignores the rights issue.

Solution

Initial calculations of the ex-rights price and the value of one right:

	£
Value of two shares (cum rights) (2 × £2.60)	5.20
Amount subscribed for one new share	2.00
Total (value of three shares after the rights issue)	7.20
Theoretical ex-rights price of one share (£7.20/3)	2.40
Rights issue price	2.00
Value of the rights offer	0.40

WORKED EXAMPLE 11.8 *continued*

(a) The shareholder takes up the rights issue (500 additional shares):

	£
Value of holding after rights issue (1,500 × £2.40)	3,600
Less cost of rights shares (500 × £2)	1,000
Shareholder's wealth	2,600

(b) The shareholder sells the rights:

Value of holding after rights issue (1,000 × £2.40)	2,400
Sale of rights (500 × £0.40)	200
	2,600

(c) The shareholder ignores the rights:

Value of holding after rights issue (1,000 × £2.40)	2,400

To this must be added any surplus when the company sells off the rights:

Value of holding before rights issue (1,000 × £2.60)	2,600

Whether the shareholder opts to purchase the rights shares or to sell the rights, the shareholder's wealth will be £2,600. However, if the shareholder ignores the rights issue, the shareholder's wealth may fall from £2,600 to £2,400. The company will sell the rights and transfer the surplus to the shareholder. The amount of this surplus cannot be predicted.

WORKED EXAMPLE 11.9

Fair2Ground plc has one billion issued ordinary shares. The share price is £3.50. It announces a 1 for 4 rights issue at a price of £2.80.

Required

Calculate the impact of the rights issue on the wealth of a shareholder who holds 1,000 shares and who:

(a) takes up the rights issue

(b) sells the rights

(c) ignores the rights issue.

11.9 *continued*

Solution

Initial calculations of ex-rights price and value of one right:

	£
Value of four shares (cum rights) (4 × £3.50)	14.00
Amount subscribed for one new share	2.80
Total (value of five shares after the rights issue)	16.80
Theoretical ex-rights price of one share (£16.80/5)	3.36
Rights issue price	2.80
Value of the rights offer	0.56

(a) Shareholder takes up the rights issue (250 additional shares):

	£
Value of holding after rights issue (1,250 × £3.36)	4,200
Less cost of rights shares (250 × £2.80)	700
Shareholder's wealth	3,500

(b) Shareholder sells the rights:

Value of holding after rights issue (1,000 × £3.36)	3,360
Sale of rights (250 × £0.56)	140
	3,500

(c) Shareholder ignores the rights:

Value of holding after rights issue (1,000 × £3.36)	3,360

To this will be added any surplus generated when the company sells the rights:

Value of holding before rights issue (1,000 × £3.50)	3,500

11.6 Open offer

This is an offer to existing shareholders to subscribe for securities; this may be in proportion to their existing shareholdings.

An open offer is a concessionary method of listing, approval being sought in principle early on. Once approval has been granted, the sponsor firm has to inform the market. The announcement will state that the proposals are subject to shareholder approval at general meeting.

11.7 Vendor share scheme or placing

Where a vendor prefers cash to shares issued to finance an acquisition by a purchaser, an issuing house can place the securities with clients for cash.

11.8 Employee share schemes

Such schemes are often used as incentives – for example, share option schemes, which give certain employees (usually directors) the chance to purchase shares in the company at a price determined in advance for, hopefully, a financial benefit.

11.9 Stock split

A stock split is the splitting of existing shares into smaller shares – for example, each ordinary share of 50p is split into two of 25p – to improve the marketability of the company's shares. It can also be used to send signals that the company is expecting significant growth in EPS and dividends per share. For this reason the resulting market price of the split shares can be higher than the simple split price would be. For example, in 2014, Apple made a 7 for 1 stock split. Prior to the stock split Apple's shares were valued at $650 each and its total market value was around $559 billion. After the split, the shares were valued at $94 each and the market value was about $562 billion. The purpose of the share split was to make the shares more accessible to a larger number of investors and to improve liquidity. In this particular case, the slight improvement in the market value was the result of improved trading in the shares rather than the effect of the split per se.

11.10 Scrip issues

A scrip issue (also known as a 'bonus' or 'capitalisation issue') involves the conversion of reserves into shares, causing a fall in the reserves. Shareholders receive additional shares in proportion to their holding. Unlike a rights issue, no additional funds are brought into the company. This results in more equity in circulation with the result that the market value will generally fall in the short term.

TEST YOUR KNOWLEDGE 11.7

List the different ways in which a company can issue shares. Which of these do not involve an inflow of funds to the company?

11.11 Advisers to share issues

The process of getting shares quoted on a stock exchange is a specialised activity in which a company generally calls on a number of professional advisers. Advisers to a share issue include the following.

- **Issuing houses**: The functions of an issuing house include: giving advice on and organising the most appropriate capital structure and time to make an issue of shares or debentures; providing publicity, marketing facilities and backing for the issue; and giving advice to a private company with regard to a decision to become a public company. Issuing houses thus play a vital role in the issuing of shares and debentures.
- **Underwriters:** These are usually issuing houses or investment banks, generally acting in a syndicate, which agree to purchase any securities not taken up at the issue price (they 'underwrite' the issue). The underwriters will charge a fee, which will be payable whether or not they are called upon to take up surplus securities. The use of underwriters removes the risk of a share issue being undersubscribed.
- **Investment banks:** Investment banks are sometimes employed to give financial advice, but may also act in the role of issuing house or sponsor.
- **Sponsors:** The Listing Rules require that a company seeking a listing has a firm of stockbrokers to act for it and to ensure that all regulations applying to the process are complied with.
- **Solicitors:** Generally two firms of solicitors will be employed, the first supervising the issue itself and the second acting for the company, ensuring the accuracy of legal documentation (e.g. the Memorandum and Articles).

- **Accountants**: Accountants are employed to give advice on the issue and to ensure that the legal requirements regarding financial information for share issues are complied with.

TEST YOUR KNOWLEDGE 11.8

List the different kinds of advisers a company may call on when it issues shares on the stock exchange.

11.12 Pricing shares for a stock market quotation

The sponsor advises on the setting of a price. The following factors have a bearing on the valuation of a company's shares:

- the business sector and its prospects
- P/E ratios of comparable companies in the same sector
- company business and prospects, including future dividends and earnings forecasts
- company size and the amount of finance required
- asset backing
- reputation of the company and its management
- factors affecting the stability of the company and the reliability of earnings, including:
  - business risk
  - financial risk, related to financial structure, in particular the level of gearing
  - degree of dependence on a small number of key individuals
- economic conditions
- market sentiment (issues are often made when the market is buoyant and expectations for the market as a whole are high)
- whether the quotation is to be on the main market or the AIM.

11.13 Estimation of issue price using P/E ratio

A share price for a stock market issue is often derived using the P/E ratio:

market share price = EPS × P/E ratio

WORKED EXAMPLE 11.10

Flower plc is planning an initial public offering of about 70% of its shares on the AIM to raise about £4 million. Sinbad plc is a company in the same business sector and has a market capitalisation of £25 million – also on the AIM. Sinbad's EPS, based on its recently published accounts, is 40p, and its shares have been quoted recently at an average of £6.40. Flower plc has a current EPS of 50p. The management of both Sinbad and Flower are highly regarded in the industry, and both have good business prospects and have published similar projections of growth in sales and earnings. Both are investing heavily to support this growth. The financial management of both companies is excellent, and both companies have their cash management well under control. Neither has any long-term debt. The sector average P/E ratio is 10.6, and companies in the sector have P/E ratios ranging from 7 to 17.

Required

Suggest an issue price for Flower plc.

WORKED EXAMPLE **11.10** *continued*

Solution

First, we have to choose a reasonable P/E ratio. The P/E ratio for Sinbad plc is 640/40 = 16. Since Flower plc is in the same sector, its P/E ratio can be based on Sinbad plc's P/E ratio, allowing for the fact that the business, management and risk profiles of both companies are very similar – although Flower is smaller. This could lead us to choose a P/E ratio for Flower slightly lower than Sinbad's. If we estimate a P/E ratio for Flower equal to 90% of Sinbad's, the P/E ratio for Flower plc is estimated as:

16 × 90% = 14.4.

A value for the shares can then be calculated as:

14.4 × 50p = £7.20

11.14 Costs of share issues

Share (and debenture) issues can be expensive, depending on the method used. Costs involved in share issues include:

- the stock exchange listing fee for the new securities
- advisers' fees, including those of the issuing house
- underwriting costs
- the compulsory advertising in national newspapers, and
- printing and distribution costs of details and prospectus.

While some costs are variable, such as the commission payable to issuing houses, most are fixed; it is therefore more economical to issue large amounts of shares, which discourages small firms.

Compliance with the Listing Rules (which vary according to the size of the issue) is also a cost to be borne by the company (the rules include the number of market-makers to use and how to issue the shares).

Issues costs are highest on the main market, but lower on the AIM. This is one reason why the AIM is favoured by smaller companies, including companies that are being listed for the first time.

12 Private Finance Initiative (PFI) and Public Private Partnership (PPP)

The Private Finance Initiative (PFI) was introduced in 1992 as a means of obtaining private finance for public sector long-term capital projects (e.g. the building of prisons, schools and hospitals).The government at the time was committed to developing this approach across a wide range of public services.

A new Commission on Public Private Partnerships – the Institute of Public Policy Research Commission – was set up in 1999. Its brief was to examine questions about specific forms of partnership between private sector firms and public sector organisations. For example, how can private firms involved in partnerships be made accountable to the public? How does this accountability fit in with achieving the best value for money? In 1997 the PFI was moved within the overall umbrella organisation of the Public Private Partnership (PPP) initiative, which also has the objective of providing private sector funding for public projects.

The advantages claimed for PFI are as follows.

- The public sector does not have to fund large capital outflows at the start of the project. In consequence, the public sector does not need to raise long-term finance by borrowing; this takes pressure off the public sector borrowing requirement.
- The public obtains valuable planning, construction and management expertise from the private sector. There may be opportunities for joint working with the public sector and this may lead to the development of ideas and the transfer of skills.

- The private sector body takes on the risks of financing and constructing the project. It is then responsible for managing the project.
- It is expected that there would be higher value for money through PFI than through public sector financing, construction and management.

However, there are also disadvantages to this approach.

- The biggest disadvantage, in hindsight, has been the high annual costs charged to the public sector body. The costs have been significantly larger than the annual cost of comparable self-funded operations. Costs have been high because firms build profit into the annual costs, an additional allowance for the risk borne by the construction company and higher borrowing costs than for public sector organisations.
- Many of the projects have been completed well over budget.
- There is a transfer of assets to the private sector. This can lead to a loss of control and accountability by the public sector.

CHAPTER SUMMARY

This chapter has examined the main sources of long-term finance available to companies. This has ranged from share issues, retention (a major source of finance), borrowing via different instruments (loans, lease finance and securitisation) and government assistance. It then examined how companies determine their financing needs. It looked at the methods of share issue, including offer for sale, tender, placing and rights issue. It also examined the pricing of a share issue. It concluded by considering PFI/PPP, a major source of long-term off-balance sheet finance in the public sector.

END OF CHAPTER QUESTIONS

11.1 (a) Distinguish between convertible bonds and warrants and explain why companies issue convertible bonds and warrants.

(b) Redbrick plc's 10% convertible loan stock is quoted at £138 per £100 nominal. The earliest date for conversion is in three years' time at the rate of 25 ordinary shares per £100 nominal loan stock. The current share price is £5.20.

(i) Calculate the conversion price.

(ii) Calculate the conversion premium.

(c) Newtown plc has issued loan stock with 4p warrants exercisable attached. Warrants give the right to purchase one ordinary share at a price of 70p for every five warrants in 2025. The current share price is 50p.

(i) Calculate the conversion premium.

(ii) Calculate the value of a warrant during the conversion period if the share price is then 150p.

11.2 Smith plc is considering issuing shares to the general public. Draft a report to the board detailing the options available and the procedures which should be adopted, including the appointment of advisers, for the option you suggest.

11.3 TT is a public limited company with a paid-up share capital of 1.2 million £1 shares and no long-term debt. The dividend has been paid at a rate of 45p per share in each of the past two years and the market price per share has not varied significantly from its current market price of £3.60.

The company now wishes to finance the expansion of its existing premises and the board has announced a rights issue of one new ordinary share at a price of £3.00 for every four shares currently held. The company forecasts that future dividends will be at a rate of 43.5p per share on the enlarged share capital and that its existing ratio of dividend cover can be maintained.

You are required to comment on the theoretical and the practical validity of the following three reactions to the announcement from various shareholders:

(a) 'I hold 5% of the equity. Whether I take up or surrender my rights, I should be getting a bargain at the offer price of £3.00.'

(b) 'As I understand the position, I should not have been out of pocket in the long run if the company had priced the rights issue at £5.00 instead of £3.00. I think they should have done that to raise a bit more money.'

(c) 'The company could have fixed a lower price for the issue if the underwriters hadn't been looking for a high amount of commission, 1.25% being the amount charged.'

The cost of capital

12

CONTENTS

1 The importance of the cost of capital
2 Cost of equity: the dividend valuation model and the dividend growth model
3 Cost of equity: the capital asset pricing model (CAPM)
4 Cost of preference shares
5 Cost of debt capital
6 Weighted average cost of capital (WACC)

1 The importance of the cost of capital

A company's cost of capital is the return that the company gives to the providers of capital. The form of the return depends on the nature of the capital. Shareholders receive dividends and usually expect capital growth from increases in the share price. The mix of dividend income and capital growth depends on the nature of the company. A high-tech company that is growing fast and is investing in research and development to support this growth is holding out the prospect of capital growth, but may pay little or none of its available cash out in dividends. A company in a mature industry, such as a water or electricity utility, may have few opportunities to invest for growth, and may pay large dividends relative to share price.

Loan stock holders receive their return in the form of regular, usually fixed, interest payments and redemption proceeds. Since the market price of loan stock varies, there is scope for capital gain, though usually less than that expected by many ordinary shareholders.

Investing in companies involves risk. Investors may lose some or all of their money. Risk is composed of two elements:

- business risk – associated with the company's area of business, its prospects and its projects, and
- financial risk – associated with the company's financial structure, in particular the amount of borrowing undertaken by the company (this is discussed in Chapter 13).

Generally, as the level of risk increases, the return expected by investors also increases. Investors expect to be compensated for bearing additional risk. This is referred to as the 'risk premium' and this acts to raise the required return above the **risk-free rate**. The larger the risk premium, the higher the return required by shareholders. The risk-free return is the return that would be required if there were no risk, which is typically taken to be the return on government bonds.

Corporate financial managers need to know the cost of capital for the following reasons.

- To make well-informed choices about capital structure and what kinds of new capital to raise, which means they need to know the cost of the alternatives. By being aware of the expectations of investors, they can attempt to meet those expectations, as far as possible.
- In making capital investment decisions, they need to know the cost of capital in order to use it as the discount rate in project appraisal. By doing this, any project giving a negative NPV will be rejected as it provides a return below the cost of capital (or the cost of raising finance). However, projects yielding a positive NPV will provide a return higher than the cost of capital and enhance returns to shareholders.

Figure 12.1 shows the relationship between the cost of capital (WACC in the diagram), used as a discount rate, and NPV, and how a positive NPV then feeds back positively into the market price of equity, when the information is published.

FIGURE 12.1 Diagrammatic overview of a public limited company

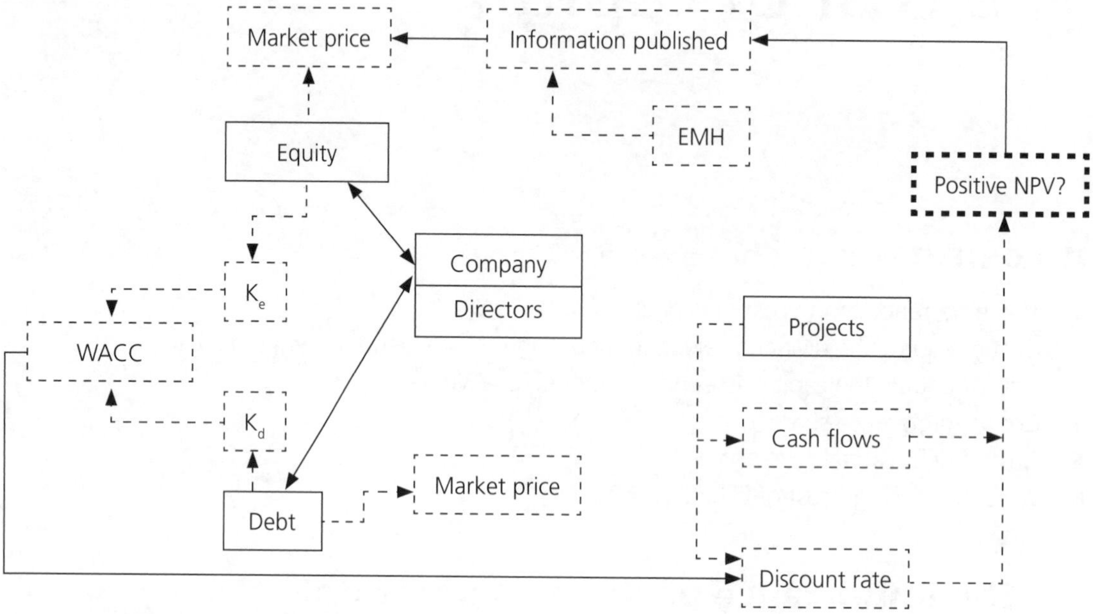

WACC = weighted average cost of capital
K_e = cost of equity
K_d = cost of debt
NPV = net present value
EMH = efficient market hypothesis

The following two sections describe methods for calculating the cost of equity capital. The first uses the dividend valuation model, which relates the dividends paid, and expected to be paid in the future, to the share price. When the cost of equity is calculated using a dividend model, it takes account of risk implicitly. This is because for higher-risk companies, either higher dividends are paid in relation to the value of the shares or dividends are expected to grow faster than for lower-risk companies. The second model for calculating the cost of equity capital is the capital asset pricing model, which takes account of risk explicitly.

The final sections of the chapter then discuss methods for calculating the cost of other forms of capital.

2 Cost of equity: the dividend valuation model and the dividend growth model

2.1 The dividend valuation model

The dividend valuation model is based on the principle that the market value of a share is the present value of the dividends paid on the share. The present value is obtained by discounting all expected future dividends to today's date. The discount rate used to discount future dividends back to equal today's share price is the cost of capital for equity. The model is used where the dividends are expected to be constant each year. The formula is:

$$P_0 = D_0 / K_e$$

The formula can be rearranged to give the cost of equity:

$$K_e = D_0 / P_0$$

WORKED EXAMPLE 12.1

Puccini plc's latest dividend is 32p per share. There has been no growth. The company's current share price is £8.00.

Required

Calculate Puccini's cost of equity:

Solution

$K_e = 32/800 = 0.04$

The cost of equity is 4%.

WORKED EXAMPLE 12.2

X plc has paid a total dividend of £40,000 per annum on its 200,000 shares, which have a nominal value of 25p per share. The company expects a similar payment for the foreseeable future. The market value of the shares is 83p per share.

Required

Estimate, using the dividend valuation model, the cost of equity capital.

Solution

Dividend per share = £40,000/200,000 = 20p

$K_e = 20/83 = 0.2409 = 24.1\%$

2.2 The dividend growth model

When dividends are expected to grow at a constant annual percentage rate, the relationship between the share price and future dividends is given by the dividend growth model.

$$P_0 = \frac{D_0 (1 + g)}{(K_e - g)}$$

where:

P_0 = current share price (ex div) (i.e. excluding the current dividend)

K_e = the cost of equity (i.e. the return shareholders require, which will be a function of factors such as the level of risk)

D_0 = dividend at year 0

g = annual rate of growth in dividends (the rate at which investors expect dividends to grow in the future).

'Ex div' means that there is no dividend payment inherent in the share price. If a dividend payment is due, a potential purchaser would have to pay for the share's capital value (denoted P_0 plus the pending dividend). Then the value of the share would be known as 'cum div'.

The formula implies that:

- higher dividends will increase the value of the company
- higher growth in dividends will increase the value of the company, and
- a lower cost of equity will increase the value of the company.

A company has just paid its annual dividend of 40p per share. Shareholders in this company require a return of 18%.

Required

Estimate the value of the shares now, assuming that dividends are expected to grow at an annual rate of 5%.

Solution

$P_0 = (40 \times 1.05)/(0.18 - 0.05) = 42/0.13 = £3.23$

This implies that if the value of a share is based on the expected future dividends then the value will increase at the rate of growth in dividends.

A company has just paid its annual dividend of 10p per share. Shareholders in this company require a return of 12%.

Required

Estimate the value of the shares now, assuming that dividends are expected to grow at an annual rate of 10%.

Solution

$P_0 = [10(1 + 0.1)]/(0.12 - 0.10) = 11/0.02 = 550p$

2.3 Estimating the cost of equity using the dividend growth model

The formula for the dividend growth model can be rearranged to be used to estimate the cost of equity:

$$K_e = \frac{D_0\,(1 + g)}{P_0} + g$$

The board of directors of Sharp plc are trying to estimate the return required by the equity shareholders. The company has just paid a dividend of 27p and dividends are expected to grow at 5% per annum. The current share price is £1.82.

Required

Estimate the firm's cost of equity.

Solution

$K_e = [27(1 + 0.05)/182] + 0.05 = 28.35/182 + 0.05 = 0.156 + 0.05 = 0.206$

The firm's cost of equity is 20.6%

WORKED EXAMPLE 12.6

The board of directors of Blunt plc are trying to estimate the return required by the equity shareholders. The company has just paid a dividend of 15p and dividends are expected to grow at 6% per annum. The current share price is £1.20.

Required
Estimate the firm's cost of equity.

Solution

$K_e = [15(1 + 0.06)/120] + 0.06 = 15.9/120 + 0.06 = 0.1925 = 19.25\%$

2.4 Growth in dividends

Occasionally we need to work out the growth in dividends over a period of time. A dividend growth rate may be estimated by taking the average past rate of growth of dividends and assume that this rate will continue in the future. For example, over a four-year period, the growth rate (g) is based on the following:

$$\text{earliest dividend} \times (1 + g)^4 = \text{latest dividend}$$

Re-arranging:

$$(1 + g)^4 = \text{latest dividend/earliest dividend}$$

and:

$$(1 + g) = \sqrt[4]{\text{latest dividend/earliest dividend}}$$

Therefore:

$$g = \left(\sqrt[4]{\text{latest dividend/earliest dividend}}\right) - 1$$

So to work out the average rate of growth we can use the following general formula:

$$\text{growth rate } (g) = \left(\sqrt[n]{\text{latest dividend/earliest dividend}}\right) - 1$$

where:
n = number of years of growth.
The process for calculating the growth rate is as follows.

1 Determine the number of years of growth (n).
2 Divide the latest dividend by the earliest dividend.
3 Find the nth root of the previous value.
4 Subtract 1 from the result.

WORKED EXAMPLE 12.7

Dividend history (£ per share)

2011	0.15
2012	0.16
2013	0.16
2014	0.18
2015	0.185

Required
Calculate the growth in dividends.

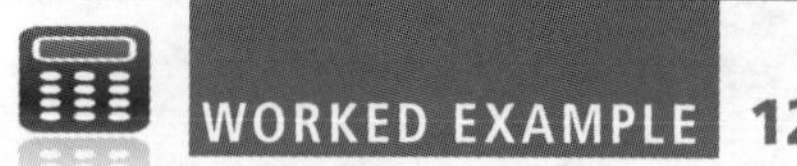
WORKED EXAMPLE 12.7 *continued*

Solution

1 n = 4 (5 years' data give 4 years of growth)
2 0.185 / 0.15 = 1.23
3 $\sqrt[4]{1.23}$ = 1.053 (we use the 4th root as there are four years of growth)
4 1.053 – 1 = 0.053

The average rate of growth in dividends is 5.3%.

WORKED EXAMPLE 12.8

Mozart's past dividends have been:

	Dividend
	Pence per share
Year 1	26
Year 2	27
Year 3	28
Year 4	32

Mozart's current share price is £4.

Required

Calculate the K_e using the dividend growth model.

Solution

n = 3; 32/26 = 1.2308; $\sqrt[3]{1.2308}$ = 1.0717 – 1 = 0.0717

K_e = [32(1 + 0.0717)/400] + 0.0717 = 34.29/400 + 0.0717 = 0.1574 = 15.74%

Another approach to estimate the growth rate was developed by Myron Gordon, an American economist. **Gordon's model of dividend growth** model is based on the growth in dividends being linked to the growth in earnings. The latter is, in turn, linked to a growing investment in a company's assets. The formula used is as follows:

growth rate (g) = r × b

where:
r = annual rate of return from investing
b = the proportion of annual earnings retained

For example, assume that a company has annual profits of £400,000 and pays dividends of £100,000. The proportion of earnings retained (b) is 75% (£300,000/£400,000). If the annual rate of return (r) is 10%, then the growth rate (g) will be 7.5% (75% × 10%).

2.5 Assumptions

The dividend valuation and dividend growth models are based on the following assumptions.

- Taxation rates are assumed to be the same for all investors.
- The costs incurred in issuing shares are ignored.
- All investors receive the same, perfect level of information.
- The cost of capital to the company remains unaltered by any new issue of shares.

- All projects undertaken as a result of new share issues have the same level of risk as the company's existing activities.
- The dividends paid must be from after-tax profits.

3 Cost of equity: the capital asset pricing model (CAPM)

The **capital asset pricing model** (CAPM) was developed in the 1960s by Sharpe (1964) and Lintner (1965) building on the work of Markowitz (1952) and portfolio theory. For our purposes, we can make the assumption that there are two basic functions associated with CAPM.

- To establish the 'correct' equilibrium market value of a company's share.
- To calculate the cost of a firm's equity (as an alternative approach to the dividend valuation model, which we considered above).

The model also implies equilibrium between risk and the expected return for each security and so can be used by financial managers to assess risk in individual company shares or a portfolio of securities.

The calculation of the cost of equity capital starts with a consideration of the different types of risk that investors face in the equity market and how those risks can be used to calculate the return that investors require from companies. Once this has been established, then one can say that companies are required to earn this return from investments if they are to satisfy their equity shareholders.

The cost of equity capital obtained under CAPM is termed the 'risk-adjusted discount rate' (RADR) and is used for purposes of investment appraisal.

This is the fundamental purpose of CAPM. Once we have established a market portfolio, we can calculate the return required for any investment – as long as we know its **beta factor** (which is explained below in section 3.2).

3.1 Unsystematic and systematic risk

Investors tend to diversify their investment portfolios to minimise risk while maintaining their return. The risk that can be diversified away in a large and well-formulated portfolio of shares is termed 'unsystematic risk'. Unsystematic risk is unique to a particular company. It is independent of political and economic factors and may arise, for example, as a result of poor labour relations, breakdown in supply lines or adverse press reports. Any of these will affect the share price of a particular company. Such risks can be diversified away because the factors causing unsystematic risk are different for different companies; they are largely uncorrelated and tend to cancel each other out. Research has shown that, if a portfolio consists of between 15 and 20 shares, selected at random, the unsystematic risk of the portfolio should be substantially eliminated.

The risk related to the economy and market that cannot be diversified away is known as 'systematic risk' or 'market risk'. Systematic risk is unavoidable. It may arise from adverse trends in the economy or from other macro external factors over which the company has no control. This non-diversifiable risk is common to all shares because all shares are exposed to macroeconomic factors. If the economy enters recession, the returns from a portfolio will fall; the converse will apply in a boom. Although all shares are affected by these macroeconomic factors, they are not equally affected. Investors will require all shares to provide an excess return over and above the risk-free rate, but the size of the risk premium will vary.

The degree of systematic risk is different for different industries. Shares in different companies and different sectors have different levels of systematic risk because some are affected more than others by macroeconomic factors. For example, food retailing has less systematic risk than the fashion industry. Income and profits for fashion companies vary much more than for food retailers. In a recession, people still have to buy food, but they can defer spending on clothes or shop for cheaper items. A portfolio that represents the market, such as a market tracker fund, is subject to the same systematic risk as the market as a whole.

Therefore, given that there is an opportunity to eliminate unsystematic risk, the only risk that an investor has to bear is systematic risk. In consequence, the risk premium obtainable in excess of the risk-free rate in the market place will be the systematic risk of the specific ordinary share.

It is possible to reduce the systematic risk of a portfolio by selecting shares with low systematic risk.

CAPM rests on the key premise that an investor can reduce overall risk by investing in an optimum portfolio and thereby eliminate unsystematic risk. All investors are assumed to be rational and it is assumed that all will behave like this.

3.2 Measuring systematic risk and calculation of the RADR

As has been explained above, CAPM splits the total risk of the security into unsystematic risk (which can be diversified away) and systematic risk. Systematic risk is relevant for determining the cost of equity and for appraising investments. Investors will require a greater return from shares with greater systematic risk.

The next steps in the development of CAPM are concerned with:

- measuring systematic risk, and
- linking systematic risk with required returns.

Measuring systematic risk

Sharpe and others examined the excess returns (in excess of the risk-free rate) of individual shares and examined the relationship of each to the excess returns of a stock market portfolio (termed the 'excess returns on the market') for each month over a 60-month period. For the stock market portfolio, one could use a stock market index such as the FTSE 100.

In order to examine the relationship scientifically, the researchers used regression analysis. Figure 12.2 is an example of a regression line, in this case showing the relationship between the excess returns on a share and the excess returns on the stock market portfolio. The gradient of this line is particularly important.

FIGURE 12.2 Excess returns on a share and excess returns on the stock market

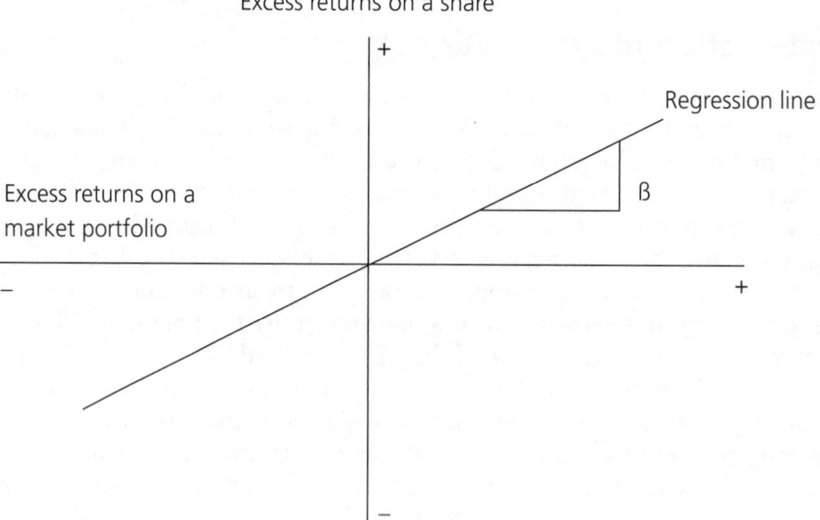

The outcomes of Sharpe's research can be summarised as follows.

- It was observed that the excess returns of a share are positively correlated with the excess returns on the market (and that both are correlated with boom/recession in the economy, i.e. they tend to rise and fall together).
- The gradient of the regression line is termed beta (β).
- If the gradient of the regression line is 45°, this indicates that the systematic risk of a share is equal to the systematic risk of the market. With a 45° gradient, the rate of increase (decrease) on the vertical axis will be identical to the rate of increase (decrease) on the horizontal axis. The variability of excess returns in both the portfolio and the specified share is identical. The share's beta equals 1.
- If the gradient of the line is greater than 45°, this indicates that the systematic risk of the share exceeds the systematic risk of the market. With a gradient greater than 45°, the rate of

increase (decrease) on the vertical axis (the excess returns on the share) is greater than the rate of increase (decrease) of the market. The share's beta is greater than 1.

- If the gradient of the line is less than 45°, this indicates that the systematic risk of the market exceeds the systematic risk of the specific share. With a gradient less than 45°, the rate of increase (decrease) on the vertical axis (the excess returns on the share) is less than the rate of increase (decrease) of the market. The share's beta is less than 1.
- The greater the beta, the greater the systematic risk and the greater the return required from the share. The size of beta is important.

WORKED EXAMPLE 12.9

The calculation of beta is shown for three different shares over a 10-month period. The table shows the excess returns for each share for each month over the period.

The results of the regression analysis are shown at the foot of the table.

For equity 1:

$y_1 = 0 + 1x$

The first term, 0, indicates the point of intercept with the vertical axis; the second term, 1, indicates that the rate of increase (decrease) of excess returns on the share is identical to the rate of increase (decrease) of the market portfolio. The systematic risk of the share is the same as the systematic risk of the market.

For equity 2:

$y_2 = -3.1 + 1.54x$

In this case, the gradient of the regression line is 1.54 times the gradient of the market line and therefore the systematic risk of the share is 1.54 times the systematic risk of the market.

For equity 3:

$y_3 = 3.8 + 0.41x$

In this case, the gradient in the regression line is 0.41 of the gradient of the market and so the systematic risk of the share is 0.41 of the systematic risk of the market.

	Market portfolio	**Excess returns (actual return – risk-free rate)**		
		Equity 1	**Equity 2**	**Equity 3**
Month	x	y_1	y_2	y_3
1	6	6	5	6.5
2	7	7	8	7
3	6.6	6.6	6.6	6.7
4	5	5	4	6
5	6	6	7	6
6	8	8	9	7
7	4	4	3	6
8	5	5	5	5.8
9	6	6	7	6
10	4	4	3	5

Regression results	Beta
$y_1 = 0 + 1x$	1
$y_2 = -3.1 + 1.54x$	1.54
$y_3 = 3.8 + 0.41x$	0.41

Linking beta with required returns: the security market line (SML)

The **security market line** (SML) – shown in Figure 12.3 – can give the cost of equity for any given share or investment. The SML indicates the risk-adjusted return required for any level of systematic risk.

FIGURE 12.3 The security market line

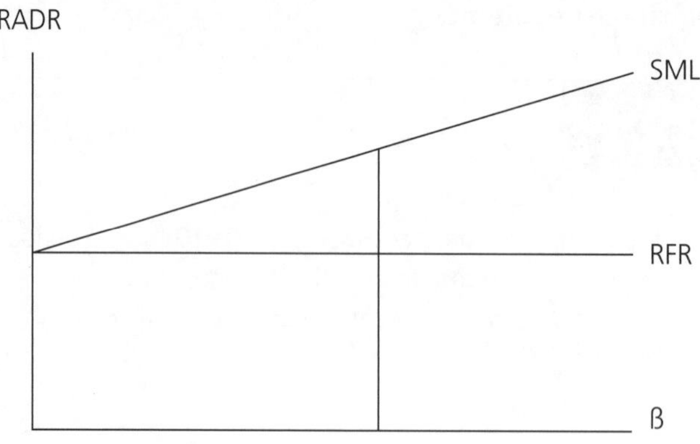

RADR = risk adjusted discount rate
SML = security market line
RFR = risk-free rate

The cost of any capital is known as the risk-adjusted discount rate (RADR). Risk-free capital (e.g. UK gilts) has a beta of 0. Any share with a beta in excess of zero will have a risk premium added to the risk-free rate. The higher the beta, the greater is the risk attached to a specific share. The beta for the market as a whole is 1; a share with a beta that is less than 1 will have an RADR lower and to the left of this. If a share has a beta greater than 1, the RADR will be higher and to the right of this.

The SML provides the opportunity to calculate a required market return for any degree of systematic risk. In a competitive market the expected risk premium varies in direct proportion to beta, therefore the returns for each share must lie on the SML. This demonstrates the excess return required when a share is added to the existing market portfolio because excess return is directly related to the systematic risk of that share.

The equation of the SML can be used to determine the cost of equity:

$$RADR = RFR + \beta(RM - RFR)$$

where:
RFR = risk-free rate of interest
RM = return on the stock market portfolio
β = the statistically derived beta of the share

WORKED EXAMPLE 12.10

We will make use of the data from Worked example 12.9. We are also informed that the risk-free rate is 3% and the return on the market portfolio is 6%.

For equity 1 (beta = 1):

$$RADR = 3\% + 1(6\% - 3\%) = 3\% + 3\% = 6\%$$

For equity 2 (beta = 1.54):

$$RADR = 3\% + 1.54(6\% - 3\%) = 3\% + 4.62\% = 7.62\%$$

For equity 3 (beta = 0.41):

$$RADR = 3\% + 0.41(6\% - 3\%) = 3\% + 1.23\% = 4.23\%$$

12.11

The risk-free rate of interest is 5% and the return on the market portfolio is 11%.

Required

Calculate the RADR for the following companies:

Company A: beta = 0.95
Company B: beta = 1.6
Company C: beta = 2.5.

Solution

A	RADR = 5 + 0.95(11 − 5)	= 10.7%
B	RADR = 5 + 1.6(11 − 5)	= 14.6%
C	RADR = 5 + 2.5(11 − 5)	= 20.0%

3.3 Assumptions underpinning CAPM

The assumptions underpinning CAPM are set out below, together with some comments on how far they hold in practice.

- Investors are rational and require greater return for taking greater risks; empirical evidence supports this.
- Individual investors can efficiently diversify away unsystematic risk. However, in practice, investors may not diversify as much as assumed by CAPM. It requires cost and effort for an investor to manage a portfolio of investments actively.
- There are equal borrowing and lending rates. In practice, however, borrowing rates are generally higher than lending rates. CAPM can be modified to accommodate this and the results remain the same.
- There are no transaction costs. However, the existence of transaction costs means that investors may not undertake all required transactions to make their portfolios efficient. Thus, the SML may be a band rather than a line.
- There are no market imperfections. Beyond the short term, the market imperfections of lack of divisibility of investments, fixed charges and imperfect information mean that the model has poor predictive ability.
- Risks of insolvency are ignored, yet these must be considered by the investor.
- Expectations are homogenous. Clearly not all investors have the same view on the prospects of securities. However, when this assumption is relaxed, it has been found that CAPM retains its predictive abilities.
- The risk-free rate is equal to the return on government bonds. In practice, there are many different government securities with different rates of return.
- There is no taxation. However, when this is relaxed, the CAPM has still been found to maintain its predictive abilities.
- There is no inflation. When this is incorporated into the model, however, it can still predict the required returns accurately.

3.4 Other criticisms of CAPM

A range of other criticisms have been levelled against the use of CAPM.

- Historically, it seems that during some periods, the linearity of the SML has been lost, with changes of gradient at different levels of beta.
- Some researchers have found a relationship between excess returns and other measures than beta, such as firm size and book/market value.

- Obtaining the beta of an investment project is operationally difficult. It is usual to use the beta of the company, but the project's systematic risk may be different, yet its beta cannot be derived statistically as the project is not traded on the stock market.
- A large company will have a number of divisions; for example, a multinational oil company will have separate divisions for exploration, production, distribution and filling stations. The company will have a single beta based on its stock market performance, yet the systematic risk is likely to be different for projects in these different divisions.
- The model is a one-year model only and requires re-computing each year. Thus long-term projects are to be appraised using a discount rate based on a one-year model.

4 Cost of preference shares

The formula for calculating the cost of preference shares is:

$$K_p = D_p/S_p$$

where:

K_p = cost of preference shares
D_p = fixed dividend based on the nominal value of the shares
S_p = market price of preference shares.

WORKED EXAMPLE 12.12

Anorak plc has 8% preference shares, which have a nominal value of £1 and a market price of 80p.

Required

What is the cost of preference shares?

Solution

$$K_p = 8/80 = 0.1$$

The cost of preference shares is 10%.

5 Cost of debt capital

Debentures can be either irredeemable or redeemable after a fixed period. It is important that you know the type of debenture a firm has in issue when calculating its cost of capital because the approach varies with the form of debentures being considered.

The 'par value' or nominal value is the face value of a security, as opposed to its market value. The par value is fixed, whereas the market value varies as supply and demand for a marketable security varies.

Corporate bonds and debentures are available in units of £100; this is the par value or nominal value and is the basis for calculating the interest payable.

5.1 Irredeemable debt

The formula for calculating the after-tax cost of debt is:

$$K_d = \frac{I(1 - t)}{S_d}$$

where:

K_d = cost of debt capital
I = annual interest
t = corporation tax rate
S_d = market price of debt.

You will notice that the formula is similar to that for calculating the cost of preference shares. Both formulae incorporate market prices and both the preference dividends and annual interest are of fixed amounts. However, the rate of corporation tax comes into the irredeemable debt formula because interest can be offset against taxation, which lowers the net rate and thus the cost of debt capital. The higher the rate of corporation tax payable by the company, the lower will be the after-tax cost of debt capital. Thus the cost of debt capital is lower than the cost of preference shares with the same coupon rate and market value as the debentures as there is no tax relief on preference dividends. The effect of tax relief on the interest cost only applies if the business has taxable profits from which to deduct its interest payments. If there is a taxable loss for the year, there is no immediate tax relief for loan stock interest, but the interest increases taxable losses, which can be carried forward and set against profits in future years.

WORKED EXAMPLE 12.13

A company has, in issue, 20% irredeemable debentures which have a market price of £96 per £100 par value. The corporation tax rate is 35%.

Required
What is the cost of debt both before and after tax?

Solution
The cost of debt before tax is:

$$K_d = \frac{20}{96} = 0.208$$

The before-tax cost of debt is 20.8%

The cost of debt after tax is:

$$K_d = \frac{20(1 - 0.35)}{96} = 0.135$$

The after-tax cost of debt is 13.5%.

WORKED EXAMPLE 12.14

A company has, in issue, 9% irredeemable debentures which have a market price of £102 per £100 par value. The corporation tax rate is 30%.

Required
What is the cost of debt?

Solution

$$K_d(1 - t) = \frac{9(1 - 0.3)}{102} = 6.3/102 = 0.062$$

The cost of debt is 6.2%.

5.2 Redeemable debt

Redeemable debt is payable at a fixed future date. The cost of debt capital can be found using the internal rate of return (IRR) (see Chapter 4).

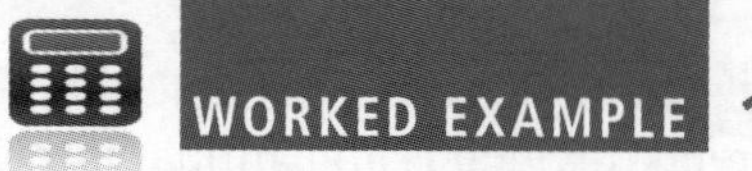

WORKED EXAMPLE 12.15

A company issues a debenture at a market price of £98.1. The debenture is redeemable in five years' time at its par value of £100. The nominal rate of interest on the debenture is 8.75%. The corporation tax rate is 20%.

Required

Calculate the cost of debt for this debenture using discount rates of 5% and 10% in arriving at your solution.

Solution

The annual after-tax cost of debt is:

= I(1 – t)
= .0875(1 – 0.2) = 0.07 = 7%

Year	Cash flow £	5% discount rate		10% discount rate	
		Discount factor	Present value	Discount factor	Present value
0	98.1	1	98.100	1	98.100
1–5	–7	4.329	–30.303	3.791	–26.537
5	–100	0.784	–78.400	0.621	–62.100
NPV			–10.603		9.463

IRR = 0.05 + [–10.603/(–10.603 – 9.463) × (0.10 – 0.05)]
= 0.05 + [0.528 × (0.10 – 0.05)]
= 0.05 + 0.0264
= 0.0764 = 7.64%

From the company's viewpoint, this debenture would cost approximately 7.64%, after corporation tax, over the five-year period.

Note: The discount rates of 5% and 10% were selected for convenience (as is the case when estimating the IRR). Other rates would have been equally acceptable and, because of the limitations of this method of estimation, would have resulted in a different answer. In deriving an IRR it is important that discount rates giving a positive and negative NPV are used.

WORKED EXAMPLE 12.16

Plop plc currently has a 6% debenture priced at £99 per £100 par value. Interest has just been paid. The debenture is redeemable at par in six years' time. The tax rate is 20%.

Required

What is the after-tax cost of debt for this debenture?

WORKED EXAMPLE 12.16 *continued*

Solution

Year	Cash flow £	4% discount rate		6% discount rate	
		Discount factor	Present value	Discount factor	Present value
0	99	1	99.00	1	99.00
1–6	–4.8*	5.2421	–25.16	5.0757	–24.36
6	–100	0.79	–79.00	0.705	–70.50
NPV			–5.16		4.14

*The after-tax cost of debt interest = 0.06(1 – 0.2) = 0.06(0.8) = 0.048 = 4.8%

IRR = 0.04 + [–5.16/(–5.16 – 4.9) × (0.06 – 0.04]

= 0.04 + [5.16/10.06) × 0.02]

= 0.0502 = 5.02%

From the company's viewpoint, this debenture would cost approximately 5.02%, after corporation tax, over the six-year period.

6 Weighted average cost of capital (WACC)

In calculating WACC, the cost of each type of capital in the company is weighted by its proportional value in the total market value of the company.

$$\text{WACC} = K_e \times \left[\frac{E}{E + D}\right] + K_d(1 - t) \times \left[\frac{D}{E + D}\right]$$

where:

K_e = cost of equity capital
K_d = cost of loan capital (or debt)
E = the total market value of equity (ex div)
D = the total market value of debt (ex interest)
t = the rate of corporation tax.

Note that in the UK, interest on loan capital (debt capital) is allowable as a charge against income. Therefore, the tax bill will be reduced if interest is paid.

Note also, that there are two ways to estimate the cost of equity:

- the dividend valuation model or dividend growth model
- the CAPM

so be prepared to use either of these two approaches when estimating the WACC.

WORKED EXAMPLE 12.17

The following is an extract from Blug plc's statement of financial position.

Ordinary share capital (issued) 20p shares	£200,000
Reserves	£700,000
Debentures 12%	£500,000

WORKED EXAMPLE 12.17 *continued*

The company has 1 million shares in issue, which are currently trading at £3.95 (ex div). The company is about to pay the annual dividend of 35p. Historically dividends have grown at 8%. The debentures, which are irredeemable, are trading at £106 per £100 nominal. The rate of corporation tax is 30%.

Required

Calculate the company's WACC.

Solution

Here the dividend growth model is used as information on dividends and growth rates permit its use. Calculate K_e:

$$K_e = [D_0(1 + g)/P_0] + g$$
$$= [0.35(1 + 0.08)/3.95] + 0.08 = 0.096 + 0.08$$
$$= 0.176$$

Calculate $K_d(1 - t)$:

$$K_d(1 - t) = 12(1 - 0.3)/106$$
$$= 0.079$$

Calculate weighted costs of capital:

		Market value: £	**Weight: %**	**K**	**K × weight**
E	1,000,000 × 3.95 =	3,950,000	88	0.176	0.155
D	500,000 × 106/100 =	530,000	12	0.079	0.009
E + D		4,480,000	100		
				WACC	0.164

The WACC of the company is 16.4%

6.1 Can the WACC be used as a discount rate for a project?

There are some potential problems with using WACC as the discount rate for new projects.

- The way the project is financed will change the company's level of gearing. This might, as we discuss in detail in Chapter 13, have an impact on the cost of capital.
- A project might have different risk characteristics to the company's existing projects. A company that diversifies into a different industry should not use the company's existing WACC because it reflects the average risk of the firm's existing projects.

WORKED EXAMPLE 12.18

Wye plc is currently evaluating a proposal to manufacture a new product, which will involve opening a new factory. A detailed discounted cash flow has been carried out, and it is envisaged that an initial capital investment of £3 million is required.

The company's current authorised share capital consists of 4 million ordinary shares, each with a nominal value of 25p. During the past few years the number of shares in issue has remained constant at 3 million, and the market price per share is 135p (ex div). The company has just paid a dividend of 16.2p per share and historically dividends have been growing at the rate of 5% per annum.

Wye plc also has irredeemable debenture loan stock of £2.2 million nominal. The current market price of these debentures is £85.50 per £100 and the coupon rate is 12%. The corporation tax rate is 20%.

WORKED EXAMPLE 12.18 *continued*

Required

(a) Calculate the WACC for Wye plc.

(b) Explain briefly to the directors of Wye plc what assumptions they are making if they use the WACC calculated in (a) above to discount the budgeted cash flows of the project.

Solution

(a) $K_e = 16.2(1.05)/135 + 0.05 = 0.176 = 17.6\%$

$K_d(1 - t) = [12(1 - 0.2)]/85.5 = 0.112 = 11.2\%$

Market value of equity = 3,000,000 × 135 = £4,050,000

Market value of debt = £2,200,000 × 0.855 = £1,881,000

	Market value £ million	Weight	K %	K(W) %
Equity (E)	4.050	0.683	17.6	12.02
Debt (D)	1.881	0.317	11.2	3.55
E+D	5.931	1.000		
			WACC	15.56

The WACC of the company is 15.56%

(b) It is assumed that:

(i) the project is of similar risk to the existing company

(ii) the gearing of the company does not change as that will change the cost of capital.

CHAPTER SUMMARY

The chapter initially explained the importance of the cost of capital and how it is related to risk. Its importance in helping to determine capital structure and in making investment appraisal decisions was discussed. The chapter went on to examine two very different approaches to the cost of equity. It looked first at the dividend valuation model and the dividend growth model. Then it examined the capital asset pricing model (CAPM). Both are important. It then considered the cost of preference shares. Determining the cost of debt is much more complex due to its tax efficiency and also its redeemable nature. The chapter ended by demonstrating how the costs of the different sources of finance are combined to give the weighted average cost of capital (WACC). WACC provides the discount rate for use in project appraisal, which was covered in Chapter 4.

END OF CHAPTER QUESTIONS

12.1 (a) Describe the purpose of the dividend growth model.

(b) Give the formula for the dividend growth model and state the underlying assumptions.

(c) A company has a share value of £1.27 ex div and has recently paid a dividend of 8p per share. Dividend growth is expected to be 3% per year into the foreseeable future. Calculate the cost of equity.

12.2 (a) Why should the WACC be used to evaluate the required return on a project?

(b) Calculate the WACC from the following information.

Capital	Statement of financial position value	Market value
Ordinary shares: 20,000 50p shares	£10,000	£1.72 per share
8% preference shares at £1 nominal value	£5,000	£0.98 per share
Non-current liabilities: 10% debentures	£7,500	£104 per £100

The cost of equity has been calculated at 9.5%. The corporation tax rate is 30%.

END OF CHAPTER QUESTIONS *continued*

12.3 You currently hold two securities that have the following features:

Security A a share with a beta value of 1.0 and an expected return of 13%.

Security B a risk-free security with a return of 6%.

Security A lies on the SML.

You now have the opportunity of acquiring the following shares:

Share	Current return	Beta
C	15%	0.8
D	20%	2.0
E	12%	1.1
F	30%	3.4

In each case indicate the relationship of the specific security (C to F) to the SML and discuss whether it is worth purchasing each of the above securities.

12.4 (a) What does the beta factor of a share tell us?

(b) Calculate the return on a particular share with a beta factor of 0.7. The return on risk-free government securities is 6.5%. The return on the market portfolio is 9%.

(c) What would happen if the return on the market portfolio increased to 12% or, alternatively, fell to 5%.

12.5 You have recently been appointed company secretary to Spider plc and have been asked by the managing director to estimate the company's WACC. You have ascertained the following information.

- The company is financed by 50 million £1 shares with a market price of £1.20 and reserves and share premium accounts totalling £100 million.
- A dividend of 2.25p has just been paid, an increase of 20% on the previous year (this is the normal annual increase in dividend).
- The rate of corporation tax is 30%.
- The company's shares have a beta of 1.6.
- The return on government stocks is 4.5% and the return on the market is 14%.
- In addition to equity, the company has £20 million (at market value) of debt in its capital structure at a pre-tax cost of 12%.

The managing director has recently read that there are different methods available for calculating the cost of equity and is particularly interested that you calculate the overall cost of capital using first the dividend growth model and then the CAPM.

Prepare a briefing note providing the managing director with the figures she requires, explaining any resulting differences.

Capital structure

13

■ CONTENTS

1 The meaning of capital structure

Capital structure refers to the make-up of the 'equity and liabilities' section of a company's statement of financial position. Specifically, it is concerned with the balance between equity (shares and retained earnings) and non-current liabilities. The non-current liabilities may be described as loans, debentures or fixed-return capital. The extent to which such liabilities contribute to a company's financing is termed 'financial gearing'. In other words, financial gearing is related to the presence of fixed-return capital, such as loans or debentures, in the capital structure of a company.

2 Measuring financial gearing

There are two complementary approaches to measuring a company's gearing: the statement of financial position basis and the earnings basis.

2.1 Statement of financial position basis

This also allows for two complementary approaches: the book value approach, using values on the face of the statement of financial position, and the market value approach, using values taken from the stock market.

The book value approach has two advantages:

- the figures are audited and reliable, and
- it reveals the managerial gearing strategy.

However, it has one disadvantage:

- it is based on historic as well as current values and this can reduce its usefulness.

The advantage of the market value approach is that it gives up-to-date valuations, which are realistic because the stock market decides what the company is worth. However:

- it can only be used for quoted companies (market values will be unavailable for private companies, partnerships and sole traders)
- this approach may not reflect the long-term position since short-term factors (such as strikes) have a temporary adverse impact on share prices and can lead to an unrepresentative gearing ratio.

Using the book value approach:

$$\text{gearing ratio} = \frac{\text{non-current liabilities}}{\text{total equity plus non-current liabilities}}$$

Using the market value approach:

$$\text{gearing ratio} = \frac{\text{market value of non-current liabilities}}{\text{market value of equity plus market value of non-current liabilities}}$$

2.2 Earnings basis

The earnings basis uses two measures. The interest cover ratio indicates how many times greater profit before interest and tax (PBIT) is than annual interest payments. The higher this is, the less risk is involved.

It is also possible to look at the impact of changes to PBIT on EPS.

$$\text{interest cover ratio} = \frac{\text{PBIT}}{\text{annual interest payments}}$$

$$\text{effect on EPS} = \frac{\%\ \text{change in EPS}}{\%\ \text{change in EBIT}}$$

2.3 Gearing ratio calculations

Financial information about two companies is as follows.

13.1

Company X: statement of financial position extract	£ million
£1 ordinary shares	100
Reserves	125
5% debenture stock	40
10% debenture stock	20
	285
Statement of profit or loss extract	
Sales	350
Variable costs	80
Fixed costs	130
PBIT	140
Interest payments	4
Market values	
£1 ordinary shares	254p
5% debenture stock	85%
10% debenture stock	96%
Company Y: statement of financial position extract	**£ million**
£1 ordinary shares	200
Reserves	28
10% debenture stock	130
12% debenture stock	80
	438

WORKED EXAMPLE 13.1 *continued*

Statement of profit or loss extract	
Sales	500
Variable costs	100
Fixed costs	320
PBIT	80
Interest payments	22.6
Market values	
£1 ordinary shares	155p
10% debenture stock	105%
12% debenture stock	110%

For both companies, the following are to be calculated:

- book value debt/total book value
- market value debt/total market value
- interest cover
- operating gearing = (revenues – variable operating costs)/PBIT.

The calculations for Company X are given below.

	Company X
Book value of non-current liabilities/ book value (non-current liabilities plus equity)	60/285 = 21%
Market value of non-current liabilities Market value (non-current liabilities plus equity) Market value of non-current liabilities/ market value (non-current liabilities plus equity	[(40 × 85%) + (20 × 96%)] = (34 + 19.2) = 53.2 (53.2) + (100 × 2.54) = (53.2 + 254) = 307.2 53.2/307.2 = 17.3%
Interest cover (PBIT/I)	140/4 = 35
Operating gearing	(350 – 80)/140 = 1.9

Required

Carry out the same calculations for Company Y:

1. book value debt/total book value
2. market value debt/total market value
3. interest cover
4. operating gearing = (revenues – variable operating costs)/PBIT.

Solution

	Company Y
1 Book value of non-current liabilities/ book value (non-current liabilities plus equity)	(130 + 80)/438 = 210/480 = 48%
2 Market value of non-current liabilities/ market value (non-current liabilities plus equity)	[(1.05 × 130) + (1.10 × 80)] = 224.5 224.5/[224.5 + (200 × 1.55)] = 224.5/534.5 = 42%
3 Interest cover (PBIT/I)	(500 – 420)/22.6 = 80/22.6 = 3.5
4 Operating gearing	(500 – 100)/80 = 400/80 = 5

3 Financial gearing and its effect on risk and return

3.1 Why do companies have financial gearing?

The reasons why a company would have financial gearing are listed below:

- fixed return securities, due to their lower risk, require a lower annual return than does equity – so, for a company, loans are cheaper than equity
- interest payments are recognised for taxation purposes as a legitimate expense item – therefore, fixed interest capital confers a tax shield benefit to the company since interest is charged before taxable profit is calculated
- to retain control of the company – this applies particularly to small companies, management buyouts and leveraged buyouts, and
- if a company wishes to expand, issuing equity will, in the shortterm, cause the dilution of earnings by sharing the company's equity among a greater number of shareholders. Issuing debt avoids this problem.

3.2 The dangers of gearing

Financial gearing has inherent dangers, as outlined below.

- The company becomes more risky – for example:
  - earnings per share will become more variable
  - there may be an increasing danger that interest may be unpaid, particularly where the interest bill becomes very high relative to PBIT.
- The company is committed to paying interest and may face difficulties in managing working capital. This is because interest payments are a significant cash drain on the business.
- At some point, the principal will need to be repaid or refinanced and the company must ensure that it is able to do this by the due dates.
- The company may be more sensitive to external or environmental changes such as:
  - supply problems which cause PBIT to fall
  - labour disputes which also cause PBIT to fall
  - increases in interest rates, which increase demands on the company's working capital.

Note that in the rest of this chapter the term 'debt' refers to 'non-current liabilities'.

13.2

For the purposes of what follows, financial gearing will be measured as:

(market value of debt/market value of equity plus debt) %

The capital structure of companies X and Y is as follows.

	Company X	Company Y
Book values	£000s	£000s
Ordinary shares of £1	8,000	1,000
Reserves	1,000	1,000
10% debenture stock	1,000	8,000
Market values		
Ordinary shares	12,000	2,000
Debentures	1,000	7,000

WORKED EXAMPLE 13.2 *continued*

There are three estimates of PBIT: £750,000, £850,000 and £1,200,000.

The corporation tax rate is 35%.

Projected income statements for both companies are as follows.

Company X:

gearing % = market value of debt/market value of equity plus debt
= 1,000/13,000 = 7.6%

	£000s	£000s	£000s
PBIT	750	850	1,200
Annual interest	100	100	100
Net profit before tax	650	750	1,100
Corporation tax (35%)	228	263	385
Available to equity	428	488	715
EPS (pence)	5.28	6.1	8.9

Company Y:

gearing % = market value of debt/market value of equity plus debt
= 7,000/9,000 = 78%

	£000s	£000s	£000s
PBIT	750	850	1,200
Annual interest	800	800	800
Net profit before tax	(50)	50	400
Corporation tax (35%)	–	17.5	140
Available to equity	(50)	32.5	260
EPS (pence)	(5)	3.25	26

Commentary

- Company X is low geared. Its earnings per share (EPS) increases slightly faster than its PBIT due to the gearing. Between £850,000 and £1,200,000 PBIT increases by [(1,200/850) - 1] = 41% whereas EPS increases by [(8.9/6.1) - 1] = 46%.
- Company Y is high geared. Its EPS increases significantly faster than its earnings before interest and tax (EBIT). Over the range £850,000 to £1,200,000, EBIT increases by 41% whereas EPS increases by [(26/3.25) - 1] = 700%.
- However, at PBIT of £750,000, Company Y makes a loss. Upside volatility is very favourable to a high-geared company, but downside volatility is very risky.
- Company X breaks even at £100,000, but Company Y breaks even at £800,000. Company Y is far riskier than Company X.

3.3 Gearing and corporate break-even

FIGURE 13.1 Relationship between EPS and PBIT

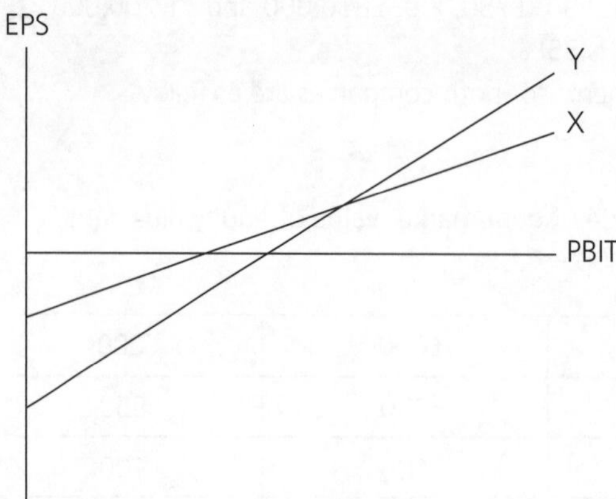

In Figure 13.1, the two diagonal lines represent the relationship between EPS and PBIT for Company X and Company Y in Worked example 13.2.

The intersection with the vertical indicates, in this case, annual interest. Annual interest payments for Company X are lower, so that at 0 PBIT, the loss is lower for Company X than for Company Y.

Company Y breaks even, returning a positive EPS, at a higher PBIT than Company X.

Company Y's line is steeper and, beyond break-even, EPS increases far more quickly with Company Y.

TEST YOUR KNOWLEDGE 13.1

Summarise the main dangers of high levels of gearing.

WORKED EXAMPLE 13.3

The capital structure of companies A and B is as follows.

	Company A	**Company B**
Book values	£000s	£000s
Ordinary shares of £1	4,000	4,000
Reserves	4,000	1,000
10% debenture stock	2,000	5,000
Market values		
Ordinary shares	8,000	7,000
Debentures	2,000	5,000

There are three estimates of PBIT: £500,000, £750,000 and £1,000,000.

The corporation tax rate is 20%.

13.3 *continued*

Required

Prepare projected income statements for both companies using the three estimates of PBIT.

Solution

Company A: Gearing % = market value debt/market value equity + debt = 2,000/10,000 = 20%

	£000s	£000s	£000s
PBIT	500	750	1,000
Annual interest	200	200	200
Net profit before tax	300	550	800
Corporation tax (20%)	60	110	160
Available to equity	240	440	640
EPS (pence)	6	11	16

Company B: Gearing % = market value debt/market value equity + debt = 5,000/12,000 = 42%

	£000s	£000s	£000s
PBIT	500	750	1,000
Annual interest	500	500	500
Net profit before tax	0	250	500
Corporation tax (20%)	–	50	100
Available to equity	0	200	400
EPS (pence)	0	5	10

4 Factors influencing the level of financial gearing

4.1 Business risk

Business risk refers to the variability of the operating profit or PBIT – the total pre-tax cash flow stream available to both debt-holders and shareholders – and the factors that cause this variability. These factors include booms, recessions, strikes, competition, machine breakdowns and other situations that can create opportunities and problems in the normal line of business. One factor that has a bearing on the level of risk of a firm's business is the percentage of fixed costs in the firm's cost structure.

A firm with a large percentage of fixed costs is said to have a higher level of **operating gearing**.

operating gearing = (revenues – variable operating costs)/EBIT

As operating gearing increases, the company's risk increases. With a high level of fixed costs, there is a danger that a relatively small decline in sales can lead to losses since the fixed costs cannot be covered. If a company has a high level of operating gearing, it will be less likely to take on the added financial risk of fixed rate debt than a company with a low level of financial gearing.

4.2 Attitudes of capital suppliers

Potential suppliers of capital or equity will take account of other factors in addition to the rate of return offered by the company.

Providers of debt capital will consider the security offered by the company and the ability of the business to meet its interest payments. In the example of Company X above, debenture interest of £100,000 is covered 7.5 times by PBIT at the lowest level of PBIT quoted. This would appeal to unsecured lenders who might look for interest cover of 3 to 5 times.

In the case of Company Y, even at the highest level of PBIT, interest is covered just 1.5 times, so lenders to Company Y will look to secure their loans on assets of the company.

Loan interest is a fixed charge and ordinary shareholders will be entitled to their dividend only after this fixed charge has been met, a consideration which will influence their decision to invest in the company.

Finally, attempts to increase returns by increasing gearing may not always be in shareholders' best interests. An influx of debt capital may help to generate additional profits, but the market may demand a higher return to compensate for what it sees as increased risk. This may result in lower share prices, reducing shareholders' capital gains.

4.3 Patterns of assets and trading

To some extent at least, the pattern of assets in most companies will dictate the gearing. The use of secured debt capital will require some tangible assets to provide security. If the business has few tangible assets, this will restrict its ability to raise debt. Thus, a research and development programme, which depends on a team of researchers, with distant and possibly uncertain returns, is risky, offers little security and is unsuitable for loan financing.

A second consideration will be the nature of the firm's business. A stable, well-established business, such as a bakery, will generally have less difficulty raising debt capital than, for example, a company engaged in biotechnology research because the market will consider the former, being tried and tested, to be less risky.

Companies in, or about to enter, risky activities, such as developing new markets overseas, will be likely to raise finance through risk capital (i.e. equity). Companies planning less risky activities, such as a large new building for their own use, will often resort to the use of debt capital because of the ease and relative cheapness with which it can be made available.

4.4 Demand patterns

Expanding on the previous point, the demand for the products of a company, or the nature of the industry as a whole, will affect how much debt capital can be raised. These issues are considered in the following three sections.

Industry and individual demand

When industry has no long-term growth prospects, no matter how well an individual company is performing within that industry it will eventually suffer the same problems as the industry as a whole. Even a relatively successful firm in a declining industry should think carefully before taking on additional debt capital, as a long-term fall in demand may make it difficult to pay interest and repay capital. This may not apply if a company in this situation raises capital to diversify into new business areas.

Sales stability

A steady sales record is likely to be taken as a pointer to future sales stability. It will give investors confidence and should make it easier to raise debt capital.

Competition

High levels of competition in an industry that demands special skills (e.g. computer-aided design), or where heavy capital investment is required, or cost-competitiveness depends on having a high level of past production, may discourage new competitors from entering the market. Established businesses in such markets may find it easier to raise debt capital, because the prospect of new competition – which might lead to pressure on profits, making it harder to service debt – is limited. Conversely, where there are few barriers to entry into a market, the prospects of increased competition may be greater and investors may be more cautious about providing debt capital.

4.5 Attitudes of management and proprietors

Many people are instinctively averse to borrowing and, even where borrowing is inevitable, they will try to limit it. Such instincts may influence managers' attitudes to capital gearing.

Secured borrowing, such as a mortgage debenture secured on the company's premises, may restrict the freedom of the business to use its buildings as it likes. Some managers prefer to use only equity so as to retain absolute control of their assets. They would see the difference between the cost of equity and the cost of debt as the opportunity cost of having unencumbered use of their assets. However, this choice may not have a valid basis, as lenders generally show little propensity to intervene unless interest payments are missed.

Other managers may borrow the maximum amount available at present interest rates. This is only limited by financing ability, availability of security and risk. Such a policy may lead to trouble if variable interest rates rise, other costs rise or sales fall. The advantage is that increased debt financing may enable the business to make full use of its resources, maximises the tax shield and, at times of raising prices, the 'real' cost of fixed-rate debt will fall.

13.2

What are the main factors that influence a company's gearing?

5 The capital structure debate

5.1 Traditional view of the relationship of the cost of capital to gearing

Gearing and the cost of equity

Risk-averse investors require:

- the risk-free rate (RFR) plus an additional return for the specific business risk
- an additional return that is related to the gearing of the company – this is regarded as the return for **financial risk**.

Gearing and the cost of debt

Initially, debt should cause the cost of capital to fall as debt is cheaper than equity, and this may be increased by the debt tax shield. However, as levels of gearing increase, the lender will require higher rates of interest in order to compensate for increased risk to interest payments and principal.

FIGURE 13.2 Capital structure and the overall cost of capital

Cost of capital

K_e (cost of equity)

WACC (overall cost of capital)

A

K_d (cost of debt)

Level of debt

Optimum point

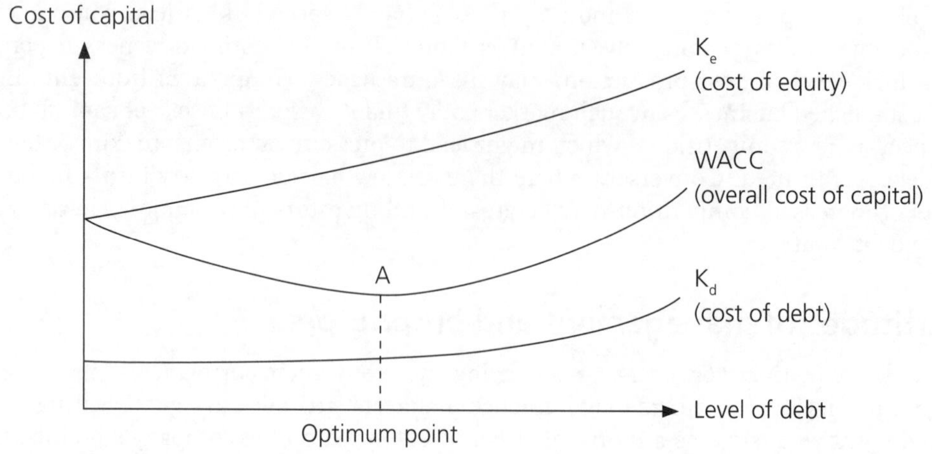

Figure 13.2 shows the traditional view of the relationship between the weighted average cost of capital (WACC) and the level of debt (or gearing) in the capital structure.

The cost of debt is initially at the risk-free rate when there is no gearing. As gearing increases, the cost of debt slowly increases but at a certain point its gradient increases as is shown by line K_d.

K_e is higher than K_d when there is no gearing. This reflects the impact of business risk. However, as gearing increases, the cost of equity increases to reflect the added financial risk of borrowing, which increases the overall risk borne by shareholders.

The combined impact of debt and equity on the WACC is shown in Figure 13.2. Initially, WACC falls due to the infusion of debt, which is cheaper than equity. The low cost of debt immediately reduces WACC. This continues, with WACC falling until a point at which the increasing cost of equity, combined with the increasing cost of debt, causes WACC to increase, and it carries on increasing as debt and gearing increase.

In the traditional approach, the financial manager should aim to manipulate the capital structure to minimise the overall cost of capital, thereby using the lower discount rate to maximise the potential number of positive NPV projects.

13.3

Why does the traditional view of capital structure argue that there is an optimum level of gearing for a company?

5.2 The net operating income approach (or Modigliani and Miller view)

This approach was originally proposed by Franco Modigliani and Merton Miller (1958).

Basic propositions

- The market value of the firm depends **only** on its capitalised future earnings. Earnings are defined as net operating income (i.e. PBIT).
- The company's overall capitalisation rate (its cost of capital) is given **only** by the risk class within which the firm is placed and is independent of the way in which investment is financed.
- The cost of equity K_e = K_e (for an ungeared company based on its risk class) + a premium for financial risk.
- The behavioural foundation for the theory lies in arbitrage, defined as:

  Two identical goods cannot continue being sold in the same market at different prices. Dealers will buy low and sell high in order to profit and this process will bring prices into equality.

FIGURE 13.3 Overall cost of capital: the net operating income approach (Modigliani and Miller 1958 view)

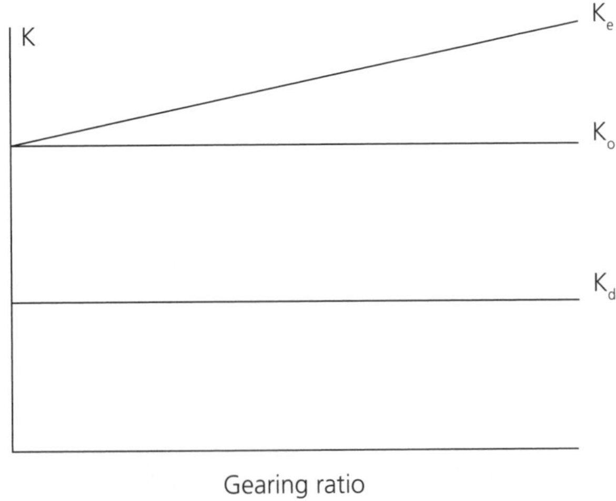

Figure 13.3 illustrates the consequences of these propositions where:

K_o = overall WACC = K_e when the company has no gearing
K_e = cost of equity
K_d = risk-free rate of interest.

According to Modigliani and Miller, as gearing increases, the K_e increases just enough to offset the benefit from cheaper debt and this ensures that WACC does not increase or decrease as gearing increases. This situation occurs because of arbitrage in the stock market and the following illustration demonstrates this at work.

Arbitrage

This example demonstrates the driving force underpinning the Modigliani and Miller model. Two companies are in the same risk class and are perfect substitutes for each other. Company A is in equilibrium. Information about them is as follows.

Equilibrium

	Company A	**Company B**
	£	£
Book values: equity (£1 shares)	100,000	70,000
Debt (5%)		30,000
Totals	100,000	100,000
Net operating income (PBIT)	10,000	10,000
Less interest on debt		1,500
Net profit (available to equity)	10,000	8,500
Assumed cost of equity	10%	11%
Therefore, market value of equity	100,000	77,272
Add market value (MV) of debt		30,000
Market value of the company	100,000	107,272
Overall cost of capital (PBIT/MV)	10%	9.3%

According to the theory, the market value and cost of capital of Company B should be identical to those of Company A because their EBITs are identical and they are in the same business risk class. However, Company B is overvalued as its market value is higher than that of Company A. The following example demonstrates that the differences in market value and cost of capital disappear when arbitrage comes into play.

Company B is geared and the holder of equity in this company is subject to financial risk.

The arbitrage process

Assume that you own 1% of the equity of Company B.

The overview of the process is as follows.

1 Sell holding in B (as it is currently overvalued and must fall in value as market forces operate).
2 Borrow to maintain financial risk at the same level as when you held shares in B (i.e. replace corporate gearing with personal gearing).
3 Invest the proceeds in A (there are an infinite number of As).

Now activate the process.

1 Sell your holding in B for 1% of £77,272 = £772.72.
2 Borrow £300 at 5% (to match the debt/equity ratio in B).
3 Invest £1,072.72 in A.

Outcomes

Process	Cash flow £	Annual returns £
Sell holding in B	+ 772.72	– (0.11 × 772.72) = –85
Borrow £300 at 5%	+ 300.00	– (0.05 × 300.00) = –15
Invest £1,072.72 in A	– 1,072.72	+ (0.1 × 1,072.72) = 107.27
Totals	0	+ 7.27

As long as a positive return can be obtained from this process, this will continue until Company B's market value falls to £100,000.

The reason that personal gearing is used to replace corporate gearing is to show that it is possible to make money while keeping all risks unchanged.

5.3 Gearing in a taxed world

Modigliani and Miller (1963) and the tax shield

The specific tax shield referred to is the reduction in a company's tax bill following the introduction of tax-deductible loan interest into its statement of profit or loss.

Three propositions can be derived from the existence of a debt tax shield.

- The value of the firm increases as the present value of the tax shield is owned by the firm.
- There is a reduction in the rate of increase in the cost of equity as the debt/equity ratio increases; this is because the tax shield reduces the financial risk associated with rising interest payments as corporate gearing increases due to the interest cost being reduced by the interest tax shield.
- As a company increases its gearing, the shareholders derive more and more benefit from the tax shield and the lower the company's tax liability becomes. This continuous and cumulative benefit from gearing results in a declining overall cost of capital for the firm. See figure 13.4.

The above scenario suggests that companies should borrow as much as possible in order to obtain maximum benefit from the tax shield and see their overall cost of capital declining.

FIGURE 13.4 Modigliani and Miller (1963): WACC in a taxed world

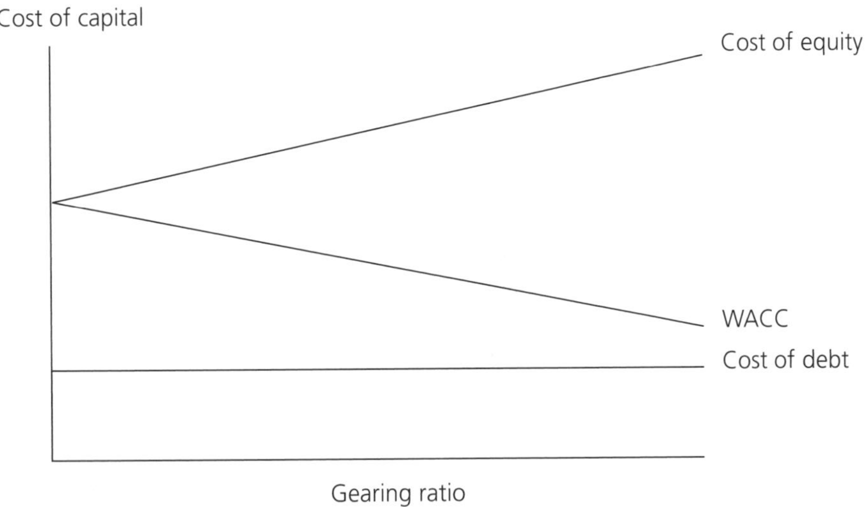

TEST YOUR KNOWLEDGE 13.4

(a) What is arbitrage?
(b) What are Modigliani and Miller's original propositions about the value of the firm and the effect of gearing on the cost of capital.
(c) How did their original propositions change when they considered the impact of the debt tax shield?

5.4 Gearing and taxation in the real world

In the real world, companies are not as highly geared as the foregoing analysis suggests; in practice there is a variety of debt/equity ratios across industries. Gearing does confer a tax shield benefit, so this section will consider other factors that mitigate the level of gearing in practice.

Agency

In this case, the principal is the lender and the agent the directors of the company. The principal will want to ensure that the agent actually uses the loan for its intended purpose.
In order to protect their position, principals may impose agency costs and place restrictions on companies with high gearing:

- They may require that loans are secured on fixed assets. However, companies that wish to borrow may lack sufficient collateral assets.
- Restrictive covenants may be employed. These are usually found within the loan documentation and are inserted to protect the lender. Some of the more common financial covenants are as follows:
  - the regular submission to the lender of financial ratios
  - a requirement that dividend growth is kept within a percentage limit in order to retain cash in the company
  - setting minimum ratios for interest cover (e.g. a minimum of 3:1)
  - restrictions on other forms of borrowing.

- Covenants may restrict managers' freedom of action; for example, a clause preventing material disposal of assets without the lender's agreement, anti-merger covenants that seek to maintain the identity of board members and key members of staff, and assets quality covenants that include obligations to repair and insure assets.

However, these steps also impose costs on suppliers of capital and their response may be to increase the rate of interest on loans.

Financial distress: liquidation

As gearing increases, the possibility of company liquidation increases and the risks of this will tend to restrain gearing. The costs of liquidation may be significant and may be measured by a reduced net asset value on liquidation due to:

- delays arising in the liquidation of assets and losses being incurred on the liquidation of assets, particularly when the assets are highly specialised
- professional fees of accountants, lawyers and liquidators eating into the value of the business
- managers and employees leaving, so the team becomes less valuable and the overall value of the firm falls
- short-term attitudes prevailing and maintenance budgets and investments being cut
- customers going elsewhere, for example to book holidays or to purchase equipment that may require spare parts in the future, and
- the probability that the firm will face problems in working capital management, which will impose costs on the firm and will also tend to drive away suppliers due to difficulties in paying them.

Tax exhaustion

In this scenario the tax shield from debt is reduced because:

- PBIT is low and is less than interest payments
- interest payments are very high, and
- other tax shields are available, such as capital allowances.

If the company is unable to obtain the full tax shield on debt, then this will result in a net increase in the cost of loans.

Lack of debt capacity

This refers to the insufficiency of collateral assets to secure debt expansion. The quality of assets as collateral depends on three factors:

- the nature of the asset – real estate will be preferred to specialised machinery
- the existence of a second-hand market in the asset, providing the lender with the opportunity to sell the asset if taken over by the lender, and
- the rate of depreciation of the asset, which should ideally be low.

If collateral is unavailable, rates of interest will increase quickly as lenders are unable to secure their loans on assets of the company.

Overall effect

The overall result of the four factors detailed above, combined with the tax shield, is that the cost of capital initially falls as gearing increases (due to the tax shield). However, these factors (agency, risks of financial distress, tax exhaustion and debt capacity) cut in to reduce the rate of decline in the cost of capital. Eventually they reverse the decline and this, in turn, leads to increases in the cost of capital when gearing rises beyond a certain level in the debt/equity ratio. This may then have a similar overall effect on the cost of capital to that shown in Figure 13.2 above.

TEST YOUR KNOWLEDGE 13.5

Explain the four factors that counteract the effect of the debt tax shield.

Pecking order theory

An alternative theory on capital structure is the pecking order theory. This theory states that firms will prefer retained earnings and will then choose debt finance followed by equity finance. The order of preference for raising finance will be:

- retained earnings
- straight debt
- convertible debt
- preference shares
- equity shares.

The reason for this is that managers prefer to use internal finance (e.g. retained earnings) rather than external finance. This is partly due to there being no issue costs if retained earnings are used. In addition, the issue costs of debt are lower than those for equity. Therefore, managers prefer to borrow only when internal sources are exhausted, and raising equity finance through the sale of new shares is seen as the last resort. The reason for the pecking order is mainly because of information asymmetry whereby managers know more about the firm than outsiders (Myers 1984). The actions of managers produce a signalling effect when raising finance. Managers are unlikely to issue new shares when they believe that the shares are undervalued. Therefore, in this situation, managers will issue debt rather than equity. This sends a signal to the market that the business is confident about the future and is able to meet the interest payments on the debt. However, managers are more likely to issue shares when they believe they are overvalued. Thus the issue of equity may be interpreted as managers believing equity to be overvalued and they are trying to maximise the sale proceeds. However, shareholders are aware of managers' actions and regard equity issues with suspicion. So if a share issue is made by managers, it sends a signal that they think that shares are overvalued and as a result, the share price is marked down, thereby increasing the cost of equity.

The implications of the pecking order theory are that firms will try to match investment opportunities with internal finance provided that dividends are not unduly affected. If internal funds are not available, then external finance will be issued in the form of debt, and finally further issues will take the form of equity. Under the pecking order theory there is no optimal debt–equity mix.

CHAPTER SUMMARY

This chapter has examined some of the most important aspects of company gearing, such as the reasons why companies borrow. It has examined the impact of gearing on risk and return. It has also discussed the concept of 'financial risk' that arises due to gearing and 'business risk' that is related to the company's area of operation and to the proportion of fixed overhead in its cost structure. The chapter has detailed how to measure gearing using both financial position and income statement measures, and the main factors that determine capital structure in companies have been discussed. Finally, it has considered the capital structure debate, including the work of Modigliani and Miller and the impact of real world factors.

END OF CHAPTER QUESTIONS

13.1 A company is to invest £10 million in a major high-technology expansion. The investment will substantially be in the costs of setting up a research team with highly specific testing equipment. The total investment will need to be raised externally. There are two ways of raising these funds:

- selling two million shares at £5 each
- selling one million shares at £5 each and borrowing the remainder at 16% per annum.

There are three possible outcomes for the PBIT:

Outcome	**A**	**B**	**C**
Probability	0.4	0.4	0.2
	£000	£000	£000
PBIT	800	1,400	2,000

Net profits after interest will be taxed at the rate of 30%.

Required

(a) Calculate EPS at each level of PBIT and weighted average EPS for both financing methods.

(b) Using your calculations in (a) where appropriate, discuss the impact of taxation, risk and asset type on the level of gearing in a company.

13.2 The following information relates to Solka plc, a company engaged in research and development work in the electronics industry.

Statement of profit or loss for year ended 31 March 2015

	£ million
Revenue	4.0
PBIT	2.5
Interest	1.2
Net profit before tax	1.3
Taxation (20%)	0.26
Net profit after tax	1.04

Appropriations

Change in equity statement

	£ million
Retained profits b/fwd	1.87
Add profit after tax	1.04
Less ordinary share dividend (6.5p per share)	0.91
Retained profits c/fwd	2.0

After-tax earnings per share were 7.4p.

Statement of financial position as at 31 March 2015

	£ million
Non-current assets (net)	11.0
Net current assets	4.0
	15.0
Equity	
Ordinary shares of 50 pence each, fully paid	7.0
Retained profits	2.0
	9.0
Add non-current liabilities	
10% debenture stock (2016–2017)	6.0
	15.0

The ordinary shares have a market value of £1.25 and the debenture stock a market value of £143.

The company plans to undertake Project 2015. The project will require an initial investment of £10 million and will provide a positive NPV. The company now has to decide how to finance the project. It is considering two alternative methods of financing: a share issue or a combined share and debenture issue. Each will incur issue costs and each will have to raise £10 million in excess of issue costs in order to provide sufficient finance for the project. Information about the two financing methods is as follows.

- Issue 8,320,000 50 pence ordinary shares at £1.25 each. Costs of issuing these shares are expected to amount to £400,000.
- Issue 2 million 50 pence ordinary shares at £1.25 each and raise £8,200,000 by issuing 7% debentures at par. Total estimated cost of issuing the shares and debentures is £700,000.

The project is estimated to generate the following annual earnings before interest and tax. The probabilities of the estimates are also provided.

Market conditions	**Probabilities**	**Annual EBIT** £ million
Good	0.3	1.1
Fair	0.5	0.75
Poor	0.2	0.65

END OF CHAPTER QUESTIONS *continued*

The company's corporation tax rate is 20%. Average ratios have been calculated for the industry in which Solka plc is positioned:

debt/debt plus equity ratio (book value basis)	39%
debt/debt plus equity ratio (market value basis)	35%
interest cover	2.3
price–earnings ratio	15

The managing director of Solka plc has asked for your advice on the method of financing to adopt.

Required

(a) Calculate for Solka the four industry ratios and comment briefly on a comparison of the two sets of ratios.

(b) For each method of financing, estimate the range of annual EPS generated by the project and the expected EPS. You should not include earnings from existing operations.

(c) Critically analyse the appropriateness of each financing method in this case and develop a reasoned recommendation for the managing director. Along with other issues, you should include in your analysis an examination of the impact of the new project on earnings, debt/equity ratios and interest cover.

13.3 Define capital gearing and give a brief explanation of what is meant by a high-geared company. Who may be interested in the gearing of a company? Give your reasons why.

13.4 Outline the main points of the theories of capital structure of Modigliani and Miller and discuss how they differ from traditional theory of capital structure.

PART **SEVEN**

Working capital management and short-term financing

■ LIST OF CHAPTERS

■ OVERVIEW

This part considers the overall place of working capital within a company and its measurement. It then examines the financial impact of working capital ratios. The components of working capital – inventories, trade receivables, trade payables and cash – are examined in detail and the critical variables with regard to the management of each are discussed. The final element of this part considers the sources of short-term financing, both external and internal.

■ LEARNING OUTCOMES

On successful completion of Part Seven, you will be able to:

- explain the importance and purpose of working capital
- analyse critically policies relating to the overall levels of working capital, inventories, receivables, cash and payables
- apply financial analysis to aid decision-making relating to issues surrounding policies within the working capital ambit, and
- assess the features of alternative and diverse sources of short-term finance and critically evaluate their appropriateness under a range of circumstances.

14 Working capital 1

■ **CONTENTS**

1 The nature and purpose of working capital

Working capital is the total amount of cash tied up in current assets and current liabilities and is calculated by deducting the total amount of current liabilities from the total amount of current assets. Thus, if A plc has current assets of £10 million and current liabilities of £6 million, then its working capital resources are £4 million.

The finance needed to fund a firm's required level of working capital can be either short or long term.

It is essential to ensure that a firm has sufficient working capital to allow it to operate smoothly and have sufficient funds to pay its bills when they arise (taking into account the effects of inflation). However, an organisation should be careful not to hold too large a sum of working capital as this has unnecessary cost implications, a phenomenon known as 'overcapitalisation'.

2 Working capital cycle

An organisation needs to control the rate of turnover of its working capital constituents. Overtrading is usually associated with increasing turnover that is not supported by sufficient working capital (see below). The rate of turnover of working capital can be determined by calculating the working capital cycle (also called the 'operating cycle', 'trading cycle' or 'cash cycle'), which shows the relationship between investment in working capital and cash flow.

Table 14.1 gives an example of a typical working capital cycle for a manufacturing company.

TABLE 14.1 Working capital cycle for a manufacturing company

Raw materials inventory	20 days
Work in progress	21 days
Finished goods inventory	38 days
Period between dispatch and invoice to customer	10 days
Period from invoicing to customer payment	60 days
Total	149 days
Less period of credit taken from suppliers	60 days
Working capital cycle	89 days

WORKED EXAMPLE 14.1

A manufacturing company has the following information relating to its working capital:

	£
Raw material inventory	19,000
Work in progress	15,500
Finished goods inventory	13,000
Trade receivables	27,000
Trade payables	10,000
Sales	140,000
Cost of sales	120,000
Material purchases	70,000

Assume that all sales and purchases are on credit terms.

Required
Calculate the working capital cycle (assume 365 days in a year)

Solution

Raw material inventory days	raw materials/ purchases × 365	19,000/70,000 × 365	99 days
Work in progress (WIP) period	WIP/cost of sales × 365	15,500/120,000 × 365	47 days
Finished goods inventory days	Finished goods/cost of sales × 365	13,000/120,000 × 365	40 days
Trade receivables days	Trade receivables/credit sales × 365	27,000/140,000 × 365	70 days
Total			250 days
Less trade payables days	Trade payables/ purchases × 365	10,000/70,000 × 365	52 days
Working capital cycle			204 days

Of course, wages and other expenses would have to be paid during the period. Steps taken to speed up the rate of working capital turnover (e.g. reducing inventory levels or improving control of trade receivables) will reduce the company's investment in working capital.

Worked example 14.2 illustrates this point.

WORKED EXAMPLE 14.2

A company sells £20 million of goods throughout the 50 weeks of the working year. As sales are partly through retail outlets and partly through mail order, daily sales from Monday to Friday can be considered to be equal.

The firm banks its takings on Thursday of each week and the incremental cost of banking is £50. The company's account is always overdrawn and it pays interest on this overdraft of 15% per annum (in this example to be applied daily on a simple interest basis).

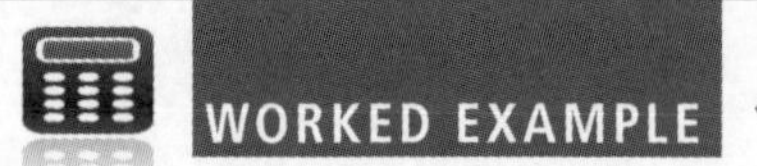

WORKED EXAMPLE 14.2 *continued*

Required

Management wishes to know whether there will be a benefit to banking twice weekly, on Monday and Thursday. Investigate the possibility.

Solution

A total of £20 million over 50 weeks of the year gives a turnover of £400,000 per week and £80,000 per day for a five-day week.

The banking alternatives being considered are assessed below:

Day	Receipts	Banking Thursday			
	£000s	Days' overdraft interest charged per week	Days' overdraft interest charged per 50-week year	Annual interest charged	£000s
Mon	80	3	150	150/365 × 15% × 80 =	4.931
Tue	80	2	100	100/365 × 15% × 80 =	3.288
Wed	80	1	50	50/365 × 15% × 80 =	1.644
Thurs	80	0			0
Fri	80	6	300	300/365 × 15% × 80 =	9.863
				Total	19.726

For interest costs we are using a calendar year.

Note: the calculation could be reduced significantly as the only difference between each calculation is the number of days' overdraft. So, we could:

- sum the number of days' overdraft interest per week = 12 days' overdraft
- calculate the number of such days over a 50-week period = 50 ×12 = 600 days
- calculate the overdraft interest thereon = 600/365 × 15% × 80 = £19,726

The costs of banking on Monday and Thursday are assessed next:

Day	Receipts	Banking Monday and Thursday
	£000s	Days' overdraft interest charged per week
Mon	80	0
Tue	80	2
Wed	80	1
Thurs	80	0
Fri	80	3

The calculations will be:

- the number of days' overdraft per week = 6 days' overdraft
- calculate the number of such days over a 50-week period = 300 days
- the overdraft interest thereon = 300/365 ×15% × 80 = £9,863

14.2 *continued*

Annual incremental banking costs at £50 per transaction are as follows:

- once weekly = 50 × £50 = £2,500
- twice weekly = 100 × £50 =£5,000

The total cost of banking on Thursdays only is = £19,726 + £2,500 = £22,226.

The total cost of banking on Mondays and Thursdays = £9,863 + £5,000 = £14,863, a saving of £7,363 per annum.

There is an even better solution, still banking twice weekly. Can you determine what it is?

Solution

Day	**Receipts**	**Banking Tuesday and Friday**
	£000	Days' overdraft interest charged per week
Mon	80	1
Tue	80	0
Wed	80	2
Thurs	80	1
Fri	80	0

The calculations will be:

- the number of days' overdraft per week = 4 days' overdraft
- calculate the number of days for 50 weeks = 200 days
- the overdraft interest thereon = 200/365 × 15% × 80 = £6,575
- total annual cost = £6,575 + £5,000 = £11,575

This produces total savings over present Thursday-only banking of £10,651.

If such an exercise were to be conducted over a period of several years, then discounted cash flows would be used (see Chapter 4).

3 Working capital needs of different forms of business

The varying needs of three different business sectors will be considered next:

- manufacturing sector
- service sector (little inventory), and
- distributive sector (wholesale and retail).

3.1 Manufacturing sector

For businesses in the manufacturing sector (such as motor manufacturers), current assets can be significant, including:

- raw materials (such as steel)
- components (such as dashboard systems)
- work in progress (such as partly constructed vehicles)
- inventory of completed vehicles, and
- trade receivables (the value of these can be high due to the value of vehicles).

Current liabilities may also be significant because there may be bulk purchases of expensive raw materials.

In manufacturing companies, there is an attempt to reduce inventory holding through just-in-time systems. In this situation, suppliers deliver precise quantities to the production line, each day at specific times, thereby significantly reducing the motor manufacturer's holdings of raw materials and components.

3.2 Service sector

In large parts of the service sector (such as universities or recruitment consultants) current assets will be much less significant and will include stationery supplies, and trade receivables will include students and customers who owe money. It is unlikely that either of these will be very significant.

Current liabilities may include amounts owed to suppliers for services and materials.

The output of a service sector organisation is characterised by the following five features:

- intangible – the service cannot be touched (e.g. an operation by a dentist to extract a tooth)
- perishable – the services cannot be stored (we cannot store the extraction)
- simultaneous production and consumption (we obtain the benefit as soon as the dentist removes the tooth)
- not transferable – you cannot own the extraction and pass it on to a friend
- heterogeneous – each procedure differs slightly.

This explains why this sector has no inventory of finished goods!

3.3 Distributive sector

In the distributive sector, finished inventory will be very high, as this enables purchasing customers to choose from a selection of goods, particularly in the retail sector. Trade receivables in retail are unlikely to be high since customers tend to pay when they acquire the goods. Trade payables may well be significant as retailers will tend to purchase from manufacturers and wholesalers on credit.

4 Ratios associated with the assessment of working capital

In attempting to control working capital, financial managers will use ratios. However, unlike someone external to the company they will not be restricted to figures in the statement of financial position, but will be able to monitor the ratios continuously.

The main ratios employed by financial managers in this area are the current ratio and liquidity ratio.

The current ratio (or working capital ratio) is measured as:

$$= \frac{\text{current assets}}{\text{current liabilities}}$$

As explained in Chapter 2, it is expressed as a ratio (e.g. 2:1).

While there is a target ratio of 2:1, the acceptability of the calculated ratio will depend on the nature of the business, but an outcome where current liabilities exceed current assets generally indicates that the business may be in trouble. In common with all ratios, it is important to monitor this trend to ascertain whether there are potential problems.

The liquidity ratio (or quick asset ratio) removes those items which cannot easily and quickly be converted into cash at their full value (i.e. inventory) and is calculated as:

$$= \frac{\text{current assets} - \text{stock}}{\text{current liabilities}}$$

Again, there is no ideal ratio; what is acceptable depends on industry practice, the company's relationships and contractual agreements with payables and receivables, and the company's working methods. The acceptability of the calculated ratio depends on the industry, although the target is 1:1. In addition, it is the trend over time that is important.

Companies with poor current and liquidity ratios need to have standby overdraft facilities to ensure that they can meet the short-term requirement to service payments of current liabilities. However, too much cash will mean that the firm is under-utilising its resources and a better return could be available elsewhere.

TEST YOUR KNOWLEDGE 14.1

What are the primary ratios used to assess working capital?

5 The financial impact of changes to working capital policies

5.1 Overtrading

This is discussed in Chapter 2 and the symptoms of overtrading, largely of a working capital nature plus the financial impact of those changes, are illustrated by Worked example 14.3.

WORKED EXAMPLE 14.3

Statement of financial position at 31 December				
	Year 1		Year 2	
	£000s	£000s	£000s	£000s
Non-current assets		80		120
Current assets				
Inventory	20		45	
Work in progress (WIP)	20		50	
Receivables	50		120	
Cash	5			
	95		215	
Current liabilities				
Payables	45		138	
Bank overdraft	20		58	
	65		196	
Working capital		30		19
		110		139

14.3 *continued*

Equity				
Share capital		100		100
Reserves		10		39
		110		139

Statement of profit or loss for the year ended 31 December				
	Year 1		Year 2	
	£000s	£000s	£000s	£000s
Sales		500		1,000
Cost of sales		400		875
Gross profit		100		125
Gross profit margin		20%		12.5%
Net profit		30		29
Net profit margin		6%		2.9%

The important points to note are detailed below.

- There has been strong growth in sales but falling profit margins. Turnover has doubled, but the gross profit margin has fallen. Discounts for quicker payment may be the cause, as could lower sale prices to win more orders, or higher unit costs as materials are bought in smaller quantities. Writing off obsolete inventory may also have contributed to a reduction in the gross profit margin.
- The net profit margin shows a big decline. Increased wages and bonuses may have caused this.
- Inventory has increased in relation to throughput. Turnover has doubled from year 1 to year 2, but the total value of inventory and WIP has more than doubled. The inventory turnover ratio has risen from 36.5 days (£40,000/£400,000 × 365) to 39.6 days (£95,000/£875,000 × 365).
- Although sales have risen by 100%, the increase in receivables is 140%. The receivable days have increased from 36.5 days (£50,000/£500,000 × 365) to 43.8 days (£120,000/£1,000,000 × 365).
- Surplus cash from year 1 has been used and bank borrowing has increased.
- Payables have increased by 206% for a rise in turnover of 100%. Credit days have risen from 41.1 days (£45,000/£400,000 × 365) to 57.6 days (£138,000/£875,000 × 365). (The cost of sales has been used to represent purchases. This is often done when calculating creditor days to provide a figure that can be compared with other companies, since published financial statements show cost of sales but may not show purchases.) There could be problems with future supplies if the increased credit from suppliers has not been negotiated.
- The increase in non-current assets may not be related to the increase in turnover. The expenditure may be part of a planned cycle and it is possible that some of the increased business volume might have been achieved through higher productivity using the existing non-current assets. It is unwise to increase capital expenditure using short-term finance such as trade credit and bank overdraft, as appears to have happened here.
- The current and liquidity ratios have fallen, indicating a worsening in the short-term financing position.

WORKED EXAMPLE 14.3 *continued*

- The proprietors' stake (shareholders' funds as a percentage of total assets) has fallen from 62.9% to 41.5%, as is shown in the following statement:

Excerpt from statement of financial position				
	Year 1		Year 2	
	£000s	%	£000s	%
Total assets	175		335	
Financed by				
Share capital and reserves	110	62.9	139	41.5
Payables	45	25.7	138	41.2
Bank overdraft	20	11.4	58	17.3
	175	100	335	100

This company needs to increase its permanent capital to match its increased investment in non-current assets and the increase in its current assets. As all its long-term capital is equity capital, with no long-term borrowing, this company may be well placed to raise long-term debt capital. It has assets to provide security, its non-current assets and current assets suggest that it may be in manufacturing or wholesaling and could have steady income. Its business is profitable, and it may have sufficiently large and steady cash flows to cover interest comfortably (although the information provided does not make this clear).On the other hand, the growth in profits suggests that it would probably be well placed to issue more ordinary shares.

5.2 Overcapitalisation

Overinvestment in working capital leading to excessive inventory, receivables and cash, coupled with few creditors, is known as overcapitalisation. Such a situation will lead to a lower return on investment and the use of long-term funds for short-term assets.

Indicators of overcapitalisation include long debtor and stock turnover periods, high liquidity ratios and a low sales/working capital ratio.

This is the situation where current asset balances are too high. In this situation, working capital is often described as 'not working hard enough'. For example, in a specific industry, key ratios are as follows:

Inventory days	40
Receivable days	35
Payable days	38

A company in this industry has the following values:

Sales	£750,000	
Cost of sales	£400,000	
Average inventory	£64,657	59 days
Trade receivables	£113,014	55 days
Trade payables	£43,836	40 days
Working capital	£133,835	

If the company is able to achieve the industry values, then this will result in a reduction in overall working capital as follows:

	Days	Values	£
Average inventory	40	£400,000 × 40/365	43,836
Trade receivables	35	£750,000 × 35/365	71,918
Trade payables	38	£400,000 × 38/365	41,644
Working capital			74,110

This shows that the company has too much finance tied up in working capital. Its overinvestment is £133,835 – £74,110 = £59,725. At a 10% rate of interest, this overinvestment costs the company £5,973 per year, as well as missing out on the potential opportunities that almost £60,000 per year can offer the company.

WORKED EXAMPLE 14.4

In a specific industry, key ratios are as follows:

Inventory days	45
Receivable days	30
Payable days	33

A company in this industry has the following values:

Sales	£700,000
Cost of sales	£380,000
Average inventory	£66,000
Trade receivables	£120,000
Trade payables	£44,000
Working capital	£142,000

Required

Calculate the working capital savings that the company would derive if it achieved the industry norms for its working capital values.

Solution

Sales		£700,000	
Cost of sales		£380,000	
	Industry norms	Using norms	£
Average inventory	45	45/365 × £380,00	46,849
Trade receivables	30	30/365 × £700,000	57,534
Trade payables	33	33/365 × £380,000	34,356
Working capital			70,027

Savings = £142,000 - £70,027 = £71,973

6 The management of inventories

6.1 The purpose of holding inventory

Manufacturing companies may hold four types of stock or inventory:

- raw materials
- work in progress
- finished goods, and
- miscellaneous items, such as tools, stationery, fuel, etc.

The reason for holding inventory is to provide:

- sufficient raw material stocks to satisfy production needs
- sufficient work in progress (part-finished production) to allow production processes to operate smoothly, and
- enough finished goods stocks to meet customers' requirements.

Stockholding involves costs (as illustrated below) and the benefits of holding inventory need to be balanced against these costs. Achieving a balance can be particularly difficult in distributive and wholesaling businesses, where customers expect a range of goods to be carried, but may only place orders for certain items infrequently. The distributor is faced with the problem of finding a balance between the ability to provide good service (and the reputation for doing so) and the need to restrict the amount of capital tied up in slow-moving lines.

Inventory management is an area where financial managers, in their broad management capacity, are concerned with what is, in fact, a specialist activity. Inventory management can involve computer-based mathematical modelling and scheduling to optimise stockholding and minimise costs.

6.2 Stockholding costs

The principal costs associated with stockholding are:

- providing finance for the money invested in inventory (the cost of the capital was discussed in Chapter 12 and may be the company's weighted average cost of capital, its overdraft rate or its opportunity cost of capital)
- the cost of storage and handling, including rent, rates, maintenance and heating costs for the space taken up, equipment costs, handling and record-keeping, insurance and security
- holding losses arising from evaporation, deterioration, obsolescence, theft and damage in stores and in transit – there may be offsetting holding gains during times of inflation, and
- higher operating costs due to the fact that a production facility that is full of materials is less efficient than one that is not.

6.3 Stock-out costs

These are the costs of running out of inventory and they include:

- loss of contribution through the lost sale caused by running out of stock of finished goods
- loss of future business or of customers
- idle time caused by interruptions to production
- overtime, rescheduling and related costs, arising from the need to expedite a rush order
- lost production, and
- higher prices paid when ordering in unusually small quantities, or with unusually short delivery times, to make good shortages.

Although some of these items may not be easy to quantify, they can all be real.

14.2

List the stockholding and stock-out costs.

6.4 Forecasting future stock levels

In order to satisfy themselves that the level of stock is being kept in proportion to the volume of business, managers use ratios that relate stock to some measure of throughput. One very commonly used measure is stock days.

Stock days are calculated as:

$$\frac{\text{average stockholding} \times \text{no. of days in period}}{\text{cost of materials purchased in the period}} = \text{no. of days' stock in hand}$$

For example, a company has an average inventory of raw materials of £32,600 and annual stock purchases of £220,700. Applying the ratio:

$$\frac{32{,}600}{220{,}700} \times 365^{*} = 54 \text{ days}$$

(*this is for a full year)

If we make the simplifying assumption that stock is consumed evenly throughout the year, we can say that the closing stock of £32,600 represented 54 days' consumption of raw materials. Alternatively, the raw material stocks are turned over every 54 days. This means that stocks are being turned over:

$$\frac{365}{54} = 6.8 \text{ times a year (the stock turnover ratio)}$$

Separate calculations may be done to find the stock days for work in progress (where the measure of throughput may be the value of production or the cost of sales instead of purchases) or for finished goods (where the measure of throughput is cost of sales).

6.5 Levels of inventory control

The 80/20 rule is known as Pareto's law after the Italian economist whose career spanned the late nineteenth and early twentieth centuries.

It is often found that a large percentage (about 80%) of stock value is accounted for by a relatively small number (about 20%) of stock lines. In these circumstances, the smaller number of high-value lines may be subjected to a detailed stock control system, while the larger number of low-value lines is controlled by a simpler and less costly system based on minimum and maximum reorder levels.

Pareto analysis is sometimes called 'ABC analysis' (not to be confused with activity-based costing). In this instance, stock is broken down into three types, depending on its value and usage:

- **A items**: Items with low volume but high cost. These are usually controlled individually and may represent 20% of the total stock lines and perhaps 80% of the total stock value, possibly also necessitating a high level of security.
- **B items**: Items that represent perhaps 30% of the items with, say, 15% of the value. Stocks will be controlled by monitoring stock levels and setting levels at which supplies are reordered.
- **C items**: High-volume, low-priced items where close control is not necessary. They can be controlled by bulk-issue methods such as 'two-bin' systems.

6.6 Inventory management and reordering

The **economic order quantity** (EOQ) provides a formula for calculating the size of order to place when stocks are replenished. It is designed to minimise the combined cost of ordering and holding stock.

Stockholding and ordering costs

Section 6.2 has illustrated the principal elements of stockholding costs. Ordering costs are the costs of obtaining inventory (apart from the purchase price) and include:

- clerical and administrative costs of procurement (e.g. salaries, purchasing office, telecommunications, letters, etc.)
- inward transport costs

- costs of receiving and checking goods when they are delivered
- costs related to setting up equipment, tooling, production scheduling, etc. associated with switching from production of one product to another when inventory is produced in response to internal orders, and
- changes in the unit costs of purchases associated with different sized orders.

The EOQ formula

The basic EOQ formula is based on the following assumptions:

- there are no bulk discounts
- there is a constant price per unit, removing the need to vary the frequency or size of orders to benefit from, for example, temporary price promotions
- there is a known and constant cost of holding each unit of inventory for a given period of time (usually a year)
- there is a known, constant cost of placing and receiving an order
- the rate of use (demand) is steady and known, and
- delivery times can be predicted accurately, so that goods can be delivered exactly when they are needed.

A new delivery of Q units can be arranged to arrive just as the inventory runs down to zero. This means that the maximum stock level, just after the delivery arrives, is Q and the average stock level is Q/2.

As the order quantity increases, the average stock level rises and so do stockholding costs. However, larger orders mean that fewer orders are placed during the year, so ordering costs are lower.

It can be proved that combined costs are minimised (i.e. the reorder quantity is most economic) when:

$$Q = \sqrt{2cd/h}$$

where:
h = cost of holding one unit of inventory for one year
c = cost of ordering a consignment from a supplier
d = annual demand in units
Q = reorder quantity.

WORKED EXAMPLE 14.5

Annual demand for material is 300 units, the ordering cost is £2 per order, the units cost £20 each and the estimated annual cost of holding a unit of inventory is 15% of its purchase cost.

Required
Determine the EOQ and the number of orders to be placed each year.

Solution

c = £2 per order
d = 300 units
h = £20 × 15% = £3 per unit

Substituting into the EOQ formula:

$$Q = \sqrt{2cd/h} = \sqrt{(2 \times 2 \times 300/3)} = \sqrt{400} = 20 \text{ units}$$

Therefore, the number of orders each year is: 300/20 = 15 orders
The total ordering costs are: 15 × £2 = £30

The assumptions made above in order to derive the EOQ formula involve some simplification of what may happen in practice. The assumptions can be modified, and EOQ calculations can be adjusted, to cope with more complicated assumptions, for example:

- discounts for large orders, and
- gradual replenishment, which may happen if items of inventory are made in-house and take a little time to produce.

The calculation of the EOQ assumes that the level of inventory runs down steadily to zero just as the next order arrives. However, because in practice the rate of demand or the date of delivery may vary, firms using the EOQ formula to set order sizes may decide to keep a 'safety stock' or 'buffer stock' to reduce the risk of running out of inventory. This does not affect the calculation of the EOQ.

WORKED EXAMPLE 14.6

Required

Calculate the total annual costs of ordering when:

c = £4 per order
d = 200 units
h = £4 per unit

Solution

$Q = \sqrt{(2 \times 4 \times 200/4)} = \sqrt{400} = 20$ units

The number of orders per year = 200/20 = 10 orders
Total ordering costs = 10 × £4 = £40

Material requirement planning systems (MRP systems)

Traditional manufacturing is organised as a rigid set of departments, processes or machines through which work flows, either following a map or route card for job or batch production or along a production line for continuous production. The time taken to meet a customer's order can be days or weeks, unless the company produces standard products, in which case inventories of finished goods can be held. The time taken to organise and set up production of a batch of products makes it appear more economical to produce large batches – either by waiting for sufficient customer orders to accumulate or by producing items for stock. During the 1980s, however, market conditions became more customer-orientated. The modern customer requires rapid responses from suppliers producing a wide variety of high-quality, low-price products.

Manufacturers have made a series of responses to the changed market environment termed 'advanced manufacturing techniques', which refers to the use of information technology to achieve higher quality and cheaper products more quickly. The techniques include MRP. This 'explodes' the materials specifications for finished products backwards through the production cycle, so that a production schedule can be designed which optimises the ordering and production of the required parts and sub-assemblies. The technique takes a 'top down' approach to the sourcing of all materials used in the production process.

Just-in-time (JIT) methods of procurement

The aim of just-in-time (JIT) procurement is to minimise the holding of inventory. It was originally introduced by Toyota and is now the norm both in the motor industry worldwide and in many other manufacturing industries. JIT procurement is complementary to modern manufacturing methods, including flexible manufacturing.

Advantages of JIT include:

- a reduction in stockholding costs
- simplification of the accounting requirements for raw materials
- a reduction in production lead times
- a reduction in labour costs per unit due to increased productivity, and
- a healthier current ratio and lower working capital requirements.

One aspect of flexible manufacturing is that inventory is minimised throughout the factory, including part-finished goods (work in progress) and finished goods, as well as raw materials and bought-in components and sub-assemblies. Items are produced when they are needed, in response to the requirements of the next stage of the production process. This means that production batches may be small and the traditional approach of maximising the length of production runs so as to reduce changeover costs is abandoned. Instead, flexible manufacturing processes, supported by technology, reduce the costs of product changes so that the costs of short-run, flexible production are kept down.

JIT procurement depends on close cooperation between customer and supplier.

The supplier has to be ready to make frequent, small deliveries, just as the components are needed by the customer. To make this possible, the customer shares information about planned production with suppliers. This includes commercially sensitive information which a traditional manufacturer would never have entrusted to a supplier in the past. Suppliers depend heavily on continuing demand from their customers and are prepared to accept guidance on such things as design and production methods. Manufacturers have fewer suppliers for a particular product than they might have chosen in the past, when they would have been more concerned about the risk of suppliers failing to deliver or using the customer's dependence on them as leverage in price negotiations. Suppliers who might, in the past, have been selected on the basis of price are now selected on the basis of service and quality rather than price.

TEST YOUR KNOWLEDGE 14.3

What are the key features of JIT systems?

CHAPTER SUMMARY

The chapter began by examining the objectives of the provision of working capital, its relationship to fixed capital and the varying needs of different forms of business. The importance of the working capital cycle and the interpretation of working capital ratios were discussed. Overtrading and overcapitalisation were then considered and procedures for forecasting future demand for inventory purposes were examined in detail. Next, the Pareto approach to the management of inventory was explained. Finally, inventory order management methods, such as EOQ and JIT, were considered.

END OF CHAPTER QUESTIONS

14.1 A manufacturing company has the following information relating to its working capital and rates of turnover and throughput:

Components of working capital	**Value**
	£
Raw material inventory	17,810
Work in progress	24,660
Finished goods inventory	37,260
Period between despatch and invoice to customer = 2 days	
Trade receivables	219,180
Trade payables	113,970

Measures of annual turnover and throughput:	
Sales	£2.0 million
Cost of sales	£1.7 million
Material purchases	£1.3 million

Required

Calculate the working capital cycle (assume 365 days in a year, and assume that the value of work in progress is equal to the cost of material plus half of the cost of converting materials into finished goods).

14.2 (a) Explain what is meant by overtrading, and suggest what symptoms you might look for to detect it.

(b) Lambda Ltd is a small computer service company with an annual turnover of £3.6 million. It is growing fast and is planning to increase its rate of growth by offering longer credit periods to its customers, many of whom are also growing fast and tend to be short of working capital. Lambda plans to allow its customers 60 days' credit. Its terms of trade are currently net payment in 30 days, but its customers are taking, on average, 36 days to pay. Lambda is confident that it can get payment in 60 days from all its customers if it implements the change, and expects it to lead to a 10% increase in the volume of business. Lambda plans to increase its long-term capital – which costs 12% – to fund the increase in working capital as a result of the new credit terms.

- Lambda's material costs are 35% of sales, and it receives, on average, 30 days' credit from its suppliers. It keeps 15 days' inventory of raw materials, but has no significant inventory of work in progress or finished goods.
- Other variable costs are 45% of sales.

Required

Evaluate the proposed change.

14.3 A company imports novelty toys for resale to retail stores. The company wishes to adopt a stock management system based upon the economic order quantity (EOQ) model. The company estimates its stock management costs for the forthcoming year to be as follows:

Ordering cost per order £150

Annual carrying cost per unit £1.50

The annual demand is estimated to be 400,000 units.

Required

Calculate the optimum order level using the EOQ.

Working capital 2

15

■ **CONTENTS**

1 The management of receivables

1.1 Introduction

The management of receivables may be even more important than the management of inventory, as inventory items are on the premises and under the control of the company, whereas receivables represent an asset (money owed by customers) over which the company has no direct control.

The issue is, as with all aspects of working capital, one of balance. With receivables, the factors to be balanced are:

- giving credit or discounts, which acts as an aid to sales and potential profitability, and the period over which credit is, or has to be, extended
- the cost of giving credit – effectively the company is lending money to its customers free of charge and needs capital, which is not free, to do so
- the cost of being unable to use that capital for more profitable projects, and
- the cost of collecting debts and writing off bad debts.

These are balanced against the additional gross margin from customers who purchase on credit.

1.2 Receivables' turnover ratio

Financial managers use receivables' turnover to monitor receivables on a daily basis. Receivables' turnover is given by:

$$\frac{\text{receivables}}{\text{annual credit sales}} \times 365 = \text{number of days' sales outstanding}$$

(Where the sales figure is for less than one year, the figure of 365 will be adjusted accordingly.)
A company with receivables of £68,400 and sales during the year of £272,500 has:

$$\frac{68{,}400}{272{,}500} \times 365 = 92 \text{ days of sales outstanding}$$

As with inventory turnover, if we assume that the statement of financial performance level of receivables is representative of the entire year and that sales arise evenly throughout the year with no seasonal trends to take into account, we can say that receivables settle on average every 92 days (i.e. some receivables will pay in less than 92 days and some will take longer).

1.3 Actions available to the company

The physical possession of capital passes from the company when the goods are transferred. Broadly, there are five areas which the company should consider in attempting to influence the level of indebtedness of its customers and the inherent risks that this brings:

- checking the credit standing of the customer and periodically rechecking for any adverse changes
- setting a limit to the level of credit granted to individual customers and laying out terms of trading clearly in writing
- implementing formal collection procedures for delinquent accounts
- negotiating cash discounts for the most valued accounts, and
- taking out credit insurance.

TEST YOUR KNOWLEDGE 15.1

How much of your company's turnover is on credit terms, and what is your average receivables turnover period?

1.4 Credit control

Credit control can be defined as minimising the risks involved in handing over goods upon the strength of a promise to pay in future.

The importance of the credit control department varies with the nature of the business. Some companies sell entirely for cash – this is generally the case with a supermarket chain, for example. Companies that deal with small retail traders usually have to grant and control credit for a large number of accounts, which is a time-consuming process.

Other firms, for example those making large industrial machines, may have a few accounts and may even receive progress (stage) payments from customers as certain stages of the project are completed.

Bearing in mind these variations, the financial manager should consider the volume of business that will be sold on credit terms, the number of customers requiring credit and the records to be maintained when organising the credit control department. Important relationships will develop between credit control and other departments, notably sales and marketing, who may resent 'their' hard-won customers being subjected to status checks.

This chapter now considers some of the most important aspects of credit control.

The credit controller

This function may be combined with the sales ledger department. This is a convenient arrangement because credit limits and the actual amount of credit permitted from one period to the next can be seen easily from the sales ledger records.

1.5 Determining which customers should receive credit and how much credit should be offered

First you should establish the integrity of the business concerned.

- You should confirm the exact name and legal status of the business. If it is a sole trader or partnership, they are personally liable so ensure that you have full details of names and addresses. If it is a limited company, you can undertake a check at Companies House.
- Beware of 'friendly' references that potential customers give you. References that you track down yourself are likely to be far more representative.

Credit limits may be set in advance, in anticipation of a new account, but often no action will be taken until the first order on credit terms has been received. At this stage a credit limit should always be set and this will generally follow enquiries into the affairs of the new customer. In addition to external reports (see section 1.6 below) some of the factors that may be taken into account in assessing a new credit limit are listed below.

- The managerial efficiency and integrity of the business concerned has to be of a high standard. You must be convinced that they will pay the invoiced amounts.

- You must be convinced that the company is able to offer facilities which are on a par with those of competitors. Also, you need to establish the usual credit terms operating within the relevant business sector.
- In order to reduce the risk of non-payment, the company may require some form of security or collateral from the purchasing business.
- The financial strength of the business is important. Look at the capital employed in the customer's business, which may give an accurate indication of this aspect. You should also look at the loans outstanding, the current assets and the current liabilities and pay particular attention to the cash position.
- You should also attempt to assess the business's overall capacity to pay for the goods it receives. As well as the cash position referred to above, do you have evidence of the company's past payments history?
- The nature of the business and the financial strength of the sector in which it operates are vital considerations. How well is that sector operating in the current financial climate? For example, firms in the holiday sector are currently suffering due to the very harsh financial climate throughout Europe.

1.6 Sources and information for assessing creditworthiness

When a new customer is involved, it is essential to check their creditworthiness. Some useful methods of carrying out these checks follow.

Direct methods

- Information can be obtained by the sales team from reports and interviews or visits to the potential customer's premises.
- The credit controller's own judgement can be applied, either based on local knowledge or gained by studying published accounts (or both). The accounts will help to identify the length of time that the potential customer takes to pay other suppliers. A rule-of-thumb check is to calculate the creditor payment period:

  $$\text{trade payable days} = \frac{\text{trade payables}}{\text{cost of sales}} \times 365$$

  using figures from the published financial statements in the annual report and accounts. Cost of sales, which is shown in the income statement, is used here as a proxy for purchases, which is unlikely to be shown.
- A valuation of the company's non-current assets can be made, comparing its liabilities and its working capital and cash position.
- A progressive and carefully managed system of credit can be established, based on the track record of the customer's ability and willingness to pay. Perhaps companies should require new customers to pay by direct debit at the end of the credit period.

Indirect methods

Sources of information on potential customers include the following:

- a report from the customer's bank – the bank is likely to exonerate itself from any liability arising as a result of the report; this may mean that it will not disclose everything that a supplier might be interested in knowing
- references from people who have had dealings with the potential customer (who may nominate suppliers with whom it has good relationships, or whom it has paid promptly for just this purpose)
- information from trade associations – which will have information on notoriously bad payers
- official records – for example, stating whether any directors have been declared bankrupt
- journals, newspapers and other publications, and
- credit reference agencies, such as Dun and Bradstreet or Experian, who will provide a report for a fee.

Generally, it is useful to have a number of opinions before granting credit, but direct methods, while efficient, are potentially time consuming. Experience is needed to interpret the guarded wording in many third-party reports. It is often what they do not say, rather than what they do commit to record, that leads the experienced credit controller to a safe conclusion. This aspect is considered in greater depth below.

Merits and drawbacks of indirect methods

- **Bank reports:** These are often slow and must be made between banks. The wording will always be guarded and it should be borne in mind that the bank may not be aware of all their customers' other commitments. Bank reports possibly have greatest value in foreign trade, where they should be the best placed of all sources to assess the potential risks of the proposed transaction.
- **Trade referees:** Some buyers 'nurse' specific accounts so that they can use them as referees and may even give friends' names without disclosing the relationship. The best use of trade references is as a gauge of potential volume.
- **Trade protection associations**: Information is generally supplied only to members for their own use. Infolink is one of the major players in this market and can provide a status report on any form of business organisation, including sole traders and partnerships.
- **Commercial credit houses**: These organisations are commercial firms which specialise in the collection of credit information. Dun and Bradstreet, Experian, Moody's, Standard & Poor's and Fitch are examples of organisations operating in the UK that provide status reports on companies. In addition to the reporting service, credit ratings are set for most businesses above a certain size and published periodically in books available to members. The rating systems use symbols (often letters) to indicate the likely credit limit that can be set for specific companies.

TEST YOUR KNOWLEDGE 15.2

How many credit checking methods can you list?

1.7 Policies for efficient collection of receivables and reducing the risk of non-payment

An important function of credit control is to ensure that debts are collected as quickly as possible. The following factors are important elements in this process.

- Ensure that you issue invoices promptly. The sooner payment is requested, the sooner it will be paid. Ensure that invoices and monthly statements are right first time. Raising and sending out revised invoices and statements costs resources and can delay the payment due date.
- The credit terms should be clearly articulated at an early stage in the negotiation with a purchaser. These terms should also be publicised on each invoice.
- Customers should be encouraged to pay by electronic transfer or direct debit, this avoids the inevitable delay while waiting for a cheque to arrive.
- If the invoice is large, call the customer before the payment due date to make sure it has been received and that there is no query. This is good customer service.
- Ensure that your credit control department is on good terms with the customer's department that is responsible for payment. It is much easier to telephone when you know who you should speak to and you are on good terms with them.
- Reports supplied to management should include details of any overdue accounts, potential bad debts emerging, volume of new business transacted on credit, previous problems which have been reconciled, and any other specific difficulties affecting credit control. Significant ratios will often be included, such as the ratio of receivables to creditors, the ratio of credit sales to receivables and the ratio of total sales to credit sales. A statement of outstanding receivables illustrating the age of those debts will also be included, termed an 'ageing schedule', but may vary considerably between different industries. A typical statement of outstanding receivables is illustrated in Table 15.1.
- To induce the customer to pay promptly, it is a common feature for the terms of payment to include a discount of around 2.5% for prompt settlement (say, within seven days). Whether

or not the discount can be justified depends on the circumstances. If the discount really does prompt settlement within a much shorter period, it may be justified, but if the money is simply added to an existing credit balance on current account, it would be much better to wait for a more usual payment period of 28 days and then receive the full, undiscounted payment.

- Irrespective of discounts, reminders should be sent out periodically unless payment on invoice is expected. One method of spreading the workload caused by sending out invoices and statements is known as cycle billing and involves sending out bills weekly or daily. This overcomes problems facing the credit control department when everything is processed, for example, in the last few days of the month.

TABLE 15.1 Statement of outstanding receivables as at 31 March 2015

A/C name	**Overdue accounts in months overdue**					**Remarks**
	>1	>2	>3	>4	>5	
	£	£	£	£	£	
Adams		1,400				Telephoned Cheque promised
Bilk				500		Court action
Davies			750			Cheque promised
Franks	3,000					
Gilbert		2,500				Cheque promised
Totals	3,000	3,900	750	500	0	
Sales: current month – March 2015: £x						
Sales: year to date – £x						
Current balances outstanding: £x						

Handling overdue debts

When payments are really overdue, it is essential to take action without delay. This may take one or more of the following forms.

- Make immediate contact when payment has not arrived. Be assertive about what you expect and when you expect it and make the consequences of non-payment clear (e.g. legal action).
- If a customer consistently pays you late or makes excuses, carry out checks on their credit-worthiness and consider whether you are prepared to continue supplying on credit terms. It may be preferable to lose an order, or even a customer, than to supply goods not yet paid for and suffer a bad debt, when you lose both the goods and the money.
- Be polite, professional and persistent. Follow up with reminders and telephone calls. Do what you said you were going to do. Keep a record of all collection activity, which will be important if you have to engage a third party.
- Put a 'stop' on supplies to purchasers who are not paying. Their need for further supplies may lead to payment.

1.8 Financial impact of changes to receivables policy

Consideration may also be given to relaxing the credit period allowed to customers if this is thought to be a profitable course of action. This scenario may be of particular benefit when interest rates are low (and therefore the cost of financing is similarly low) to rebuild trade which has fallen off as a result of recession. However, care should be taken to ascertain the degree of risk in such a course of action. To assess the viability of extending the credit periods offered to customers, the company would undertake a calculation along the lines shown in Worked example 15.1.

WORKED EXAMPLE 15.1

A company with annual credit sales of £1.2 million allows, on average, two months for payment. It is considering changing its terms of trade to require quicker payment. It expects this course of action to lead to customers paying on average in one month, but also anticipates that it will result in a 5% reduction in its annual sales. At the same time, it is planning to offer a discount of 1% for payment in 15 days and expects this offer to be taken up by customers purchasing 30% of its reduced turnover. The company's marginal profit on sales is 20% (before any discounts for prompt payment) and this is not expected to change if the new credit policy is introduced.

Required

If the company requires a return of 16% on its investments, would the planned changes in credit allowed to customers and the discount for prompt payment be worthwhile?

Solution

Reduction in credit to customers and associated reduction in volume of business		
Reduction in working capital		
Present	2 months' credit = 2/12 × £1.2 million	£200,000
New	1 month's credit = 1/12 × 0.95 × £1.2 million	£95,000
	Reduction in working capital	£105,000
	Annual saving in financing cost at 16%	£16,800
	Loss of marginal profit: 20% × (£1.2 million × 5%)	£12,000
Conclusion: the reduction in credit allowed from two months to one month would be worthwhile if the consequent loss of business were limited to 5%.		
Discount for prompt payment		
Reduction in working capital		
30% of new annual credit sales = 0.3 × 0.95 ×£1.2 million		£342,000
Credit: 1 month = 1/12 × £342,000		£28,500
Credit: 15 days = 15/365 × £342,000		£14,055
Reduction in working capital		£14,445
Annual saving in financing cost at 16% × £14,445		£2,311
Cost of discount: 1% of £342,000		£3,420
Conclusion: the discount would not be worthwhile.		

WORKED EXAMPLE 15.2

A company plans to extend its credit period from one to two months, with the intention of increasing its sales by £0.5 million on top of its current level of £1.25 million. The current profit is about 5% of sales and the increased sales would require increased working capital of £50,000 (excluding the trade receivables). The required rate of return is 15%. The company assumes that all customers will take advantage of the new terms.

15.2 *continued*

Required

Calculate whether the new credit policy would be worthwhile for the company.

Solution

The company assumes that all customers will take advantage of the new terms and it calculates that the increased level of debtors would be:

(£1,750,000 × 2/12) – (£1,250,000 × 1/12) = £187,500

So, the total increase in working capital is £50,000 + £187,500 = £237,500.
The financing costs are £237,500 × 15% = £35,625.
The increased profits from the new policy are £500,000 × 5% = £25,000.
Therefore, the new credit policy would not be worthwhile as its implementation would result in a reduction in profit of £10,625.

1.9 Credit insurance

When customers pay late, suppliers may need to find additional short-term capital. This may be available from banks or accepting houses. Some agencies provide short-term capital in combination with insurance against the risk of default. A provider of non-recourse finance takes on the credit risk (the possibility that the customer will not pay) as well as providing short-term funding. In the UK, these services may be offered by banks or by specialist companies, including factors and invoice discounters (whose role and functions are described in Chapter 16).

2 The management of cash

Supplier credit represents a legitimate, and usually very important, source of business credit. However, every organisation must have adequate cash resources (including undrawn bank overdraft facilities) available to meet the financial commitments of day-to-day trading (e.g. wages and taxation). Cash is also required to meet contingencies, to take advantage of discounts and other opportunities available and to finance expansion. Firms should avoid holding too much cash, with the resulting under-utilisation of resources. The quality of working capital management can make the difference between survival and failure, by ensuring that the firm always has sufficient funds to pay what it owes and avoid liquidation. Time spent in credit control can be as important as time spent developing new business.

2.1 Cash flow planning

To understand cash management you need to be aware of the difference between profits and cash flow. From your accountancy studies you will be aware that profit is the amount by which income exceeds expenditure when both are matched on a time basis. Cash flow, however, is the actual flow of cash in and out of the organisation with no adjustments made for prepayments or accruals.

A business which has insufficient cash may be forced into liquidation by its unpaid creditors even if it is profitable. Profitability and liquidity are complementary, and are both crucial. While planning and controlling the use of resources to achieve profitability is essential for a company's long-term success, planning and controlling the use of cash to achieve liquidity may be essential for the company's short-term survival.

A lack of cash can be seen in increasingly late payment of bills. Managers need to plan and control cash flows to ensure liquidity, so that the company can pay what it owes. In the short term, this is done by cash flow budgeting, which can be daily, weekly, monthly or yearly, ensuring that the organisation has sufficient cash inflows to meet its outflows as they become due. Such budgets should fit in with the overall budgetary scheme that the company operates. If a shortfall is expected, then the firm can arrange finance, perhaps by increasing its overdraft.

Other remedies that can be used to deal with short-term cash shortages include:

- accelerating cash inflows from trade receivables
- postponing cash outflows by delaying payment to trade payables – while this is considered to be a cheap alternative (trade payables rarely charge interest), such an alternative increases the risk of insolvency of the firm
- postponing capital expenditure (or negotiating extended payment terms with the supplier)
- reversing past investment decisions, such as selling non-essential assets
- rescheduling loan repayments (with the lender's agreement)
- reducing the level of dividend to be paid, and
- deferring tax payments (after discussion with HMRC), which may incur an interest cost.

Despite it being bad policy to finance long-term assets with short-term funding, where the financial manager can determine from the cash budget that sufficient funds will become available it may be possible to operate such a policy without detriment to the firm.

To help cash management of groups, a facility called 'cash pooling' may be requested by the group's bank. The process of cash **pooling** allows the offsetting of surplus and deficits held at the bank by the group's companies using a dummy account. The net balance is the one on which interest is payable or receivable and the group can then decide how to allocate this cost or income.

For groups which have overseas subsidiaries involved in intra-group trading, the group may net off the transactions between its members on a multilateral basis. While there are some countries which limit or prohibit netting (e.g. Italy and France), the groups should benefit from reduced transaction costs.

A further method of cash management that may be adopted by a multinational firm is to centralise cash management, holding funds in one of the major financial centres such as London or New York, with only the minimum level required for day-to-day purposes being held by subsidiaries. The remittance of funds back to the parent can be done via the group's bank or telegraphic transfer, but restrictions may be imposed by overseas governments on the level of remittances.

2.2 Factors affecting the amount of cash held

The amount of cash that an organisation holds can be affected by a number of unforeseen events:

- new competitors and/or new products on the market may adversely affect demand for a company's products
- consumers may change their purchasing habits (e.g. people are becoming increasingly aware of benefits derived from the use of environmentally friendly products)
- upward movements in interest rates will reduce the amount of cash available to firms that are in a net borrowing situation
- businesses involved in international trade will be affected by movements in foreign exchange rates
- strikes or natural disasters may halt production, or at least significantly reduce it, with a resultant fall in sales volume
- a firm which is growing may need to finance new assets to replace old and obsolete ones; alternatively, if a business continually trades at a loss for a protracted period, cash problems will materialise
- the replacement costs of stock will be at a higher price during periods of inflation; however, competitive pressure may prevent a corresponding increase in selling prices, with resultant pressure on cash resources
- payment delays, due to either the business's inefficiency or external delays, can affect cash flow
- bad debts, for example those caused by a large customer going into liquidation, can create severe problems for a company's cash flow

- large items of expenditure, such as fixed asset purchases or the redemption of loans, can drain cash resources rapidly if planning for the expenditure has been inadequate, and
- seasonal trading can cause short-term difficulties, particularly if a retailer's stocks, bought in specifically for seasonal trading (e.g. Christmas), prove unpopular and do not sell.

There is often a considerable amount of money tied up in the 'float' (i.e. the process of converting a cheque sent by a customer into cash in the supplier's bank). Delays inherent in the process include those in receiving the cheque (transmission delay) and in lodging and clearing it. The use of systems such as bank giro, BACS (Bankers' Automated Clearing Services), standing orders, direct debits and CHAPS (Clearing House Automated Payments System) help to reduce these delays. In addition, local cheques could be collected in person and should certainly be banked on the day of receipt whenever possible.

Margin of safety

No forecast will ever be completely accurate and the further into the future the projections are made, the greater the margin of error. In cash budgeting, the balance at the end of each period represents a margin of safety, whereby the company buys peace of mind at the expense of profitable utilisation of cash. The size of the balance must be related to the certainty or otherwise of the predicted inflows and outflows and the availability of back-up resources, such as overdraft facilities. A cash-based business, such as a food supermarket, will be more certain of its cash inflows than a business selling principally on extended trade terms. Where cash inflows can be predicted with greater accuracy, margins of safety can be smaller.

TEST YOUR KNOWLEDGE 15.3

What can a company do if its cash budget gives advance warning of impending cash shortages?

2.3 Cash management models

A number of models have been developed to help companies manage their cash. These range from simple spreadsheets to more complicated models, such as the Miller–Orr (1966) model and Baumol's (1952) model (see below).The aim of the Miller–Orr model is to trade off the loss of interest involved in holding idle cash balances against the risk of having insufficient cash. The model sets optimal minimum and maximum levels of cash holding.

When these levels are reached, the firm either sells or buys short-term marketable securities to adjust the cash levels. To set these levels, the variability of cash flows needs to be determined, together with the costs of buying and selling securities and the interest rate.

The steps in using the model are detailed below:

1 Determine the lower limit of cash that the firm is happy to hold. This is generally set at a minimum safety level, which in theory could be zero.
2 Determine the statistical variance of the firm's cash flows (perhaps over a three- or six-month period). This measures the variability of the firm's cash flows.
3 Calculate the spread of transactions, using the following formula:

$$\text{spread} = \frac{3 \times \sqrt[3]{(0.75 \times \text{variance of cash flow} \times \text{transaction cost})}}{\text{interest rate}}$$

4 Calculate the upper limit (the lower limit plus the spread).
5 However, to minimise the costs of holding cash, securities should be sold when a pre-calculated level (the return point) is reached. The return point is the lower limit plus one-third of the spread.

WORKED EXAMPLE 15.3

Pat Ltd incurs an overdraft interest rate of 0.1% per day and its brokers charge £75 for each transaction in short-term securities. The managing director has stated that the minimum cash balance that is acceptable is £2,000 and the variance of cash flows on a daily basis is £16,000.

Required

What is the maximum level of cash the firm should hold and at what point should it start to purchase or sell securities?

Solution

Following the above procedure:

1 Determine the lower limit of cash that the firm is happy to hold – this has been set at £2,000.

2 Determine the variation in the firm's cash flows – this has been found to be £16,000.

3 Calculate the spread of transactions:

$$\text{spread} = \frac{3 \times \sqrt[3]{(0.75 \times \text{variance of cash flow} \times \text{transaction cost})}}{\text{interest rate}}$$

$$= \frac{3 \times \sqrt[3]{(0.75 \times 16{,}000 \times 75)}}{0.001}$$

$$= 3 \times \sqrt[3]{900{,}000{,}000} = £2{,}496$$

4 Calculate the upper limit – this is the sum of the lower limit and the spread:

upper limit = £2,000 + £2,496= £4,496

5 Securities should be sold when the return point is reached. The return point is the sum of the lower limit and one-third of the spread:

return point = £2,000 + 1/3(2,496) = 2,832

Thus, the firm is aiming for a cash holding of £2,832 (the return point). Therefore, if the balance of cash reaches $4,496, the firm should buy £4,496 - £2,832 = £1,664 of marketable securities; if it falls to £2,000 then £832 of securities should be sold.

The Miller–Orr model is useful in that it considers:

- the level of interest rates (higher rates give a narrower spread, so less cash needs to be held before the return point and the upper limit are reached)
- transaction costs (higher transaction costs increase the spread and therefore reduce the number of transactions), and
- variability of cash flows (more variable cash flows allow a greater degree of freedom for cash levels).

A drawback of the model is that it assumes that cash flows vary randomly and does not take account of the fact that some cash flows (for example, dividend payments) can be predicted accurately.

The Baumol model of cash management is based on the economic order quantity (EOQ) model for inventory management (see Chapter 14). The model assumes that the firm has cash available in a bank current account for day-to-day transactions. In addition, the firm has funds invested in a short-term deposit account which can be used to top up the current account when required. Any surplus cash can be invested in the deposit account. In the case of cash, the EOQ model can be used, where Q represents the amount of optimum cash injection from the deposit account into the current account. The EOQ equation is:

$$Q = \sqrt{2cd/h}$$

where, for the cash model:

h = cost (i.e. interest rate of holding cash)

c = transaction cost for the sale of short-term securities from the deposit account

d = annual demand for cash.

The model works where cash drawings are uniform and there is certainty. However, its main weakness is that it assumes a regular pattern of cash flow. In reality, cash flow is rarely constant. Therefore, the Miller–Orr model of cash management may be more realistic.

WORKED EXAMPLE 15.4

Pete Ltd expects to have cash payments of £15,000 per week. The interest rate for its short-term investments on deposit is 7%. Transaction costs are fixed at £50 per transaction.

Required
What is the most economic amount of cash to be drawn from the deposit account and transferred into the current account?

Q = √2cd/h
= √2 x £50 x £780,000/0.07
= £33,381

Thus, the firm should draw £33,381 from the deposit account. The frequency of the transfer will be £780,000/£33,381 = 23.4 or about 23 times a year or roughly every 16 days.

TEST YOUR KNOWLEDGE 15.4

What are the key elements of the Miller–Orr model?

2.4 The use of cash flow statements in managing cash

The primary cash flow statement used in managing cash is the cash budget, an example of which is shown below:

Cash budget for a three-month period				
Month	Jan.	Feb.	Mar.	Total
	£	£	£	£
Cash inflows				
Sales				
Loans				
Total cash inflows				
Cash outflows				
Materials				
Wages and salaries				
Repairs				
Total cash outflows				
Monthly net cash flow				
Opening cash balance				
Closing cash balance				

The key features of the cash budget are as follows:

- it emphasises cash, not profits
- the budget shows the planned cash inflows (or receipts) for each month and the planned cash outflows (or payments)
- the effects of these are summarised for each month in the 'Monthly net cash flow' figure
- for each month, the monthly net cash flow figure is added to the 'Opening cash balance' to give the month's 'Closing cash balance'
- as each month passes, the budget can be compared with the actual cash inflows and outflows for the period, and
- it serves as an early warning of cash surpluses so that plans can be made for their investment. It also warns of cash shortages so that the company may be able to delay purchases of capital equipment or contact its bank well in advance of the month during which a loan will be required.

Worked example 15.5 illustrates these features.

WORKED EXAMPLE 15.5

Set out below is Grubacre Ltd's budgeted receipts and payments for the next four months. The company has a bank overdraft of £118,000 at 31 December.

Month	Jan.	Feb.	Mar.	Apr.
	£000s	£000s	£000s	£000s
Receipts from trade receivables	425	380	510	480
Other receipts	20	27	14	93
Payments to materials trade payables	114	153	144	130
Payments for variable overheads	76	102	96	104
Wages and salaries	153	144	156	132
Payments for fixed overheads	41	41	41	41

Required

Prepare the company's cash budget for January to April.

Months	Jan.	Feb.	Mar.	Apr.	Total
	£000s	£000s	£000s	£000s	£000s
Cash inflows					
Trade receivables	425	380	510	480	1,795
Other	20	27	14	93	154
Total cash inflows	445	407	524	573	1,949
Cash outflows					
Materials payables	114	153	144	130	541
Variable overheads	76	102	96	104	378
Wages and salaries	153	144	156	132	585
Fixed overheads	41	41	41	41	164
Total cash outflows	384	440	437	407	1,668
Monthly net cash flow	61	(33)	87	166	281
Opening balance	(118)	(57)	(90)	(3)	(118)
Closing balance	(57)	(90)	(3)	163	163

Solution

Note that bracketed figures are negative and in the 'Total' column, the opening cash balance is that at the start of the period, in this case a negative £118,000.

TEST YOUR KNOWLEDGE 15.5

What are the primary benefits offered by a cash budget?

WORKED EXAMPLE 15.6

Manufactures Co. Ltd issued £300,000 of share capital for cash on 1 January 2015, the date of its incorporation. In the following two weeks it raised an additional £50,000 by way of a loan from its local bank and spent £200,000 on machinery. The machinery is expected to last ten years. The company rents a factory at a cost of £10,000 per month, paid on the last day of each month. Additional fixed costs (excluding depreciation) of £10,000 are paid monthly.

During its first six months of trading, the company expects to sell the following numbers of small, high-quality digital headphones:

January	1,000
February	3,000
March	5,000
April	7,000
May	9,000
June	12,000.

Of these sales, 10% each month will be cash sales, the remainder are on credit with customers paying 40% in the month following the sale and 60% in the month following that. The selling price of each unit is £12.

The company will produce the following number of headphone sets each month:

January	4,000
February	5,000
March	7,000
April	9,000
May	12,000
Jun	15,000.

Materials cost £3 per set of headphones and are purchased in the month of production on one month's credit. Labour costs at £3 per unit are paid in the month of production, as are other variable overhead costs of £1 per unit.

Required

Prepare a monthly cash budget for the company for its first six months of trading. Show clearly the closing cash balance each month and the total cash flows over the period.

15.6 *continued*

Solution

Cash budget:

	Jan.	Feb.	Mar.	Apr.	May	June	Total
	£000s	£000s	£000s	£000s	£000s	£000s	£000s
Cash inflows							
Share capital	300.00						300.00
Loan	50.00						50.00
Cash sales	1.20	3.60	6.00	8.40	10.80	14.40	44.40
Credit sales Month 1		4.32	12.96	21.60	30.24	38.80	108.00
Credit sales Month 2			6.48	19.44	32.40	45.36	103.68
Totals	351.20	7.92	25.44	49.44	73.44	98.64	606.08
Cash outflows							
Machinery	200.00						200.00
Rent	10.00	10.00	10.00	10.00	10.00	10.00	60.00
Fixed costs	10.00	10.00	10.00	10.00	10.00	10.00	60.00
Materials		12.00	15.00	21.00	27.00	36.00	111.00
Labour	12.00	15.00	21.00	27.00	36.00	45.00	156.00
Variable overheads	4.00	5.00	7.00	9.00	12.00	15.00	52.00
Totals	236.00	52.00	63.00	77.00	95.00	116.00	639.00
Net Cash Flow	115.20	(44.08)	(37.56)	(27.56)	(21.56)	(17.36)	(32.92)
Opening balance	0	115.20	71.12	33.56	6.00	(15.56)	0
Closing balance	115.20	71.12	33.56	6.00	(15.56)	(32.92)	(32.92)

2.5 The cash conversion cycle

The cash conversion cycle is the average number of days between the date on which inventory of raw material is paid for and the date when the sales revenue is received in cash.

The longer the cash cycle, the greater the amount of cash that the company needs to finance that cycle. If a company's cash cycle increases from 50 to 60 days, the firm will need to finance cash for an additional ten days.

The cash cycle may be reduced by:

- maximising (or delaying) the time taken to pay creditors for inventory; however, the supplier may refuse to supply goods until payment is made
- holding inventory for a shorter time before it is sold – one benefit of just-in-time processes is that they tend to minimise the inventory holding period
- speeding up the production process so that inventory is turned into saleable goods more quickly, and
- minimising the debt collection period; this can be achieved by putting pressure on trade receivables by sending reminder letters, etc.

Different businesses have different cash conversion cycles, as illustrated below.

- For a retail firm which sells to the public, sales are paid for immediately by customers while wholesalers allow a period of credit. In this situation the cash cycle is relatively short but is influenced by the speed with which in-store stock is sold.
- A manufacturing company selling on credit will tend to have a long cash conversion cycle. It will tend to have a longer inventory holding period as it carries raw materials, partly completed work in progress and finished goods. Because it sells on credit, this introduces an additional period compared with the retail firm selling to the public.

The cash cycle may be measured as follows:

> average inventory turnover period + average rate of payment of trade receivables – average rate of payment of trade payables

Worked example 15.7 illustrates this method of calculation.

WORKED EXAMPLE 15.7

The cash balance of Block Ltd has declined and is causing concern to management. The following information is available:

	2014	**2015**
	£000s	£000s
Sales	573.0	643.0
Raw materials purchases	215.0	264.0
Raw materials consumed	210.0	256.4
Balances at 31 December		
Trade receivables	97.1	121.5
Trade payables	23.9	32.5
Inventory of raw material	22.4	30.0

All purchases and sales are on credit.

Required

(a) Calculate the cash conversion cycles for 2014 and 2015.

(b) Prepare a brief comment on the implication of any changes.

Note: assume a 360-day year.

Solution

(a)	**2014**		**2015**	
		Days		Days
Raw materials	22.4/210 × 360	38	30/256.4 × 360	42
Credit to customers	97.1/573 × 360	61	121.5/643 × 360	68
		99		110
Less credit from suppliers	23.9/215 × 360	(40)	32.5/264 × 360	(44)
Cash conversion cycle		59		66

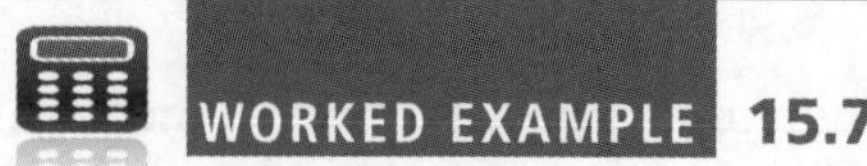

WORKED EXAMPLE 15.7 *continued*

(b) The cash operating cycle has increased from 59 days to 66 days, an increase of seven days or 12%. The increased investment in working capital may be calculated as follows:

	2014	2015
	£000s	£000s
Inventory	22.4	30.0
Accounts receivable	<u>97.1</u>	<u>121.5</u>
	119.5	151.5
Less accounts payable	<u>23.9</u>	<u>32.5</u>
	95.6	119.0

The increase in the inventory holding period is balanced by the increase of four days in the credit received from suppliers (accounts payable). However, credit taken by trade payables increased by seven days and is wholly responsible for the increase in the cash conversion cycle over the two-year period.

TEST YOUR KNOWLEDGE 15.6

Explain what is meant by the cash conversion cycle.

3 The management of payables

3.1 The benefits of taking trade credit and the problems of taking excessive credit

Trade credit is a fully accepted part of business and most transactions are credit-based. The benefit is that it provides a way of gaining credit that does not require the approval of the bank. Once a supplier accepts a firm as a credit customer, trade credit tends to follow automatically as long as the customer makes payment by the due dates.

Moreover, trade credit represents a form of interest-free loan; the customer is given time to pay for the product but interest is not charged during that prearranged period. Trade credit is regarded as a 'free' source of finance in much of the business world, although the necessary system of accounting for payables does represent an overhead cost for business.

However, if excessive credit is taken by, say, failing to pay the outstanding debt by the due date, the following consequences may arise.

- Delayed payment may be taken as a sign of financial difficulty and your supplier may decide to cease supply. You may then be forced to use other suppliers who are not your first choice, which may reflect in quality of supplies or the timeliness of deliveries.
- If goods are in short supply then you will probably be relegated to the back of the queue.
- You may be regarded as a credit risk and credit rating agencies may pass this information on to other potential suppliers.

3.2 The efficient management of trade payables

A firm needs to determine what policy to adopt in the management of its trade payables. In making this decision it must consider the following factors:

- the need to ensure continuing supplies as and when required, by maintaining good relations with regular suppliers
- the level of credit required and the ability to extend it when the firm has a cash flow shortfall
- the advantages of having a high level of trade credit as a method of reducing the level of working capital required
- the possibility of extending credit (although this may lead to the firm having a poor credit rating with resultant problems in obtaining additional credit)
- whether the supplier will charge interest on overdue accounts, and
- whether to accept or reject early payment discounts – this decision is made in the same way as offering discounts to a firm's customers; in this case, the benefits of accepting the discount must outweigh the costs (i.e. additional interest cost) of paying the debt early.

Management can use the following ratio to help monitor the level of trade payables:

$$\frac{\text{average trade payables}}{\text{credit purchases}} \times 365 \text{ days}$$

It can also use an ageing schedule as was described for controlling trade receivables in section 1.7 above.

3.3 The cost of discounts for prompt settlement

Companies often see trade credit as free capital, but it is not free if trading credit means losing a discount for prompt payment. The customer must balance the discount received against the potential interest cost. In order to do this it has to work out the annual cost of the discount that is on offer, which it can then compare with the costs of borrowing.

The general expression for the cost of early payment discounts forgone is:

$$s/(100 - s) \times 365/t$$

where:
s = percentage discount offered for early payment
t = the reduction in days in the payment period required to earn the discount.

Worked example 15.8 demonstrates the calculation.

15.8

A company's supplier offers a discount of 2% for payment in ten days as an alternative to payment in 30 days with no discount. The effect of paying in 30 days is to pay £100 instead of £98 and to receive an extra 20 days' credit. The company is unsure whether it is worth taking the discount offered. The cost of the extra 20 days' credit to the business will be the 2% discount forgone. If we annualise the cost of this discount, we have:

$$\frac{2}{98} \times \frac{365}{20} = 0.372 = 37.2\%$$

The annualised cost of forgoing the discount is very high, probably well in excess of the cost of borrowing, and so it should be profitable to pay the supplier within the discount period, even if the company has to borrow to enable it to do so.

A company's supplier offers a discount of 2.5% for payment in 12 days as an alternative to payment in 35 days with no discount. The company can borrow short-term at an annual rate of 13%. The company doesn't know whether to pay early and take the discount.

Required

Advise the company on whether to accept the discount.

Solution

If the cost of this discount is annualised, it gives:

$$\frac{2.5}{97.5} \times \frac{365}{23} = 0.4069 = 40.7\%$$

This is a very high interest rate and far exceeds the short-term borrowing rate of 13%. So it is worthwhile to pay in 12 days and collect the 2.5% discount. Even if this necessitates borrowing at 13% to cover the early payment, it will be worthwhile.

CHAPTER SUMMARY

First, this chapter considered the management of receivables and dealt with the following issues:

- actions available to the company
- the selection of which customers should receive credit
- sources of information on potential customers (direct and indirect)
- policies for efficient collection, and
- the financial impact of changes to receivables policy.

The chapter then discussed the management of cash, including cash flow planning, factors influencing the amount of cash held, cash management models and the cash conversion cycle.

Finally, it dealt with the management of payables, including the benefits of trade credit, the efficient management of trade payables and the cost of discounts for prompt payment.

END OF CHAPTER QUESTIONS

15.1 (a) Discuss possible methods of assessing the creditworthiness of a new customer, identifying potential weaknesses as well as advantages.

(b) The cash balance of Davids Ltd has declined and is of concern to management. The following information is available.

	2014	2015
	£000s	£000s
Sales	690.0	624.0
Raw materials purchases	295.0	264.0
Raw materials consumed	240.0	218.4
Balances at 31 December		
Trade receivables	108.1	118.5
Trade payables	53.9	52.5
Inventory of raw material	42.4	50.0

All purchases and sales are on credit.

Required

(i) Calculate the cash conversion cycle for 2014 and 2015.

(ii) Prepare a brief comment on the implication of these changes.

Note: assume a 360-day year.

15.2 In order to celebrate the birthdays of its most famous living painters, David and Jill, Pontypont Council is planning to hold an arts festival next summer with the intention of making it an annual event should this initial festival be a success. Financially, it has been stipulated that the festival should not make a loss and that it should plan to make a small surplus. A separate bank account has been set up for the festival. Sponsorship has been sought and a number of local businesses have given their support.

The festival will take place in June 2017 and estimated receipts and payments up to the end of June 2017 are listed below:

END OF CHAPTER QUESTIONS *continued*

Pontypont Festival – estimated receipts and payments

	£	£
Receipts		
Ticket sales	42,000	
Sponsorship	54,000	
Bar franchise	20,000	
Sale commissions on paintings	6,000	122,000
Payments		
Upgrade of facilities for the festival	22,000	
Project support team	36,000	
Festival materials	24,000	
Fees to artists	12,000	
Hospitality	8,000	
Publicity	10,000	112,000
Planned surplus		10,000

The payments and receipts are scheduled as follows over the period January to June 2017:

- the receipts from ticket sales are expected to arise as follows:
  - February 5%
  - March 10%
  - April 25%
  - May 25%
  - June 35%
- 40% of sponsorship is expected to be received in April and the balance in May
- the bar receipts and sales commissions will be received in June
- the upgrade to facilities will take place in January and February and will be paid in March
- the payments to the project support team will be phased over the six-month period from January to June
- festival materials will be paid for in two equal instalments in April and May
- fees to artists will be paid in June
- hospitality will be paid during June
- publicity payments will be made in the following instalments: 10% in April, 60% in May and 30% in June.

The project manager is concerned to ensure that the cash flow position does not exceed the overdraft of £10,000 that he has arranged with a local bank. If a cash deficit does arise in any month, overdraft interest of 2% per month will be charged and this should be included in the cash flow statement in the following month.

Required

(a) Prepare a statement showing the monthly cash flow over the six-month period January to June 2017.

(b) Provide a commentary identifying any significant issues arising from the cash flow statement.

(c) Indicate the monitoring procedures that should be adopted with reference to the budgeted cash flow statement over the period January to June 2017.

16 Short-term financing

■ **CONTENTS**

1 Bank lending and overdrafts

Bank lending to companies is predominantly short-term, although it is also now a valuable source of medium-term finance.

There are two forms of short-term finance.

- **Short-term loans:** Fixed rates of interest are available for up to five years.
- **Overdrafts negotiated with the bank:** Interest is charged on a daily basis, depending on how much the company is overdrawn each day. Interest rates on overdrafts are usually higher, but it is a very flexible method of finance, particularly when a company has to provide for seasonal variations in cash flow which will require facilities for short periods of time only. There is no penalty for repayment of an overdraft, unlike the early repayment of a medium-term loan, which is generally for a fixed period.

The interest rate for small companies on medium-term loans may either be at a fixed rate or at a margin above the bank's base rate. For larger companies, the interest rate on medium-term loans may again be fixed for up to five years, but is usually at a margin above the London Interbank Offered Rate (LIBOR), adjusted every three, six, nine or 12 months in line with LIBOR movements, the size of the margin being determined by risk and the credit standing of the company.

2 Bills of exchange and acceptance credits

The cost of trading transactions may be settled by means of bills of exchange (also called 'trade bills'): the seller draws up a bill specifying the name of the buyer and requesting payment, on a certain future date, of the price of the goods; the purchaser 'accepts' the bill of exchange by signing it and returning it to the seller, thus formally acknowledging a debt to the seller. The seller can either:

- hold the bill until maturity (the date specified on the bill), at which time the bill is presented to the buyer who pays and settles the debt, or
- use the bill of exchange to obtain money from its own bank or a discount house. The discount house or a bank will agree to pay the face value of the bill, less a discount. The discount house or bank will then arrange to collect payment from the buyer at maturity. The more secure the bill (such as from a bank (see below) rather than a trader), the 'finer' or lower the discount.

The advantage of the bill of exchange is that it provides the seller with immediate funds (from a bank) while allowing the buyer a period of credit.

Whereas bills of exchange are drawn on the buyer of the goods by the seller, acceptance credits (also called 'bank bills') are drawn by a company on a bank. The bank grants a credit facility to the company which enables the company to draw up bills that the bank will accept and honour when presented for payment at a predetermined future date. The accepted bills are sold on the discount market at a relatively 'fine', or low, discount. In effect, the company is obtaining finance from the buyer of the discounted bills using the reputation of the bank as security. The minimum amounts are normally £250,000 and acceptance credits have maturity periods of 30, 60, 90 or 180 days.

3 Customer credit

In the home market, customer credit can be financed through debt factoring and invoice discounting. We shall look at each of these in turn.

3.1 Factoring

Factoring grew as a way to facilitate trade credit and is now an important part of commercial life. Two main forms of factoring agreement exist: recourse factoring, where the factor assumes no responsibility for bad debts, and non-recourse factoring, where the factor accepts responsibility for bad debts, subject to the payment of an additional fee. Thus, subject to the factor's approval, debts can be transferred free of recourse and therefore the company passing its debts to the factor will:

- not have to deal with bad debts
- lose the administrative burden of the supervision of trade credit, which may be important for small and growing businesses and can lead to savings in the credit management process, and
- have an assured cash flow; generally, the factor will advance around 80% of the value of the debt within two or three days of an approved debt being passed to the factor. The factor collects from those trade receivables and subsequently pays over the balance, less its administration costs, to the company.

Factoring is particularly useful to firms trading in markets that require a considerable period of trade credit and to companies that are expanding rapidly, as it will leave other lines of credit open for use elsewhere in the business.

Costs will vary with the perceived level of risk, the volume of business and the period over which credit is granted. A monthly facility fee will usually be payable by the customer, whether or not funds are drawn from the facility. Another downside is that the factor's debt collecting activities may have a detrimental effect on the company's relations with its customers. Factoring can be expensive with costs running at 2% to 3% of sales revenue.

3.2 Sales aid financing

As an alternative to offering their own trade credit, suppliers of capital equipment and vehicles to both the home market and abroad may offer finance at the point of sale through a third-party finance company. This is known as 'sales aid finance' and is especially common in the UK retail motor trade, where credit may be subsidised by the manufacturer, the dealer, or both, to attract business and private customers by easing the burden of expenditure on a major capital item.

3.3 Invoice discounting

Invoice discounting is a variant of factoring where a company borrows from the invoice discounter on the security of its own debts, but continues to collect debts itself. The amount advanced may be up to 80% of the amounts invoiced. The advance has to be repaid within a relatively short period. Many companies prefer this arrangement because they do not hand over the management of their relationships with their customers to a third party. Additionally, costs are much lower than with a factor, typically about 0.2% to 0.4% of sales revenue.

Worked example 16.1 examines the relative costs and benefits of factoring and invoice discounting.

WORKED EXAMPLE 16.1

Trades Supplies Ltd has annual sales revenue of £2.5 million, all of which is on credit, and which includes bad debts amounting to £0.05 million per year. The business currently has an overdraft of £0.5 million at an interest rate of 16%. The average period for which trade receivables are outstanding is 50 days, although the usual credit terms in the business are for payment in 40 days.

The business is currently reviewing its credit policies and has received the following quotations.

- A factoring company has offered to carry out non-recourse factoring. The factor will advance 80% of trade receivables at an interest rate of 15%. The factor will undertake collection of all trade receivables and the factor will charge a fee of 3% of sales revenue for this service. The factoring service will lead to annual credit control savings amounting to £25,000 per year. The factor also undertakes to reduce the settlement period for trade receivables to 40 days.
- An invoice discounting firm has offered to advance 75% of the value of approved sales invoices for 50 days. It will charge interest of 14% over this period. It will also charge a fee of 0.2% of sales invoices. In conjunction with this option, the company also plans to strengthen credit control by spending an additional £25,000 per year and believes that it will be able to reduce bad debts to 10% of their current level.

Required

Make appropriate calculations and advise the company.

Solution

	£000s
Current costs	
Bad debts	50.00
Interest cost of average receivables (£2.5 million × 50/365 × 16%)	54.79
	104.79
Factoring option	
Interest cost of average receivables (£2.5 million × 40/365 × 80% × 15%)	32.88
Interest cost of balance (£2.5 million × 40/365 × 20% × 16%)	8.77
Cost of factor (3% × £2.5 million)	75.00
	116.65
Less: credit control savings	25.00
	91.65
Invoice discounting option	
Bad debts	5.00
Interest cost of average receivables (£2.5 million × 50/365 × 75% × 14%)	35.96
Interest cost of balance (£2.5 million × 50/365 × 25% × 16%)	13.70
Cost of invoice discounter (0.2% × £2.5 million)	5.00
Credit control costs	25.00
	84.66

The calculations show that invoice discounting, together with strengthening of the credit control function, is the cheapest option. The company may also judge that this is preferable as the invoice discounting option allows it to keep a continuous, unbroken link with its customers.

WORKED EXAMPLE 16.2

Extra Ltd has annual credit sales of £7 million and its customers pay, on average, in 35 days, although the agreed credit period is 30 days. It currently has an overdraft of £500,000 at 15%. It suffers minimal bad debts.

The company is considering three options:

1. A factor has offered a recourse package. The factor will advance 85% on receipt of sales invoices and reduce the collection period to 30 days. Its interest rate is 14%. It also charges a fee of 2.5% of credit sales. This will lead to savings in credit control of £60,000 per year.
2. A firm of invoice discounters has offered to advance 80% of the value of sales invoices for 30 days. The company charges 0.3% of credit sales. Its interest rate is 14%. The company also plans to rent a new software system at a cost of £7,500 per year that it believes will allow it to reduce the average settlement period of debtors to 30 days.
3. The company would rent the new software system at a cost of £7,500 and work with it to achieve an immediate reduction in the average settlement period to 30 days.

Required

Make appropriate calculations and advise the company.

Solution

	£000s
Current costs	
Interest: £7 million × 35/365 × 15%	100.68
Factor	
Interest cost: £7 million × 30/365 × 0.85 × 14%	68.47
Interest cost of balance: £7 million × 30/365 × 0.15 × 15%	12.95
Cost of factor: £7 million × 2.5%	175.00
	256.42
Less credit control savings	60.00
	196.42
Invoice discounters	
Interest cost: £7 million × 30/365 × 0.8 × 14%	64.44
Interest cost of balance: £7 million × 30/365 × 0.2 × 15%	17.26
Cost of invoice discounting: £7 million × 0.3%	21.00
Software	7.50
	110.20
Rent software and work to reduce average payments period to 30 days	
Interest: £7 million × 30/365 × 15%	86.30
Software	7.50
	93.80

The standalone new system is the cheapest. However, other factors apart from cost might influence the decision, such as an overdraft limit to be avoided or alternative uses for cash. Both options 1 and 2 would reduce the overdraft significantly.

4 Retained profits and provisions

4.1 Introduction

Typically, internally generated funds represent some 60% of the sources of long-term capital used by a company.

A company uses its funds in the pursuit of profit and, where that profit is sufficiently large, it will pay a dividend to shareholders. The surplus remaining is referred to as 'retentions' and will be available to finance growth and the replacement, as necessary, of the company's assets. These retentions of profits which are ploughed back into the business are internally generated capital.

Retentions of profit arise in two forms.

- Provisions are expenses used to calculate profits prior to determining the amount available for dividends.
- After shareholders' dividends have been paid, the surplus funds are regarded as retained profits – one could argue that these funds represent an investment on the part of shareholders who have forgone their dividends.

4.2 Availability of internal funds

The obvious advantage of internally generated funds is that they become available without the formalities of issuing houses, brokers, requirements to provide security, and so forth. However, it can be difficult to generate the precise amount of financing needed at the optimum time for the business, as profits arise from trading and will often fluctuate with economic conditions.

4.3 Provisions used to calculate profit

Depreciation

The charge for depreciation in the income statement does not arise as an outflow of cash at the time the charge is made. The cash outflow relating to a new fixed asset usually occurs when the asset is first brought into use. The outflow is treated as capital expenditure and recorded in the statement of financial position. The depreciation charges 'filter' the capital expenditure from the statement of financial position to the statement of profit or loss periodically. You should, however, note that the charge in the statement of profit or loss is not a cash-based item. It is the apportionment of a historic cost incurred on earlier occasions.

Other items

There are many items which do not involve any actual cash outlay and examples include provisions for bad and doubtful debts, for plant maintenance etc.

The effect of creating provisions for depreciation and other items is to reduce the profit available to pay out dividends and/or make retentions. For this reason, amounts of cash are held back in the business and not distributed to shareholders.

However, these are largely related to the purchase of fixed assets rather than working capital and generally represent sources of long-term, finance but they could be used to increase working capital on a long-term basis.

4.4 Internal sources of short-term finance

There are three main sources of short-term finance, all deriving from working capital items. They are derived specifically from the savings made by:

- reducing the levels of inventory held by the company
- implementing tighter credit control with the object of reducing the size of trade receivables balances, and
- delaying payment to trade payables as long as possible.

5 Reducing levels of inventory

Chapter 14 showed how large inventory can be in a manufacturing company and demonstrated how it can be reduced by just-in-time activities. The amount of cash that can be released by this type of action can be significant, as inventory can consume large amounts of finance.

Worked example 16.3 shows how much finance can be released when balances of inventory are reduced.

WORKED EXAMPLE 16.3

Flek Ltd, a manufacturing company, has the following balances of inventory:

Finished goods £200,000
Raw materials £350,000

Its annual cost of sales is £800,000 and its annual consumption of raw materials is £400,000.
It wishes to reduce its finished goods stock to 60 days' cost of sales and its raw materials cost to 45 days' consumption.

The company has an overdraft of £500,000 and the rate of interest is 16%.

Required
Estimate the potential financial benefit of these changes.

Solution

	Current		Reduced	
		£000		£000
Finished goods	200/800 × 365 = 91 days	200,000	Target = 60/365 × £800,000	131.51
Raw materials	350/400 × 365 = 319 days	350,000	Target = 45/365 × £400,000	49.32
		550,000		180.83

If the company is successful, it will release cash of (£550,000 – £180,830) £369,170. This could be used to reduce the company's overdraft significantly, saving (£369,170 × 16%) £59,067 per year in interest charges.

WORKED EXAMPLE 16.4

Trik Ltd, a manufacturing company, is about to introduce just-in-time processes. Its current inventory balances are as follows:

Finished goods £256,000
Work in progress £145,000 (on average 60% complete)
Raw materials £168,000

Annual cost of sales is £1.2 million and annual raw materials consumed are £300,000.
As a prelude to introducing just-in-time processes, Trik Ltd wishes to reduce its finished goods stock to 40 days' cost of sales, its work in progress also to 40 days' consumption (on average 60% complete) and its raw materials to 20 days' consumption.

The company's cost of capital is 14%.

WORKED EXAMPLE 16.4 *continued*

Required

Estimate the potential financial benefit of these changes.

Solution

	Current		Reduced	
		£000s		£000s
Finished goods	256/1,200 × 365 = 78 days	256	Target = 40/365 × £1.2 million	131.51
WIP	145/(1,200 × 0.6) × 365 = 73 days	145	Target 40/365 × £1.2 million × 0.6	78.90
Raw materials	168/300 × 365 = 153 days	168	Target = 20/365 × £300,000	16.44
		569		226.85

If the company is successful, it will release cash of (£569,000 – £226,850) £342,150. This could be used to reduce the company's overdraft significantly saving (£342,150 × 14%) £47,901 per year in interest charges.

6 Tighter credit control over trade receivables

This is discussed in Chapter 15, which stresses the care needed in the selection of creditworthy customers and the efficient collection of income from receivables. As with inventory, high levels of trade receivables represent a large commitment of finance and a significant opportunity cost in interest. In order to reduce this investment, as well as good collection procedures, use may be made of discounts to encourage early payment. However, the company has to balance tighter credit control against the potential loss of business. Worked example 16.5 illustrates these issues.

WORKED EXAMPLE 16.5

Fidelity Ltd sells a component with the following cost and revenue structure:

	Per component
	£
Selling price	15
Less variable costs	6
Contribution	9
Less fixed costs (apportioned)	4
Profit	5

(The fixed cost is apportioned from a central pool and will not change as sales increase or decrease, so the relevant figure in determining the effect of changes in sales is the contribution.)

WORKED EXAMPLE 16.5 *continued*

Sales revenue is £15 million per year. The credit period is 30 days and most customers settle within that period, with the average receivables payment period of 33 days.

The company's credit control department has indicated that it wishes to pursue a policy whereby all customers pay within 30 days and senior management supports this policy. It is estimated that sales revenue will fall by £0.5 million per year as a result of the policy. The credit control department is also going to offer a 3% discount to all customers who pay in 10 days; it is estimated that 40% of clients, at the revised sales level, will take up this offer.

The company finances trade payables by overdraft and its annual cost is 16%.

Required

Calculate the financial effects of the change in policy by credit control.

Solution

		Annual cost	
Current system	£000s		£000s
Receivables balances: 33/365 × £15 million	1,356.16	0.16 × 1356.16 =	216.99
Revised system			
Receivables: 30/365 × £14.5 million × 0.6	715.07	0.16 × 715.07 =	114.41
Discounted receivables: 10/365 × £14.5 million × 0.4	158.90	0.16 × 158.90 =	25.42
Discount: 3% × £14.5 million × 0.4			174.00
Loss in contribution: 9/15 × £0.5 million			300.00
Total receivables balances	873.97		
Total cost of revised system			613.83

The new system is a disaster! Although the receivables balances are lower, the discount and the loss of contribution totally outweigh this saving. The company should keep the current system.

WORKED EXAMPLE 16.6

Bank Ltd sells a component with the following cost and revenue structure:

	Per component
	£
Selling price	20
Less variable costs	12
Contribution	8
Less fixed costs (apportioned)	4
Profit	4

16.6 *continued*

Sales revenue is £20 million per year. The credit period is 40 days but the average receivables payment period is 56 days.

The company's credit control department has indicated that it wishes to pursue a policy whereby all customers pay within 40 days and senior management supports this policy. It is estimated that sales revenue will fall by £0.2 million per year as a result of the policy. The credit control department is also going to offer a 2% discount to all customers who pay within five days; it is estimated that 20% of clients, at the revised sales level, will take up this offer.

The company finances trade payables by overdraft and its annual cost is 15%.

Required

Calculate the financial effects of the credit control department's change in policy.

Solution

		Annual cost	
Current system	£000s		£000s
Receivables balances: 56/365 × £20 million	3,068.49	0.15 × 3068.49 =	460.27
Revised system			
Receivables: 40/365 × £19.8 million × 0.8	1,735.89	0.15 ×1,735.89 =	260.38
Discounted receivables: 5/365 × £19.8 million × 0.2	54.25	0.15 × 54.25 =	8.14
Discount: 2% × £19.8 million × 0.2			79.20
Loss in contribution: 8/20 × £200,000			80.00
Total receivables balances	1,790.14		
Total cost of revised system			427.72

The new system is considerably cheaper and should be adopted. It will save the company an estimated £32,550 per year.

7 Delaying payment to trade payables

This subject is also discussed in Chapter 15. While a company would be urged to take the full credit period before paying, to delay beyond that period would be dangerous. Issues such as loss of supply and the reputation of being a poor credit risk can arise if a company delays payment beyond the agreed credit period.

CHAPTER SUMMARY

This chapter has considered short-term financing. Initially, financing that is obtained external to the company and then finance that is generated internally.

The chapter has examined sources of short-term financing. These sources have been classified as follows:

- external sources including bank overdrafts, bills of exchange and acceptance credits, factoring and invoice discounting, and
- internal sources including retained profits and provisions for depreciation, reducing inventory balances, implementing tighter credit control and delaying payments to payables.

END OF CHAPTER QUESTIONS

16.1 Limpa plc services lifts on a nationwide basis. Recently, the Board of the company has been alerted by its bankers with reference to the size of the company's overdraft. The company has traditionally been on good terms with the bank and its overdraft has been 'rolled over' for several years at a level of £300,000. However, in the last six months it has increased to £450,000. The bank charges interest of 16% per year. The finance director has indicated that this is largely due to the upward drift in the payment period taken by trade receivables; this is against the background of an increasingly difficult financial situation.

An extract from the company's income statement for the year ended 31 March 2015 and its statement of financial position as at 31 March 2015 are shown below:

Statement of profit or loss for the year ended 31 March 2015	
	£000s
Sales	6,000
Cost of sales	1,800
Gross profit	4,200
Operating profit	1,500
Finance costs	140
Net profit before tax	1,360
Tax (20%)	272
Net profit for the period	1,088

Statement of financial position as at 31 March 2015		
	£000s	£000s
Non-current assets		
Property, plant and equipment		2,450
Current assets		
Inventory	400	
Trade receivables	900	
Total current assets		1,300
Total assets		3,750
Equity		
Share capital	1,000	
Retained earnings	1,400	
		2,400
Non-current liabilities		
Loans (secured on property) 10% interest		800
Current liabilities		
Trade payables	100	
Bank overdraft	450	
Total current liabilities		550
Total equity and liabilities		3,750

The finance director has indicated to the board that there appear to be two ways of dealing with the overdraft problem, both involving a reduction in current asset balances:

- Increase the efficacy of credit control by spending an additional £30,000 on strengthening the credit control system. The credit control department would be tasked with reducing trade receivables so that all receivables pay within the normal 40-day period. It is accepted that there may be bad debts totalling as much as £35,000. Management would also focus on reducing the average inventory holding to six weeks of the cost of sales.
- A factor has offered a non-recourse factoring agreement for 3% of sales invoices; the factor will advance 80% of sales invoices and charges interest at 14%. The factor will pay net balances over after 40 days. It has undertaken to collect all debts in 40 days. The company has never employed a factor. This option could be combined with the internal operation to reduce inventory.

Required

Write a briefing note for the Board of Limpa plc in which you:

1 outline the services provided by factors and refer to any potential disadvantages for the company
2 calculate the financial effects of both options for dealing with the overdraft problem

END OF CHAPTER QUESTIONS *continued*

3 make a recommendation to the Board of Limpa plc.

16.2 (a) Discuss possible methods of assessing the creditworthiness of a new customer, identifying potential weaknesses as well as advantages.

(b) Outline the services provided by factors.

(c) Suggest actions that a company can take to deal with late payers.

PART **EIGHT**

Corporate risk management

LIST OF CHAPTERS

OVERVIEW

This part examines the diverse nature of risks facing organisations and the different responses to risk. The relationship between risk and return is again explored, as this is a key concept within this syllabus. It discusses enterprise-wide approaches to managing risk. Finally, it examines a variety of financial strategies for hedging financial risk: futures, options, forward rate agreements, swaps and a money market hedge.

LEARNING OUTCOMES

On successful completion of Part Eight, you will be able to:

- explain the importance of risk and risk management to organisations
- demonstrate a conceptual understanding of the financial methodologies used to hedge risk, and
- apply financial analysis to the diverse financial hedging techniques.

17 Corporate risk management

■ **CONTENTS**

1 The nature of risk

Financial decision-making is undertaken in conditions of risk. Risk can be distinguished from uncertainty as follows.

- **Uncertainty:** This occurs when there is insufficient information to say what will probably happen in the future. Any estimates of future values (sales, costs etc.) are unlikely to be accurate. Uncertainty can be reduced by obtaining more reliable information about the future.
- **Risk:** This also occurs when there is volatility in future returns, but the probability of each possible outcome can be assessed with reasonable accuracy. Risk often cannot be removed and it must be taken account of in decision-making. In investment decisions, risk is particularly important because of the duration of projects (there is more time for things to go wrong) and the scale of projects (if anything does go wrong, it can have a serious impact on the company).

2 Operating and financial risk

2.1 Operating risk

Sometimes known as 'business risk', operating risk refers to the variability of the operating profit or profit before interest and tax (PBIT) – the total pre-tax profits available to debt-holders and shareholders – and the factors that cause this variability. These factors include booms, recessions, strikes, competition, machine breakdowns and other things that can create opportunities and problems in the normal course of business. One factor that has a bearing on the level of risk of a firm's business is the percentage of fixed costs in the firm's cost structure. Fixed costs include rent, salaries, insurance premiums and depreciation. This is important because fixed costs have to be covered whatever the trading conditions. If trading activity declines, sales will fall, variable costs will also fall, but fixed costs will remain unchanged.

A firm with a high percentage of fixed costs is said to have a higher level of operating gearing:

operating gearing = contribution/PBIT

where:

contribution = sales – variable costs

The higher the operating gearing, the greater the operating risk, as is demonstrated in Worked example 17.1.

WORKED EXAMPLE 17.1

	£000s	£000s	£000s
Sales	200	160	100
Variable costs	100	80	50
Contribution	100	80	50
Fixed costs	40	40	40
PBIT	60	40	10
Degree of operating gearing	100/60 = 1.67 times	80/40 = 2 times	50/10 = 5 times

2.2 Financial risk

Financial risk is the additional risk borne by shareholders when the firm takes on fixed-rate debt. A firm with a large percentage of debt is said to have a high degree of financial gearing, which is a measure of a firm's financial risk (see Chapter 13).

The cost of any type of capital is a function of the risk-free rate and a risk premium for each type of risk that is taken on. Therefore, an equity investor expects a higher return than does a debt-holder, with a fixed rate of interest, as the equity holder is subject to financial risk (as well as operating risk).

3 Key risk concepts

This section considers the four key risk concepts facing companies:

- exposure
- volatility
- severity
- probability.

3.1 Exposure

Exposure is a measure of the extent to which a company faces risk. This risk can be operating risk and/or financial risk. It can also refer to the extent to which a company faces foreign exchange risk due to its import, export and foreign investing activities.

3.2 Volatility

Volatility is the extent to which expected returns vary. The more they are expected to vary, the more volatile or the more risky they are said to be. Variance and standard deviation are used to measure volatility. Another term for volatility is 'dispersion'. A risk-free return has no volatility and may be pictured as an undeviating straight line.

3.3 Severity

One way of looking at risk is as follows:

$$\text{risk} = \text{probability of hazard} \times \text{severity of outcome when hazard occurs}$$

Thus, severity is defined as follows: if a hazard occurs, how bad is the outcome? If severity is low then, possibly, we will give a low priority to preventing this risk from occurring. However, if severity is high then, even if the probability of the hazard is low, prevention has a high priority. For, example, computer files are so important that a company will undertake regular back-ups so that the costs of computer failure are minimised. Furthermore, back-up material will often be kept in an alternative location, in case the building housing the computer and back-ups is subject to a disaster, such as a fire.

3.4 Probability

Probabilities that are assigned to future events can be either objective or subjective. Objective probabilities are based on the accumulation of past information. For example, if we have a number of machines that have run for several years, we may be able to evaluate likely breakdown rates, annual machine running costs and so on. However, there are two difficulties with using past experience to derive probabilities relating to future events. One of these is that changes in technology can mean that past information is out of date. Another difficulty is that capital investment projects are one-off or unique projects for which it may be impossible to derive historic data.

Subjective probabilities are based on subjective opinion. They can be derived from the opinions of experts or the judgements of managers with experience in these areas. However, there is always the danger due to bias as personal experience may be limited and subjective interpretation of it may be flawed.

17.1

What is the connection between probability and severity?

4 Risk responses

This section considers the four principal responses of companies towards risk:

- risk transfer
- risk reduction
- risk avoidance
- risk retention.

4.1 Risk transfer

Risk transfer is the process of transferring risk to another party, usually by payment of a fee. For example, with foreign exchange risk, risk can be reduced by purchasing currency on the forward market. More generally, taking out insurance is a method of risk transfer: the risk is transferred from the company to the insurance company on payment of a fee (the insurance premium).

4.2 Risk reduction

Risk reduction is the process of reducing overall risk. One way of achieving this is by investing in a portfolio of assets rather than in one or two assets. Another approach is to carry out market research to provide more certainty in estimates of future sales revenue.

4.3 Risk avoidance

Given two projects with identical returns, the risk-averse investor will choose the project with the lowest risk. Risk-averse people continually take risks, but only where the expected return is sufficiently high to compensate them for taking those risks. Unnecessary risks are not appealing. Most people are risk averse.

4.4 Risk retention

Risk retention involves accepting the gains or losses from a risk when it occurs. Risk retention would be a viable strategy for risks with low severity, where the cost of insuring the risk over time would be greater than any loss incurred by the company. Also, any potential risk in excess of a ceiling imposed by the insurance company is retained risk. Some risks have to be retained as they cannot be invested against, such as the risk of war.

17.2

Define risk transfer, risk reduction, risk avoidance and risk retention.

5 The relationship between risk and expected return

Because most investors are risk-averse, any increased risk must be balanced by increased return. This is why the average returns in the market for equities (which are risky) are higher than the average returns from investments in government savings schemes, which are assumed to be risk free. The more risk, the higher the return, as illustrated in Figure 17.1.

FIGURE 17.1 Risk and return

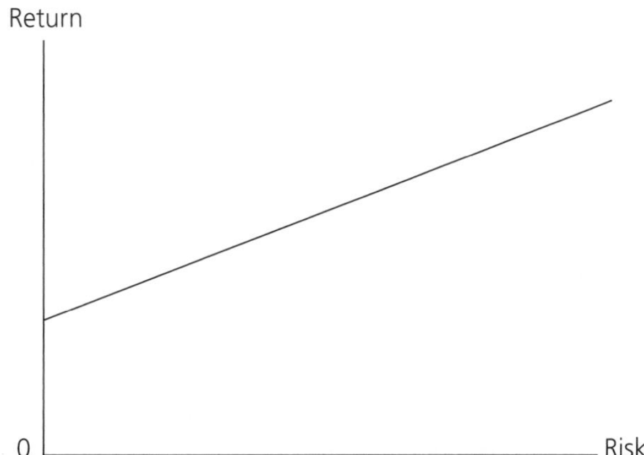

In Figure 17.1, the return is the percentage return on an investment. Risk would be measured by the standard deviation of return, so the higher the standard deviation, the higher the volatility and the higher the risk. The line slopes up to the right to indicate the additional return required by the risk-averse investor to compensate for additional risk, measured on the horizontal axis. Where the sloping line cuts the vertical axis, risk is zero – this point is known as the risk-free rate. The additional return available over the risk-free rate is known as the 'risk premium', the return for taking on risk. The risk premium increases as risk increases.

6 Risk management policies

Risk management involves identifying the risks faced by the business and then ensuring that such risks are assessed and managed. As has been indicated above, risks arise from operational and financing decisions. In consequence, risk management must also involve taking account of risk in operational and financing decisions.

Risk management is allied with the values of the business and the extent to which it enters fields with high degrees of risk.

Risk assessment provides a mechanism for identifying which risks represent opportunities and which represent serious threats. Risk assessment must be related to the objectives and values of the business, which are critical in the assessment of the impact of risks facing the company.

A business may have a low appetite for risk, but in order to compete in the marketplace it may have to take it on. For example, consider a manufacturing company in the UK which has been making good profits for many years and has successfully introduced modern manufacturing techniques and new products. However, the company has recently experienced increased competition from low-cost, high-quality imports from the Far East. As a result, the company may need to relocate manufacturing to one of the Far East countries, partly to benefit from lower wage rates; but this would increase its operational and financial risks significantly.

6.1 Enterprise risk management

Enterprise risk management (ERM) is an example of a framework for a company's risk management processes. ERM is a system for integrating and formalising risk management processes within the organisation. It also involves using the risk management processes to find profitable opportunities related to the company's objectives. By identifying and addressing risks and opportunities, companies are able to create value.

There are different responses to risk within ERM, which can be categorised as follows.

Category	Description
1	Avoidance of activities related to risk
2	Action to reduce the impact of risk
3	Share or transfer a portion of risk
4	Accept and take action based on risk assessment

Companies are advised to take a portfolio approach to risk. Financial portfolio theory provides a framework for evaluating the risk from a collection of financial instruments and also the contribution to risk and return of an additional security. Within ERM, these concepts have been generalised beyond financial risks to include all risks that an organisation faces. The principles of portfolio risk are as follows.

- Portfolio risk is not the simple sum of the individual risk elements.
- Portfolio risk is based on the elements of the portfolio and their interaction.

There is a growing recognition that risks must be managed with the total organisation in mind. An overall approach gives companies a perspective on the magnitude and importance of different risks.

The risk management processes of ERM involve the following.

1. Establish the current risk management environment within which the company operates.
2. Identify the risks that face the organisation, analyse those risks and, if possible, establish probabilities relating to the risks.
3. Prioritise the risks facing the organisation.
4. Take a portfolio approach to risks.
5. Develop strategies for controlling the risks and (or) for exploiting the opportunities that are available.
6. Ensure there is a monitoring and reviewing process. This involves reviewing the risk management performance of the company.

WORKED EXAMPLE 17.2

Assessing risk severity: an illustration

A company may instigate a process whereby:

- the company considers separately the impact and likelihood of each risk:
  potential severity score = potential impact × likelihood of adverse outcome
- the process distinguishes between inherent risk and residual (mitigated) risk
- the company regularly reviews the effectiveness of controls applied to inherent risk and the consequent levels of residual risk, and
- the company reports evidence of how it actively manages risks.

Assessment and scoring of impact

Impact may be assessed within five levels:

Probability	Score	Magnitude of impact
Low	1	Minimal loss; easily remedied
Low/medium	2	Minor loss; short-term effect
Medium	3	Significant waste of time and resources; medium-term effect
Medium/high	4	Major impact on costs and objectives; medium- to long-term effect
High	5	Critical impact on objectives; long-term impact

Assessment and scoring of likelihood

Likelihood may also be assessed within five levels:

Probability	Score	Likelihood
Low	1	Rare; the risk will materialise only in exceptional circumstances
Low/medium	2	Unlikely; it will probably not materialise
Medium	3	Possible
Medium/high	4	Likely; the risk will probably arise
High	5	Almost certain; this will materialise in most circumstances

Risk management matrix

The individual impact and likelihood scores can then be multiplied to produce a risk management matrix, in which the resultant scores equate to different categories of risk:

Overall Score	Company approach to risk
1–3	Manageable risk: the company may elect to carry the risk
4–14	Material risk: the company will need to manage the risk
15–25	Significant risk: a high-profile risk which the company must treat as a risk management priority

Risk summary table

The next step is to prepare a table summarising risk identification, assessment and response. Two items are provided as examples: staffing and a major power loss.

WORKED EXAMPLE 17.2 *continued*

Risk description	Inherent risk			Risk-control measures	Residual risk		
	I	L	O		I	L	O
If key staff leave there may be insufficient skilled staff to support efficient operations	4	3	12	Staff training, appraisal, delegation, succession planning	3	3	9
A power loss (due to equipment failure, terrorist attack etc.) may lead to loss of information systems files	5	4	20	Data are backed up daily at a disaster recovery centre Emergency back-up lines are in place	5	1	5

I = impact score, L = likelihood score, O = overall score.

As may be seen, the summary table shows the action taken to mitigate risks and the resulting residual risk.

TEST YOUR KNOWLEDGE 17.3

Why are corporate strategy and values important in corporate risk management?

7 Credit risk and market risk

'Credit risk' is the risk of loss arising from a borrower or trade receivable who fails to make the necessary payments. This is referred to as a 'default'. Losses include lost principal and interest, bad debts, decreased cash flow and increased collection costs.

'Market risk' is the risk that the value of a portfolio will decrease due to the change in equity values or, more broadly, due to the change in value of the market risk factors. The associated market risk factors are:

- equity risk – the risk that equity prices will change significantly; this may be measured by an index
- interest rate risk – the risk that interest rates will change, affecting equity prices and portfolio valuations
- currency risk – the risk that foreign exchange rates will change, and
- commodity risk – the risk that commodity prices (copper, oil etc.) will change.

8 Methods for hedging financial risk

Hedging involves offsetting or reducing potential losses from financial risks. There are five principal methods for hedging:

- futures
- options
- forward rate agreements
- swaps
- money market hedges.

The first four in this list are derivatives. A derivative security is a security whose existence is dependent, or contingent, upon the existence of another security.

Future and option contracts can be used to hedge the risk arising from future contracts. Table 17.1 summarises the differences between futures and options; these differences will be explained below.

TABLE 17.1 Key differences between futures and options contracts

Future contract	Option contract
Standardises: price quality time	Specifies: price quality time
Both parties are obligated to complete a future contract.	Rights of the purchaser: no obligation to complete the contract. The writer (or originator of the option) has an obligation to complete if the holder of the option wants to complete.

8.1 Futures

A **future contract** is an agreement between two counterparties that fixes the terms of exchange that will take place between them at some future time. The counterparties are obligated to complete the transaction. The agreement may relate to currency or to the rate of interest on a loan. Other features of futures are as follows.

- Interest rate futures are traded on an exchange and their prices depend upon prevailing interest rates. The greater the interest rates, the lower the value of the future, and vice versa.
- All futures are traded on a regulated exchange; to permit trading, all categories of transactions are in set amounts (e.g. a standard amount of currency or a standard amount of loans (the unit of trading is £500,000)). We will consider three-month contracts.
- The rule is that if you want to hedge against an increase in interest rates (because you want to borrow) then you should hedge by selling futures (known as 'going short'). If you want to hedge against a fall in interest rates (because you want to lend) then you hedge by buying futures (known as 'going long').
- With interest rate futures, the future relates to the interest rates on a notional underlying sum of money.
- The price for future contracts is quoted as an index:

  price = 100 – annual interest rate

- The futures exchange removes almost all the risk of running an exchange. Every day the profits or losses accruing to the counterparties to the transaction as a result of that day's movement in interest rates or exchange rates must be paid in to the exchange by one of the counterparties.

In the UK, all financial future contracts are run through the London International Financial Futures and Options Exchange (LIFFE) which is owned by NYSE Euronext.

Worked example 17.3 illustrates the use of financial future contracts to hedge interest rate risk.

17.3

A company wishes to borrow £50 million for three months starting in three months' time. The rate of interest will be LIBOR +2%. LIBOR is currently 6%. However, the company is concerned that interest rates may increase between now and the start of the loan. So, the company should hedge by selling financial futures. By doing this, it can lock in the current interest rate on the loan that it will take out in three months' time. The steps are as follows.

1. The company treasurer sets up a target interest cost using the amount that will be borrowed:
   = £50 million × 3/12 × 8% = £1 million.
2. The company treasurer identifies the number of future contracts that are needed:
   = £50 million/£500,000 = 100 contracts
   and their start date in three months' time.
3. The company treasurer sells 100 future contracts at 92 (100–8%).
4. If in three months' time interest rates have increased to 9% then the actual interest charge payable by the company is:
   = £50 million × 3/12 × 9% = £1.125 million
   This is £125,000 more than was planned. The company will make a profit on its future contract that will compensate for this extra interest cost.
5. The company treasurer now 'closes out' the futures position. They now buy 100 three-month future contracts at a price of 91 (100–9%).

The net effect is as follows:

Future contracts	**Interest**	
Sold interest at 8% on £50 million for three months	£1 million	Sold
Bought interest at 9% on £50 million for three months	£1.125 million	Bought
Overall, one set of future contracts cancels out the other set of future contracts (both 100 contracts for the same period) and the company receives the balance of interest bought less interest sold and this compensates for the additional interest cost incurred.	£0.125 million	

By using the financial futures market the company treasurer has been able to protect the company from the feared increase in interest rates for the three-month period.

17.4

A company wishes to borrow £20 million for three months starting in three months' time. The rate of interest will be LIBOR +1.5%. LIBOR is currently 7%. However, the company is concerned that interest rates may increase between now and the start of the loan.

Required

Show how the company treasurer can set up future contracts and show the outcome if the actual rate of interest is 9.5%.

Solution

1. The company treasurer sets up a target interest cost using the amount that will be borrowed:
   = £20 million × 3/12 × 8.5% = £425,000.
2. The company treasurer identifies the number of future contracts that are needed:
   = £20 million/£500,000 = 40 contracts
   and their start date in three months' time.

17.4 *continued*

3 The company treasurer sells 40 future contracts at 91.5 (100–8.5%).

4 If in three months' time interest rates have increased to 9.5% then the actual interest charge payable is:
= £20 million × 3/12 × 9.5% = £475,000
This is £50,000 more than was planned.

5 The company treasurer now 'closes out' the futures position. They now buy 40 three-month future contracts at a price of 90.5 (100–9.5%).

The net effect is as follows:

Future contracts	Interest	
Sold interest at 8.5% on £20 million for three months	£425,000	Sold
Bought interest at 9% on £20 million for three months	£475,000	Bought
Overall, one set of future contracts cancels out the other set of futures contracts (both 40 contracts for the same period) and the company receives the balance of interest bought less interest sold.	£50,000	

The futures' net interest covers the additional interest paid by the company.

A forward contract is similar to a futures contract in that it is an agreement to buy or sell an asset at a fixed price at a fixed time in the future. However, whereas future contracts are traded on an exchange, forward contracts are over-the-counter (OTC) instruments which fall outside of the regulation of an exchange. One of the uses of a forward contract may be to hedge foreign currency risk. For example, a forward exchange contract is a binding agreement to buy or sell an agreed amount of currency at a specified time in the future at an agreed exchange rate. Forward contracts are tailor-made to suit the requirements of the parties. However, a forward contract exposes the parties to the default risk whereby one party fails to deliver.

8.2 Options

An **option contract** confers the right to buy or sell a given underlying asset at a specified price sometime before (or on) a specified date. It is important to understand that the owner of the contract has the right, but not the obligation, to buy or sell; it is this which differentiates an option from a future. In the case of a future there is an obligation to complete the contract; the holder of a future must buy or sell a specified asset or, more probably, buy or sell the future contract.

Convertible loans provide an example of an option contract. A convertible loan offers the holder, at some future point in time, the option to exchange the loan for ordinary shares at a predetermined price, termed the 'exercise price'. The company that issued the bond has an obligation. Loans with warrants attached to such bonds can carry similar rights.

As well as examples such as convertible bonds, there is a 'traded options' market in which option trading is regulated by an exchange; in the UK this is LIFFE.

The purchaser of a traded option contract pays a seller (or 'writer') of the option a premium that gives the purchaser the right, but not the obligation, to purchase from or sell to the writer a specified volume of a specified security at the specified price (termed the 'striking price' or the 'exercise price') and by a specified date. The option premium is not a deposit on the purchase of a share.

There are two types of option contract:

- a call contract – which confers upon the holder of the contract the right to purchase from the original seller of the option a fixed number of shares or units at a specified price within a specified period/or at a certain date, and

- a put contract – which confers upon the holder the right to sell to the original seller of the option a fixed number of shares or units at a specified price within a specified period or by a certain date.

Risk

The risk implications of option contracts are as follows.

- **Buying:** Exposure is limited to the option premium that has been paid, but in a traded option market the option can readily be resold.
- **Writing:** The writer of the option is the originator or creator of the option contract, either put or call. The writer sells the contract and receives a fee for this – the 'option premium'. The writer's exposure to risk is open ended as the potential loss may be unlimited. The writer bears the ultimate responsibility for providing or buying the shares at the exercise price at or by the agreed date.
- **The contract:** On LIFFE, the option contract is for nine months, at the end of which the contract becomes void; and each option contract is for 1,000 shares, or options may be generated relating to the FTSE 100 index.

WORKED EXAMPLE 17.5

On 2 April the following information was available on the September traded options in the ordinary shares of Excal plc (all prices in pence):

Current share price	Exercise price	Call option price	Put option price
345			
	300	53	1
	350	15	10
	400	3	40

The current share price is 345p and the table gives the price of option contracts in the shares of Excal plc. Prices are given for call contracts and put contracts. As the exercise price increases, the price of call options falls, but the price of the put option contracts increases. The option contracts will become void in September. These option prices are not for newly generated options as there is less than nine months to September. Instead, they are the prices for September options in the market on 2 April.

From one perspective, purchasing a September call option with an exercise price of 300p, and paying out 53p for this, will only be worthwhile if the share price exceeds 353p between now and September. The more volatile the underlying share price, the more valuable will be the option as there is more chance that the share price will reach the desired level before the option contract expires.

TEST YOUR KNOWLEDGE 17.4

In Worked example 17.5 why do the call option prices fall, and the put option prices increase, as the exercise price increases?

Worked example 17.6 shows how options may be used to hedge a position.

WORKED EXAMPLE 17.6

You currently own 1,000 securities. Their market price is £2.00 each. The shares were acquired under an executive compensation plan and may not be sold until July of this year. You are concerned about a drop in value of the security before July, when you plan to sell the shares.

The following information is available:

	Call	Put
July traded options: 200p series	10p	15p

There are two ways in which you can protect your position.

(a) Purchase a put option contract that gives you the right to sell your shares at 200p in July; cost 1,000 × 15p = £150.

- The current value of your portfolio is £2,000. The payment of £150 protects you from any further loss.
- The £150 is made up of 15p premiums, which means that you are bearing the loss in value from £2 to £1.85. After that, the loss is covered by the option (e.g. if the price falls to 150p, you can still sell your shares for 200p but you have incurred a cost of 15p per share).
- If the share price stays at 200p or appreciates in value then you would not exercise your put option.

(b) Write a call option contract; the premium obtained is 1,000 × 10p = £100.

- The current value of your portfolio is £2,000 but you have an additional 10p per share, which compensates you for a decline in share price down to 190p. Below this price, the loss in the value of your portfolio is borne entirely by you.
- If the price falls below 200p, the buyer will not exercise the option to purchase from you at 200p.
- If the price appreciates above 200p, the buyer will exercise the option to buy the shares from you for 200p. The premium protects you from losses for increases in share price up to 210p, but beyond this price your losses are potentially unlimited; this is an opportunity cost as you lose the opportunity to sell your shares for a price in excess of 200p.

If your portfolio is made up of a variety of shares and, say, you fear a drop in the stock market, you may be able to secure a partial hedge using the FTSE 100 index option.

WORKED EXAMPLE 17.7

It is April and you currently own 5,000 shares in Excal plc. The current share price is 345p and you must keep these for another three months, when you will sell them. The following information is available (all prices in pence):

Current share price	Exercise price	Call option price	Put option price
345			
	300	53	1
	350	15	10
	400	3	40

The share price of Excal plc is particularly volatile and you want to protect the value of your holding.

Required

Set out the different ways in which you can protect your holding of shares in Excal plc.

17.7 *continued*

Solution

You can protect your holding in the following ways.

(a) Buy put contracts.

You need to buy five contracts as you have 5,000 shares.
If you buy put options with a 350p exercise price, the cost will be 10p × 5,000 = £500.
If the share price does not rise above 350p, you will exercise the put contracts:

Sell 350p × 5,000	£17,500
Less	£500
Bring in 340p per share	£17,000

Alternatively, buy put options with a 400p exercise price, the cost will be 40p × 5,000 = £2,000.
If the share price does not exceed 400p, you will exercise the put contracts:

Sell 400p × 5,000	£20,000
Less	£2,000
Bring in 360p per share	£18,000

However, if you bought options with a 350p exercise price sold at 400p:

Sell 400p × 5,000	£20,000
Less	£500
Bring in 390p per share	£19,500

Of course, this is not guaranteed.

(b) Write call contracts

You write five call contracts at 350p.
The premium will be 15p × 5,000 = £750.
If the share price falls, this protects down to (345p–15p) = 330p.
Below 330p, you must bear the losses.
Below 350p, buyer will not exercise the option.
If the share price increases, this protects you up to (350p + 15p) = 365p.
If the price exceeds 365p, then you lose the opportunity to sell shares above 365p.

8.3 Forward rate agreements

A forward rate agreement (FRA) is issued by a bank and tailored to the specific needs of the purchaser. The key features of an FRA are as follows.

- The bank will agree to enter into a notional loan or accept a deposit from a customer for a specified period of time and to settle with the customer the difference between the interest rate agreed with the customer and the actual interest rate when the notional loan/deposit is deemed to start.
- The FRA is quite separate from the actual contract to borrow money, which may be from another source.
- If a loan is involved and the actual interest rate is greater than that specified in the FRA, the bank will pay the difference to the customer.
- If the reverse occurs and the actual interest rate is less than that specified under the FRA, the customer compensates the bank.

- FRAs are not traded on an exchange and so have the advantage of being tailored to the needs of the purchaser. However, there is the potential of the counterparty failing to complete the transaction.
- FRAs can be used by companies whose business is severely hit by increases in interest rates. Such companies can use FRAs to protect themselves when interest rates rise and demand falls off.

Worked example 17.8 illustrates the use of FRAs.

WORKED EXAMPLE 17.8

A company is to take out a £5 million loan for a year, starting in two months' time. Interest rates are currently 5%, but the company is concerned that rates might increase to 6.5% in the near future because of the rate of inflation.

The company secures an FRA with a bank. The bank has quoted a rate of 6.25%. The company agrees to this.

Scenario 1

Interest rates actually increase to 6.5%. As a result the bank compensates the company by providing it with:

(6.5% – 6.25%) × £5 million = £12,500

The company's net interest bill will be:

6.5% × £5 million	£325,000
less compensation	£12,500
	£312,500

The next interest of £312,500 is 6.25% of £5 million for one year.

Scenario 2

Interest rates actually increase to 6.1%. As a result the company compensates the bank by paying:

(6.25% – 6.1%) = 0.15% × £5 million = £7,500

The company's interest bill will be:

6.1% × £5 million	£305,000
add compensation	£7,500
	£312,500

As before, the net total interest of £312,500 is 6.25% of £5 million for one year.

WORKED EXAMPLE 17.9

A company is to take out a £10 million loan for six months, starting in three months' time. Interest rates are currently 7%, but the company is concerned that rates might increase to 8% in the near future. The company secures an FRA with a bank. The bank has quoted a rate of 7.45%. The company agrees to this.

Required

Set out different scenarios for the outcome using actual rates of 7.9% and 7.3%.

WORKED EXAMPLE **17.9** *continued*

Solution

Scenario 1: Interest rate 7.9%

		£
Bank compensates company	(7.9%–7.45%) × £10 million × 6/12	22,500
Company pays	7.9% × £10 million × 6/12	395,000
Less compensation		22,500
	7.45% × £310 million × 6/12	372,500

Scenario 2: Interest rate 7.3%

		£
Company compensates bank	(7.45%–7.3%) × £10 million × 6/12	7,500
Company pays	7.3% × £10 million × 6/12	365,000
Add compensation		7,500
	7.45% × £310 million 6/12	372,500

8.4 Swaps

Interest rate swaps involve two counterparties. They agree to swap their liabilities for interest rate payments on a given capital sum. This is usually a swap between a fixed interest rate liability and a variable interest rate liability. The end result is similar to an FRA, with the parties securing a reduction in exposure to interest rate changes. A swap can be agreed directly between two counterparties or with the aid of intermediaries.

Worked example 17.8 illustrates an interest rate swap.

WORKED EXAMPLE **17.10**

Company X has £15 million of variable rate loans tied to LIBOR +2%. LIBOR is currently 6% and the company is paying interest at 8%. The company treasurer is concerned that interest rates are about to rise but the company is unable to escape its variable rate loans as there is a five-year agreement with expensive escape clauses.

Company Y has £15 million of five-year fixed interest loans at 10%. The company treasurer does not feel that interest rates will increase significantly and wishes to get out of the straightjacket of a fixed 10% interest rate. Company Y is also locked into a five-year loan agreement.

If the two companies agree to swap their interest obligations, both achieve their aims. Company X will now be paying 10% fixed interest, happy in the knowledge that it is insulated from higher interest rates for the next five years. Company Y is free of the fixed-rate regime and is now paying interest at just 8%.

TEST YOUR KNOWLEDGE **17.5**

What is the objective of interest rate swaps?

8.5 Money market hedges

If a firm needs to obtain finance for a short period of time it can secure a loan against future income. This is often used where a company is involved in buying and selling in foreign markets. Instead of using the forward exchange market for currency, this contract uses the money market, where the price is the interest rate. The firm taking the loan borrows money in one currency and exchanges the resulting proceeds for another currency. Obviously, the borrower must have the funds to repay the loan. The cost of the money market hedge is determined by differential interest rates.

Worked example 17.11 demonstrates money market hedging.

WORKED EXAMPLE 17.11

A US firm sells telecoms equipment to a UK firm in March for £1 million. Payment is due three months later, in June.

The US company receives quotes as follows:

Spot exchange rate:	$1.7640/£
UK three-month borrowing interest rate:	10% (= 2.5% per quarter)

If the rate of exchange in three months is the same as the current spot exchange rate then the payment will be:

£1 million × 1.7640 = $1.764 million

The US firm's foreign exchange analyst forecasts that the spot rate in three months will be $1.76/£. This would give the US company $1.76 million, but there is no guarantee of this.

The US firm has low margins, like most manufacturing firms. The US firm would be happy if pound sterling appreciates against the dollar as this would give more dollars. The US firm is worried about pound sterling depreciating and giving fewer dollars. The US firm has calculated that to cover its costs it needs $1.7 million from the sale. Any depreciation in sterling below this will result in losses for the company.

A money market hedge strategy for the US firm in our example would be as follows.

- The US firm borrows sterling, for three months, in London as soon as the transaction is agreed.
- The company then immediately converts the borrowed pounds into dollars.
- The loan will then be repaid in three months' time using the money from the UK company's payment. In effect, the UK company's cash repays the sterling loan in pounds sterling – which means that all foreign exchange exposure is removed.

In this example, the US company hedges the sale proceeds from a foreign receivable by setting up a liability (i.e. borrowing). If a company imports and wants to hedge a purchase then it would need to set up a receivable (i.e. lend (see Worked example 17.13)).

How does the US company decide on the amount to borrow?

The US company should borrow an amount which will be exactly repaid with the proceeds from the UK company's payment in three months' time. We need to work out the exact amount. As the borrowing interest rate in the UK is 10%, or 2.5% per quarter, then we can find the amount to borrow as follows:

(1 + borrowing rate) × (amount to be borrowed by US company)	= amount payable
(1.025) × (amount to be borrowed)	= £1,000,000
thus, amount to be borrowed = £1,000,000/1.025	= £975,610

To summarise, the US company must borrow £975,610 for three months from a UK bank as soon as the transaction is created. The amount payable by the UK company in three months' time will cover £975,610 **plus** the bank interest (£24,390) (i.e. £1 million). The amount borrowed should be changed into dollars immediately.

This amount gives:

($1.764 × £975,610) = $1,720,976

and the net amount shown above exceeds the minimum of $1.7 million that the US company requires from the sale.

WORKED EXAMPLE 17.12

The same US company has concluded a second, larger, sale of telecoms equipment to Regency (UK). Total payment of £3 million is due in 90 days. Due to banking credit concerns, the US company will be able to borrow in the UK, but at a rate of 14% per annum. The following information is available.

Spot rate	$1.7620/£
90 day £ borrowing rate	14% per annum

Required

Prepare calculations to show how the company can carry out a money market hedge.

Solution

1. As soon as the equipment is delivered, borrow from a UK bank for 90 days.
2. 14% for 90 days = 3.5%. Therefore, borrow (£3 million/1.035) = £2,898,551.
3. Convert immediately to $ = £2,898,551 × 1.762 = $5,107,246.

WORKED EXAMPLE 17.13

A UK firm imports computer equipment costing $500,000 from a US company. Payment is due in three months time. The three-month US interest rate is 12% (= 3% per quarter). The spot rate of exchange is $1.6540/£.

If the rate of exchange in three months time is the same as the current spot exchange rate, then the payment will be:

$500,000/1.6540 = £302,297

The UK firm is concerned about the dollar strengthening against the pound, which will make the import more expensive.

A money market hedge strategy would be as follows:

- the UK firm buys US dollars at the spot rate at the time of the transaction
- the company places the US dollars on deposit for three months, and
- the amount placed on deposit will be received in three months' time and used to pay the amount owing to the US company.

The amount to be placed on deposit will be $500,000/1.03 = $485,436. The UK company pays $485,436/1.654 = £293,492 at the time of the transaction.

To summarise, the UK company buys $485,436 at the spot rate costing £293,492.The US dollars are placed on deposit and, in three months' time, the amount receivable will be $485,436 plus the interest ($14,564) i.e. $500,000, which will be used to pay the amount owing to the US company.

CHAPTER SUMMARY

The chapter has discussed the nature of risk and key risk concepts, such as operating risks, financial risks, risk exposure and risk responses. These represent important building blocks in your understanding of risk in financial decision-making. The chapter then discussed the relationship between risk and return, which is important and has been referred to elsewhere within this text.

The chapter then examined frameworks for managing risk within companies, with emphasis on enterprise risk management (ERM).

After discussing credit risk and management risk, the chapter considered hedging methods. These contained examples to explain the methods more fully – you should ensure that you understand these five hedging methods.

END OF CHAPTER QUESTIONS

17.1 You are employed in a large demolition and construction company. The company has no risk management policies or practices in place. Prepare a briefing paper in which you outline key risk concepts (namely, the nature of risk, exposure, volatility, severity and probability) and key risk responses including risk transfer, risk reduction, risk avoidance and risk retention.

17.2 Your company is involved in manufacturing wind turbines and is based in the UK. It has a contract to deliver 50 turbines in one month's time to a company in France; the French company will have a further three months to pay for the turbines. Prepare a briefing note outlining the main forms of financial risk and explaining how the company may use a money market hedge to protect its interests in the sale of turbines to the French company.

17.3 Juniper plc is a UK firm which manufactures and sells farm equipment. It exports mostly to the USA. At the end of June, Juniper sold equipment with an invoice value of $200,000 to a US firm. Payment is due three months later at the end of September. Juniper has received the following quotes:

Spot exchange rate:
$1.5940/£
US three-month borrowing interest rate: 9% per annum

Required

Prepare calculations to show how the company can carry out a money market hedge.

APPENDIX 1

Discount factor tables

Present value table

Present value (in £) of a single payment of £1, n years from now, discounted at a rate of r% per annum

Discount rate (r)

Years (n)	1%	2%	3%	4%	5%	6%	7%	8%	9%	10%
1	0.990	0.980	0.971	0.962	0.952	0.943	0.935	0.926	0.917	0.909
2	0.980	0.961	0.943	0.925	0.907	0.890	0.873	0.857	0.842	0.826
3	0.971	0.942	0.915	0.889	0.864	0.840	0.816	0.794	0.772	0.751
4	0.961	0.924	0.888	0.855	0.823	0.792	0.763	0.735	0.708	0.683
5	0.951	0.906	0.863	0.822	0.784	0.747	0.713	0.681	0.650	0.621
6	0.942	0.888	0.837	0.790	0.746	0.705	0.666	0.630	0.596	0.564
7	0.933	0.871	0.813	0.760	0.711	0.665	0.623	0.583	0.547	0.513
8	0.923	0.853	0.789	0.731	0.677	0.627	0.582	0.540	0.502	0.467
9	0.914	0.837	0.766	0.703	0.645	0.592	0.544	0.500	0.460	0.424
10	0.905	0.820	0.744	0.676	0.614	0.558	0.508	0.463	0.422	0.386
11	0.896	0.804	0.722	0.650	0.585	0.527	0.475	0.429	0.388	0.350
12	0.887	0.788	0.701	0.625	0.557	0.497	0.444	0.397	0.356	0.319
13	0.879	0.773	0.681	0.601	0.530	0.469	0.415	0.368	0.326	0.290
14	0.870	0.758	0.661	0.577	0.505	0.442	0.388	0.340	0.299	0.263
15	0.861	0.743	0.642	0.555	0.481	0.417	0.362	0.315	0.275	0.239
	11%	12%	13%	14%	15%	16%	17%	18%	19%	20%
1	0.901	0.893	0.885	0.877	0.870	0.862	0.855	0.847	0.840	0.833
2	0.812	0.797	0.783	0.769	0.756	0.743	0.731	0.718	0.706	0.694
3	0.731	0.712	0.693	0.675	0.658	0.641	0.624	0.609	0.593	0.579
4	0.659	0.636	0.613	0.592	0.572	0.552	0.534	0.516	0.499	0.482
5	0.593	0.567	0.543	0.519	0.497	0.476	0.456	0.437	0.419	0.402
6	0.535	0.507	0.480	0.456	0.432	0.410	0.390	0.370	0.352	0.335
7	0.482	0.452	0.425	0.400	0.376	0.354	0.333	0.314	0.296	0.279
8	0.434	0.404	0.376	0.351	0.327	0.305	0.285	0.266	0.249	0.233
9	0.391	0.361	0.333	0.308	0.284	0.263	0.243	0.225	0.209	0.194
10	0.352	0.322	0.295	0.270	0.247	0.227	0.208	0.191	0.176	0.162
11	0.317	0.287	0.261	0.237	0.215	0.195	0.178	0.162	0.148	0.135
12	0.286	0.257	0.231	0.208	0.187	0.168	0.152	0.137	0.124	0.112
13	0.258	0.229	0.204	0.182	0.163	0.145	0.130	0.116	0.104	0.093
14	0.232	0.205	0.181	0.160	0.141	0.125	0.111	0.099	0.088	0.078
15	0.209	0.183	0.160	0.140	0.123	0.108	0.095	0.084	0.074	0.065

Annuity table

Present value (in £) of a series of n equal annual payments of £1 a year, starting one year from now, discounted at a rate of r% per annum

Discount rate (r)

Years (n)	1%	2%	3%	4%	5%	6%	7%	8%	9%	10%
1	0.990	0.980	0.971	0.962	0.952	0.943	0.935	0.926	0.917	0.909
2	1.970	1.942	1.913	1.886	1.859	1.833	1.808	1.783	1.759	1.736
3	2.941	2.884	2.829	2.775	2.723	2.673	2.624	2.577	2.531	2.487
4	3.902	3.808	3.717	3.630	3.546	3.465	3.387	3.312	3.240	3.170
5	4.853	4.713	4.580	4.452	4.329	4.212	4.100	3.993	3.890	3.791
6	5.795	5.601	5.417	5.242	5.076	4.917	4.767	4.623	4.486	4.355
7	6.728	6.472	6.230	6.002	5.786	5.582	5.389	5.206	5.033	4.868
8	7.652	7.325	7.020	6.733	6.463	6.210	5.971	5.747	5.535	5.335
9	8.566	8.162	7.786	7.435	7.108	6.802	6.515	6.247	5.995	5.759
10	9.471	8.983	8.530	8.111	7.722	7.360	7.024	6.710	6.418	6.145
11	10.37	9.787	9.253	8.760	8.306	7.887	7.499	7.139	6.805	6.495
12	11.26	10.58	9.954	9.385	8.863	8.384	7.943	7.536	7.161	6.814
13	12.13	11.35	10.63	9.986	9.394	8.853	8.358	7.904	7.487	7.103
14	13.00	12.11	11.30	10.56	9.899	9.295	8.745	8.244	7.786	7.367
15	13.87	12.85	11.94	11.12	10.38	9.712	9.108	8.559	8.061	7.606

Years (n)	11%	12%	13%	14%	15%	16%	17%	18%	19%	20%
1	0.901	0.893	0.885	0.877	0.870	0.862	0.855	0.847	0.840	0.833
2	1.713	1.690	1.668	1.647	1.626	1.605	1.585	1.566	1.547	1.528
3	2.444	2.402	2.361	2.322	2.283	2.246	2.210	2.174	2.140	2.106
4	3.102	3.037	2.974	2.914	2.855	2.798	2.743	2.690	2.639	2.589
5	3.696	3.605	3.517	3.433	3.352	3.274	3.199	3.127	3.058	2.991
6	4.231	4.111	3.998	3.889	3.784	3.685	3.589	3.498	3.410	3.326
7	4.712	4.567	4.423	4.288	4.160	4.039	3.922	3.812	3.706	3.605
8	5.146	4.968	4.799	4.639	4.487	4.344	4.207	4.078	3.954	3.837
9	5.537	5.328	5.132	4.946	4.772	4.607	4.451	4.303	4.163	4.031
10	5.889	5.650	5.426	5.216	5.019	4.833	4.659	4.494	4.339	4.192
11	6.207	5.938	5.687	5.453	5.234	5.029	4.836	4.656	4.486	4.327
12	6.492	6.194	5.918	5.660	5.421	5.197	4.988	4.793	4.611	4.439
13	6.750	6.424	6.122	5.842	5.583	5.342	5.118	4.910	4.715	4.533
14	6.982	6.628	6.302	6.002	5.724	5.468	5.229	5.008	4.802	4.611
15	7.191	6.811	6.462	6.142	5.847	5.575	5.324	5.092	4.876	4.675

APPENDIX 2

SOLUTIONS TO END OF CHAPTER QUESTIONS

1 Objectives and governance

1.1 The purpose of financial management is to ensure the company achieves its financial objectives. It involves deciding what investments to make and choosing sources of funds for investment and payment of dividends. Financial objectives should be set as part of the company's strategy in furtherance of its corporate objectives. While corporate objectives are likely to remain reasonably stable over an extended period of time, the chosen strategies, and the shorter-term targets set as part of the implementation of these strategies, may vary with circumstances, including the economic situation. Financial strategy and financial objectives will also need to vary in conjunction with, and as part of, corporate strategy. For example, capital investment activity will be linked to the prospects for businesses and to the availability of funding. Both will be affected by a general recession, so financial objectives concerning investment will change.

The form of investment will change because the relative costs of direct investment in assets and acquisition of companies will change, and the cost of debt capital and equity will also change. So the form and financing of investment will be affected.

Bank of England interest rates, and with them the cost and availability of debt capital, will be influenced by the economic situation; so will stock market sentiment and the availability and cost of new equity capital. Sales are likely to be less buoyant, or to fall, in a recession, and the company may trade down to adjust to changed consumer behaviour. This will affect the availability of internally generated funds. So objectives concerning the sources, as well as the amounts, of capital required for investment will be affected.

Shareholders will understand, in differing degrees, the significance of the above considerations for dividend policy. The company may wish to maintain dividends so as to signal to the financial community that any downturn in business and profits is temporary. It may also be aware, at times of economic downturn, of an increased desire on the part of investors to maintain their cash flow. On the other hand, it may wish to conserve cash and may believe that it has communicated effectively to shareholders that a dividend cut is a prudent measure in straitened circumstances.

The economic situation may thus affect dividend policy and objectives.

1.2 The attitudes of a company's shareholders have a major effect on the availability and cost of capital. If they sell their shares, the share price is likely to fall and the cost of equity capital will rise. If the stock market is poorly informed about the company's prospects, the share price may not fully reflect these prospects. In addition, the uncertainty arising from imperfect information will increase the perceived risk associated with investment in the shares, and the required rate of return will rise (this is discussed in more detail in Chapter 9). Similar considerations apply to lenders, though these may be more sophisticated investors, such as banks and other financial institutions, who are better placed to inform themselves.

It is therefore important for a company to ensure that its shareholders and other investors understand the business and its prospects, so that they can fully value the company's securities and interpret bad news in context, rather than taking ill-informed decisions in situations where, according to theorists, the market is least likely to form a rational view of the information available to value shares.

In some respects, UK industry and commerce has been aware for many decades of the need to keep investors properly informed. In the 1960s, asset strippers gained control of companies whose shares were undervalued because those companies had not revalued their land and buildings, so that the net assets were understated in their balance sheets.

Directors realised that they had to provide more up-to-date information about asset values or risk falling victim to a hostile takeover bid. In more recent years (i.e. since the

1980s) this understanding has become more general and sophisticated. The growth of consultancies specialising in corporate communication, financial public relations and investor relations bears testimony to this. A major part of the purpose of these consultancies is to advise their clients so that their companies' share can be fully valued and the cost of capital kept to a minimum.

The Combined Code published by the Hampel Committee on the Principles of Good Governance, incorporating the work of the Cadbury Committee and the Greenbury Committee, was concerned with relationships with shareholders, as well as the constitution of the board and directors' remuneration. It formulated good practice concerning dialogue with, and accountability to, shareholders, particularly institutional shareholders. This was reinforced in the UK Corporate Governance Code.

The audit, which is at the heart of mechanisms controlling corporate governance, is a form of communication with shareholders. The auditors' report to shareholders and the shareholders' vote in the annual general meeting to accept the accounts, together with the auditors' report, confirm that shareholders can rely on what the directors tell them in the accounts.

1.3 The agent–principal problem arises because no two groups will have identical objectives. The closest match may be the management and shareholders of a private company, where the board and the shareholders may be substantially or completely the same. Otherwise the interests of managers may not even closely match the interests of other stakeholder groups. In one sense the interests of all stakeholder groups may coincide, since all stakeholder groups have an interest in the success of the company. However, different stakeholders may define success in different terms.

Shareholders will measure success by the long-term growth of profits and share values; employees may be interested in secure and growing employment opportunities; customers may want a stable, high-quality, low-cost supplier; banks may want a company that is profitable and solvent; the government may want a good corporate citizen that generates a stable and increasing level of economic activity and pays its taxes; and specialist interest groups may want a company that protects the environment, sells safe or ethically acceptable products or services or trades fairly with developing countries.

Managers may want to do all these: partly because they are laudable things that commend themselves to reasonable and decent people, and partly because they are consistent with the long-term maximisation of shareholder returns, but also because they are consistent with the achievement of managers' own specific aims. The latter could include: increased job scope and responsibility, associated with financial and other material rewards, power, prestige and job satisfaction.

Sometimes there will be inconsistencies and conflicts between management's objectives and those of other stakeholders. For example, on occasion, managers will judge it necessary to cut jobs. This is likely to conflict directly with the interests of other employees. Unmediated and unreconciled disputes with suppliers or customers are likely to lead to a gain by one party at the expense of the other (e.g. a company that minimises its tax bill will frustrate the purposes of the government).

In a more general sense, management objectives will be in line with those of shareholders. Managers who maximise shareholder value will encourage shareholders to buy or keep their shares, thereby reducing the cost of capital. They will also improve their own career prospects. So by furthering shareholders' objectives, managers will either make it easier to do their own job well or improve their chance for personal gain.

2 Management performance measurement

2.1 (a)

1 Management of working capital			
Current ratio	current assets/current liabilities	700/635 =	1.1
Liquidity ratio	(current assets – inventory)/ current liabilities	465/635 =	0.73
Rate of inventory turnover	(average inventory/cost of goods sold) × 365	235/2,700 × 365 =	32 days
2 Profitability			
Gross profit ratio	(gross profit/sales) × 100	2,800/5,500 × 100 =	51%
Operating profit percentage	(operating profit/sales) × 100	1,250/5,500 × 100 =	23%
ROCE	(operating profit /current equity) × 100	1,250/6,065 × 100 =	21%
3 Gearing			
Balance sheet (using the suggested approach in the question)	(non-current liabilities/ total equity) × 100	3,000/3,065 × 100 =	98%
Interest cover	operating profit/interest	1,250/300 =	4.2

(b) **Commentary**

1 The current ratio is 1.1 and, as it is more than 1, this is positive. However, if it was higher and nearer 2, this would give more assurance to the company's short-term liquidity. Commentary is limited by the absence of trend data or comparative figures from a comparative company.

2 The liquidity ratio is 0.73. This would be a cause for concern as a norm of 1 is recommended and the payment of dividends and taxation may require overdraft facilities. However, inventory turns over very quickly in this company (just 32 days), so we can accept that the liquidity ratio is not as risky as it first appears.

3 The gross profit ratio is 51%, which is in line with the expectations for the business.

4 The operating profit is 23%. This is approximately 46% of gross profit, so that overheads amounted to approximately 54% of gross profit. This is significantly lower than the expected figure of overheads at two-thirds of gross profit. This suggests that the company is being run more efficiently than expected.

5 ROCE seems acceptable at 21%, but comparative figures from previous years and from other companies would provide useful reference points.

6 Non-current liabilities are 98% of equity. The expected gearing ratio is 25% of equity, so the company is far more highly geared, with much more borrowing, than expected. This implies the possibility of financial problems if profits decline, but relatively high returns for investors in Merino when profits are buoyant.

7 Interest cover is at 4.2, which is good. The expected figure is 5 so the actual level of interest cover is slightly below the expected figure. Despite the very high level of gearing, the company's efficiency in keeping overheads relatively low means that interest cover is stronger than might be expected, given the gearing level.

2.2 (a)

	£000s	Ackworth	Cohn
Gross asset turnover	7,200/2,400	3	
	9,000/6,000		1.5
Operating profit percentage	600/7,200 × 100	8.3%	
	1,200/9,000 × 100		13.3%
Rate of return on gross assets	600/2,400 × 100	25%	
	1,200/6,000 × 100		20%

(b) Typical comments might include the following:

- The directors of Cohn follow business policies that result in a ratio of gross asset turnover in line with that achieved, on average, by members of the trade association. The directors of Ackworth have succeeded in achieving twice the level of asset turnover, reflecting a much greater ability to 'make assets sweat'.
- The operating profit percentage of Cohn is closely in line with the trade association average, indicating a price and cost structure in line with what might be regarded as the 'typical' firm in this industry. The operating profit percentage of Ackworth is significantly lower, possibly reflecting a lower pricing policy designed to increase the level of sales and asset utilisation.
- The rate of return earned by Cohn on gross assets is marginally below that of the average for members of the trade association, reflecting the slightly lower operating profit percentage. The rate of return by Ackworth is significantly higher, indicating the success of their combined strategy of lower prices and higher asset utilisation compared with the average firm.

2.3 (a)

Ratio		Euro		Dollar
Profitability	Workings		Workings	
ROCE %	104/856 × 100	12.15	104/655 × 100	15.88
Return on equity %	51/792 × 100	6.44	41/400 × 100	10.25
Gross profit ratio %	193/570 × 100	33.86	199/747 × 100	26.64
Operating profit %	104/570 × 100	18.25	104/747 × 100	13.92
Efficiency				
Total asset turnover	570/(785 + 271)	0.54	747/(563 + 252)	0.92
Non-current asset turnover	570/785	0.73	747/563	1.33
Current asset turnover	570/271	2.10	747/252	2.96
Average inventories (days)	94/377 × 365	91.01	112/548 × 365	74.60
Rate of collection of receivables (days)	166/570 × 365	106.30	124/747 × 365	60.59
Rate of payment of payables (days)	132/381 × 365	126.46	97/568 × 365	62.33
Short-term solvency				
Current ratio	271/200	1.36	252/160	1.58
Liquidity ratio	175/200	0.88	130/160	0.81
Gearing				
Book value gearing %	64/856 × 100	7.48	255/655 × 100	38.93
Market value gearing %	64/[64 + (470 × 3.5)] × 100	3.74	255 [255 + (250 × 4.65)] × 100	17.99
Interest cover	104/7	14.86	104/27	3.85
Investment ratios				
Dividend payout ratio %	37/51 × 100	72.55	30/41 × 100	73.17
Dividend cover ratio	51/37	1.38	41/30	1.37
Dividend per share (pence)	37/470 × 100	7.87	30/250 × 100	12.00
Dividend yield ratio %	7.87/350 × 100	2.25	12/465 × 100	2.58
EPS (pence)	51/470 × 100	10.85	41/250 × 100	16.40
P/E ratio	350/10.85	32.26	465/16.4	28.35

(b) **Profitability**

Dollar makes better use of its resources with a higher ROCE, and it also makes a higher return on equity. However, Euro's gross profit ratio and operating profit percentage are higher.

Efficiency

- Dollar's asset turnover is better than Euro's, which explains why Dollar's ROCE is higher despite its lower gross profit and operating profit percentages.
- Dollar holds inventory for 75 days, or almost 11 weeks, but Euro holds stock for 16 days longer than this. Dollar collects receivables in 61 days and Euro in 106 days. Dollar is much more efficient in its management of inventory and trade receivables.
- Euro takes 126 days (18 weeks) to pay receivables, but Dollar pays them off in half the time: 62 days.

Short-term solvency

Dollar's current ratio is higher than Euro's, but at 1.58 is lower than might be preferred. Euro's liquidity ratio (0.88) is slightly higher than Dollar's (0.81), but both give cause for concern as they are below 1 and both companies might suffer liquidity problems with recourse to bank overdraft. This might apply particularly to Euro as it takes so long to collect its trade receivables.

Gearing

Euro's gearing is much lower than Dollar's. Dollar's gearing may help to explain its higher ROCE, using cheaper loan finance. Euro's interest cover gives a higher level of security than Dollar's.

Investment ratios

Payout ratio and dividend cover ratio for both companies are almost identical. Dollar's dividend yield ratio is slightly higher than Euro's. Dollar's EPS is higher, but this needs to be related to the share price. Euro's P/E ratio is higher than Dollar's, reflecting higher market expectations of Euro.

3 Distribution

3.1 (a) The argument that the pattern of dividends is important was first raised in the early literature on dividend policy. It rests on the assumption that investors would prefer to receive a certain amount of money today rather than have this amount reinvested in the business. This is because investors value certainty: they view amounts received today more highly than amounts to be received in the future. Future dividends are uncertain and so will be discounted to reflect this uncertainty. If this argument is accepted by the directors of Upton, the dividend policy should be to distribute as much as possible in order to maximise shareholder wealth.

Modigliani and Miller (MM) rejected this view of dividends. Starting from the assumption of perfect and efficient markets, they argued that the pattern of dividends will have no effect on shareholder wealth. It will simply represent a movement of cash from inside to outside the business. They argued that the value of a business is determined by the investments that it undertakes. To maximise shareholder wealth, a business must seek out profitable opportunities and accept all those that yield a positive NPV. The way in which the benefits of these investments are allocated between retention and distribution will have no effect on shareholder wealth. Thus, the dividend decision does not matter. MM point out that if investors wish to receive dividends, they can create their own dividend policy by selling a portion of the shares held. Although the logic of the MM position is compelling, their argument rests on a number of restrictive assumptions. In particular, it assumes a world where there are no share transaction costs, no share issue costs and no taxation.

In the real world, there is little doubt that the pattern of dividends is regarded by investors and directors as important. One possible explanation is the 'clientele effect'.

It is argued that investors will seek out companies with dividend policies that are in line with their needs. Thus, a business with a high dividend policy may attract investors that require dividends to supplement their income. On the other hand, a business that pays very low, or no, dividends may attract investors who prefer capital gains to dividend income. This may be because, in some countries, capital gains are treated differently for tax purposes than dividends. In the UK, for example, only capital gains beyond a threshold of £11,100 (2015/16) are liable to taxation. This may be of particular value to high-rate taxpayers.

A further possible reason is that the directors of a company may have information relating to the future prospects of the business that shareholders do not have. The directors may wish to transmit this information indirectly though the dividends announced. Hence, confidence in future profitability may be signalled by an increase in the level of dividends announced. Although this is an expensive method of signalling confidence in the future, it is more likely to be taken seriously by shareholders than announcements to this effect. Research studies that monitor the reaction of share prices to changes in dividend policy suggest that these changes are interpreted as important signals regarding future prospects. Share prices rise or fall depending on whether increases or decreases in dividends are announced.

(b) In practice, the amount paid out by a business in dividends may be determined by various factors, including the following.

- **Market expectations:** Investors may develop expectations concerning the amount of dividends that a business will pay each year. These expectations may be formed by earlier announcements or by the pattern of dividends that has occurred in the past. If these expectations are not fulfilled, there may be a loss of investor confidence, leading to serious repercussions.
- **Legal restrictions:** To protect creditors, the law limits the amount that can be distributed by a business in the form of dividends. For example, a UK private limited company can only pay dividends out of realised profits.
- **Earnings stability:** Where a business has a stable and predictable pattern of earnings over time, it should be better placed to make higher dividend distributions than a business with unstable and unpredictable earnings. This is partly because there will be less need to retain earnings to allow for unexpected events.
- **Financing options:** In certain situations, such as an economic recession, it may be difficult to raise finance from external sources. Where this is the case, a business may have to rely on retained earnings to fund new investment opportunities. As a result, the amounts available for dividends will be restricted.
- **Loan covenants:** Where a business has loan capital, conditions may be contained within the loan agreement that restrict the amount of dividend to be paid during the period of the loan. Such restrictions are designed to protect the interests of the lenders.

3.2 (a) Report to: Finance director
From: Company secretary
Date: 30 November 20XX
Subject: Returns to shareholders

As requested, I give below comments on the financial management implications of the three approaches to shareholder payments:

(i) Increase dividend per share

- Cash is returned to shareholders.
- The market may respond positively as this can indicate improved future profitability.
- As the product is maturing, less investment is required, so returns can increase.
- The company may face liquidity problems due to increased cash pay-outs.
- It may cause concern to existing shareholders who bought shares for growth rather than income. Increased dividends may indicate that the company has no new profitable investment opportunities.

(ii) Repurchase shares
- Increase in future EPS as profits will be earned by fewer shares.
- Existing shareholders increase their voting power.
- It may make it harder for an outsider to make a takeover bid.
- Cash flow problems may occur as repurchase requires cash.
- Existing shareholders must approve the repurchase.
- Gearing is increased.

(iii) Continue existing policy
- Cash flow will not be affected by additional payouts.
- Resources are maintained within the company for future investment.
- Shareholders invest in companies to receive dividends; they may resent the company holding onto resources.
- The company may be retaining resources for which it has no profitable use.

(b) In order to stimulate business growth Atherton may:
- try to increase market share of its existing business by advertising
- develop new products with subsequent investment requirements
- expand its markets, possibly in other EU countries
- maintain quality, but try to reduce costs to meet price competition
- go further up-market to increase differentiation.

4 Investment appraisal 1

4.1 (a)

Year	Additional fee income	Additional running costs	Net cash flow	Cumulative cash flow
	£000s	£000s	£000s	£000s
0				–500
1	125	120	5	–495
2	170	120	50	–445
3	215	120	95	–350
4	215	120	95	–255
5	215	120	95	–160
5	Additional resale value		700	+540

Notes:

Fees

The existing membership will pay an additional 80% of £250 = £200; new members will pay 180% × 250 = £450

Year 1 = (400 × £200) + (100 × £450) = £125,000

Year 2 = (400 × £200) + (200 × £450)= £170,000

Years 3, 4 and 5 = (400 × £200) + (300 × £450) = £215,000

Additional running costs = £200,000 – £80,000 = £120,000

Payback period = five years (when the club is sold for £1.7 million, an increase of £700,000 on its undeveloped value).

(b) NPV

Year	Net cash flow	10% discount factors	Present value
	£000s		£000s
0	–500	1	–500
1	5	0.909	+4.545
2	50	0.826	+41.300
3	95	0.751	+71.345
4	95	0.683	+64.885
5	95	0.621	+58.995
5	700	0.621	+434.700
		NPV	175.770

(c) Assuming that the projections are realistic, the positive NPV suggests that it is worth investing in the swimming pool. However, the positive NPV is almost entirely due to the enhanced resale value at the end of year 5. If this does not occur, the NPV would be a negative £258,930 (175.77 – 434.7). So, the additional net cash flow from installing the swimming pool does not provide for a positive return over five years. To proceed with this project would be very risky unless Rowena Hull is absolutely confident that the increase in the resale value will be as she has indicated.

4.2 Viernes Ltd.

(a) Capital allowances and tax saved:
(It is assumed that tax is paid or saved one year in arrears.)

Year	Calculations	Capital allowances	Reducing balance	Tax saved on capital allowances
		£	£	£
1	£125,000 × 0.25	31,250	93,750	
2	£93,750 × 0.25	23,437	70,313	9,375
3	£70,313 × 0.25	17,578	52,735	7,031
4	£52,735 × 0.25	13,184	39,551	5,273
5	£50,000 – £39,551	–10,449		3,955
6				–3,135

Year	12% discount factor	Capital	Tax saving	ANCF	Present value
		£000s	£000s	£000s	£000s
0	1	–125		–125	–125
1	0.893				
2	0.797		9.375	9.375	7.472
3	0.712		7.031	7.031	5.006
4	0.636		5.273	5.273	3.354
5	0.567	+50	3.955	53.955	30.592
6	0.507		–3.135	–3.135	–1.589
NPV					–80.165

(b)

Year	12% discount factor	Lease	Tax saving	ANCF	Present value
		£000s	£000s	£000s	£000s
0	1	–35		–35	–35
1	0.893	–35		–35	–31.255
2	0.797	–35	10.5	–24.5	–19.538
3	0.712	–35	10.5	–24.5	–17.447
4	0.636	–35	10.5	–24.5	–15.580
5	0.567		10.5	10.5	5.953
6	0.507		10.5	10.5	5.323
NPV					–107.544

(c) The figures show that the purchase option is cheaper than the lease option; in present value terms, it is over £27,000 cheaper than lease over the appraisal period.

4.3 Annual WDA and ANCFs
(It is assumed that tax is paid or saved one year in arrears.)

Year	Opening balance	WDA (25%)	Closing balance	Tax saved (30%)	Contribution	Tax on annual contribution	ANCF
1	200,000	50,000	150,000		75,000		75,000
2	150,000	37,500	112,500	15,000	75,000	–22,500	67,500
3	112,500	28,125	84,375	11,250	75,000	–22,500	63,750
4	(84,375 – 40,000) = £44,375			8,437	75,000	–22,500	60,937
5				13,312		–22,500	–9,188

(a) Payback and discounted payback

1	2	3	4	5	6	7
		Cash flow	Cumulative cash flow	8% discount factor	Present value (col. 3 × col. 5)	Cumulative present value
Year	0	–200,000	–200,000	1.000	–200,000	–200,000
	1	+75,000	–125,000	0.926	+69,450	–130,550
	2	+67,500	–57,500	0.857	+57,847	–72,703
	3	+63,750	+6,250	0.794	+50,617	–22,086
	4	+100,937		0.735	+74,189	
	5	–9,188		0.681	–6,257	
				NPV	+45,846	

Payback period = 2 years + (57,500/63,750× 52 weeks) = 2 years 47 weeks
Discounted payback = 3 years + [22,086/(60,937 × 0.735) × 52 weeks] = 3 years 26 weeks (£ 60,937 is used as £100,937 contains £40,000 that arrives at the end of the year).

(b) See calculation of NPV with 'Discounted payback' in (a). NPV at 8% = £45,846

(c) Calculation of IRR:
NPV at 8% = £45,846
NPV at 18%:

Year	18% discount factor	ANCF	Present value
		£	£
0	1.000	–200,000	–200,000
1	0.847	75,000	63,525
2	0.718	67,500	48,465
3	0.609	63,750	38,824
4	0.516	100,937	52,083
5	0.437	–9,188	–4,015
		NPV	–1,118

IRR = 8% + (45,846/(45,846 – (–1118))) × (18% – 8%)
= 8% + (45,846/46,964) × 10% = 8% + 9.76% = 17.76%

(d) Main points of the briefing note:

1. The scheme attracts significant capital allowances.
2. It has a positive NPV of £45,846 using the cost of capital of 8%.
3. The project pays back in 2 years and 47 weeks and has a discounted payback period of 3 years and 26 weeks.
4. It is recommended that the company proceeds with this project.

4.4 (a) Statement of profit or loss for year ended 31 March 2015

	£
Revenues	
Ticket sales (note 1)	9,131,250
Sponsorship	1,250,000
	10,381,250
Less expenses	
Players' wages	2,200,000
Management costs	1,000,000
Training ground rent	100,000
Other overheads	1,500,000
Advertising	200,000
Depreciation (note 2)	2,050,000
Total	7,050,000
Net profit	3,331,250

Note 1: ticket sales	(£)
6,000 × £800 =	4,800,000
1,750 × 25 × £30 =	1,312,500
4,200 × 25 × £25 =	2,625,000
1,050 × 25 × £15 =	393,750
Total	9,131,250

Note 2: depreciation	(£)
Cost of stadium	10,000,000
Gymnasium	250,000
Total	10,250,000

Annual depreciation = £10,250,000/5 = £2,050,000

(b) ANCF = £3,331,250 + depreciation (£2,050,000) = £5,381,250.

Capital allowances

Cost b/f	Allowance	Bal c/f	Tax saved	Year	
£	£	£	£		
10,250,000	2,562,500	7,687,500	512,500	1	
7,687,500	1,921,875	5,765,625	384,375	2	
5,765,625	1,441,406	4,324,219	288,281	3	
4,324,219	1,081,055	3,243,164	216,211	4	
3,243,164	3,243,164	0	648,633	5	
0	0	0	0	6	Allowances
	10,250,000		2,050,000		

NPV

Year	0	1	2	3	4	5	6
	£	£	£	£	£	£	£
Capital cost	−10,250,000						
ANCF		5,381,250	5,381,250	5,381,250	5,381,250	5,381,250	
Tax on ANCF			−1,076,250	−1,076,250	−1,076,250	−1,076,250	−1,076,250
Tax savings			512,500	384,375	288,281	216,211	648,633
Net cash flow	−10,250,000	5,381,250	4,817,500	4,689,375	4,593,281	4,521,211	−427,617
Discount factor	1	0.870	0.756	0.658	0.572	0.497	0.432
Present value	−10,250,000	4,681687	3,642,030	3,085,608	2,627356	2,247,042	−184730,
NPV	5,848,933						

(c) The new stadium produces a positive NPV of £5,848,933 and does seem an attractive proposition. However, the offer to renew the rental agreement on the existing stadium, albeit at a higher rent, places a different complexion on things.

The existing stadium produces a higher NPV over five years and should be preferred. However, it produces a slightly lower annual net profit than the new stadium: £3,325,000, compared with £3,331,250. Yet, in project appraisal, the DCF approach is superior to annual net profit comparisons.

The existing stadium is a less risky alternative as it does not require the club to engage in a high level of capital expenditure; while the existing stadium is filled to capacity, there is no guarantee that the ticket sales projected for the new stadium would actually be realised.

However, the new stadium does provide an opportunity for the club to grow.

5 Investment appraisal 2

5.1 Evaluation of projects

Project:	Borune	Honeth	Rane	Vordue
	£	£	£	£
Annual cash flow	330,000	290,000	230,000	200,000
10% present value of annuity	4.355	4.355	4.355	4.355
Present value of annual cash flow	1,437,150	1,262,950	1,001,650	871,000
Outlay	1,200,000	1,100,000	840,000	700,000
NPV	237,150	162,950	161,650	171,000
Profitability index (NPV/outlay)	0.20	0.15	0.19	0.24

(a) Assuming all projects are independent, the order of preference for the products should be as follow:

Rank	Product	Cost (£)
1	Vordue	700,000
2	Borune	1,200,000
3	Rane	840,000
4	Honeth	1,100,000

Given the capital expenditure limit of £1,600,000 the company should therefore undertake full production of Vordue and 75% of Borune. The total NPV of this solution is £348,862.

(b) Assuming Borune and Vordue are mutually exclusive, the products can be split into two groups, one excluding Borune and the other excluding Vordue. The order of preference for each group will be as follows:

Excluding Borune				Excluding Vordue			
Rank	Product	Cost £000s	NPV £000s	Rank	Product	Cost £000s	NPV £000s
1	Vordue	700	171.00	1	Borune	1,200	237.15
2	Rane	840	161.65	2	Rane	840	**76.980
3	Honeth	1,100	*8.89	3	Honeth	1,100	
Total			341.54				314.13

* Can afford 60/1,100 of Honeth's capital cost producing 60/1,100 of its NPV.
** Can afford 400/840 of Rane's capital cost producing 400/840 of its NPV.
The first option produces the higher NPV and should be accepted.

(c) **Limitations**

1 Pro rata investment and pro rata NPV rest on the highly simplistic assumption of divisibility.

2 Pro rata investment may be impossible for technical reasons (e.g. a bridge) or for reasons of efficient scale (e.g. a power station).

3 It also assumes constant returns to scale with no efficiencies for large-scale production.

If any of these assumptions do not apply, the profitability index does not work. Instead we have to look at total NPV values of all the possible alternative combinations of whole projects.

5.2

	£	10% discount factor	Present value
Gas boiler			
Capital cost	6,000	1.000	6,000.0
Annual cost (10 years)	3,000	6.145	18,435.0
NPV of cost			24,435.0
Annual equivalent cost = £24,435/6.145 =			3,976.4
Electric boiler			
Capital cost	3,000	1.000	3,000.0
Annual cost (7 years)	4,000	4.868	19,472.0
NPV of cost			22,472.0
Annual equivalent cost = £22,472/4.868 =			4,616.2

The gas boiler has the lowest annual equivalent cost (AEC) and is the recommended option.

5.3 (a) A post-completion appraisal (or audit) provides an opportunity to check the assumptions that were made, the information used and the evaluations done when the project was proposed and assessed before it was accepted. This may lead to a learning process for individuals and the organisation. If similar projects are likely to be undertaken in future, it may help to improve the collection and interpretation of information for evaluation, avoid over-optimistic projections by project advocates and provide guidance on how to implement and operate similar projects in future. To be effective, it needs to be carried out in a spirit of enquiry and learning, rather than being focused on the apportionment of blame. Organisations with good reputations for the successful management of projects, including meeting deadlines within budget, carry out this kind of review as a matter of course.

Issues to be considered before initiating procedures to carry out post-completion audits include the following.

- Will the organisation be able to approach the exercise with the objectives outlined, and with a sufficient degree of cooperation to make the process constructive and useful, rather than inquisitorial and destructive?
- How much it will cost? (More detailed records will have to be kept during the life of projects, and time will have to be spent on the audit.)
- How relevant will the results be? (There needs to be a prospect of applying the lessons learnt to future investments.)
- What is the balance between cost and return? (This could lead a company to restrict audits to large or repeatable projects, or to audit only a random sample of smaller projects.)
- How long will it be necessary to wait after implementation before auditing? (It may not be necessary to wait until the end of the life of the investment, which will mean that results can be available faster and the cost of collecting and analysing information kept down.)

(b) (i) The costs of machines A and B can be compared by calculating annual equivalent costs (AECs), since one or other of the machines will be needed for the foreseeable future and therefore whichever machine is purchased will need to be replaced at the end of its useful life.

The present value of operating each machine for its economic life is calculated, and then expressed as an AEC using an annuity factor, as follows:

Present value of operating machine for economic life

AEC can be used to compare machines A and B, even though they have different economic lives, provided that at the end of its life the asset is replaced by a similar one. We need to assume that the prices of A and B remain constant, or use a 'real' cost of capital adjusted for price changes. The cost of capital, whether the money cost or the real cost, is assumed to remain constant.

Calculation of AECs is as follows:

	Machine A	Machine B
Present value of costs	£	£
Initial cost	50,000	90,000
Running cost		
£10,000 × 3.170 (4 years at 10%)	31,700	
£8,000 × 4.868 (7 years at 10%)		38,944
Less salvage value £5,000 × 0.683	–3,415	
£7,000 × 0.513		–3,591
Total present value of costs (a)	78,285	125,353
Annuity factor (b)	3.170	4.868
Equivalent annual cost (a/b)	24,696	25,750

On the assumptions stated, machine A will be replaced on a four-year cycle, with costs equivalent to identical annual cash flows of £24,696 repeating on a four-year cycle and continuing indefinitely into the future. Machine B will be replaced on a seven-year cycle, with costs equivalent to annual cash flows of £25,750 repeating on a seven-year cycle and also continuing indefinitely into the future. Since the annual cash flows for machine A are less, machine A should be chosen.

(b) (ii) For the two machines to be equally financially attractive, the initial cost of machine A needs to rise until the AEC of A is £25,750, the same as for machine B. An AEC of £25,750 for machine A would make the present value of the total costs over the four-year cycle for machine A:

£25,750 × 3.170 = £81,628
Deduct present value now £78,285
Increase in present value of total costs = £3,343

If this increase is due to an increase in the initial cost of machine A, this initial cost needs to rise from £50,000 to £50,000 + £3,343 = £53,343.

5.4 (a) Real cost of capital = [(1 + 0.21)/(1 + 0.1)] – 1 = 0.1 = 10%

Option 1 present machine	£000s
Sales	288
Variable costs of manufacture	200
Contribution	88
Present value of contribution over four years = £88,000 × 3.17	278,960
Option 2 using the new machine	
Sales	288
Variable costs of manufacture	140
Contribution	148
Present value of contribution over four years = £148,000 × 3.17	469,160
Less cost of new machine	190
Add sale of existing machine	12
NPV of new machine	291,160

(The development and installation costs of £150,000 for the existing machine are not relevant to the decision on whether to buy the new machine. These costs are sunk costs which are not affected by the decision. We are only concerned with costs where there is a difference between the two alternatives.)

(b) The present machine makes a contribution of £88,000 per annum for four years, with a present value of £278,960. The new and more efficient machine will increase the contribution to £148,000 per annum. Allowing for the initial cost of £190,000 and the £12,000 proceeds from the sale of the existing machine, the NPV of buying and operating the new machine is £291,160. The small proportional increase in NPV (£12,200 on £278,960) needs to be carefully weighed against the risks of the project:

- Will the market for plastic cricket bats continue to be buoyant?
- Might the variable production costs increase?

Either possibility could easily eliminate any advantage, so it is probably better not to invest in the new machine.

The initial net outlay of £178,000 on the new machine generates an increase of £60,000 in the annual contribution, which gives a payback period of 2.97 years, as compared with the new machine's total useful life of four years; it takes almost 75% of its productive life to pay back its cost. This indicates a high level of risk for the investment required to buy the new machine.

6 Project appraisal and risk

6.1 (a) NPV using the best estimate figures:

Year	0	1–20
	£ millions	£ millions
Capital costs	–40	
Annual net revenues (1,200 – 500) × 32,000		22.4
Less annual fixed costs		15.0
		7.4
10% discount factor	1.000	8.514
Present value	–40	63
NPV = 63 – 40 = £23 million		

(b) Two-way sensitivity table: NPV figures

Annual number of passengers	Revenue per passenger		
	£800	£1,200	£2,000
	£ millions	£ millions	£ millions
15,000	(1) –129.397	(4) –78.313	(7)23.855
32,000	(2) –85.976	(5) 23	(8) 240.962
40,000	(3) –65.542	(6) 70.682	(9) 343.130

Working calculations for NPVs:

1 Annual net revenue (ANR) = [(800 – 500) × 15,000] – 15m = 4.5m – 15m = –£10.5m
NPV = (–10.5m × 8.514) – 40m = –£129.397

2 ANR = (300 × 32,000) – 15m = 9.6m – 15m = –£5.4m
NPV = (–5.4m × 8.514) – 40m = –£85.976m

3 ANR = (300 × 40,000) – 15m = 12m – 15m = –£3m
NPV = (–3m × 8.514) – 40m = –£65.542m

4 ANR = (700 × 15,000) – 15m = 10.5m – 15m = –£4.5m
NPV = (–4.5m × 8.514) – 40m = –£78.313m

5 See the answer to (a)

6 ANR = (700 × 40,000) – 15m = 28m – 15m = £13m
NPV = (13m × 8.514) – 40m = £70.682m

7 ANR = (1,500 × 15,000) – 15m = 22.5m – 15m = £7.5m
NPV = (7.5m × 8.514) – 40m = £23.855m

8 ANR = (1,500 × 32,000) – 15m = 48m – 15m = £33m
NPV = (33m × 8.514) – 40m = £240.962m

9 ANR = (1,500 × 40,000) – 15m = 60m – 15m = £45m
NPV = (45m × 8.514) – 40m = £343.130m

(c) Pivot approach

Sensitivity table				
Variable	Original estimate	Maximum or minimum value	% change	Notes
Capital cost	£40 million	£63 million max.	57.5	(1)
Fixed costs	£15 million	£17.7 million	18.0	(2)
Annual number of passengers	32,000	28,140 min.	–12.06	(3)

Notes:

1 NPV = £23 million; capital costs can rise by £23 million to £63 million before we get to a zero NPV. This is an increase of (23/40 × 100) 57.5%.

2 Present value of fixed costs = £15 million × 8.514 = £127.71 million. The maximum increase is £23 million before NPV becomes zero. This is an increase of (23/127.71 × 100) or 18%. Therefore, annual fixed costs can increase by a maximum of 18% to (15 ×1.18) £17.7 million.

3 Present value of revenue is £22.4 million × 8.514 = £190.714 million. The maximum decrease is £23 million or (23/190.714 × 100) 12.06%. Therefore, the annual number of passengers must not fall below (32,000 × 87.94%) 28,140 per year.

(d) The key points of the briefing note:

1 The projection using the best estimate figures shows an NPV of £23 million over the 20-year life of the vessel.

2 The two-way sensitivity table shows how important it is to maintain passenger revenues at least at £1,200 per passenger and, preferably, higher. This is because even at £1,200 per passenger, at the lowest level of demand (15,000 passengers per year), a negative NPV of £78 million results. At all other combinations with revenues at £1,200 or £2,000, positive NPVs are returned.

3 The pivot approach shows that capital costs can increase by £23 million or 57.5% before a zero NPV is earned. However, it is important that the ship is acquired within budget if we are to achieve our projected NPV. Annual fixed costs can increase by a maximum of 18%, assuming that everything else is on target. Again, it is important that they are kept within budget if the company is to achieve its target NPV. The annual number of passengers can fall by just 12% before we make a zero NPV. Clearly, it is important that the project is marketed successfully in order to ensure that we obtain at least 32,000 passengers per annum and at a price of at least £1,200.

6.2 Expected returns:

	Existing		Project B	
p	Returns (R)	p × R	Returns (R)	p × R
0.3	17	5.1	25	7.5
0.5	18	9.0	20	10.0
0.2	23	4.6	15	3.0
	Expected value	18.7		20.5

The expected value of the risk-free security is 5%.
Portfolio returns:
Existing (0.9) + project B (0.1) = 18.7(0.9) + 20.5(0.1) = 16.83 + 2.05 = 18.88%
Existing (0.9) + risk-free (0.1) = 18.7(0.9) + 5(0.1) = 16.83 + 0.5 = 17.33%

Portfolio risks:
Existing (0.9) + project B (0.1)

p	Return	Mean	d	d^2	pd^2
0.3	17.8*	18.88	−1.08	1.1664	0.3499
0.5	18.2	18.88	−0.68	0.4624	0.2312
0.2	22.2	18.88	3.32	11.0224	2.2045
				Variance	2.7856
				Standard deviation	1.669

* (0.9 × 17) + (0.1 × 25) = 17.8

Existing (0.9) + risk free (0.1)

p	Return	Mean	d	d^2	pd^2
0.3	15.8	17.33	−1.53	2.3409	0.7023
0.5	16.7	17.33	−0.63	0.3969	0.1985
0.2	21.2	17.33	3.87	14.9769	2.9954
				Variance	3.8962
				Standard deviation	1.9739

Existing plus project B gives a higher return, 18.88% as compared with 17.33% from existing plus risk-free. Existing plus project B also results in less risk with a lower standard deviation, which is attributable to the negative correlation in the returns of the existing investment and project B.

6.3 NPV at different levels of savings:

		NPV
£15,000 × 6.145 =	£92,175 – (£63,000 + £6,000) =	£26,175
£12,000 × 6.145 =	£73,740 – (£63,000 + £6,000) =	£7,740
£10,000 × 6.145 =	£61,450 – (£63,000 + £6,000) =	–£4,550

p	NPV £000s	p × NPV	d	d^2	pd^2
0.2	26.175	5.235	18.435	339.849	67.970
0.5	7.740	3.870	0	0	0
0.3	–4.550	–1.365	12.290	151.044	45.313
	EV	7.740		Variance	113.283
				Standard deviation	£10.643

Coefficient of variation = £10,643/£7,740 = 1.375

7 Shareholder value analysis

7.1

	£000s	£000s
Turnover		10,000
Less		
Cost of sales	8,000	
Operating expenses	700	8,700
Operating profit		1,300
Less taxation		220
		1,080
Less incremental investment in non-current assets		200
		880
Less increased investment in working capital		
Inventory	–300	
Accounts receivable	–200	
Accounts payable	+200	300
Free cash flow		580

The company's free cash flow for the year is £580,000.

7.2 (a)

Year:	1	2	3	4
	£ millions	£ millions	£ millions	£ millions
Sales	40.00	44.00	49.00	55.00
Operating profit	4.80	5.28	5.88	6.60
Less taxation (0.2)	0.96	1.06	1.18	1.32
	3.84	4.22	4.70	5.28
Less additional investment in non-current assets		0.80	1.00	1.20
Less additional working capital		0.40	0.50	0.60
	3.84	3.02	3.20	3.48
14% discount factors	0.877	0.769	0.675	0.592
Present value	3.37	2.33	2.16	2.06
NPV of planning period = £9.92 million				
NPV of terminal value = (5.28/0.14) × 0.592 = £22.33 million				
Total shareholder value = 9.92 + 22.33 = £32.25 million				

(b) A briefing paper on SVA.
Shareholder value analysis (SVA) has at its core the objective of managing the business so as to maximise shareholder value. In place of conventional profit, it supports the concept that the total return for the year is the increase in the value of the business over that one-year period. It has several advantages and disadvantages, as follows.

Advantages:

- SVA can be used in a strategic way within a business. For example, if the company is making a decision about launching a new product, SVA will help to analyse the project from the perspective of whether or not it increases the value of the business. In doing this, it will explicitly take account of risk; there are several ways of doing this but one way is by increasing the discount rate used in evaluating the project.
- SVA is relatively easy to use and interpret. It emphasises the concept of 'free cash flow', which can be derived from the company's conventional financial accounting system.
- It is consistent with the methodology of discounted cash flow (DCF) project evaluation and also with the DCF approach to ordinary share valuation.
- The value drivers are made explicit. This means that targets can be set for each of the drivers; each target should aim to increase shareholder wealth.
- Because the value drivers are made explicit, they can be benchmarked against other companies and this can form the basis of a learning experience designed to improve total returns.

Disadvantages:

- SVA assumes a constant change in the various cash flow elements and that they are related to the level of sales. This may not be the case and it is very unlikely that a linear relationship will be observed; for example, many costs will be fixed or have fixed components and so will not increase proportionately with sales.
- The assumption of a constant percentage increase in value drivers lacks realism. In practice, estimates would need to be more realistic, but where would the information come from? Forecasting elements of cash flows years ahead is very difficult.

- Possibly, the accounting system may be unable to provide the required information; for example, the value driver percentage would not be generated by any conventional accounting system.

8 Business combinations 1

8.1 (a) Different advantages are derived by different stakeholder groups. The nature and extent of the advantages depend partly on what a successful takeover bid means.

If success is interpreted as meaning that the acquisition is completed, this means that Company A gains control of Company B to form New A, and almost certainly has to pay a premium over the pre-bid price of B's shares to do so. The stakeholder groups that benefit immediately are B's shareholders, who receive a price for their shares, or a consideration paid in shares of the merged company greater than the value before the bid, and A's management, which succeeds in gaining control of additional resources that it believes it can use profitably in the combined company.

Success may mean, in addition, that the resources of the two companies are successfully combined. New A is able to use B's resources, such as tangible assets, products, brands, know-how, management skills, access to markets and customers and other intangible assets. New A benefits if the value of its assets grows or can be made greater than in A and B separately. This is synergy. It may mean that more income can be generated from the same resources that A and B had before the merger, or that the same can be achieved with fewer resources. Often it means the latter, and this usually means cost savings, almost invariably including job losses.

In this context, the original shareholders of A benefit if the synergy was valued correctly and B acquired at a premium less than the synergy realised after the merger.

Research suggests that there is little evidence, on average, that this happens. However, if synergy benefits are achieved after the merger to an extent not reflected in the acquisition price of B, the old B shareholders may benefit further. So will the management of A, which stands to be rewarded for controlling the larger company and for achieving the aims on which the merger was based. In the event of a hostile takeover, the management of B will probably do very badly. If the merger is friendly – recommended to B's shareholders by the B board – some or all of the top management of B may keep jobs in New A.

The employees of B may lose, since they are likely to bear the brunt of job cuts.

Those that remain may benefit from job opportunities in New A, which is potentially stronger than either A or B. The employees of A may also suffer from job cuts, and may also benefit from being in a larger company. They may do better on the whole than the employees of B because of established relationships with the management of New A.

Customers of both companies may benefit from a wider range of products and services, although a combination of operations and the search for synergies may mean product simplification and the withdrawal of products they had bought previously.

(b) If a bidder had made an offer to my company's shareholders without the agreement of my company's board and I was satisfied that it was in the best interests of the company and its shareholders to reject the offer, my task would be to persuade my shareholders not to accept the offer. If the bidder was requisitioning a general meeting of the company to consider its proposal, I would need to gain sufficient proxy votes to defeat the motion to accept the offer.

I would need to persuade my shareholders that the new offer was not in their best interests. Since the bidder would have offered them a premium over the pre-offer market price of shares, probably combined with calculations showing how their income would increase if they accepted, I might wish to persuade them that the advantages offered would not last. I might do this by throwing doubt on the income calculations and, if the consideration was offered in the form of the bidder's shares, on the stability or prospects of the bidder's share price. If the bidder was offering cash, I might claim that he was not in a position to raise the finance required. However, I might need to demonstrate that, if shareholders stayed loyal, the prospects for the company under the management of the existing board were worth more than the short-term gain offered by the bidder. This argument, convincingly put, should raise the share price and make the hostile offer less attractive. (I might initiate a review of asset valuations to see whether asset values needed to be updated.)

I would, therefore, need to develop a convincing case and communicate it persuasively to my shareholders. I would retain merchant bankers and corporate communication consultants, whom I might already have on retainer as a contingency measure. My board would develop and communicate the counter-case with the help of these advisers. The communication channels used would include letters, financial advertising and any general meeting of the company and financial public relations to gain media coverage of our company's case. The company's advisers would ensure that any actions taken by the company in response to the unwelcome bid were in line with the City Code on Takeovers and Mergers.

Other tactics could include referring the bid to the Competition and Markets Authority or making a counter-bid for the bidder.

I might believe that the reason for rejecting the offer was that it was too low. I would therefore have to investigate whether the bidder was willing to make a higher offer, which I might have to recommend to my shareholders.

Another reason for rejecting the offer might be that, while I believed that the company ought to stick to its existing strategies, which would not be possible if the bidder gained control, it did not have the resources to remain independent. In this case, I might look for a defensive merger with a 'white knight' company: one that would be able to offer greater financial security while allowing the company to continue operating as at present. The 'white knight' would make a counter-offer for the shares, with the agreement and support of the board.

8.2 (a) The behaviour of companies in a takeover bid is regulated by the Takeover Code which is issued by the City Panel on Takeovers and Mergers (the Panel). The Code applies to offers for all listed and unlisted public companies as well as resident statutory and chartered companies. The Code has statutory backing. Those who fail to conduct themselves in accordance with its rules may, by way of sanction, have the facilities of the securities markets withdrawn. The Code is made up of a number of general principles, which are statements of good commercial conduct, together with 38 Rules, supported by substantial notes. The Rules are not written in technical language and should be interpreted in terms of their underlying spirit and purpose rather than as a legal framework.

The Code describes itself as the collective opinion of those professionally involved in the field of takeovers on a range of business standards. It is not concerned with the financial or commercial advantages or disadvantages of a takeover, which are a matter for the company and its shareholders, or with those wider questions which are a matter for government.

The purpose of the Code is to ensure that all shareholders are treated fairly and equally. It sets out general principles and detailed rules which must be observed during a takeover or a merger. The Code deals with:

- the approach, announcements and independent advice
- dealings and restrictions on the acquisition of shares and rights over shares
- the mandatory offer and its terms
- conduct during an offer, and
- substantial acquisition of shares.

There is a general prohibition against a company giving financial assistance for the purchase of its own shares, so as to avoid manipulation of the share price. It also makes provision for an acquiring company to compulsorily purchase the remaining shares once it has acquired 90% of the shares. Insider trading (dealing in shares by a person who has price-sensitive information that is not public) is a criminal offence at any time, including during a bid.

The Enterprise and Regulatory Reform Act 2013 merged the Office of Fair Trading and the Competition Commission to form the Competition and Markets Authority (CMA). The CMA considers bids and decides whether or not they are in the public interest. The CMA then makes recommendations to the Department for Business, Innovation and Skills, which may include rejection of the bid.

The European Commission has the power to block large mergers (defined as large on the basis of their worldwide or EU-wide turnover) which it considers to be incompatible with the objectives of the Single European Market.

(b)

	Blue plc	Yellow plc
Number of shares	£50,000/£0.10 = 500,000	£300,000/£1 = 300,000
Value of shares for merger	£200,000/500,000 = 40p	£92,280/300,000 = 30.76p
Market value = P/E ratio × EPS	40p × 15 = £6	30.76p × 13 = £4

If Green plc is to have ordinary share capital of (£500,000 + £300,000) £800,000, the holdings of ordinary shares in the new company could be divided between the former companies' shareholders as follows:

Blue plc	500,000 × £6 =	£3,000,000
Yellow plc	300,000 × £4 =	£1,200,000

This allocation gives a proportion of 3:1.2
This leads to a division of the new shares in Green plc as follows:

Blue plc	571,429 shares	(approx. 114 for 100)
Yellow plc	228,571 shares	(approx. 76 for 100)
	800,000 shares	

The expected earnings per share (EPS) for Green plc would be:
£292,280/800,000 = 36.535 pence
The proportions attributable to Blue and Yellow would therefore be:

Blue plc	571,429 × 36.535p =	£208,772
Yellow plc	228,571 × 36.535p =	£83,508
		£292,280

In this scheme, Blue gains some earnings contributed by Yellow and Yellow loses earnings to Blue. The critical point to both sets of shareholders will be the rating placed on the shares of Green by the market. Gains and losses in EPS will be mitigated by movements in the new share prices.

As an alternative to the above, the shares in Green could be apportioned on the basis of input of earnings without heeding the market price situation. This would penalise Blue in the sense that the market appears to favour its development and growth potential more highly than it does Yellow's. A straight proportional split would not acknowledge the apparent difference in market rating.

9 Business combinations 2

9.1 (a) If the company is short of cash, a rescue package may involve improving the cash situation by reducing working capital. This can be done by reducing stocks, reducing the credit granted to customers and taking increased credit from suppliers (probably by agreement or negotiation). Increased working capital can be raised by raising cash against invoices through factors or invoice discounters or, preferably in the short term, by a bank overdraft. Other actions may include deferring capital investment expenditure, using leasing or borrowing rather than cash for capital expenditure and financing working capital increases through debt or equity issues.

Drastic action along these lines might be described as a rescue package.

If cash shortages are caused by poor profitability, or cash shortages arising from it, changes are needed in the management of the business. This may mean making cost reductions or focusing on the most profitable businesses (in the short term those that generate most cash). It may mean the appointment of new managers, which could be achieved by the appointment of a new board, through a resolution passed by a general meeting of the company, or by the appointment of new managers by the board.

However, a rescue package to avoid liquidation is most likely to mean a capital reconstruction scheme. This involves raising new capital or converting liabilities into different forms which defer or reduce cash payments (such as payments to suppliers, payments of interest and repayment of loans). Since different kinds of creditors have different requirements, it may be possible to make changes that they will find acceptable by offering something they want. For example, trade creditors may be willing to wait for payment if interest is paid on what they are owed, or if the alternative to waiting for payment is a liquidation in which they may receive nothing.

Loan stock holders may be willing to have interest payments increased but deferred, or to exchange some of their loan stock for equity. Equity shareholders who believe that the company has a future may be willing to accept a reduction in the nominal value of their equity and subscribe for more shares.

The principle underlying a capital reconstruction is that the company gains the agreement of shareholders and of all classes of creditors to vary their rights by altering the capital structure in a way that allows the company to continue in business and leaves them better off than if the company had been liquidated. This may mean that secured creditors, who might get their money in the event of a liquidation, have to be paid in full.

A capital reconstruction scheme must treat all groups of shareholders and creditors fairly, and not favour one group over others. This will involve protecting the voting rights of all groups, and as far as possible maintaining their income.

Calculations need to be presented to show how the reconstruction protects the interests of each group as compared with their situation in a liquidation. The different classes of creditors and shareholders are placed in order of priority in the event of liquidation, with secured creditors first and ordinary shareholders last. The order of priority affects how much creditors in each different class stand to receive, and will be a factor in their judgement of whether the capital reconstruction is acceptable.

Each class of creditors votes in a separate class meeting on the capital reconstruction proposals, and each meeting needs to agree to the proposals by a 75% majority. Given this agreement, the company can apply to the court for approval, after which the reconstruction is binding on all parties.

(b) The success of a management buyout (MBO) can be influenced by:

- the ability of the management team, which may not have expertise in all of the functions (such as legal or financial) needed to run an independent company, to acquire these skills for itself or through advisers
- the ability of the new management team to cut costs sufficiently to pay debt interest and redemption payments
- cash control
- the ability of the management team to maintain output at the same time as cutting costs

- the willingness of the workforce, some of whom may lose their jobs as part of cost cutting, to cooperate in the new venture
- the commitment of the management team, who will be coping with new management challenges as well as stresses caused by personal financial pressures
- whether the buyout team overpaid, and
- the ability of the management team to work effectively with the financial backers, who will wish to intervene to protect their investment.

9.2 (a) Taking only the financial factors into account, the divestment decision usually depends on whether or not the expected cash flows from the retention of the light engineering division have a present value greater than the £6.5 million offer.

Estimated liability to tax (£000s):

	Year 3	Year 4	Year 5	Year 6	Year 7
Turnover	13,416	13,953	14,511	15,091	15,695
Less					
Direct costs	10,368	11,197	12,093	13,060	14,105
Overheads	1,716*	1,888	2,077	2,285	2,513
Depreciation	500	500	500	500	500
	12,584	13,585	14,670	15,845	17,118
Taxable profit	832	368	–159	–754	–1,423
Taxation	–250	–110	48	226	427

* Overheads year 3 = 2400 × 0.65 × 1.1

Expected cash flows (£000s):

	Year 3	Year 4	Year 5	Year 6	Year 7
Cash inflows					
Turnover	13,416	13,953	14,511	15,091	15,695
Taxation			48	226	427
Land, buildings plant and machinery					6,491*
Other					1,000
	13,416	13,953	14,559	15,317	23,613
Cash outflows					
Direct costs	10,368	11,197	12,093	13,060	14,105
Overheads	1,716	1,888	2,077	2,285	2,513
Taxation	250	110			
Redundancy		500			
	12,334	13,695	14,170	15,345	16,618
Annual net cash flow	1,082	258	389	–28	6,995
17% discount factors	0.855	0.731	0.624	0.534	0.456
Present value	925	189	243	–15	3,190
NPV	4,532				

* Land, buildings etc. = $[(2{,}100 \times 80\%) + (3{,}650 \times 75\%)] \times 1.08^5$

Notes:

1 The overhead attributable to the division is 65% of the allocated £2.4 million increasing at 10% per annum.
2 It is assumed that divisional losses can be offset against other income of the business in the years in which they arise, so that losses give rise to tax savings.
3 Finance charges and their tax impact are taken into account in the discount rate.
4 A discount rate of 17% has been used as the cash flows are inflated.

If the division is sold, redundancy payments of £1.5 million are deducted leaving net sale proceeds of £5 million. The expected present value of retaining the division is £4.532 million. On financial grounds the offer should be accepted. Check whether the division might fetch more if production ceased and the assets were sold:

	£000
Estimated market value of land and buildings	1,680
Plant and machinery	2,738
Net value of current assets	120
Total	4,538

If production stopped, the redundancy payments and other closure costs would probably be higher than £1.5 million, giving a net value of less than £3.038 million.

(b) Divestment may occur for the following reasons.

- The part of the business to be divested generates losses or fails to hit profit objectives.
- The business has a cash shortage in its main operations.
- The part sold is not considered part of the core activities.
- Individual parts of a company may be worth more sold separately than would be the case were the business to be sold as a whole.
- A strategic decision to restructure results in the need to divest certain activities.
- Disposal of a very profitable sector of the business could ward off otherwise hostile takeover bids.
- Some types of divestment, such as spin-offs (de-mergers) and MBOs, offer particular advantages. A spin-off, where two or more companies are formed to replace the original business, may result in improved control and greater definition of management responsibility. It may also allow risky parts of the business to be hived off. An MBO often creates a climate for a speedy sale and for good relations with mutually beneficial trading opportunities thereafter.

(c) The financial manager defending a company against an unwelcome takeover bid will be constrained to act in accordance with the City Code. General principles of the Code that are of relevance to the financial manager, in such circumstances, include the following.

- Information may not be provided only to selected shareholders; it must be available to all.
- Shareholders must be allowed sufficient information to make an informed decision. Relevant information should not be withheld.
- The directors or managers of a company must not prevent a bid succeeding without giving the shareholders the opportunity to decide on the merits of the bid for themselves.

Rules of the Code concern the conduct of all parties during the offer period. The company that has been bid for must:

- notify shareholders of the identity of the bidder and the terms and conditions of the bid
- seek independent advice (e.g. from a merchant bank)
- not issue new shares or purchase or dispose of major assets of the company (unless agreed prior to the bid) without the agreement of a general meeting
- not influence or support the market price of its shares by providing finance or financial guarantee for the purchase of its own shares.

Directors and managers must disregard their own interests when advising their shareholders. Where it is part of a company's defence to state that certain assets are undervalued, the accounting conventions must be reported on by the firm's auditors or other qualified external accountants.

9.3 (a) The break-up value can be computed in two ways, depending on whether the investments, together with plant worth £225,000, are sold:

	Retain investments and all plant	Sell investments and some plant
Value at 30 September 2015	£000s	£000s
Land and buildings	900	900
Plant	600	375
Investments	675	–
Inventories	750	750
Trade receivables	600	600
Cash	300	300
Sum due on sale of investments/assets or cash proceeds realised	–	900
	3,825	3,825
Less: Debentures	(750)	(750)
Creditors	(300)	(300)
Value of business to ordinary shareholders	2,775	2,775

Potential future profitability is not reflected in the break-up figure. To allow for this, a value would need to be calculated for goodwill as a certain number of years' purchase of average annual profits less an allowance for the cost of capital. The number of years' profits would be a number typical for XYZ's industry.

(b) The cash flows represent the projected flows excluding investment and debenture interest. They compare, therefore, with the adjusted profits assessments of value. Discounted cash flow (DCF) looks at the value of the company as a discounted stream of future cash flows available to the purchaser.

This gives the NPV, as follows:

Year	Cash flow £000s	10% discount factor	Present value £000s
2016	450	0.909	409.1
2017	600	0.826	495.6
2018	450	0.751	338.0
2019+	570	0.751/0.1 =7.51*	4,280.7
	NPV		5,523.4

*For a perpetuity starting in four years' time, using a discount rate of 10%.

The maximum price which ABC Ltd should be prepared to pay for XYZ Ltd on each of the bases is:

(a) Break-up value: £2.775 million.
(b) DCF: £5.523 million.

10 Financial markets and institutions

10.1(a) A company that meets the Listing Rules, contained in the UK Listing Authority's guidelines, can apply for a full listing on the Main Market of the London Stock Exchange. The Listing Rules include the following requirements.

- The market capitalisation must be at least £700,000, and 25% of the shares must be held by persons unconnected with the company.
- The company must have a successful audited track record of at least three years.
- The company must have sufficient working capital for 12 months.
- Sufficient shares (with a price that is not so high as to discourage trading) must be made available to the public to allow a free market in the company's shares.
- The directors and senior managers must have suitable experience, and must be able to act independently of any one controlling shareholder.

The costs of entry into the Main Market and the continuing cost of compliance are high, and smaller companies, and those which wish to avoid these costs, can apply for listing on AIM (the Alternative Investment Market), which has less stringent entry requirements and regulations. Firms on AIM are still subject to regulation by the Stock Market, and must normally publish a prospectus, publish interim reports and give details of directors' share dealings. A company that wishes to enter AIM must select a nominated adviser from an official list, who will advise the company on compliance, and a nominated broker, who will deal with investors and support trading when there is no market-maker.

Shares can also be traded in the 'over-the-counter' market, which is not regulated by the Stock Exchange, and therefore provides less protection for the investor, but offers lower dealing costs.

(b) The advantages of a full listing are that a company has access to the largest source of funds from subscribers for new shares. This makes it easiest to raise large sums, and gives the best chance of issuing shares at a high price. After the issue, a full listing on the Main Market gives the most active market, and the marketability of shares is maximised. This means that it is the easiest market in which to sell shares.

Paradoxically, since shareholders like liquidity, this means the highest share price. A full listing gives the company the largest amount of media attention. This provides opportunities for a company to communicate with investors and potential investors.

All of the above considerations provide opportunities for a company to issue its shares at a high price and for the price to remain higher than it would in less liquid markets that are subject to less attention and analysis. This means that the cost of capital can be kept to a minimum.

The price that the company has to pay for these advantages is the cost involved in making an application, including the cost of professional advice and the preparation of listing documentation, and the continuing cost of compliance with listing requirements. The disclosure requirements and the corporate governance requirements of the UK Corporate Governance Code, which is designed primarily for listed companies, are more wide-reaching for listed companies than for unlisted companies. Larger companies are likely to be better placed to cope with the costs and requirements associated with a full listing.

10.2 Taking a company private avoids the disadvantages of a stock market listing, including issue costs and reporting costs, disclosure requirements and scrutiny by shareholders and analysts (which may be salutary but will certainly tie up management time) and the possibility of losing voting control. There is also scope for value creation due to closer management involvement, and reduction or elimination of the agency problem (the managers are likely to be the controlling shareholders). Since a large amount of debt is usually raised to buy out the other shareholders, there are tax benefits (but increased financial risk) associated with higher gearing. Increased debt gives managers an incentive to maximise profits, specifically by cutting unnecessary costs, which managers familiar with the business are well placed to judge. The company may benefit from the greater freedom of action of managers who are no longer accountable to market investors

10.3 (a) Efficient capital markets have the following characteristics.

- No one individual dominates the market.
- Transaction costs do not significantly discourage trading.
- Prices respond quickly to all information available to those dealing in securities.

Efficient markets exhibit three types of efficiency.

- **Allocative efficiency:** Funds are allocated in the way that maximises economic prosperity.
- **Operational efficiency:** Transaction costs are low, which can occur when there is free and open competition within the market.
- **Information processing efficiency:** Prices quickly and accurately reflect relevant information, preventing speculation driving prices up or down.

(b) Three levels of information processing efficiency have been identified.

1 **The weak form:** Prices reflect all past price information.

2 **The semi-strong form:** Prices reflect all publicly available information (which means that investors assess and take account of the relevance and reliability of, for example, public statements by the company and accounting presentation).

3 **The strong form:** Prices reflect all relevant information, whether published or not. This means that unpublished price sensitive information – which it is illegal for insiders to use as a basis for trading – is reflected immediately in share prices.

Research suggests that the weak and semi-strong forms apply. Counter-examples are provided by sudden large price changes that do not appear to be triggered by specific new information. Some evidence against the strong form is provided by the fact that prices often change quickly but not instantaneously over short periods before price-sensitive information – such as merger announcements – is released by companies.

11 Main sources of long-term finance

11.1 (a) Convertible loan stock is stock that pays a fixed rate of interest, and may be converted into shares at a specified time, or times, in the future. The share price at which the stock can be converted may increase for later conversion dates, reflecting expected share price growth. At the conversion date or dates, the convertible stock holder can decide whether to convert the stock into ordinary shares or do nothing and continue to receive interest on the stock. The price of the convertible stock in effect includes an option to buy the ordinary shares.

As a result, the interest cost to the company is lower than for conventional, non-convertible stock. The benefits for the investor are the potential value of the conversion rights, combined with interest income which would not be received if the investor simply bought a call option on the shares.

A warrant is an entitlement given to a purchaser of loan stock to buy shares at a predetermined price at some future date. It is issued in conjunction with loan stock, but can be traded separately. It is a long-term option on the ordinary shares, and warrants are often issued to make loan stock issues more attractive. The value of a warrant to investors in loan stock is the same as the value of any option. Because the warrant is issued at the same time as the stock, the investor receives interest on the stock, whereas a purchase of options by themselves would not generate income up to the exercise date. Because the exercise date is some years ahead, the value of the warrant at the issue date is often small, so that it reduces only slightly the return that needs to be offered on the loan stock. It does not involve any immediate dilution in shareholders' earnings or voting rights. Warrants are sometimes described as 'sweeteners' for loan stock issues.

(b) (i) The conversion price is the amount of stock required to obtain each ordinary share. For Redbrick plc this is:

£100/25 = £4

i.e. £4 of stock is necessary for each share.

(ii) The conversion premium is:

(£138/25) – £5.20 = £5.52 – £5.20 = £0.32 per share

(c) (i) To calculate the conversion premium:

Cost of one share at exercise price	70p
Cost of five warrants	20p
Cost of acquiring one share using warrants	90p
Current share price	50p
Conversion premium	40p

The conversion premium as a percentage of current share price is therefore:

(40p/50p) × 100 = 80%

(ii) The value of a warrant during the exercise period if the share price is then 150p is:

(150p – 70p) × 1/5 = 16p

11.2 Report to: Board of Smith plc
From: Company secretary
Date: 30 November 20XX
Subject: Options for Public Share Issue
The options for a public share issue are:

1 Offer for sale
2 Tender offer
3 Bought deal
4 Placement
5 Stock Exchange introduction
6 AIM (Alternative Investment Market)

Offer for sale

The company would appoint an issue house, and possibly also separate financial advisers. The issue house would prepare a prospectus, seek listing approval, advertise the issue, receive subscriptions for shares, allot and issues shares and return surplus subscriptions.

The company would have to pay fees to the issue house, which would cover the work described, as well as the costs of printing and advertising. It would also have to pay a listing fee and fees for any other financial advisers and for legal and other advisers. If the company wished to have the issue underwritten, where underwriters would guarantee to buy the shares at the issue price if there were insufficient public demand, it would need to pay an underwriting fee.

This option would maximise the publicity for the company, would give the best chance of a good issue price (although the issue house is likely to press for a price low enough to make demand for shares comfortably exceed supply) and would involve the highest fees. If the board wishes to choose this option, it is recommended that we seek quotations from AB Merchant Bank, BC Merchant Bank and the corporate finance arm of CD Finance. We can expect the total expenses to amount to between 10% and 15% of the capital raised by the issue.

Tender offer

This would be similar to an offer for sale. Potential investors would be required to state the maximum number of shares they want to purchase and the maximum price they are prepared to pay. The normal arrangement would be that the issue house would set a price at which there are sufficient tender applications to clear the whole issue and to sell all the shares at this price. Subscribers tendering less than this price would receive no shares.

Tender offers are designed for slightly more sophisticated investors (who have to decide for themselves what price they are prepared to pay, as well as for how many shares, and who will realise that they will receive no shares if their tender price is too low). It is a form of auction. For a well-established company, particularly where there is already a market price for the shares, it should offer the prospect of a price close to the best that can be achieved. Since the company is coming to the market for the first time, this may not be a suitable choice for Smith plc.

Bought deal
The company would sell the shares that it plans to issue to a merchant bank or other financial institution, which would sell the shares on in the market. The company would still need to gain listing authority, but the issuing process would be simplified.

We would certainly need to retain additional financial advisers, who could help us to negotiate the price at which we sell the shares to the issuing house.

Placement
This would be similar to a bought deal. The institution that bought the shares would sell them on to a limited number of investors. Both a placement and a bought deal would keep down expenses if the purpose was to sell only a small number of shares (e.g. to establish a market value, or allow part of the shares to be sold for estate planning or inheritance tax purposes).

Stock Exchange introduction
A limited number of shares would be sold on the Stock Exchange in order to establish a price.

AIM (Alternative Investment Market)
AIM might be ideal for us. Listing requirements would be less onerous than on the Main Market, where the company's short track record might make it hard to get listing approval. It would still be necessary to prepare a prospectus. The company would gain a listing by being sponsored by a nominated adviser (nomad), which would typically be a corporate finance specialist. The company could transfer to the Main Market in a few years' time.

Recommendation
We should negotiate the appointment of the corporate finance arm of our bank as nomad to sponsor the entry of Smith plc into AIM through a public offer of shares. We should seek the nomad's advice on the appointment of specialist legal advisers and financial PR consultants.

11.3(a) Investor who holds 60,000 ordinary shares (5% equity):

Present position	Shareholder	
	Takes up rights	Sells rights
Value of investment: 60,000 shares × £3.60 = £216,000	Current investment: £216,000	Current investment: £216,000
	Add rights: 15,000 × £3 = £45,000	Less sale of rights: 60,000 ×12p* = –£7,200
New level of investment	£261,000	£208,800
Dividend received: 60,000 × 45p = £27,000 Return on investment = 27/216 = 12.5%	Dividend received: 75,000 × 43.5p = £32,625 Return on investment = 32.625/261 = 12.5%	Dividend received: 60,000 × 43.5p = £26,100 Return on investment = 26.1/208.8 = 12.5%

*Theoretical ex-rights price would be shares = £3.48. Thus the value of one right = 12p

From these calculations, the shareholder will be no better or worse off after the rights issue. The investor's action is determined by whether they wish to increase or decrease their investment.

(b) The idea of a rights issue is to encourage existing shareholders to invest more funds in a company so as not to dilute further their membership interest. To achieve this, the share price set for the rights issue is at a discount to the market price. This is designed to ensure that the price paid will be less than the market price, even if prices fall before the issue. The rights issue cannot be above market price, since this would mean that it would be cheaper to buy shares in the market and nobody would subscribe.

(c) As the total sum to be raised is £900,000, calculated as:

1,200,000/4 × £3 = £900,000 (300,000 new shares)

the underwriting commission will be:

£900,000 × 1.25% = £11,250.

It would have been possible to price the rights issue below that, at say £2.50, to raise the same sum on a 3 for 10 issue at £2.50 as follows:

1,200,000/10 × £2.50 × 3 = £900,000 (360,000 new shares).

The underwriting commission will still be £11,250 (£900,000 × 1.25%) and will be payable whether the issue is fully subscribed or not.

An underwriter agrees to take up the remainder of an issue if it is not altogether successful. This ensures that the company raises the sum required. The underwriting commission is an insurance premium against the risk that not all the rights will be taken up.

Underwriting commission is usually between 1.25% and 2%. Shares can be offered in the rights issue at a lower price if a lower rate of commission is negotiated or if the issue is not underwritten.

12 The cost of capital

12.1 (a) The dividend growth model has developed from the dividend valuation model, which gives a formula for the share price in terms of the dividend and the cost of equity capital. This can be rearranged to give the cost of equity capital in terms of the dividend and the share price.

The dividend growth model incorporates the annual rate of dividend growth in a formula for the share price. It can also be rearranged to give an expression for the cost of equity capital in terms of the dividend, the share price and the annual rate of dividend growth.

(b) The dividend growth model gives the cost of equity capital as:

$K_e = [D_0 (1 + g)/ P_0] + g$

where:
K_e = cost of equity shareholder's expected return on shares
D_0 = current dividend payable
P_0 = current ex-div share price
g = the expected annual growth in dividends.

The dividend growth model is based on the following assumptions.

- Taxation rates are the same for all investors, and in particular higher rates of tax are ignored. The dividends used are the gross dividends paid out from the company's point of view.
- No costs are incurred in a share issue.
- All investors receive the same, perfect level of information.
- The cost of capital to the company remains unaltered by any new issue of shares.
- All projects undertaken as a result of new share issues have the same level of risk as the company's existing activities.
- The dividends paid must be from after-tax profits – there must be sufficient funds to pay the shareholders from profits after tax.

(c) $K_e = [0.08(1 + 0.3)/1.27] + g = 0.065 + 0.03 = 0.095$
The company's cost of equity is 9.5%.

12.2 (a) The WACC represents the average cost of capital for a company. Where an investment project has a level of risk typical of the company's investments, it should give the same return as the whole of the company's investments and should be evaluated using the average rate of return required to recover the average cost of capital. This argument does not hold if the project risk is not typical or if special funding arrangements for the project mean that its cost of capital is not typical.

(b) WACC using statement of financial position values:

	Value £	Weight	Return	Weight × return
Equity	10,000	0.45	0.095	0.0428
Preference shares	5,000	0.22	0.080	0.0176
Debentures	7,500	0.33	0.070*	0.0231
	22,500	1.00		0.0835
WACC				8.35%

* Return on debentures = 0.1(1 – 0.3) because of the tax shield.

WACC using market values:

	Value £	Weight	Return	Weight × return
Equity	34,400	0.73	0.0950	0.0694
Preference shares	4,900	0.10	0.0816*	0.0082
Debentures	7,800	0.17	0.0673**	0.0114
	47,100	1.00		0.0890
WACC				8.90%

*Cost of preference capital = 8/98 = 8.2%
** Cost of non-current liabilities = 10(1 – 0.3)/104 = 6.73%

12.3

Security		Required %	Actual %	Comment
C	= 6 + (13 – 6)0.8	11.6	15	C's actual return is in excess of the return required by its degree of systematic risk. It is positioned above the SML and is certainly worth adding to the portfolio. The market should soon respond and this will push the share price up and the return down.
D	= 6 + (13 – 6)2.0	20	20	D's return is in line with its expected return. It is in equilibrium and it is positioned on the SML. It is worth adding to the portfolio.
E	= 6 + (13 – 6)1.1	13.7	12	E's actual return is less than its required return. It is positioned below the SML and should not be added to a portfolio. The market should respond by selling this share, forcing its price down and return up.
F	= 6 + (13 – 6)3.4	29.8	30	In this case the actual return marginally exceeds the required return. It is positioned slightly above the SML and is worth adding to a portfolio. However, a risk avoider may be concerned about the very high beta.

12.4 (a) The beta factor of a share shows the variability of the return on a share (its risk) in relation to the variability of the return on a market average investment. In the CAPM equation it is used to calculate the expected return on a share to compensate for the level of risk:

$$R_s = R_f + \beta(R_m - R_f)$$

where:
R_s = expected return from an individual investment
R_f = the risk-free rate of return
R_m = the market rate of return (the return on the all share index)
β = the beta factor of the investment.

(b) $R_s = 6.5 + 0.7(9 - 6.5) = 8.25$

The return on the share is 8.25%.

(c) If the market rate of return increased to 12%:

$R_s = 6.5 + 0.7\ (5.5) = 10.35$

the return on the share would be 10.35%.

If the market rate of return increased to 12%:

$R_s = 6.5 + 0.7\ (-1.5) = 5.45$

the return on the share would be 5.45%.

12.5 Report to: Managing director
From: Company secretary
Date: 1 December 20XX
Subject: Cost of capital

One common method of calculating the cost of equity is the dividend growth model, which uses the current level of dividend, the current market price of our shares and the annual growth in dividends.

This model states:

$$K_e = [D_0\,(1 + g)/P_0] + g$$

where:
P_0 = the current ex-div market price
D_0 = the current dividend
g = the expected annual growth in dividends
K_e = the shareholder's expected return on the shares.

The cost of equity can also be calculated using the capital asset pricing model (CAPM):

$$R_s = R_f + \beta(R_m - R_f)$$

where:
R_s = the cost of equity
R_f = the risk-free rate
β = the beta factor for the share
R_m = the expected return on the market portfolio.

Differing results may arise from using the two models because of the differing assumptions underlying them.

The dividend growth model is based on the following assumptions.

- Taxation rates are constant across all investors, and as such the existence of higher rates of tax is ignored. The dividends used are the gross dividends paid out from the company's point of view.
- No costs are incurred in a share issue.
- All investors receive the same, perfect level of information.
- The cost of capital to the company remains unaltered by any new issue of shares.
- All projects undertaken as a result of new share issues are of equal risk to that existing in the company.

Assumptions underlying the CAPM include the following.

- Investors are risk-averse and require greater return for taking greater risks.
- There are equal borrowing and lending rates.
- There are no transaction costs.
- There are no market imperfections.
- Expectations are homogeneous.
- There is no taxation.
- There is no inflation.

One method of dealing with the different results from the two models is to calculate the cost of equity using both models and to use an average of the two results in calculating the overall cost of capital.

Calculations

WACC using the dividend valuation model:
$K_e = [2.25(1.2)/120] + 0.2 = 0.2225 = 22.25\%$
$K_d = 12\ (1 - 0.3)$ (the debt tax shield) $= 8.4\%$

WACC

	Market value £ million	Weight	Return	Weight × return
Equity	60	0.75	0.2225	0.16875
Debt	20	0.25	0.084	0.0210
	80	1.00		0.19125
WACC				18.975%

WACC using CAPM
$R_s = 4.5 + 1.6(14.0 - 4.5) = 19.7\%$

	Market value £ million	Weight	Return	Weight × return
Equity	60	0.75	0.197	0.14775
Debt	20	0.25	0.084	0.0210
	80	1.00		0.17025
WACC				16.875%

13 Capital structure

13.1(a) (i) Financing with equity (2 million shares = £10 million)

Outcome	A	B	C	
	£000s	£000s	£000s	
PBIT	800	1,400	2,000	
Taxation (0.3)	240	420	600	
Available to equity	560	980	1,400	
EPS (pence)	28	49	70	
probabilities	0.4	0.4	0.2	
P(EPS)	11.2	19.6	14	44.8

(ii) Financing with equity (1 million shares = £5 million) and debt (£5 million)

Outcome	A	B	C	
	£000s	£000s	£000s	
PBIT	800	1,400	2,000	
Interest	800	800	800	
PBT	0	600	1200	
Taxation (0.3)	0	180	360	
Available to equity	0	420	840	
EPS (pence)	0	42	84	
probabilities	0.4	0.4	0.2	
P(EPS)	0	16.8	16.8	33.6

(b) Taxation
- Method (ii) benefits as the tax shield is 30% × £800,000 = £240,000 per year.

Risk
- Both methods suffer from business risk, but method (ii) also suffers financial risk.
- Method (ii) has a 40% probability of break-even or less; the break-even is £800,000.

Asset type
- Very specialised assets with a low collateral value and possibly a delay in sale.
- Possibly not suitable for borrowing against.

Other points
- Less dilution of control and earnings with method (ii).

13.2(a)

	Solka plc		Industry
D/(D+E) book	6/15	0.40	0.39
market	8.58/26.08	0.33	0.35
Interest cover	2.5/1.2	2.08	2.3
P/E ratio	125/7.4	16.89	15

Solka plc is in line with industry ratios on book (D + E), market (D + E) and P/E ratio. Interest cover is below a weak industry interest cover rate.

(b) Share issue:

No. of shares = £10,400,000/£1.25 = 8,320,000

Market conditions	Good	Fair	Poor	
Probability	0.3	0.5	0.2	EV
EBIT (£000s)	1,100	750	650	
Tax (£000s)	220	150	130	
Profit after tax (£000s)	880	600	520	
EPS (pence)	10.58	7.21	6.25	
Expected EPS (pence)	3.17	3.61	1.25	8.03

Share and debenture issue:

Value of debentures = £8,200,000
No. of shares = 2,000,000

Market conditions	Good	Fair	Poor	
Probability	0.3	0.5	0.2	EV
EBIT (£000s)	1,100	750	650	
Interest (£000s)	574	574	574	
Profit before tax (£000s)	526	176	76	
Tax (£000s)	105.2	35.2	15.2	
Profit after tax (£000s)	420.8	140.8	60.8	
EPS (pence)	21.04	7.04	3.04	
Expected EPS (pence)	6.31	3.52	0.61	10.44

The range of EPSs under the debt-finance method is greater than under equity finance. Under good market conditions, debt gives double the EPS as compared with equity. However, equity gives higher returns under fair and poor market conditions

(c) The impact on debt/(equity + debt) ratios is shown in the following table.

Equity	Book	6/(9 + 10 + 6)	0.24
	Market	8.58/(17.5 + 10.4 + 8.58)	0.24
Debt + equity	Book	(6 + 8.2)/(6 + 9 + 8.2 + 1.8)	0.57
	Market	(8.58 + 8.2)/(17.5 + 8.58 + 8.2 + 2.5)	0.46

Under debt finance, the debt/equity ratios increase significantly and will become much greater than the industry averages.

Interest cover for the project under debt and equity finance is shown immediately below.

Good 1.92

Fair 1.31

Poor 1.13

The impact on overall interest cover is shown in the table below:

	Current	Plus new project		
		Good	Fair	Poor
PBIT	2,500	3,600	3,250	3,150
Interest	1,200	1,774	1,774	1,774
Interest cover	2.08	2.03	1.83	1.78

As can be seen, interest cover will fall as compared with existing interest cover.

With regard to Industry and asset type: the company is unlikely to have collateral assets. The company's strength is in its staff and expertise.

Recommendation: finance by equity rather than debt.

13.3 Capital gearing is the ratio of long-term debt to shareholders' funds of a company. A highly geared company has a high ratio. The expression 'highly geared' may imply, depending on the context, that the level of borrowing is such as to cause a significant risk of insolvency. The level of gearing at which this happens depends on the nature of the business, and in particular the steadiness of operating cash flow from which to pay interest.

The level of gearing of a company is significant because the interest on debt is payable whatever the operating profit of a company, whereas dividends on ordinary share capital can only be paid when there are sufficient distributable profits, and can be passed (not paid) or reduced if the directors think it sufficiently important to conserve funds.

A company's financial managers will be interested in the company's level of gearing because it is a major component of the funding decision, and a determinant of the cost of capital (although the Modigliani–Miller hypothesis states that capital structure is irrelevant, and the reduction in the cost of capital associated with gearing is exactly balanced by increased financial risk).

Shareholders are interested in gearing because it affects the risk associated with equity capital and consequently the return that equity holders require.

Lenders are interested in gearing for similar reasons. Debt capital may be low risk for holders when the level of gearing is low, but the risk rises with gearing. They may require a higher interest return to compensate for this.

Other stakeholders who have an interest in the profitability of the company, and perhaps more importantly those who have an interest in its stability and solvency, including employees, customers and particularly creditors, will also be interested in the level of gearing.

13.4 MM's first and second propositions state in different ways that capital structure is irrelevant. This means that efforts to reduce the cost of capital by gearing cannot succeed. The first proposition is that the value of the geared firm is equal to:

- the value of the ungeared firm which is equal to:
- the earnings before interest divided by WACC.

This means that the value of WACC is constant. The second proposition puts this forward because savings from debt being cheaper than equity are equal to the increase in the cost of equity due to increased risk arising from gearing.

Later developments in the theory deal with the fact that debt interest is tax-deductible in several countries, including the USA and UK, whereas ordinary share dividends are not. The conclusions were that debt is, in fact, cheaper than equity, and that there is no optimum level of debt.

The differences of the MM theory from traditional theory are that traditional theory considers that tax relief on debt interest reduces the WACC. It argues that WACC can change as gearing changes, and that there is an optimum level of debt.

The traditional and MM theories make some common assumptions, but MM makes some further assumptions.

- Individuals can borrow at the same interest rates as companies, and there are no transaction costs in borrowing to do this (these assumptions are necessary for MM's argument that the value of companies cannot be changed by gearing, because arbitrage by individual investors would remove any differences in value).
- Bankruptcy and the consequent risk of debt are ignored (which weakens the argument concerning high levels of gearing).

14 Working capital 1

14.1 Working capital cycle:

Raw material inventory days = £17,810/£1.3 million × 365 days	= 5 days
Work in progress (WIP) days (based on material cost of WIP: see below)	
= £21,369/£1.3 million × 365 days	= 6 days
Finished goods inventory days = £37,260/£1.7 million × 365 days	= 8 days
Period between dispatch and invoice to customer	= 2 days
Trade receivables days = £219,180/£2.0 million × 365 days	= 40 days
Total	= 61 days
Less trade payables days =£113,970/£1.3 m × 365 days	= 32 days
Working capital cycle	= 29 days

Calculation of material cost of work in progress:
Annual cost of sales £1.7 million
Annual material cost £1.3 million
Annual conversion cost £0.4 million = 0.4/1.3 of material cost = 30.8% of material cost
Value of WIP (conversion half-complete) = material cost + half of conversion cost = 100% + (0.5 × 30.8% of material cost) = 115.4% of material cost
Material cost included in WIP = 100%/115.4% × £32,000 = £21,369

14.2(a) Overtrading occurs when a company grows rapidly but does not provide long-term capital to fund the increased working capital, in the form of trade receivables and inventory, needed to support sales growth. The result may be constrained growth, extended credit taken by taking longer to pay suppliers or an increasing bank overdraft. Overtrading can lead to liquidity problems and even insolvency. It can occur when a company is trading profitably.

The signs of overtrading include:

- rapidly increasing sales
- a reliance on short-term finance to fund growth in working capital
- a corresponding lack of growth in long-term finance
- reduced cash balances
- increased trade receivables

- increases in the level of trade payables and the payables payment period
- large stock changes (either increases in anticipation of higher sales, or decreases because the company cannot cope with demand)
- lower profit margins if the company is gaining sales by cutting prices or by disproportionate increases in expenses
- increased levels of short-term borrowing
- a higher asset turnover ratio if sales growth is being achieved without a corresponding increase in assets.

(b) Changes in components of Lambda Ltd's working capital and margin:

	Old	New	Change
	£000s	£000s	£000s
Sales	3,600	110% of 3,600 = 3,960	360
Material purchases	35/100 × 3,600 = 1,260	35/100 × 3,960 = 1,386	126
Trade receivables	36/365 × 3,600 = 355	60/365 × 3,960 = 651	296
Material inventory	15/365 × 1,260 = 52	15/365 × 1,386 = 57	5
Trade payables	30/365 × 1,260 = (104)	30/365 × 1,386 = (114)	(10)
Change in working capital			291
Cost of increase in long-term capital		12% of 291	35
Increased margin		20% × 360	72
Increase in profit			37

Conclusion

Provided the new terms of trade can be enforced, the increased volume of business will lead to an increase in margin of £72,000 with an increased cost of capital for the increased working capital (mainly due to increased credit) of £35,000, increasing profit overall by £37,000. The change is worthwhile.

14.3 The EOQ is:

c = £250 per order
d = 500,000 units
h = 30p per unit
EOQ = $\sqrt{2cd/h}$ = $\sqrt{(2 \times 150 \times 400{,}000/1.50)}$ = $\sqrt{80{,}000{,}000}$ = 8,944 units

15 Working capital 2

15.1(a) Methods for assessing the creditworthiness of a new customer include the following.

- Reports by sales staff based on visits to or interviews with the customer. This can take account of up-to-date observation of trading conditions, but may not be comprehensive.
- The judgement and experience of the credit controller, based on local knowledge or checking the potential customer's published accounts. This may also be based on up-to-date knowledge, although local knowledge may need to be supplemented by further enquiries to focus on the customer. Published accounts

will not be up to date, and may be manipulated at year end, so that the creditor's payment times give a flattering figure.

- Valuation of the company's fixed assets. This may give some idea of the company's standing, although it will not necessarily show all financial liabilities – such as operating leases – and fixed assets will not guarantee payment to a particular supplier if the customer becomes insolvent.
- Checking the track record of past payments. This needs access to other companies' information in the case of a new customer (and see below).
- Reports from the customer's bank. The bank may not give a full report, and will word its report in such as way as to avoid responsibility for any omissions.
- References from other suppliers. The customer may nominate suppliers that it has paid on time for this purpose.
- Trade association references. Trade associations will know who is a bad payer.
- Credit reference agencies will provide a report, which should be reliable, for a fee.
- Creditworthiness can include the amount of credit that should be allowed as well as whether the potential customer should be allowed credit at all. Credit limits can be based on judgement, taking account of the nature and size of the business and an assessment of the customer's management. More sophisticated methods use scoring methods based on statistical models reflecting past credit risk experience.

(b) (i)

	2014		2015	
		Days		Days
Raw materials	42.4/240 × 360	63.6	50/218.4 × 360	82.4
Credit to customers	108.1/690 × 360	56.4	118.5/624 × 360	68.3
		120.0		150.7
Less Credit from suppliers	53.9/295 × 360	–65.8	52.5/264 × 360	–71.6
Cash conversion cycle		54.2		79.1

The cash conversion cycle has increased from 54.2 days to 79.1 days, an increase of 24.9 days or 46%.

(ii) The increased investment in working capital may be calculated as follows:

	2014	2015
	£000s	£000s
Inventory	42.4	50.0
Trade receivables	108.1	118.5
	150.5	168.5
Less trade payables	53.9	52.5
	96.6	116.0

The increase in the inventory holding period is 18.8 days while credit to customers increased by 11.9 days, resulting in an increased investment in working capital of £18,000 in respect of these two items. The overall increase in working capital was £19,400 as accounts payable fell by £1,400. Accounts payable days increased, but the value fell because purchases fell by over £30,000 over the two-year period.

15.2 (a)

	Jan.	Feb.	Mar.	Apr.	May	June	Totals
	£000s	£000s	£000s	£000s	£000s	£000s	£000s
Cash inflows							
Tickets		2.10	4.20	10.50	10.50	14.70	42.00
Sponsorship				21.60	32.40		54.00
Bar						20.00	20.00
Sales commission						6.00	6.00
Totals	0	2.10	4.20	32.10	42.90	40.70	122.00
Cash inflows							
Upgrade			22.00				22.00
Project support	6.00	6.00	6.00	6.00	6.00	6.00	36.00
Materials				12.00	12.00		24.00
Fees						12.00	12.00
Hospitality						8.00	8.00
Publicity				1.00	6.00	3.00	10.00
Interest		0.12	0.20	0.68	0.432	0.063	1.495
Totals	6.00	6.12	28.20	19.68	24.432	29.063	113.495
Net cash flow	–6.00	–4.02	–24.00	12.42	18.468	11.637	8.505
Opening balance	0	–6.00	–10.02	–34.02	–21.60	–3.132	0
Closing balance	–6.00	–10.02	–34.02	–21.60	–3.132	8.505	8.505

(b) The significant features are as follows.

- The closing balance is negative for each of the first five months. This will result in the project incurring interest.
- Overall the project is expected to have a positive net cash flow.
- The positive net cash flow could be increased if interest costs were reduced. This could be achieved by bringing forward the sponsorship and by putting in a marketing effort to achieve higher ticket sales in the early months.

(c) The monitoring procedures that should be put in place in order to ensure that the closing balance of £8,505 is achieved are as follows.

- Each month the actual cash flows should be compared with the budgeted cash flows and where there are differences, they should be investigated and, if the impact is negative, they should be corrected.
- The actual figures should replace the budgeted figures as each month passes and this will allow the manager to see the effect of divergences between budget and actual. In order for this to be achieved, the budget should be set up as a spreadsheet.

16 Short-term financing

16.1 Briefing note to: Board of Limpa plc
From: Company secretary
Date: 30 May 20XX
Subject: Options for dealing with the overdraft

1. The services offered by factors are:
   - Sales administration: The factor takes over elements of the sales administration. It collects payments from the company's customers and pays over balances, less its interest and charges to the company.
   - Short-term finance: It advances, in this case, 80% of sales invoices and reduces the need for company to use bank overdraft facilities.
   - Credit assurance: If a factor offers a non-recourse service, it pays its client, whether or not it receives payment from the customer. This means that it accepts the risk of any bad debts and is providing a form of insurance against non-payment.

   Disadvantages are the cost of the service plus a danger that the factor comes between the company and its clients. This may result in a deterioration in relationships.
2. The financial effects of both options:

	Annual costs	£000s
Existing		
Trade receivables interest	£900,000 × 0.16	144.00
Inventory interest	£400,000 × 0.16	64.00
		208.00
Internal option		
Trade receivables interest	£6 million ×4 0/365 × 0.16	105.21
Inventory interest	£1.8 million × 42/365 × 0.16	33.14
Credit control staff		30.00
Bad debt		35.00
		203.35
Factor		
Advance interest	£6 million × 0.8 × 40/365 × 0.14	73.64
Balance interest	£6 million × 0.2 × 40/365 × 0.16	21.04
Cost of factor	£6 million × 0.03	180.00
Inventory interest	£1.8 million × 42/365 × 0.16	33.14
		307.82

Effect on cash balances:

	Current	Proposed	Increase in cash balances
Trade receivables	£900,000	£6 million × 40/365 = £658,000	£242,000
Inventory	£400,000	£1.8 million × 42/365 = £207,000	£193,000
Totals	£1.3 million	£865,000	£435,000

3. Recommendation
   - The internal option to achieve reductions is cheaper than current costs and cheaper than using the factor. In consequence it is recommended that we increase credit control by £30,000 per year and require that they reduce receivables to 40 days on average. Additionally, inventory should also be reduced to 42 days.
   - The actions projected are estimated to increase cash balances by £435,000, which will allow the company to reduce overdraft balances significantly.

16.2(a) Methods for assessing the creditworthiness of a new customer include:
- Reports by sales staff based on visits to or interviews with the customer. This can take account of up-to-date observation of trading conditions, but may not be comprehensive.
- The judgement and experience of the credit controller, based on local knowledge or checking the potential customer's published accounts. This may also be based on up-to-date knowledge, though local knowledge may need to be supplemented by further enquiries to focus on the customer. Published accounts will not be up to date, and may be manipulated at year end, so that the creditors' payment times give a flattering figure.
- Valuation of the company's fixed assets. This may give some idea of the company's standing, though it will not necessarily show all financial liabilities such as operating leases; fixed assets will not guarantee payment to a particular supplier if the customer becomes insolvent.
- Checking the track record of past payments: needs access to other companies' information in the case of a new customer (and see below).
- Reports from the customer's bank. The bank may not give a full report, and will word its report in such as way as to avoid responsibility for any omissions.
- References from other suppliers. The customer may nominate suppliers that it has paid on time for this purpose.
- Trade association references. Trade associations will know who is a bad payer. Credit reference agencies will provide a report, which should be reliable, for a fee.
- Creditworthiness can include the amount of credit that should be allowed as well as whether the potential customer should be allowed credit at all. Credit limits can be based on judgement, taking account of the nature and size of the business and an assessment of the customer's management. More sophisticated methods use scoring methods based on statistical models reflecting past credit risk experience.

(b) The services offered by factors are:
- Sales administration: the factor takes over all the sales administration. It issues invoices and collects payments from the company's customers. It may use its own or the client company's invoices.
- Invoice discounting: the factor advances cash to the company on the security of invoices that it approves. The use of this service used to be seen as a sign of financial distress, but it is rapidly growing, often costing less than an overdraft, and is now one of the main sources of short-finance.
- Credit insurance: If a factor offers a non-recourse service, it pays its client whether or not it receives payment from the customer. This means that it accepts the risk of any bad debts, and is providing a form of insurance against non-payment.

(c) Actions to deal with overdue payments include:
- sending reminders
- telephone calls from the credit controller
- sending a member of the sales staff in person to collect payment
- threatening to cut off supplies
- making good this threat
- threatening legal action
- appointing debt collectors
- solicitor's letters, and
- legal action.

17 Corporate risk management

17.1 To: The Board
From: Company Secretary
Date: 10 May 20XX
Subject: Briefing note on key risk concepts and responses

When considering a risk management policy for the company, the following key concepts must be taken into account.

The nature of risk

Risk occurs when there is volatility in future returns, but the probability of each possible outcome can be assessed with reasonable accuracy. Risk often cannot be removed and it must be taken account of in decision-making. In investment decisions, risk is particularly important because of the duration of projects (there is more time for things to go wrong) and the scale of projects (if anything does go wrong, it can have a serious impact on the company).

Exposure

Exposure is a measure of the extent to which a company faces risk. This risk can be operating risk and/or financial risk. It can also refer to the extent to which a company faces foreign exchange risk due to its import, export and foreign investing activities.

Volatility

Volatility is the extent to which expected returns vary. The more they are expected to vary, the more volatile or the more risky they are said to be. Variance and standard deviation are used to measure volatility. Another terms for volatility is 'dispersion'. A risk-free return has no volatility and may be pictured as an undeviating straight line.

Severity

Severity is defined as follows. If a hazard occurs, how bad is the outcome? If severity is low then, possibly, we will give a low priority to preventing this risk from occurring. However, if severity is high then, even if the probability of the hazard is low, prevention has a high priority. For, example, computer files are so important that a company will undertake regular back-ups so that the costs of computer failure are minimised.

Probability

Probabilities that are assigned to future events can be either objective or subjective. Objective probabilities are based on the accumulation of past information. For example, if we have a number of machines that have run for several years, we may be able to evaluate likely breakdown rates, annual machine running costs and so on.

Subjective probabilities are based on subjective opinion. They can be derived from the opinions of experts or the judgements of managers with experience in these areas. However, there is always the danger due to bias as personal experience may be limited and subjective interpretation of it may be flawed.

There are also key risk responses that the company can take when faced with the above risks and these are summarised below:

Risk transfer

Risk transfer is the process of transferring risk to another party, usually by payment of a fee. For example, with foreign exchange risk, risk can be reduced by purchasing currency on the forward market. More generally, taking out insurance is a method of risk transfer: the risk is transferred from the company to the insurance company on payment of a fee (the insurance premium).

Risk reduction
Risk reduction is the process of reducing overall risk. One way of achieving this is by investing in a portfolio of assets rather than in one or two assets. Another approach is to carry out market research to provide more certainty of estimates of future sales revenue.

Risk avoidance
Given two projects with identical returns, it is possible to avoid risk by selecting the project with the lowest risk. Risk-averse people continually take risks, but only where the expected return is sufficiently high to compensate them for taking those risks. Unnecessary risks are not appealing. Most people are risk-averse.

Risk retention
Risk retention involves accepting the gains or losses from a risk when it occurs. Risk retention would be a viable strategy for risks with low severity, where the cost of insuring the risk over time would be greater than any loss incurred by the company. Also, any potential risk in excess of a ceiling imposed by the insurance company is retained risk. Some risks have to be retained as they cannot be invested against, such as the risk of war.

17.2 To: The Board
From: Company Secretary
Date: 20 June 20XX

Subject: Briefing note on the financial risks attached to the turbine supply contract.

1. Financial risk is the additional risk borne by shareholders when the firm takes on fixed-rate debt. A firm with a large percentage of debt is said to have a high degree of financial gearing, which is a measure of a firm's financial risk.
2. In order to use a money market hedge to protect our interests in the sale of turbines to the French company:
   (a) As soon as the turbines are delivered to the French company, we approach for a loan from a French bank, using the sale proceeds (in three months' time) as security. The amount we can borrow will need to be discounted for three months at the bank's interest rate in order to ensure that the proceeds will cover the bank's advance in three months' time.
   (b) Immediately convert the loan from the French bank to sterling at the current spot exchange rate, thereby ensuring a reduction in our financial risk.
   (c) In three months' time use the euros received from the French company to repay our loan at the French bank.

17.3 Juniper will need to borrow dollars for three months at the time of the transaction. The borrowing rate is 2.25% for the quarter. Therefore, Juniper will need to borrow $200,000/1.0225 = $195,599. This is converted immediately into pounds to realise $195,599/1.5940 = £122,710. In three months' time, Juniper will receive $200,000 from the US company which will cover the borrowed amount of $195,599 plus the interest of $4,401.

Glossary

accounting rate of return (ARR) A traditional method of evaluating capital investment projects which expresses the profit from an investment as a percentage of the investment. The profit is the accounting profit, calculated as in the statement of financial position, and may be calculated before or after tax. It is usually the average profit over the life of the project. The investment includes fixed assets and working capital specific to the project, valued in the same way as in the statement of financial position, and is usually also averaged over the life of the project. The ARR for the project is usually compared with a company, group or divisional target.

allocative efficiency The optimum allocation of funds within financial markets (i.e., that which will maximise economic prosperity).

AIM (Alternative Investment Market) AIM was launched by the London Stock Exchange in June 1995. It has less stringent entry requirements and regulations than the Main Market, or the Unlisted Securities Market, which it replaced. AIM provides a market for smaller growth companies that either do not wish, or fail to qualify, to join the Official List.

Argenti's failure model A measure used to forecast company failure, based on the calculation of scores related to company defects, management mistakes and other symptoms of failure.

bear Somebody who has a pessimistic view of the prospects of a share, or of share prices in general.

beta factor (ß) A measure of the relationship between the return on a share and the market return. A high beta share has a high risk and a high expected return to compensate for this risk.

bought deal A major investment bank buys all the shares in a new issue at a slightly discounted price. This offers an alternative to underwriting as a way of protecting against the risk that an offer for sale will be undersubscribed.

bull Somebody who has an optimistic view of the prospects of a share, or of share prices in general.

capital asset pricing model (CAPM) Equation expressing the relationship between the degree of risk of an investment and the expected return on the investment.

capital rationing The situation of an organisation when it has insufficient funds to accept all projects with a positive net present value (NPV).

capital reconstruction A company gains the agreement of its shareholders and creditors to vary the rights of its members and creditors, by altering its capital structure in a way that allows the existing company to continue in business.

commercial paper Short-term promissory note with a fixed period of less than one year. The rate of interest is the difference between the face price and the discounted issue price.

concentric diversification The development of products that offer synergies with current products.

conglomerate diversification The development of products with no marketing, technology or product synergy with the business's current products. The firm may, however, aim to obtain management synergies.

convertible loan stock Loan stock that can be converted into ordinary shares at a set date or dates at a predetermined price. The conversion price is the price of ordinary shares at which loan stock can be converted. The number of ordinary shares received by a loan stock holder on conversion of £100 nominal of convertible loan stock is £100 divided by the conversion price.

convertible preference shares Preference shares that can be converted into ordinary shares. A company may issue them to finance major acquisitions without increasing the company's gearing or diluting the earnings per share (EPS) of the ordinary shares. Preference shares potentially offer the investor a reasonable degree of safety with the chance of capital gains as a result of conversion to ordinary shares if the company prospers.

cost of capital The cost to a company of the return offered to different kinds of capital. This may be in the form of interest (for debt capital) or dividends and participation in the growth of profit (for ordinary shares) or dividends alone (for preference shares) or conversion rights (for convertible loan stock or convertible preference shares).

debt Long-term capital consisting of money lent by investors. May be called loan stock, loan notes, debentures or bonds. Return on debt consists of interest (usually at a fixed rate) which is payable irrespective of the financial performance of the company. Secured loan stock holders rank before ordinary shareholders for repayment of capital in the event of a liquidation of the company.

discount rate Cost of capital used to define interest rates or to discount cash flows to find present values (*see* Discounted cash flow analysis).

discounted cash flow (DCF) analysis Technique for evaluating investment projects by identifying the future cash flows attributable to the project and calculating their present values so that they can be compared on a like-for-like basis. The present value of a future cash flow is the amount of money at today's date that has an equivalent value. The present value is calculated by discounting the future cash flow to allow for its timing and the cost of capital. The sum of the present values of all the project's cash flows is the net present value (NPV) of the project. The discount rate that makes the NPV of a project zero is the project's internal rate of return.

divisible project A capital investment project that can be undertaken either as a whole or in part.

economic order quantity (EOQ) A formula for calculating the size of order to place when stocks are replenished. It is designed to minimise the combined cost of stockholding and stock reordering.

enterprise risk management A framework for risk management throughout the organisation.

equity shares With equity shares the payment of dividends is not guaranteed, and the amount of dividends depends on the company's financial performance. Equity shareholders are last in line for payment of dividends and for repayment of capital in the event of a liquidation of the company. Equity shareholders accept these risks and disadvantages because they are the legal owners of the company and have voting control and own any remaining funds after other claims have been met. They expect to benefit, through growth of dividends and share prices, from the company's future success.

financial gearing Ratio of debt to equity (shareholders' funds) – a measure of a firm's financial risk.

financial risk The additional risk borne by shareholders when a firm takes on fixed rate debt.

Fisher equation States that: (1 + money or nominal discount rate) = (1 + real discount rate) x (1 + inflation rate).

Forward contract An agreement to buy or sell an asset at a fixed price at a fixed time in the future. Forward contracts are similar to future contracts except that the former fall outside the regulation of an exchange.

future/future contract An agreement to purchase or sell a set quantity of currency at a date in the future (used to hedge against, or speculate on, currency movements).

gilts UK government stock. There are a large number of different stocks with different maturity dates and different rates of interest (which are usually fixed, though index-linked stocks have both the interest rate and the redemption price linked to the retail price index).

goal congruence Occurs when the objectives of the agents match those of the principals. In a company, the management is the agent and the shareholders are the principals.

Gordon's model of dividend growth Equation relating the ex-dividend ordinary share price to the dividend, the expected annual growth in dividends and the cost of equity capital.

hard rationing Limits on the availability of capital for investment due to a lack of sources outside the company.

hedging The external management of risks, where two or more parties make an agreement in which their risks cancel each other out. This is used in areas outside the company's control (e.g. exchange rate and interest rate risk). The parties involved may be those facing the same risk but in opposite directions, or may be speculators. The costs to a party undertaking a hedging transaction are any fee payable to the counterparty, and any profit forgone if the outcome of the hedged risk would have been favourable.

horizontal integration A firm finds new markets for its existing products or introduces new products into its current markets, with the objective of gaining economies of scale or scope.

information processing efficiency Quick and accurate pricing of securities, preventing speculation pushing prices to unrealistic levels.

interest rate swap An exchange of two currencies between two or more parties for a predetermined length of time and at a predetermined price.

internal rate of return (IRR) The discount rate that makes the net present value (NPV) of a project zero – equal to the rate of return on capital invested in the project (*see* Discounted cash flow analysis).

internally generated funds Retained earnings, together with cash generated by the business other than profit (e.g., provisions for depreciation).The preferred source of investment funds for many companies.

net present value (NPV) The sum of the present values of all the cash flows associated with an investment project (*see* Discounted cash flow analysis).

nominal cost of capital The cash return (in the form of dividends, interest or capital growth) actually paid out or received or required by providers of capital. It includes an allowance for expected price changes (*see* Fisher equation).

Non relevant factors In project appraisal, are those factors which do not affect the decision under consideration.

offer for sale Issue of shares to the public, either by an existing plc or by a company that is going public.

operating gearing A measure of a firm's business risk, reflecting the proportion of a company's operating costs that are fixed.

operational efficiency The lowest level of transaction costs in financial markets, which can occur when there is open and free competition within the market.

option/option contract The right (but not the obligation) to sell or buy (a 'put' or 'call' option) a specific asset at a specific price at a specific time. The set price is called the 'strike' or 'exercise' price.

over-the-counter (OTC) market A market, outside regulated exchanges, which allows contracts to be tailor-made to meet individual requirements.

pooling The internal management of risks, where risks are aggregated and offset against each other. This is the general method of dealing with normal business risks, and is used in areas such as insurance and portfolio diversification.

preference shares Non-equity shares, with a (usually fixed) dividend paid – subject to the availability of distributable profits – before ordinary share dividends can be paid. Preference shares do not normally have voting rights, but rank before ordinary shares for distribution of capital in the event of liquidation.

present value The amount of money at today's date that is equivalent to a sum of money in the future. It is calculated by discounting the future sum to reflect its timing and the cost of capital (*see* Discounted cash flow analysis).

profitability index Ratio for a capital investment project used to put capital investment projects in order of priority for allocation of funds, since it shows how much surplus a project offers over the cost of capital for every £ invested.

Relevant factors In project appraisal, are those factors that are significant to the decision under consideration.

retained earnings Profits reinvested in the business instead of being paid out as dividends. They belong to the shareholders and form part of shareholders' funds, together with equity capital subscribed by shareholders and reserves. The cost of retained earnings is the same as the cost of other forms of equity capital included in shareholders' funds.

rights issue An issue of shares to existing shareholders, usually at a discount to the market price.

risk Risk is associated with the variability of operating costs, sales and profits and is caused by factors such as economic conditions, competition, operational problems and by the company's cost structure (*see* Operational gearing).

risk-free rate The rate offered with certainty. There is no prospect of volatility.

sale by tender Form of share issue that tends to be used for larger first-time issues. People who wish to buy shares submit tenders stating how many shares they wish to buy and the maximum price they are willing to pay. Shares are usually issued at the same price to all successful tenderers. The sale price is the highest price at which all the shares can be sold.

satisficing Since managers have objectives that are not identical with those of shareholders, they may be tempted to pursue their own agendas, while doing only enough to provide a return that shareholders consider adequate, rather than maximising shareholder returns.

scenario analysis Scenario analysis involves preparing net present value (NPV) calculations according to different possible 'states of the world'. A common form of scenario analysis is to present three possible states of the world that provide a most likely view, an optimistic view and a pessimistic view.

security market line (SML) The line that shows the relationship between risk, as measured by the beta factor, and required returns. Its gradient reflects the gradient provided by the following equation: gradient = risk-free rate + β (return on the market – risk-free rate).

sensitivity analysis Calculation of the degree to which different factors can affect the outcome of a project (may be presented as the amount by which the project NPV will be changed by a given change in a factor, or the proportional change in a factor needed to bring the project just to breakeven in NPV terms).

share option The right, but not the obligation, to buy (a call option) or sell (a put option) shares at a future date (generally three months forward) at a fixed price agreed now. A double option – called a 'put and call' option or 'straddle' – gives the right either to buy or to sell. Bargains are agreed at a 'strike price' or 'exercise price' (the price at which shares can be bought or sold at the end of the option period).

simulation model A method for evaluating projects and investigating risk that uses equations programmed on a computer to relate project inputs to project outcomes. The model is used to test statistically a number of possible variations in the inputs to find what variations these may cause in the outcome. It can be used to test the vulnerability of outcomes to possible variations in uncontrolled factors, or to evaluate possible changes in the project specification.

soft rationing Limits on the availability of investment funds as a result of internal management decisions.

stag Somebody who subscribes for shares in an initial public offering of shares, with the expectation that trading will start at a premium to the issue price and the intention of selling immediately to make a short-term profit.

stakeholder A person who has made some kind of investment in a company, and consequently expects a return, and as a result has an interest in the success of the company.

standard deviation The square root of the variance. The standard deviation of the return on a portfolio can be calculated to give a measure of the variability of the return.

stock option scheme An incentive scheme for managers which gives senior managers the right to buy a certain number of the company's shares at a fixed price at a specified time in the future. This is designed to provide rewards for managers that encourage them to behave in such a way as to maximise the shareholders' wealth by maximising long-term share price growth.

strategy The ways in which a company commits its resources in furtherance of its objectives. It is likely to involve decisions about products, markets, customers, competitive positioning and organisation, together with the corporate finance decisions.

synergy The concept that, by combining activities, it is possible to achieve more than would be possible if the activities remained separate.

Tax shield The reduction in a company's taxation liability because of the existence of loan interest which is a tax-deductible expense.

underwriter Somebody (usually an issuing house or an investment bank) who agrees, for a fee, to purchase any shares that are not taken up at the issue price in a share issue. Underwriters are often used in initial public offerings (IPOs) of shares.

value drivers Factors that increase shareholder value.

vertical integration A firm expands along the supply chain. This can be either backwards (supply of components or raw materials) or forwards (being one step closer to the end customer).

volatility The variation in future returns, reflecting the risk of those returns.

warrants Rights given to lenders allowing them to buy new shares in a company at a future date at a fixed price. This price is known as the exercise price, and the time within which they can be used to obtain shares is known as the exercise period.

weighted average cost of capital (WACC) A weighted average of the costs of different kinds of long-term capital, calculated to reflect the amounts of different kinds of capital (most importantly shareholders' funds and debt) in the company's capital structure. The weightings used for the different kinds of capital may be either the book values or the market values. The WACC is commonly used as the cost of capital in evaluating projects. It represents the cost of capital for projects with a normal level of business risk and where funds are raised in similar proportions to the existing capital structure.

Z score A measure of company financial stability, used to forecast company failure, calculated using financial ratios.

Directory

References

Chapter 2

Altman, E. I., 'Financial ratios, discriminant analysis and the prediction of corporate bankruptcy', in *Journal of Finance*, 23:589–609 (1968)

Argenti, J., *Corporate Collapse, The Causes and Symptoms* (McGraw Hill, 1976)

Beaver, W. H. 'Financial ratios as predictors of failure', in *Journal of Accounting Research*, 4:71–111 (1966)

Brealey, R. A., Myers, S. C. and Allen, F., *Principles of Corporate Finance*, 11th edition (McGraw Hill, 2014)

Taffler, R. J., 'Forecasting company failure in the UK using discriminant analysis and financial ratio data', in *Journal of the Royal Statistical Society*, 145(3):342–58 (1982)

Chapter 3

Becker, B., Ivkovic, Z. and Weisbenner, S., 'Local dividend clienteles', in *Journal of Finance*, 66:655–83 (2011)

Brav, A., Graham, J.R., Harvey, C.R. and Michaely, R., 'Payout policy in the 21st century', in *Journal of Financial Economics*, 77:483–527 (2005)

Elton, E.J. and Gruber, M.J., 'Marginal stockholder tax rates and the clientele effect', in *Review of Economics and Statistics*, 68–74 (February 1970)

Graham, B. and Dodd, D. L., *Security Analysis: Principles and Techniques*, 3rd edition (McGraw Hill, 1951)

Gordon, M.J., 'Dividends, earnings and stock prices', in *Review of Economics and Statistics*, 41:99–105 (May 1959)

Lintner, J., 'Distribution of incomes of corporations among dividends, retained earnings and taxes', in *American Economic Review*, 46:97–113 (May 1956)

Miller, M.H. and Modigliani, F., 'Dividend policy, growth and the valuation of shares', in *Journal of Business*, 34:411–433 (October 1961)

Woolridge J. R. and Ghosh, C., 'Dividend cuts: Do they always signal bad news?', in J. M. Stern and D. H. Chew (eds), *The Revolution in Capital Finance* (Blackwell Business, 1998)

Chapter 10

Alexander, S., 'Price movements in speculative markets: trends and random walks', in *Industrial Management Review*, 7-26 (May 1961)

Amihud, Y. and Mendelson, H., 'Liquidity and asset prices: Financial management implications', in *Financial Management*, 17(1):5–15 (Spring, 1988); reprinted with amendments in Stern J. M. and Chew, D. H., *The Revolution in Corporate Finance*, 3rd edition (Blackwell,1998)

Ball, R. and Brown, P., 'An empirical evaluation of accounting income numbers', *Journal of Accounting Research*, 159-78 (Autumn 1968)

Fama, E. F., 'The behaviour of stock market prices', in *Journal of Business*, 34–106 (January 1965)

Fama, E. F., 'Efficient capital markets: A review of theory and empirical evidence', in *Journal of Finance*, 383–417 (May 1970)

Fama, E. F., 'Efficient capital markets II', in Journal of Finance, 46(5):1575–617 (December 1991)

Fama, E. F., Fisher, L., Jensen, M., and Roll, R., 'The adjustment of stock prices to new information', in *International Economic Review*, 10:1–21 (February 1969)

Finnerty, J. E., 'Insiders and market efficiency', in *Journal of Finance*, 31(4):1141–48 (September 1976)

Jaffe, J. F., 'Special information and insider trading', in *Journal of Business*, 47(3):410–428 (1974)

Jensen, M., 'The performance of mutual funds in the period 1945–64', in *Journal of Finance*, 389–416 (May 1968)
Kendall, M., 'The analysis of economic time-series prices', in *Journal of the Royal Statistical Society*, 96:11–15 (1953)
Roberts. V. H., 'Stock market "patterns" and financial analysis: Methodological suggestions', in *Journal of Finance*, 1–10 (March 1959)

Chapter 12

Lintner, J., 'The valuation of risky assets and the selection of risky investments in stock portfolios and capital budgets', in *Review of Economics and Statistics*, 47:13–37, (February 1965)
Markowitz, H.M., 'Portfolio selection', in *Journal of Finance*, 7:77–91 (1952)
Sharpe, W. F., 'Capital assets prices: a theory of market equilibrium under conditions of risk', in *Journal of Finance*, 19:425–42 (September 1964)

Chapter 13

Modigliani, F. and Miller, M. H., 'The cost of capital, corporation finance and the theory of investment', in *American Economic Review*, 48:261–97 (June 1958)
Modigliani, F. and Miller, M. H., 'Corporate income taxes and the cost of capital: A correction', in *American Economic Review*, 53: 433–43 (June 1963)
Myers, S. 'The capital structure puzzle', in *Journal of Finance*, 39:575–92 (1984)

Chapter 15

Baumol, W., 'The transactions demand for cash: An inventory theoretic approach', in *Quarterly Journal of Economics*, 66:545–56 (November 1952)
Miller, M. and Orr, D., 'A model of the demand for money by firms', in *Quarterly Journal of Economics*, 80:413–35 (August 1966)

Further reading

Arnold, G., *Corporate Financial Management*, 5th edition (Pearson, 2013)
Atrill, P., *Financial Management for Decision Makers*, 7th edition (Pearson, 2014)
Blake, D., *Financial Market Analysis*, 2nd edition (Wiley, 1999)
Brealey, R. A., Myers, S. C. and Allen, F., *Principles of Corporate Finance*, 11th edition (McGraw Hill, 2014)
Lumby, S. and Jones, C. *Corporate Finance Theory and Practice*, 9th edition (Cengage, 2015)
McLaney, E., *Business Finance: Theory and Practice*, 9th edition (Pearson 2011)
Pike, N., Neale, B. and Linsley, P., *Corporate Finance and Investment: Decisions and Strategies*, 8th edition (Pearson, 2015)
Watson, D. and Head, A., *Corporate Finance: Principles and Practice*, 6th edition (Pearson, 2013)

Magazines, journals and newsletters

There is a wide variety of magazines and journals servicing the accounting and finance market. They range from academic to regular magazines and newsletters produced by the accountancy professional bodies and all are worth regular review. In many cases, article archives are posted on these organisations' websites; see below for details. Journals, magazines and newsletters, including those specifically targeted at professional accounting students, are also often available in downloadable format.

Accountancy

This is the monthly journal of the ICAEW. It covers a wide range of topics.

CA Magazine

This is the monthly magazine of the ICAS.

Accounting & Business

This is the monthly magazine from ACCA. It covers business and professional developments worldwide.

Financial Management

This is CIMA's professional magazine. It focuses on management accounting methods and technology, and has good coverage of some of the topics in the ICSA course (e.g. capital investment appraisal). It is available from the Magazine Department at the CIMA's headquarters.

Public Finance

This is the monthly magazine on public sector financial management from CIPFA.

Professional bodies and useful organisations

The specialist financial accounting bodies in the UK are the Institute of Chartered Accountants in England and Wales (ICAEW) and the Institute of Charted Accountants of Scotland (ICAS). Other professional accounting bodies are the Association of Chartered Certified Accountants (ACCA), the Chartered Institute of Management Accountants (CIMA) and the Chartered Institute of Public Finance and Accountancy (CIPFA).

All these accounting bodies include financial management elements in their examination schemes and many of their members are employed in financial management roles in industry, commerce and the public sector.

All the organisations listed below post additional information and resources on their websites. Many of the professional bodies also have international sites and offices that can provide students with additional local or regional material.

Association of Chartered Certified Accountants (ACCA)
The Adelphi
1–11 John Adam Street
London WC2N 6AU
Tel +44(0)141 582 2000
www.accaglobal.com

Chartered Institute of Management Accountants (CIMA)
The Helicon
One South Place
London EC2M 2RB
Tel +44(0)20 8849 2251
www.cimaglobal.com

The Chartered Institute of Public Finance and Accountancy (CIPFA)
77 Mansell Street
London E1 8AN
Tel +44(0)20 7543 5600
www.cipfa.org.uk

The Institute of Chartered Accountants in England and Wales (ICAEW)
Chartered Accountants' Hall
Moorgate Place
London EC2R 6EA
Tel +44(0)20 7920 8100
www.icaew.com

The Institute of Chartered Accountants of Scotland (ICAS)
CA House
21 Haymarket Yards
Edinburgh EH12 5BH
Tel +44(0)13 1347 0100
www.icas.com

Index